Bangladesh

From Stabilization to Growth

The World Bank
Washington, D.C.

World Bank Country Studies are among the many reports originally prepared for internal use as part of the continuing analysis by the Bank of the economic and related conditions of its developing member countries and of its dialogues with the governments. Some of the reports are published in this series with the least possible delay for the use of governments and the academic, business and financial, and development communities. The typescript of this paper therefore has not been prepared in accordance with the procedures appropriate to formal printed texts, and the World Bank accepts no responsibility for errors. Some sources cited in this paper may be informal documents that are not readily available.

The World Bank does not guarantee the accuracy of the data included in this publication and accepts no responsibility whatsoever for any consequence of their use. The boundaries, colors, denominations, and other information shown on any map in this volume do not imply on the part of the World Bank Group any judgment on the legal status of any territory or the endorsement or acceptance of such boundaries.

The complete backlist of publications from the World Bank is shown in the annual *Index of Publications*, which contains an alphabetical title list (with full ordering information) and indexes of subjects, authors, and countries and regions. The latest edition is available free of charge from the Distribution Unit, Office of the Publisher, The World Bank, 1818 H Street, N.W., Washington, D.C. 20433, U.S.A., or from Publications, The World Bank, 66, avenue d'Iéna, 75116 Paris, France.

ISSN: 0-0253-2123

Library of Congress Cataloging-in-Publication Data

Bangladesh : from stabilization to growth.
    p.   cm. — (A World Bank country study)
"Prepared in mid-1994 by a team led by Shekhar Shah, under the
overall guidance of Pradeep Mitra"—P.   .
    Includes bibliographical references (p.   ).
    ISBN 0-8213-3227-9
    1. Public investments—Bangladesh.   2. Exports—Bangladesh.
3. Privatization—Bangladesh.   4. Economic stabilization—
Bangladesh.   5. Bangladesh—Economic policy.   I. Shah, Shekhar,
1955–   . II. Mitra, Pradeep.   III. Series.
HC440.8.Z9P833   1995
338.95492— dc20   95-13326
                                                          CIP

Contents   Page No.

PART I: RECENT ECONOMIC PERFORMANCE
AND MACROECONOMIC PRIORITIES FOR GROWTH

PART II: REFORM PRIORITIES FOR
PRIVATE SECTOR MANUFACTURING GROWTH

List of Tables, Figures and Boxes   Page No.

ABSTRACT

Bangladesh has achieved much in its quest for economic and social development, but much is left undone. Significant achievements in population, food production, and stabilization of the macroeconomy have not been accompanied by the faster economic growth and employment generation needed to alleviate massive poverty. Raising economic growth to a sustainable level approaching 7 percent over the medium term remains the overriding policy goal for the country. *How Government policy and actions can help achieve the goal of faster growth by promoting an export push in manufacturing by the private sector is the basic theme of this report.* The Government has successfully stabilized the economy. This affords an unprecedented window of opportunity to accelerate pro-growth reforms in four priority areas. The Government's *first priority* must be to raise investment: by giving the private sector the reform confidence necessary to invest in export-oriented manufacturing activities, and by urgently and substantially improving implementation of public investment in infrastructure and human resource development. Faster trade liberalization would go far toward increasing the private sector's confidence in the reforms. To further reduce the costs of policy uncertainty for the private sector, the Government's *second priority* should be to make the deregulation of the private sector much more effective, giving it the flexibility to make unfettered business decisions relating to investments, production, trade, international payments, and employment. The Government's *third priority* should be to enter into long-term arrangements with domestic and overseas private investors in infrastructure and the utilities to promote their entry, enhance competition, raise efficiency, and improve service quality; in the shorter term, the Government must rapidly complete the long-delayed privatization of state-owned enterprises in the manufacturing sector. To support an export push by the private sector, financial and industrial labor markets must function efficiently: therefore, the Government's *fourth priority* should be to implement fundamental reforms aimed at easing its dominant ownership of the financial sector, further improving financial supervision and regulation, and substantially increasing competition and the quality of intermediation. In labor markets, government dealings with labor and employers must emphasize the overriding importance for international competitiveness of keeping wages and employment adequately flexible to adjust to productivity growth, skill requirements, and the market outlook for final products.

ACKNOWLEDGEMENTS

This World Bank Country Study on Bangladesh was prepared in 1994 by a team led by Shekhar Shah, under the overall guidance of Pradeep Mitra. Members of the team comprised Charles Draper, Hafez Ghanem, Ashok Khanna, Syed Nizamuddin, Nadaraja Ramachandran, and Vidya Shetty. Valuable contributions were received from Shamsuddin Ahmad, Anne Ching, Forrest Cookson, Clara Else, Woldai Futur, Juan Gaviria, Zamir Hasan, Reazul Islam, Janet Koch, Francis Ng, Arvind Panagariya, Rajesh Pradhan, Martin Ravallion, Owaise Saadat, Binayak Sen, Pankaj Thampil, Sona Varma, Peter Wogart, Kamil Yilmaz, and Nancy Zhao. The Study was processed by Soon-Won Pak, with assistance from Jennifer Feliciano and Hera Sutrisna. The statistical appendix was prepared by Vidya Shetty, with assistance from Veena Khaleque and Anthony Stanley. The internal peer reviewers were Ataman Aksoy, Carl Dahlman, and Shahid Yusuf. The excellent cooperation of many officials of the Government of Bangladesh in preparing this Study is gratefully acknowledged. The Study was discussed with the Government of Bangladesh in February-March 1994.

ABBREVIATIONS AND ACRONYMS

ADB	-	Asian Development Bank
ADP	-	Annual Development Programme
BADC	-	Bangladesh Agricultural Development Corporation
BAPEX	-	Bangladesh Petroleum Exploration Company
BB	-	Bangladesh Bank
BBC	-	Bangladesh Biman Corporation
BCA	-	Banking Companies Act
BCIC	-	Bangladesh Chemical Industries Corporation
BEPZA	-	Bangladesh Export Processing Zone Authority
BFDC	-	Bangladesh Film Development Corporation
BFDC	-	Bangladesh Fisheries Development Corporation
BFIDC	-	Bangladesh Forest Industries Development Corporation
BFFWT	-	Bangladesh Freedom Fighter Welfare Trust
BHB	-	Bangladesh Handloom Board
BIWTA	-	Bangladesh Inland Water Transport Authority
BIWTC	-	Bangladesh Inland Water Transport Corporation
BJC	-	Bangladesh Jute Corporation
BJMC	-	Bangladesh Jute Mill Corporation
BKB	-	Bangladesh Krishi Bank
BOI	-	Board of Investment
BOO	-	Build-operate-own
BOGMC	-	Bangladesh Oil, Gas & Minerals Corporation
BOT	-	Build-operate-transfer
BPC	-	Bangladesh Petroleum Corporation
BPDB	-	Bangladesh Power Development Board
BPRC	-	Bangladesh Parjaton Corporation
BRTA	-	Bangladesh Rural Telecommunications Authority
BRTC	-	Bangladesh Road Transport Corporation
BSB	-	Bangladesh Shilpa Bank
BSB	-	Bangladesh Sericulture Board
BSC	-	Bangladesh Shipping Corporation
BSCIC	-	Bangladesh Small and Cottage Industries Corporation
BSEC	-	Bangladesh Steel and Engineering Corporation
BSFIC	-	Bangladesh Sugar and Food Industries Corporation
BSRS	-	Bangladesh Shilpa Rin Sangstha
BTB	-	Bangladesh Tea Board
BTMC	-	Bangladesh Textile Mills Corporation
BTTB	-	Bangladesh Telegraph and Telephone Board
BWDB	-	Bangladesh Water Development Board
CBA	-	Collective bargaining agents
CD	-	Customs duty
CDA	-	Chittagong Development Authority
CPA	-	Chittagong Port Authority
CWASA	-	Chittagong Water Supply and Sewerage Authority
DEDO	-	Duty Exemption and Drawback Office
DESA	-	Dhaka Electricity Supply Authority
DFI	-	Development finance institution
DSE	-	Dhaka Stock Exchange
DWASA	-	Dhaka Water Supply and Sewerage Authority
EPB	-	Export Promotion Bureau
ERER	-	Equilibrium real exchange rate
FFW	-	Food for Work Scheme
FY	-	Fiscal year
GATT	-	General Agreement on Tariffs and Trade
GDP	-	Gross domestic product

HBTL	-	Hutchison Bangladesh Telecom Limited
HYV	-	High yielding variety
ICB	-	Investment Corporation of Bangladesh
ICOP	-	Inter-Ministerial Committee on Privatization
IDA	-	International Development Association
IOC	-	International oil company
IPO	-	Import policy orders
IRO	-	Industrial Relations Ordinance
JBC	-	Jiban Bima Corporation
MFA	-	Multi-fibre Agreement
MOPT	-	Ministry of Post and Telecommunications
MPA	-	Mongla Port Authority
MT	-	Metric ton
NBR	-	National Board of Revenue
NCB	-	Nationalized commercial bank
NGO	-	Non-governmental organization
NMWB	-	National Minimum Wages Board
NPO	-	National Productivity Organization
NTB	-	Non-tariff barrier
NWPC	-	National Wage Productivity Commission
OC	-	Operating company
PBS	-	Palli Bidyut Samiti (rural electricity cooperative)
PSC	-	Production sharing contract
PSI	-	Preshipment inspection
RAJUK	-	Rajdhani Unnayan Kartipakhya
RAKUB	-	Rajshahi Krishi Unnayan Bank
RDA	-	Rajshahi Development Authority
REB	-	Rural Electrification Board
RER	-	Real exchange rate
RMG	-	Readymade garments industry
RMP	-	Rural Road Maintenance Program
SBC	-	Sadharan Bima Corporation
SBW	-	Special bonded warehouse
SD	-	Supplementary duty
SEC	-	Securities Exchange Commission
SKOP	-	Sramik Karmachari Oikya Parishad (Council of labor union federations)
SLR	-	Statutory liquidity ratio
SOE	-	State-owned enterprise
SRD	-	Statutory rate of duty
SRTC	-	Silk Research Training Centre
TA	-	Technical assistance
TCB	-	Trading Corporation of Bangladesh
TCC	-	Tripartite Consultative Committee
TPC	-	Tripartite Productivity Committee
TV	-	Tariff value
TYRIP	-	Three-Year Rolling Investment Programme
UNDP	-	United Nations Development Program
UNFPA	-	United Nations Fund for Population Activities
USAID	-	United States Agency for International Development
VAT	-	Valued added tax
VGD	-	Vulnerable Group Development Scheme

CURRENCY EQUIVALENTS

The external value of the Bangladesh Taka (Tk) is fixed in relation to a basket of reference currencies, with the US dollar serving as the intervention currency. The official exchange rate on January 27, 1994 was Tk 40.07 per US dollar.

US $ 1	=	Tk 40.07
Tk 1	=	US $ 0.025

Following local convention, expenditures and revenues are sometimes denominated in units of *crore* (abbreviated Cr), which is equal to Tk 10 million. At the current official exchange rate, Tk 1.0 Cr = US $ 250,000.

In this report, US $ is sometimes abbreviated as $.

WEIGHTS AND MEASURES

kWh	=	kilo watt-hour
MCF	=	million cubic feet
MMCFD	=	million cubic feet per day
MT	=	metric ton
MW	=	megawatts

FISCAL YEAR (FY)

July 1 - June 30

COUNTRY DATA - BANGLADESH

AREA
148,393 km²

POPULATION   (1991)
111.455 million
Rate of Growth: 2.17%

DENSITY
751 per km² (1991)
959 per km² of cultivable land (1991)

POPULATION CHARACTERISTICS (1991)

Crude Birth Rate (per '000)	31.6
Crude Death Rate (per '000)	11.2
Infant Mortality (per '000 live births)	90.6

HEALTH (1992)

Population per physician	5,304
Population per hospital bed	3,243

INCOME DISTRIBUTION (1988/89)

% of national income, highest quintile	46.2
% of national income, lowest quintile	6.6

DISTRIBUTION OF LAND OWNERSHIP (1978)

% owned by top 10% of owners	49
% owned by smallest 10% of owners	2

ACCESS TO DRINKING WATER (1992)

% of population - urban (piped water)	42
% of population - rural (tubewell)a/	80

ACCESS TO ELECTRICITY (1991/92)

% of population - urban	56.7
% of population - rural	4.7

NUTRITION

Calorie intake as % of requirements (1988)	88
Per capita protein intake (grams/day, 88/89)	64

EDUCATION (1991)

Adult literacy rate (%)	35
Literacy rate for all ages (%)	24.9
Primary school enrollment (%)	70

GNP PER CAPITA IN 1992: US$220 b/

GROSS DOMESTIC PRODUCT (1992/93)   ANNUAL RATE OF GROWTH (%, constant prices)

	US$ Million	%	FY75-80	FY81-88	FY89-93
GDP at Market Prices	24,753	100.0	4.12	4.58	4.2
Gross Domestic Investment	3,144	12.7	..	..	..
Gross National Saving	2,609	10.5	..	..	..
Current Account Balance	535	2.2	...	...	...
Exports of Goods, f.o.b.	2,383	9.6	4.7	7.7	11.0
Imports of Goods, c.i.f.	3,986	16.1	6.2	3.5	0.3

OUTPUT IN 1992/93 BY SECTOR

	Value Added c/ US$ Mill	%	Labor Force d/ Mill	%	Value Added/Worker d/ US$	%
Agriculture	8,204	33.1	32.6	65	251	51
Industry	4,221	17.1	7.8	16	541	110
Services	12,328	49.8	9.8	19	1258	255
Total	24,753	100.0	50.2	100	493	100

CENTRAL GOVERNMENT FINANCE

	Taka Billion FY93	% of GDP FY88	% of GDP FY93
Current Revenue	113.6	8.9	11.7
Current Expenditure	83.6	8.1	8.6
Current Surplus	30.0	0.8	3.1
Capital Expenditure	82.6	7.9	8.5
External Assistance (net)	52.9	6.9	5.5

a/ Based on 150 meter distance to tubewell.
b/ World Bank Atlas methodology; base 90-92.
c/ At market prices.
d/ Data is for 1989/90 civilian labor force.
.. = not available.
... = not applicable.

COUNTRY DATA - BANGLADESH

MONEY, CREDIT AND PRICES	June 86	June 87	June 88	June 89	June 90	June 91	June 92 a/	June 93 a/
	(Billion Taka outstanding, end of period)							
Money and Quasi-money	123.4	138.6	164.1	190.8	223.0	250.0	285.2	315.3
Bank Credit to Public Sector	58.2	60.5	60.8	59.0	70.3	75.5	76.0	84.5
Bank Credit to Private Sector	83.6	89.6	109.0	133.6	160.0	178.2	191.2	199.6
	(Percentages or Index Numbers)							
Money and Quasi-money as % of GDP	26.5	25.7	27.5	28.9	30.2	30.0	31.5	32.6
General Price Index (1970=100)	436.0	481.2	536.0	578.9	632.7	689.3	724.4	734.0
Annual Percentage Changes in:								
General Price Index	9.9	10.4	11.4	8.0	9.3	8.9	5.1	1.3
Bank Credit to Public Sector	11.7	4.0	0.5	-2.9	19.1	7.4	0.7	-8.8
Bank Credit to Private Sector	21.3	7.2	21.7	22.6	19.8	11.4	7.3	11.3

BALANCE OF PAYMENTS	(US$ Million)	
	1987/88	1992/93
Exports of Goods, f.o.b.	1,231	2,383
Imports of Goods, c.i.f.	-2,986	-3,986
Trade Gap (deficit = -)	-1,755	-1,603
Non-Factor services, net	-11	76
Worker's Remittances	737	942
Other Factor Payments (net)	-82	50
Current Account Balance	-1,111	-535
Direct Foreign Investment	0	10
Net MLT Borrowing	713	742
(Disbursements)	906	1,006
(Amortization)	193	264
Capital Grants	824	657
IMF facilities, net	-18	2
Other Capital, net	-264	-358
Change in Reserves (- = increase)	-144	-518
Gross Reserves (end of year)	897	2,197

RATE OF EXCHANGE (January 27, 1994)

US$1.00 = Taka 40.07

MERCHANDISE EXPORTS (1992/93)

	US$ Million	%
Raw jute	74	3
Jute goods	294	12
Tea	41	2
Leather	148	6
Fish and shrimp	165	7
Garments	1,240	52
Others	421	18
Total	2,383	100

EXTERNAL DEBT, June 1993

	US$ Million
Public Debt, incl. Guaranteed Private Debt	13,331
Non-Guaranteed Private Debt	..
Total Outstanding and Disbursed	13,331

DEBT SERVICE RATIO FOR 1992/93 a/

	%
Public Debt, incl. Guaranteed Private Debt	12.1
Non-Guaranteed Private Debt	..
Total	12.1

IBRD/IDA LENDING, June 1993 (US$ Million)

	IBRD	IDA
Outstanding and Disbursed	60.6	4,739
Undisbursed	0.0	1,522
Outstanding incl. Undisbursed	60.6	6,261

a/ Credit data adjusted for industrial loan write-offs and recapitalization of nationalized commercial banks by the Government through the issue of bonds.
b/ Including IMF.
.. = not available.

EXECUTIVE SUMMARY

Introduction

Bangladesh is at a crossroads in its quest for economic and social development. It has achieved much, but much is left undone. Population growth is lower, rice output has increased dramatically, a structural reform program has been underway for four years, the macroeconomy is stable, the balance of payments is sound, investments in education and health are proceeding, and democratic institutions are stronger today than ever before. And yet, the absolute number of poor in Bangladesh has grown steadily every year since Independence in 1971. Half its population of 111 million entered the 1990s with incomes below the poverty line. Bangladesh's progress on poverty reduction has been among the slowest in Asia, and poverty incidence appears to have declined only modestly during the 1980s. This Country Economic Memorandum describes the choices that Bangladesh faces at these crossroads.

The choice of the road ahead will determine the pace and quality of development over the next decade and beyond. This report emphasizes the importance of choosing the high road of faster policy and institutional reforms, leading to a GDP growth approaching 7 percent a year from the current 4.5 percent. This would require investment levels relative to GDP to rise to 18-20 percent from the current rate of under 13 percent. Only then will the economy be able to raise the poor out of poverty through a virtuous circle of rising employment, incomes, and human capital accumulation. In contrast, on the current road of slow reforms and growth, large segments of the population will remain in poverty well into the next century

The road of accelerated reforms must be based on the best medium- to long-term sources of growth in Bangladesh. These sources are anchored in both the agricultural and manufacturing sectors. Given its size, the agricultural sector's growth is clearly important for both its contribution to overall GDP growth, to poverty alleviation, and to absorbing the growing labor force. Agricultural growth has so far been fueled by foodgrains, mainly rice and some wheat. With approaching rice self-sufficiency, further growth led by foodgrains must now also depend crucially on the further growth of domestic demand and overall GDP growth. Likewise, to be sustainable, diversification and total factor productivity growth in agriculture will require further increases in the domestic demand for agricultural products or exports. There is also an untapped potential for off-farm output and employment growth, but this will require prior increases of rural farm incomes. Similarly, the services sector's expansion, though important, is likely to be led by, rather than lead, non-services growth.

Taken together, these considerations suggest that while agriculture can and should make an important contribution to overall growth, accelerated GDP growth will need to be driven largely by the growth of the manufacturing sector. The engine of manufacturing growth must also be export oriented, given the as yet small size of the domestic market for manufactures caused by low incomes. And it must come as an export push by the private sector, given the dismal failure of state-owned manufacturing in Bangladesh and worldwide. How Government policy and actions over the medium term facilitate an export push in manufacturing by the private sector is the basic theme of this report.

Bangladesh currently enjoys an unprecedented window of opportunity for achieving a dramatic breakthrough in the pace of pro-growth reforms. Inflation is at a record low, external reserves are at an all-time high, and the Government's domestic resource position is favorable. Macroeconomic stability and improved public resource management are the hard won gains of accelerating structural adjustment, they reduce the danger of macroeconomic strain, and they provide the potential resources for a safety net for the poor during the transition to a higher growth path.

Four principal questions need to be addressed for a medium-term growth agenda that relies on an export-oriented, private, manufacturing sector. *First*, how can business confidence be strengthened, leading to a substantial rise in efficient private investment in manufacturing for exports? Furthermore, while this is happening, how can public investment in priority areas be stepped up without sacrificing its quality? This is the essential investment challenge for the Government -- raising total investment from 13 percent of GDP to 18-20 percent. *Second*, how can the enabling environment for an outward-oriented private sector be enhanced? In particular, how can trade, payments, and direct investment links with the international economy be made much more effective by removing the impediments on the ground that still act as a disincentive to export? More generally, while broader reforms are underway, how can the high "cost of doing business" in specific lines of export activity be lowered (as appears to have happened in the successful readymade garments sector) to broaden and deepen the export orientation of the economy? *Third*, how can the Government deal expeditiously with the poor performance of the state-owned enterprise (SOE) sector, with the bulk of its assets in public utilities and infrastructure, and the remainder in manufacturing? The privileged position of SOEs has stifled private initiative, raised private costs, wasted scarce public resources, and sorely burdened the banking system and the budget. *Finally*, how can the present deep difficulties in the financial sector be untangled, and the distortions in industrial labor markets be resolved, so that these markets can function efficiently in support of an export push by the private sector?

There has been significant, though uneven, political commitment for tackling the early elements of the reform agenda. This political commitment must not be allowed to falter. The political economy of reforms in other adjusting countries suggests that opposition tends to resurface toward the middle of reform programs, at a stage when reforms have not yet reached a critical, self-sustaining mass. There is a strong rationale for reinvigorating the political commitment for reforms in Bangladesh, for broadening its political base to take advantage of the window of opportunity, and for staying the course without giving in to macroeconomic populism. More public awareness and advocacy of reforms are needed: reforms are still better known to those who stand to lose from them, but not to those who will gain. Unless implementation quickens and the Government takes both bolder and swifter actions, there is a danger that the expected industrial supply response, on which the growth objectives of the structural adjustment program are premised, may not materialize. Such an outcome would repudiate the excellent performance on stabilization, and put increasing political pressure on the Government as it approaches the next general election. Reform complacency now, through its political fallout over the medium term, could therefore threaten the entire reform effort with failure and potential reversal.

The four questions highlighted above, and addressed in the rest of this summary and the report, form the core objectives of policy reform. Set against the current window of opportunity, they provide the policy and institutional framework for choosing the high road of accelerated reforms, and therefore of rapid growth and poverty alleviation.

Private Credibility and Public Implementation: Meeting the Investment Challenge

As against this framework for faster growth, Bangladesh currently faces a central problem of stagnant domestic demand. Economic activity remains weak, and investment growth is feeble. Highly successful fiscal reforms since FY90 have raised domestic resources through the value added tax (VAT), curbed public consumption, and set priorities for public investments in the Annual

Development Programme (ADP). But the reforms have not been able to raise public investment, which has stagnated at around 5.7 percent of GDP for the past six years. Private investment has done no better, stagnating at a slightly higher average of 6.5 percent. Thus, the highly commendable success in public resource management, but the failure of private and public investment to rise in tandem, have jointly led to a problem of low aggregate demand. In FY93, this problem may have been exacerbated by the Government's financial operations. On the one hand, the Government has been borrowing from the private sector through the sale of savings certificates with interest rates well above market. On the other hand, it has been retiring its debt -- a reduction of Tk 12 billion in FY93 -- to the banking system, which is fragile and unable to lend aggressively to private industry. Preliminary information for FY94 suggests that the Government is continuing to retire its debt to the banking system.

Breaking out of this problem of low aggregate demand as soon as possible is the most important macroeconomic challenge for the Government. It is a challenge that will require the private sector's investment response to the Government's economic liberalization measures over the medium term, but for which bolder Government actions must start now. It is also a challenge that the Government can substantially tackle on its own in the short term through public investment, while private investment gathers momentum.

Private Investment. To attain a higher growth path that is sustainable, as well as to alleviate the current aggregate demand problem, private investment must rise. For this, it is critical that the Government ensure that its medium- to long-term macroeconomic policy framework and its specific reform actions and pronouncements are credible to the private sector. Entrepreneurs must be firmly persuaded that the reforms are irreversible, and likely to be effective, before they will begin to invest substantially in internationally competitive, export-oriented manufacturing. Adjustment experience elsewhere has shown that private investment responds to a complex set of policy and business expectations, including confidence, which can take long to consolidate. Bangladesh is no exception to this experience. The Government needs to address three areas of policy concern in bolstering its reform credibility.

First, the Government can greatly enhance confidence in its reforms by accelerating its trade liberalization program. Non-tariff barriers have been mostly removed. Ongoing tariff liberalization has brought customs duties plus import license fees down to a weighted-by-imports rate of 30 percent in FY93, further reductions have taken place in FY94, and the Government has announced its intention to continue rationalizing the tariff structure over FY95-97. Accelerating this schedule -- possibly reaching the nominal protection levels of 10 to 15 percent prevailing in internationally competitive developing countries within the next year -- would act as a precommitment device to ensure the consistency of future Government actions, as well as to lay out clearly an outward-oriented adjustment path for the private sector. Experience in East Asia suggests the critical difference such precommitment has made to the success of economic policies. In its absence, private enterprises may perceive a high probability that exports will fail to develop, and consequently that the reforms would be reversed.

Although customs revenues appear to have gone up during the first four months of FY94, faster tariff liberalization could, depending on the buoyancy of imports, reduce customs revenue. Tariff liberalization, whether it is done decisively now or incrementally over a number of years, will inevitably present a potential short-run tradeoff with tax revenues. It should be recognized that the Government, despite its best efforts and the existence of a well-prioritized ADP over the past three years, has found itself repeatedly unable to spend public revenues as planned. Hence, an accelerated, decisive trade liberalization in the near future, and the underlying objective of accelerating structural adjustment, should not be held hostage to short-run revenue needs that may have been established in relation to unrealistic targets for the ADP. This is particularly so if the Government adheres to its highly desirable objective of consolidating the gains from tax reform and strengthening tax administration and collection (particularly from the VAT). As private investment and ADP implementation lift the economy out of its current low aggregate demand, imports will increase, not least because of the high import intensity of investment, thereby further reducing possible losses of customs revenue from accelerated tariff liberalization. Finally, accelerated tariff liberalization would provide a quicker replacement of trade-distorting customs duties with trade-neutral VAT and income taxes.

It should be emphasized that trade liberalization and the Government's export-oriented growth strategy, even if well-implemented, cannot succeed unless competitiveness improves. This requires that there must be flexible management of the exchange rate, steps to link real wages with productivity, and other domestic cost reducing measures. All three elements are necessary if export competitiveness vis-a-vis actual and potential competitors is to be maintained and enhanced.

Second, the Government should liberalize interest rates further, removing or reducing the deposit rate floor so that lending rates can have one less reason to remain as high as the present 10 to 12 percent real levels. The Government should also lower the interest rates on virtually risk-free postal and savings certificates, since this causes financial disintermediation from the banking system, and potentially dampens interest in equity markets. Given overlapping and complex weaknesses in the enabling environment for the private sector, it is difficult to estimate the private sector's investment response, but evidence clearly suggests that it would be positive, particularly in conjunction with the crowding-in effect of prioritized ADP expenditures and their fiscal stimulus. While the Government's concern about raising private saving and offering high returns to households is welcome, the evidence is clear that total saving (meaning saving not just in financial instruments but all income that is not consumed) responds more to income growth than to interest rates. Thus, to the extent that further lowering deposit interest rates will bring down lending rates and boost investment and income growth, total saving over the medium term would be higher.

Third, there is a vital need to ensure that the Government follows a steady policy toward the private sector. The more consistent Government policy actions and pronouncements relating to the private sector are, the more impact will accelerated trade liberalization and a decline in lending rates have on private investment decisions. There is still a strong tendency for Government statements to leave its policy stance toward the private sector unclear. This lack of clarity and consistency clouds private business expectations. Worse still, policy changes that promise effective decontrol of private enterprise, but which are then delayed or retracted, shake the confidence of the private sector and therefore must be avoided.

Public Investment. In the short run, the Government can best meet the investment challenge by making an urgent, all-out effort to improve the implementation of the ADP. The early indications for the first half of FY94 are not encouraging. Much effort has been spent on prioritizing the ADP so that its quality can be high and it can be focussed on infrastructure, education, health, and population. In the past, the binding constraint has been local taka resources. This is no longer the case, with the VAT bringing in considerable additional revenues. But, with its failure to expand the ADP rapidly (the FY93 ADP was Tk 70 billion, Tk 16.5 billion short of the originally planned ADP, and 85 percent of the subsequently lowered operational ADP target), the Government has failed to reap the benefits of its past good work. This represents a fundamental shortcoming of public administration, located principally in the line ministries and agencies that are responsible for project implementation, as well as in the overall policy framework for infrastructure and the utilities. This public investment failure spills over into private investment decisions, since there is strong evidence to suggest that as in other countries, high quality public investment in Bangladesh crowds in private investment.

The Government has introduced several procedural changes over the past two years to improve ADP project execution. It has tried to simplify procurement decisions, improve personnel policies relating to key project staff, and has increased financial authorities for contract awards and project expenditures. However, a recent survey of project management during FY93 showed that on average procurement decisions continue to take 8 to 34 months, nearly half of all projects were still managed by a part-time director, and decisions on contracts of less than Tk 5 crores still continue to be sent to the Ministries for approval. Action is now urgently required in three areas. *First*, high-level intervention, monitoring, and follow-through are needed to ensure that procedural reforms are effectively implemented. *Second*, selective administrative and civil service reforms that impact the ADP should be expedited, particularly in agencies that sit on the critical path of ADP implementation; this could be done, for example, by selectively posting only high-performing civil servants to these agencies and ensuring the stability of their tenure. *Third*, the private sector should be actively encouraged to play a greater role in executing ADP projects, through, for example, contracting out project supervision, and by drawing them into the planning of projects. ADP execution is also affected by policy and institutional weaknesses in infrastructure and the utilities sectors. Feeble capacity for reform in these Government agencies, and the need to develop appropriate sector strategies before private entry can start, is holding back more aggressive public investment through new public-private partnerships. Faster progress in dealing with the deep-rooted problems in these agencies is therefore all the more important (see below).

If, instead of raising public investment substantially, the Government takes the easier route of returning to the public consumption profligacy of earlier years (for example, through generous public wage awards), or to wasteful, low-quality projects in the ADP, the hard work of public resource management will have been wasted. Similar slides into macroeconomic populism have had disastrous consequences, in terms of low growth and fiscal imbalances, in Latin America and Sub-Saharan Africa, and must be avoided. This will require that the political commitment to the reforms not be allowed to weaken. Otherwise, without a solid foundation of physical and human capital on which to sustain long-term growth, the current window of opportunity for accelerated reforms would inexorably close, as the economy fails to make a successful transition from stabilization to rapid growth.

To sustain the rapid acceleration of the ADP, it is imperative that the Government maintain the policy momentum on tax reforms, particularly in the administration of the VAT. The expansion of the VAT in the early years was easier because it was replacing excise duties. Efforts to extend its domestic coverage and improve compliance now need to be redoubled. Tax revenue collection needs to be monitored carefully. Preliminary evidence for the first five months of FY94 shows that tax revenue collection from domestic indirect taxes may be slowing down relative to the previous year and the Government's annual tax target. Unless there is a pickup in the second half of FY94, such a slowdown would be a cause for concern.

Effective Deregulation: Meeting the Challenge of an Export Push by the Private Sector

Rapid growth in Bangladesh will require a substantial export push spearheaded by the private manufacturing sector. Both to keep pace with its competitors and to raise the confidence of the private sector in the reform process, there is now an urgent need to take the high road of accelerated pro-private sector reforms. Economic liberalization in South Asia, rapid change in China and the high-performing East Asian economies, and emerging competition from low labor-cost countries such as

Vietnam, pose a challenge that Bangladesh must meet. There is likely to be intense competition among these countries for overseas export markets and foreign investment. To be well positioned, Bangladesh needs to offer the same or better enabling environment for the private sector as these countries do. While enjoying its window of opportunity, the Government has successfully reduced overall macroeconomic uncertainty. It must now rapidly reduce uncertainties relating to trade liberalization, availability of tradable and nontradable inputs at world prices, investment deregulation, and efficient availability of credit and labor. Action is required at the general level of the policy and business environments, and in specific subsectors where Government policies or poorly functioning institutions constrain rapid export development.

At the economy-wide level, the Government's structural adjustment reforms are seeking to alter the incentive framework decisively in favor of the private sector's greater integration with world markets. This will provide the basis for an export push, as well as force efficiency more generally in the domestic economy. The current round of reforms has achieved much, but much remains to be tackled yet. Most non-tariff barriers have been lifted; investment controls have been largely swept aside; foreign companies can invest freely; the taka is now partially convertible. But the financial sector remains underdeveloped, caught between excess liquidity on the one hand and depressed private investment demand on the other; tariffs have been lowered, but, as argued above, there is a clear rationale for accelerating their further reduction; problems of service provision by power, water, and gas utilities are still a far cry from being solved; foreign investment is still a trickle; labor reforms have not yet gotten off the ground. Even where the rules have changed on paper, there is often a large effectiveness gap on the ground. Serious attention needs to be devoted to removing such effectiveness gaps where reforms relating to the private sector are being implemented poorly. For example, little progress has been made on improving clearance procedures, which continue to bedevil the import process. The 1992 voluntary preshipment inspection scheme (PSI) did not work, since it failed to require certified PSI values to automatically overrule Customs assessments. The Government has recently tried to improve the scheme to give it a green channel aspect. While this is welcome, the Government must return to its original intention of instituting a compulsory, off-shore PSI scheme in order to break the essential problem of rent-seeking and delays in import clearance, and to enhance customs revenue.

There have been recent improvements in the export incentives relating to the access to bonded warehouse facilities and the simplification of duty drawback procedures. But, effectiveness gaps remain, with frequent delays reported still in obtaining duty drawbacks, and problems in using bonded warehouses outside the readymade garments industry. The rule attempting to force bonded warehouse users to raise domestic value added (by limiting the proportion of export value that can be imported) has been modified partially, but is not yet being implemented. This effectively prevents exporters from working with higher value inputs and targeting up-market exports. It also forces them to forego potentially lucrative export opportunities for high-volume exports that have a low domestic value added on a per-unit basis. Other rules on consignment sales, now rendered obsolete by the convertibility of the taka on the current account, need to be discarded. These lurking effectiveness gaps need to be closed by concerted, high-level insistence on clear and transparent action, and by random checks of effectiveness.

In attempting to put its private entrepreneurs on the same footing as their international competitors, rapid progress may not be possible on all fronts despite the best intentions of the Government. It is therefore imperative that the Government also explore the possibility of making more modest changes to the policy framework (akin to bonded warehouses and the back-to-back letters of credit for readymade garments) that can alleviate the one or more critical constraints that may be holding back the potential development of an export subsector. As the readymade garments sector has shown, effective deregulation of the private sector and a supportive policy environment can make a dramatic difference. An important principle that must be followed in supporting such private sector prospects is to first consider the possibility of establishing a firm export foothold, and only then moving upstream to exploit backward linkages. Industrial policy has often sought to go the other way, as in the case of textiles, with little success.

Public-Private Partnerships: Meeting the Challenge of State-Owned Enterprises

The gross FY93 losses of all state-owned enterprises including the railways amounted to about Tk 20 billion, a staggering 27 percent of the ADP, 45 percent of external aid disbursements and 2 percent of GDP. Such a vast public failure spanning both industry and finance has raised private industrial costs, stymied faster private sector-led growth, and hurt the banks and the Budget. The Government needs to quickly develop, enunciate, and begin implementation of a policy vision to deal with this morass, building on the *Industrial Policy of 1991*. Such a vision should be based on a clear conceptual framework that pairs market circumstances (whether competitive, natural monopoly, or quasi-monopoly) with the desired sector structure, for example, in the power sector. Such a vision must also be tempered by the Government's regulatory capabilities, preferring simple, rule-based structural regulation to much more demanding negotiated, conduct regulation.

In line with such a vision, the Government should adopt a three-pronged strategy to deal with the problems of the non-financial SOEs. *First*, the privatization of selected SOEs, initially in manufacturing, should be accelerated. *Second*, enterprises likely to remain in the hands of Government over the foreseeable future should be pushed to commercialize and face the market. *Third*, private sector entry must be encouraged, particularly in power, gas, and water utilities, and in telecommunications and transport. The last prong of the strategy, and by far the most important for raising overall efficiency in the economy, will require new forms of public-private partnership designed to promote private entry in infrastructure and utilities, improve sector efficiency, and force existing public monopolies to compete. Such arrangements will require both an enabling environment and appropriate regulatory regimes.

Privatization. Progress on privatization has so far been tardy, and the Government has been unable to meet its own divestiture targets. Delays have been caused by difficulties in setting up the Privatization Board, making it fully operational, and wavering political commitment. No concerted efforts have been made to build a political constituency for privatization, consisting of the public, labor unions, and SOEs. The choice of poorer performing units for initial privatization may have cooled the interest of potential purchasers. Rapid action is needed to correct all three problems, starting with the strengthening of the technical capabilities, decision-making authority, and transparent autonomy of the Privatization Board. Only then can the Board be well positioned to undertake the major, privatization of the jute sector that is in the offing, and which will be a test case for the Government's commitment to private sector development. A major public education campaign (particularly aimed at workers) to provide information on the benefits of privatization is needed, as is an expanded focus to include the early privatizations of the more successful SOEs. There has been some modest progress on privatization during the latter half of FY94, but this progress needs to be consolidated rapidly.

Restructuring. Progress on SOE restructuring during FY93 largely took the form of increased retrenchment through voluntary separation to deal with the severe problem of overmanning, particularly in the Railways and in the jute sector. While this needs to be continued and extended to other sectors, the overall uncertainties and delays surrounding SOE reforms have resulted in a loss of direction for many SOEs, and thereby worsened their performance. Therefore, while it pushes ahead with traditional SOE reforms such as commercialization and improved management autonomy, the development of a policy vision as noted above will help to clarify the transition from the current structure of the SOE sector to a largely private manufacturing sector, and to joint involvement with the private sector in the utilities and infrastructure.

Private Entry. The most urgent need for initiating private entry in the utilities and infrastructure is to formulate the regulatory frameworks within which such entry can take place. These regulatory regimes must emphasize the principles of procedural transparency, competitive behavior on the part of both public and private entities, and simple rule-based regulation that will not exceed the regulatory capacity for monitoring and enforcement. Without such regimes, Government agencies on occasion appears to be rudderless in their dealings with potential partners, at times acting at cross-purposes to each other. The actual forms such public-private partnerships can take (management contracts, leases, and concessions such as production sharing contracts and build-operate-transfer) are well known, and there is a good base of international experience to build on once the regulatory framework is made clear.

Financial and Labor Reforms: Meeting the Challenge in Factor Markets

Financial Markets. There appears to be a stalemate in commercial bank lending to the private sector, caused by factors affecting the supply and demand for funds. On the supply side, the nationalized commercial banks (NCBs) are hesitant to lend because new prudential regulation has exposed their financial weaknesses and they face an uncertain future that may include restructuring or privatization. The NCBs also do not have the expertise to make project loans or develop new financial instruments. The two development finance institutions have been moribund for some time. On the demand side, the factors dampening demand for credit include the weakness of economic activity and the current problem of low aggregate demand, high real interest rates, low SOE activity due to the slow pace of privatization and their own uncertain prospects, and an apparent dearth of creditworthy borrowers with acceptable collateral. Tackling the demand-side problems is likely to be easier in the short run, as compared to the harder institutional problems on the supply side.

The major barrier to financial sector development in Bangladesh has been the Government's ownership of the main financial institutions, and, in the past, its interventions in credit allocation. This has led to an uncompetitive and oligopolistic financial sector, providing poor quality intermediation. Weak supervision by Bangladesh Bank in the past has allowed these difficulties to deepen, particularly in the private banks. The Government has recognized that fundamental reform to increase competition in the financial sector is now inevitable. Past attempts to cure the sector have resulted in temporary alleviation of the symptoms of its malaise, but, without fundamental change, capital adequacy and other problems have reappeared. Progress on these reforms needs to accelerate, since much difficult and complex work of institutional sorting out lies ahead.

Using an integrated strategy comprising strengthened bank supervision, privatization, and new private bank entry, the long-overdue fundamental reform of the financial sector is now possible, but this will require a renewed political commitment for rapid implementation. Progress will depend on the speed with which the Government can take the necessary steps to privatize the NCBs (starting with the announced privatization of Rupali Bank, but taking care that the poor experience of the previous bank privatizations of Pubali Bank and Uttara Bank are not repeated), license new private banks, push the two denationalized banks to restructure and become an effective competitive presence in the market, and continue the strengthening of Bangladesh Bank. It will also depend on the speed with which it can tackle the reform of the non-financial SOEs. Imposing hard budget constraints and restructuring the SOEs (as proposed in the jute sector) will vastly improve the portfolios of the NCBs and the two denationalized banks. Finally, progress will also clearly depend on the pace at which the economy can overcome the current weakness in aggregate demand. A pickup in the pace of economic activity, and therefore of private demand for investment funds, would ease the task of restructuring relative to the current lending standstill in the financial sector.

Labor Markets. Labor markets in Bangladesh are the crucial link in converting its comparative advantage in low labor cost into a successful export push. They are also the crucial link between productive job opportunities and the poor, whose only asset may be their labor. Experience in other low-income countries that have successfully achieved an export push shows that both these links require labor markets to be flexible. This implies that wages and employment must be free to adjust in line with productivity growth, skill requirements, and the market outlook for final products, and must not be held hostage to vested interests. It also implies that labor markets should send appropriate signals to workers and employers about the skill mixes that are likely to be required.

Excessive and misguided Government intervention has prevented Bangladesh's industrial labor markets from playing this role. Public wage policies and minimum wage regulations have allowed real wages to increase faster than productivity, and the spillover effects of this on private sector wages have resulted in a loss of international competitiveness. Labor legislation concerned more with job security than job creation has hampered firms seeking to restructure their operations in response to shifts in the market outlook for their products. The Government has permitted an excessive political orientation of labor relations. In the absence of more conventional channels of negotiation between employers and workers, trade unions affiliated with political parties have come to use general strikes and political agitation to seek their demands directly from the Government. The perception of militant labor activity, whether based in fact or not, has potentially acted as a strong disincentive to new investment, particularly from overseas.

Attention must also be devoted to medium-term concerns about the appropriate skill-mix requirements of the private sector in Bangladesh to mount a sustained export push. It would be highly desirable for the Government to enter into a dialogue with the private sector to identify processes by which these skills may be supplied without waiting for the much needed, but longer-term, process of increases in the general educational attainment of the population. If real wages reflect productivity, then workers should be willing, barring specific market failures, to acquire training in anticipation of higher productivity and wages, and a market-based supply of such training is to be preferred. Where workers are cash-constrained to obtain such services, training credit and safety net programs can help alleviate the problem.

Bangladesh's comparative edge should be its low labor costs, adjusted for labor productivity differentials due to different capital-labor ratios. If real wage growth is allowed to outpace productivity growth in either the public or the private sector as a result of excessive and misguided Government interventions, this edge will be lost. Thus, success in supporting rapid, private-sector led growth will depend on minimizing the extent to which public sector wage policies subvert a market-based wage determination process in the private sector. This link between public and private sector wages will be weakened the faster the Government proceeds with worker retrenchment, privatization, and commercial restructuring of SOEs, including the dilution of its monopoly in the utilities and infrastructure through new partnerships with the private sector.

Synergies and Implementation Priorities in the Reform Program

This executive summary started out by asking four questions relating to how Government policy and actions over the medium term can facilitate accelerated growth. As the discussion here and in the report shows, the resulting agenda for promoting an export push by the private manufacturing sector is an ambitious one, requiring simultaneous progress on many fronts.

First, breaking out of the current aggregate demand problem and stimulating weak economic activity is the most important challenge facing the Government. Quicker tariff reductions and lower real interest rates are needed to spur private investment, raise confidence, and precommit the Government to the irreversibility of an outward-oriented adjustment process. In the short-run, faster ADP implementation is the primary fiscal instrument at the Government's disposal to raise investment. *Second*, improvements in the policy and business environments are needed to reduce large effectiveness gaps that still keep the "cost of doing business" in Bangladesh high, and act as a potential deterrent to greater domestic and foreign investment. *Third*, clearing the regulatory underbrush and rapidly initiating public-private partnerships in the utilities and infrastructure are required to bring much needed new investment, management styles, and technology to Bangladesh. Completing the Government's privatization program expeditiously is also important, as much to demonstrate its commitment to the private sector as to raise public efficiency and ameliorate the problem of bad debts in commercial banks. *Fourth*, the financial restructuring of the NCBs (in conjunction with the imposition of hard budget constraints on SOEs) and the private banks, and further empowering Bangladesh Bank for effective regulation, need to start in earnest. Both will take time, and the structural transition from dominant Government ownership to efficient private control must be managed carefully. For industrial labor markets to translate rapid growth into rapid employment, the Government must look to both its own potentially misguided interventions and the effect of public sector wage policies. When such policies create a mismatch between increases in real wages and productivity, they potentially render ineffective Bangladesh's comparative advantage in low labor costs. To raise productivity, greater investments in both human capital and plant and machinery are necessary.

It is important to emphasize that these four elements form a package, with the effect of the whole likely to be greater than the sum of its parts. Implementing this agenda will require a renewed political commitment and attention to bureaucratic capacity for accelerated reforms. Fortunately, there are powerful synergies between the various elements of the reform program, which should make progress on several fronts mutually reinforcing. Two such synergies are highlighted below.

Synergies. *First*, rapid implementation of the ADP in the priority areas of infrastructure and the social sectors will help crowd in private investment. The fiscal stimulus from lifting aggregate demand will, through its stimulation of private investment demand for investible funds, also break the current lending standstill in the financial sector, and make restructuring that much easier in a growing market than in a stagnant one. Similarly, it would ease industrial labor market frictions as employment rises in response to higher economic activity. Greater private investment in plant and machinery will enable faster increases in labor productivity.

Second, faster progress on restructuring problem SOE sectors, such as jute and textiles, should have a profound effect on cleaning out the portfolios of the affected NCBs. This will facilitate privatization and restructuring of the NCBs, and increase the effectiveness of financial intermediation for the private manufacturing sector as a whole. In particular, it will lower loan loss provisioning costs, and thereby reduce lending rates. Downsizing the SOE sector, including the voluntary separation of labor, will progressively reduce the demonstration impact of public sector wage policies on the private sector. Private entry in utilities and telecommunication will bring large, lumpy investments that should work toward ameliorating the problem of weak aggregate demand. New entry, particularly foreign investment in technologies, management and marketing, will not only bring competitive pressure on the public monopolies, but also a new ethos to industrial management, labor relations and productivity, and new technology.

Besides synergies, the reform program also implies some short-run tradeoffs. Faster tariff reductions may, depending on the buoyancy of imports, slow down the growth of tax revenues. The Government's comfortable domestic resource position makes this tradeoff less important than it might otherwise be deemed. Liberalizing interest rates on deposits and rationalizing them on savings certificates may cause temporary declines in financial savings. However, total saving responds more to income growth than to interest rates, and will pick up with rising incomes.

Implementation Priorities. As adjustment experience elsewhere shows, completing this ambitious reform agenda will take time, and it is imperative that policymakers stay the course until a critical mass of self-sustaining reforms develops. In order to put the synergies in the reform program to work as soon as possible, and to develop an early policy momentum while Bangladesh enjoys the current window of opportunity, the Government should consider the following priority actions.

In the *short* run:

(a)   accelerate ADP implementation urgently, while maintaining its quality, to lift the economy out of its low aggregate demand problem, as well as to lay the foundation for private sector development;

(b)   complete tariff liberalization within the next 12 to 18 months to precommit the Government to the pace and direction of reform, and manage costs and prices so as to maintain competitiveness;

(c)   liberalize interest rates further, by removing or further lowering the floor on deposit rates and rationalizing returns on risk-free Government instruments, so that real lending rates decline and, in conjunction with the fiscal stimulus, raise private investment;

(d)   conclude the much-delayed privatization of manufacturing SOEs quickly by empowering the Privatization Board and requiring it to make the rapid progress that would clearly signal to the private sector the direction and underlying commitment of Government policy toward private sector development; and

(e)   support those subsectors that can significantly enhance their export prospects (as happened in the readymade garments industry) by small and easily implementable improvements in the policy environment.

Over the *short* to *medium* term:

(f)   encourage private entry in the utilities and infrastructure in order to attract foreign investment and improve domestic service provision;

(g)   privatize Rupali as soon as feasible to show the way for future banking privatizations, enhance bank supervision, license new banks, and restructure the two denationalized banks so that competition can increase at the same time as bank portfolio quality improves with the imposition of hard budget constraints on SOEs and their restructuring in sectors such as jute;

(h)   make deregulation of the private sector genuinely effective, removing the implementation and credibility gaps that exist between policies and their outcomes; and,

(i)   enhance the flexibility of industrial labor markets by ensuring that Government interventions are kept to a minimum and they do not impede the decentralized setting of wages in the private sector in line with productivity gains.

PART I

RECENT ECONOMIC PERFORMANCE AND
MACROECONOMIC PRIORITIES FOR GROWTH

CHAPTER I: RECENT ECONOMIC DEVELOPMENTS AND REFORM PRIORITIES

A. INTRODUCTION

Bangladesh is at a crossroads in its quest for economic and social development. It has achieved much. Population growth is lower, self-sufficiency in rice production is today a reality that was hard to imagine just a decade ago, macroeconomic stability and improved use of public resources are the hard won gains of stabilization, GDP growth has averaged 4 percent over the past two decades, and democratic institutions are more robust today than ever before during the first two decades of nationhood. And yet, the absolute number of poor in Bangladesh has steadily increased each year since Independence in 1971. Two decades of sustained aid flows and emphasis on the social sectors have still left Bangladesh's social indicators amongst the lowest in the world. Poverty, and poor rural infrastructure, leave large parts of the population exposed to repeated natural disasters. Much precious time has been lost in state sponsored industrial and agricultural ineptitude and wasteful public consumption.

At these crossroads, the choices for Bangladesh seem clear. Choose the high road and accelerate policy reforms, removing the constraints to faster income and employment growth led by the private sector. Or continue on the low road of incremental and ineffectively implemented reforms, accompanied by a modest growth of around 4 to 4.5 percent that will leave large segments of the population in poverty well into the next century. This Country Economic Memorandum highlights the need to accelerate reforms aimed at generating faster growth led by the private sector in Bangladesh.

Experience with poverty alleviation over the past four decades has yielded several lessons. The World Bank's *World Development Report 1990:Poverty* provides an overview of this experience, and draws conclusions that reflect a broad consensus. The UNDP's first *Human Development Report*, which also came out in the same year, can be interpreted as reaching the same broad conclusions. The WDR conclusions are summarized in Box 1.1, and Table 1.1 compares Bangladesh's long-term progress on reducing poverty incidence with other developing countries. The main lesson of global experience is that no country has achieved and sustained any significant reduction in poverty without sustained, high growth. Even in China, with its strong pre-reform commitment to egalitarianism, it took a decade of sustained, rapid growth generated by market-oriented reforms to reduce the number of the absolute poor from 270 million to the current level of around 97 million people.

Rapid economic growth is critical to reducing poverty in Bangladesh. To illustrate the orders of magnitude, it would take 25 years for an average poor person in Bangladesh to cross the poverty line[1] if real per capita income continues to grow as it has in the past.[2] This "crossover time" could be more than halved, to 10 years, if real per capita income growth rose above 4 percent (6 to 7 percent real income growth and 2 percent population growth). The connection of poverty alleviation

---

[1] The "crossover time" is the time it would take, in the absence of income redistribution policies, for the average poor person at the mean level of income below the poverty line to cross the poverty line if his or her income grows at the national average per capita rate. See Ravi Kanbur, "Measurement and Alleviation of Poverty," *IMF Staff Papers*, Vol. 34, March 1987, pp. 60-85. Martin Ravallion, "The Challenging Arithmetic of Poverty in Bangladesh," *Bangladesh Development Studies*, Vol. XVIII, September 1990, pp. 35-53.

[2] Real per capita income has grown at an average rate of 1.6 percent per annum over the past two decades: 4.2 percent real income growth and 2.6 percent population growth.

Box 1.1: *WORLD DEVELOPMENT REPORT 1990*:
CORRELATION BETWEEN GROWTH AND POVERTY ERADICATION

Three East Asian countries--Indonesia, Malaysia, and Thailand--demonstrate the benefits of an appropriate balance between policies that spur growth and policies that enable the poor to participate in growth. All three achieved and sustained annual GDP growth rates of more than 6 percent. This growth--relatively labor intensive--generated demand for the factors of production owned by the poor. These countries also provided for adequate social spending. As a result, they have achieved universal primary education, and their infant mortality rates are lower than those of many countries with similar incomes. The improvement in skills and quality of the labor force enabled the poor to seize the opportunities provided by economic growth.

Indonesia was able to combine accelerated economic growth with impressive progress in reducing poverty. Besides addressing economic imbalances and distortions, this was basically the result of a strong focus on public investment in rural development and an emphasis on public expenditures concerning the welfare and productivity of the poor. Broadly speaking, policies stimulated investment in labor-intensive, export-oriented production. The enabling macro environment of trade liberalization, agricultural diversification, and the development of financial and infrastructural support services was complemented by initiatives to generate income-earning opportunities for the poor and to enhance their productive resources by improving their access to physical assets, human capital, credit, and inputs. Sustained employment creation--especially in small-scale enterprises and expansion of rural development programs into the more remote areas--provided the necessary requirements for poverty alleviation.

In Malaysia strong economic growth in the 1970s and 1980s was accompanied by significant achievements in poverty reduction. The development of a labor-intensive manufacturing sector, an open trade and price regime and a flexible labor market enabled the poor to expand into all branches of economic activity. Increased public spending on social services, especially public health and education, promoted equity and endowed the poor with the human capital needed to benefit from the new employment opportunities and to participate in the economic growth.

In other countries the creation of opportunities for the poor and the development of their capacity to respond have not always been well balanced. Brazil's GDP growth exceeded that of every other country in Table 1.1, and Pakistan's equaled the 6 percent annual growth achieved by the East Asian countries. Yet in neither country did social indicators improve rapidly. Brazil has one of the highest mortality rates for children under five among the middle income countries, and Pakistan has one of the lowest rates of primary enrollment in the world. The failure to improve the skills of the labor force has limited poor people's ability to benefit from growth. In each case the headcount index fell, but less quickly than in Indonesia or Malaysia.

So, it is possible to have economic growth without much social progress. The converse is also true: social indicators can be improved even in the absence of rapid economic growth. The experience of Sri Lanka shows that remarkable social progress can be achieved even at low levels of income. Yet, as the experience of India, Morocco, and Sri Lanka shows, low GDP growth makes it difficult to reduce poverty.

A key conclusion emerges from all this: the countries that have been most successful in attacking poverty have encouraged a pattern of rapid growth that makes efficient use of labor and have invested in the human capital of the poor. This two-part approach, proposed in the *World Development Report*, should be the basic strategy for the reduction of poverty. Both elements are essential. The first provides the poor with easily accessible opportunities to use their most abundant asset -- labor. The second improves their immediate well-being and increases their capacity to take advantage of the newly created possibilities. Together, they can improve the lives of the poor.

Source: *World Development Report 1990.*

---

with faster growth can be illustrated in another way: household expenditure survey data indicate that merely to prevent the absolute number of poor in Bangladesh from increasing, as they have done for the past 23 years, real national income would consistently have to grow at least two and a half times as fast as the rate of population growth (currently just above 2 percent per annum). As against this need for faster growth, Bangladesh's progress on poverty alleviation has been slow and uneven during the past decade, and the incidence of poverty still remained high at the start of the 1990s. This adds urgency to the need to accelerate pro-growth reforms.

In assessing Bangladesh's opportunities and obstacles to faster growth, three issues deserve particular attention. *First*, Bangladesh is enjoying unprecedented macroeconomic stability, providing a window of opportunity for accelerating economic growth based on a rapid structural adjustment of the economy. Inflation is extremely low, foreign reserves are at an all-time high, and the Government's domestic resource position is favorable. Whereas rapid structural change can cause macroeconomic strain and endanger stability, Bangladesh currently has a cushion of comfort. Policymakers can now ill afford to pursue a "business as usual" approach. Complacency, bred either by political expediency or bureaucratic lethargy, will only worsen the problem of poverty, as the aspirations of the poor mount.

Table 1.1: Poverty Reduction: Variation in Country Experience

	Average annual reduction			
Country and Period	Headcount index (percentage points)[a]		Under-five mortality (percent)[b]	
Indonesia (1970-87)	2.34	(58)	3.3	(146)
Malaysia (1973-87)	1.66	(37)	3.7	(46)
Brazil (1960-80)	1.45	(50)	2.8	(107)
Pakistan (1962-84)	1.43	(54)	1.8	(200)
Costa Rica (1971-86)	1.41	(45)	9.3	(35)
Thailand (1962-86)	1.40	(59)	4.4	(70)
India (1972-83)	1.04	(54)	1.8	(199)
Colombia (1971-88)	0.91	(41)	7.2	(64)
Morocco (1970-84)	0.64	(43)	5.6[c]	(136)
Sri Lanka (1963-82)	0.51	(37)	2.8	(66)
Bangladesh (1984-1992)	0.29	(52)	4.7	(211)

[a]   Initial level in parentheses.
[b]   1975-80 rate in parentheses, except 1981 for Bangladesh.
[c]   1977-81.
Source: *World Development Report 1990*; and Staff estimates for Bangladesh.

Second, in seeking higher growth, the highest priority must be given to raising private and public investment, without which growth will not accelerate even if macroeconomic policies remain prudent. Private investment responds worldwide to a complex set of policy and business factors, including confidence, which can take long to consolidate: Bangladesh is no exception to this experience. Using the current window of opportunity, the overall macroeconomic policy climate must be such as to support rapid private investment. This requires, among other things, that Bangladesh not let its international competitiveness slide. While private investment gains strength, the major burden of raising investment in the interim must fall on the Annual Development Programme (ADP), whose lackluster implementation performance in recent years still leaves much to be desired. The ADP, no longer constrained by local taka resources as in the past, and now better prioritized, is hampered by weak implementation capacity in line ministries. This implies continuing attention to the many small impediments that thwart ADP implementation. At the heart of the problem of ADP implementation, however, is a fundamental failure of public administration in Bangladesh. Changing this will require stronger political and bureaucratic commitment to do what it takes to raise public investment through the ADP.

Third, the quest for accelerated growth must focus on the best medium- to long-term sources of growth in the economy. These sources are anchored in both the agricultural and manufacturing sectors. Given its size, the agricultural sector's growth is clearly important for both its contribution to overall GDP growth, to poverty alleviation, and to absorbing the growing labor force. Agricultural growth has so far been fueled by foodgrains, mainly rice and some wheat. With approaching rice self-sufficiency, further growth led by foodgrains must now also depend crucially on the further growth of domestic demand and overall GDP growth. Likewise, to be sustainable, diversification and total factor productivity[1] growth in agriculture will require further increases in the domestic demand for agricultural products or exports. There is also an untapped potential for off-farm output and employment growth, but this will require prior increases of rural farm incomes. Similarly, the services sector's expansion, though important, is likely to be led by, rather than lead, non-services growth. Taken together, these considerations suggest that while agriculture can and should make an important contribution to overall growth, accelerated GDP growth will need to be driven largely by the growth of the manufacturing sector. Unlike China and the rest of the high-performing East Asian economies,[2] faster manufacturing growth and a major push for exports has not followed improved agricultural performance in Bangladesh. The manufacturing sector's growth has been slow, and its size remains small. This is because the reform agenda for private manufacturing development in Bangladesh has trailed considerably behind agricultural reforms, has never had the same political commitment as the drive for self-sufficiency in food, has often been misguided, and has had to deal with the dismal legacy of state-owned enterprises (SOEs). The public failure of the SOE sector, and the limited size of the domestic market as a result of low incomes, both imply that the engine of sustained growth in Bangladesh must be centered in an export-oriented, private manufacturing sector.

Effectively changing the structure of what was until recently a highly protected and inward-looking economy continues to pose stiff challenges. The current round of reforms have achieved much, but much remains to be done. Industrial controls have been considerably unwound; foreign companies can invest freely; the taka is now partially convertible; most non-tariff barriers have been swept aside; a previously constrained agriculture has been freed. But privatization has barely started; the financial sector remains underdeveloped, fragile, inefficient and uncompetitive, caught between excess liquidity on the one hand and depressed private industrial credit demand on the other; tariffs, although lower than they were, remain high; foreign investment remains negligible; labor reforms have not yet gotten off the ground. Dithering on reforms, announcing policy actions and then delaying or retracting them, is clouding private sector expectations. Even where the rules have changed on paper, in many instances there is in practice a yawning effectiveness gap. Having pushed the easier bits of reform, the Government is finding it difficult to drive the program home. This is slowing down the emergence of an outward-oriented private manufacturing sector that can spearhead rapid growth in industrial output. It is also slowing down improvements in total factor productivity and their potential growth impact, which can be significant.

The policy agenda framed by this concern for faster, private-sector led, outward-oriented growth is the main theme of this Country Economic Memorandum. The agenda is centered around four short- to medium-term core objectives for policy reform. These objectives are, *first*, to stimulate private investment and to implement public investment; *second*, to strengthen the enabling environment for the private sector; *third*, to raise public sector efficiency; and *fourth*, to make factor markets for finance and labor function more efficiently.

This report is organized as follows: in Part I the focus is on the first of the above priorities, the need to raise investment. In Part II, the focus is on the need to remove the impediments to private sector development. **Chapter II** discusses the need to effectively deregulate the private

---

[1] Total factor productivity (TFP) growth is often defined as the rate of technical progress, or that part of economic growth that can be explained by improvements in efficiency rather than the accumulation of factors of production. Econometric evidence suggests that TFP growth in agriculture can be just as rapid as in the rest of the economy. See *Global Economic Prospects and the Developing Countries, 1994*, The World Bank, 1994; and W. Martin and P.G. Warr, "Explaining the Relative Decline of Agriculture: A Supply Side Analysis for Indonesia," *The World Bank Economic Review*, Vol. 7, No. 3, pp. 381-403.

[2] *The East Asian Miracle: Economic Growth and Public Policy*, World Bank, 1993.

sector, **Chapter III** deals with efforts to downsize the public sector and increase its efficiency, and **Chapter IV** focusses on the problems that affect the private sector in financial and labor markets.

This Chapter contains five further sections. **Section B** shows how Bangladesh currently enjoys a window of opportunity for accelerating reforms. Readers interested in a more detailed review of recent economic developments should turn to **Section C**. **Section D** deals with the central reform priority for faster growth, raising private and public investment. It discusses the short- and medium-term macroeconomic policy implications of raising investment, and reviews progress on improving ADP implementation and the considerable work that lies ahead. Finally, **Section E** discusses the medium-term growth and aid implications of accelerated reforms. It also highlights the costs of continuing on the current path of slow reforms. At the April 1993 Aid Group Meeting in Paris, the Government reaffirmed its commitment to the broader reform agenda focussing on the private sector, public sector efficiency and the effectiveness of human resource development programs. Readers interested in understanding the progress on this agenda discussed at the Aid Group Meeting should turn to the **Annex** to Chapter I.

B. MACROECONOMIC STABILITY: A WINDOW OF OPPORTUNITY FOR ACCELERATED REFORMS

Successful stabilization during the past four years is a highly commendable achievement, both when viewed against Bangladesh's own record over the 1980s, and the record of other adjusting countries. The progress on stabilization--involving a fundamental tax reform and tight controls on current spending--is all the more commendable because at the very start, the reforms could have been derailed by exogenous shocks (the Middle East crisis in 1990 and the 1991 cyclone) and political instability leading to the return to parliamentary democracy under the current Government. As the summary Figure 1.1 (and the discussion of Section C) shows, after FY90 both inflationary and balance of payments pressures were sharply contained, the current account deficit relative to GDP fell rapidly, national saving rose beyond expectations, fueled largely by rising public saving as a result of fundamental fiscal reforms.

Bangladesh's recent stabilization record is also commendable when viewed against the experience of other adjusting countries. Table 1.2 presents average data on the fiscal deficit and inflation rate for 77 countries classified by their adjustment lending in the mid-to-late 1980s. Bangladesh's recent stabilization efforts commenced in FY89; its policy outcomes, as shown in Figure 1.1, compare highly favorably with these countries.

The shift from stabilization to sustained growth is neither automatic nor easy, as experience around the world shows.[1] Prudent macroeconomic policies, and sustained foreign aid inflows, though necessary, will not by themselves achieve the move to accelerated growth and employment generation. Despite successful stabilization, GDP growth and investment over the past three years in Bangladesh have consistently remained low (Figure 1.2). Macroeconomic stability now presents a window of opportunity for accelerating the structural reforms required for rapid growth. There are both domestic and external reasons to capitalize on this opportunity.

---

[1] Rudiger Dornbusch, "Policies to Move From Stabilization to Growth," in *Proceedings of the World Bank Annual Conference on Development Economics, 1990*, Supplement to the *World Bank Economic Review* and the *World Bank Research Observer*, 1991.

Figure 1.1: Successful Stabilization
(percent)

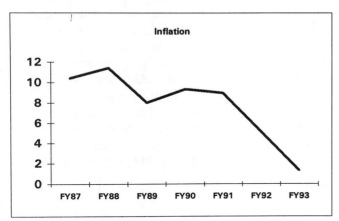

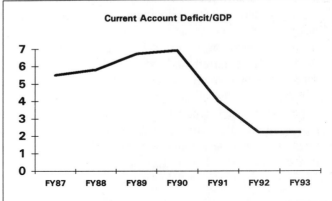

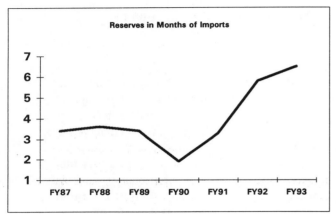

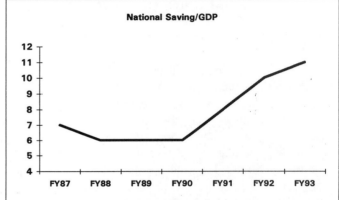

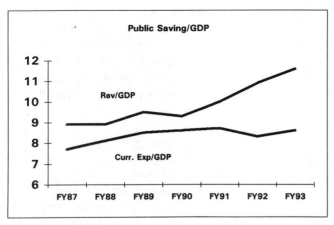

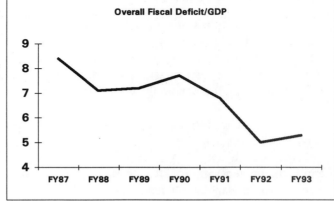

Note: FY93 are preliminary.
Source: Government of Bangladesh and Staff Estimates.

Table 1.2: Selected Indicators of Policy Performance in Adjusting Countries, 1971-90

Country Group	Fiscal deficit (percentage of GDP; average)				Annual rate of inflation (percent; median)			
	1971-80	1981-82	1983-85	1986-90	1971-80	1981-82	1983-85	1986-90
All Countries								
IAL	5.9	8.4	6.4	4.2	15.0	14.8	20.0	17.0
OAL	4.9	6.4	7.3	8.0	10.7	12.9	9.9	11.4
NAL	4.4	7.5	6.5	6.3	10.9	10.4	10.0	15.5
Middle-income countries								
IAL	3.2	6.1	4.7	3.0	16.6	14.5	20.8	15.1
OAL	3.9	4.0	4.5	5.1	8.7	12.0	9.0	9.7
NAL	5.1	8.3	6.8	5.3	10.9	13.3	15.7	22.5
Low-income countries								
IAL	8.8	10.9	8.3	5.5	12.3	15.4	14.7	19.5
OAL	5.9	8.6	9.8	10.5	11.4	14.4	10.7	13.2
NAL	3.0	6.7	6.5	9.0	10.9	9.1	8.6	6.2
Sub-Saharan Africa								
IAL	8.9	11.1	7.3	5.6	12.2	14.3	13.2	15.4
OAL	5.2	5.3	6.6	8.0	11.4	13.3	9.8	6.4
NAL	3.9	7.2	4.0	6.7	11.9	9.5	8.9	6.2

Note: IAL comprises 27 intensive adjustment lending countries, OAL represents 30 other adjustment lending countries, and NAL comprises 20 non-adjustment lending countries.
Source: *Adjustment Lending and Mobilization of Private and Public Resources for Growth*, Country Economics Department, The World Bank, 1992.

The pending reform agenda, aimed at attaining a virtuous circle of accelerated growth and rising opportunities for the poor, is large. Furthermore, even with intense adjustment and accelerated reforms, experience elsewhere suggests that it takes several years for private investment to take off, and establish such a virtuous circle.[1] The Government has shown a considerable political commitment for tackling the reform agenda, but this commitment has been highly uneven and hesitant. There is a strong rationale for raising this commitment, for broadening its base to take advantage of the window of opportunity and for avoiding the temptation of macroeconomic populism. Such populism has had disastrous consequences in Latin America and Sub-Saharan Africa.[2] Unless implementation quickens and the Government takes both bolder and swifter actions, there is a danger that the expected industrial supply response, on which the structural adjustment program is premised, may not materialize. Such an outcome would put increasing political pressure on the Government as it approaches the next general election. Reform complacency now could therefore threaten the entire reform effort with failure and potential reversal.

At least three external developments also force the conclusion that Bangladesh cannot afford to let time slip away. *First*, though Bangladesh continues to make a strong case for concessional aid, it cannot afford to ignore the world-wide tightening of aid budgets, and the rising claims of other

---

[1] *Adjustment Lending and Mobilization of Private and Public Resources for Growth*, Policy and Research Series, No. 22, Country Economics Department, The World Bank, 1992.

[2] Rudiger Dornbusch and Sebastian Edwards, *Macroeconomic Populism in Latin America*, University of Chicago Press, 1991.

low-income countries.[1] *Second*, economic liberalization in South Asia, particularly in India and Pakistan, is accelerating. This, combined with rapid change in China, in the high-performing East Asian economies, and in emerging competitors such as Vietnam, poses a challenge that Bangladesh must meet. There is likely to be intense competition among these countries for overseas export markets, as well as for attracting foreign direct investment. To be well-positioned, Bangladesh must strive to offer the same or better enabling business environment for the private sector as these countries.

Figure 1.2: Low Investment and GDP Growth

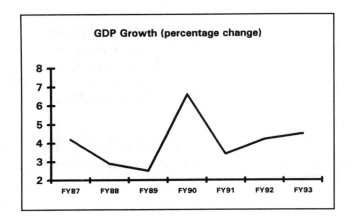

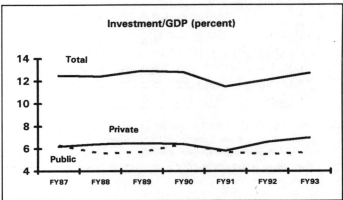

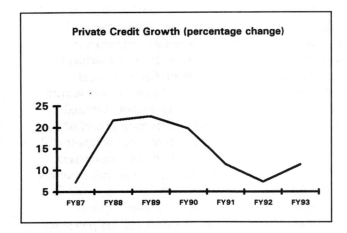

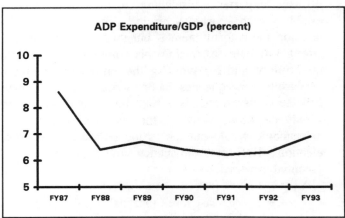

Note: FY93 is preliminary. Private credit data are adjusted for loan write-offs and bank recapitalization.
Source: Government of Bangladesh and Staff estimates.

---

[1] *Global Economic Prospects and the Developing Countries, 1993*, The World Bank, 1993.

Third, Bangladesh's links with the international trading system are at the moment predominantly tied to a single product, readymade garments. With the signing of the Uruguay GATT accord, the eventual dismantling of the quota system under the Multi-Fibre Arrangement (MFA) will allow industrial agglomeration in the most efficient garments producers. The global garments industry has typically moved rapidly from one generation of industrializing countries to the next. Countries, including Bangladesh, to the extent that they offer only quota dispersion and not internationally competitive production, may lose out.[1] Other processed exports, such as frozen fish, leather goods, and jute products suffer from a structural problem in that their export prices are affected by large swings or secular declines in their raw materials prices on volatile world commodity markets. The new GATT accord holds the promise of a general increase, over the next decade, in world incomes and trade and in the distribution of output and trade. But to take advantage of this, Bangladesh must be well-positioned as a low labor cost production center. Faster reforms must create a push for exports diversification over the medium term in line with Bangladesh's comparative advantage.

Bangladesh remains highly prone to natural disasters. Even though the ability to handle the macroeconomic and balance of payments effects of such shocks has improved in recent years, as evidenced by the response to the April 1991 cyclone, there can be no illusion that the potential for very large losses of life and property, and hence large emergency claims on public resources for rehabilitation and reconstruction, remain high. A robust and dynamic economy will be better able to weather such exogenous shocks.

Thus, all three elements of the current economic situation -- macroeconomic stability, the domestic economic and political imperatives for accelerated growth, and external developments -- argue for much faster implementation of the Government's reform agenda.

C. RECENT ECONOMIC DEVELOPMENTS: SECTORAL DETAILS

GDP growth in FY93, as in the past four years, was below expectations. Domestic investment remained sluggish, and even though public saving increased, the ADP did not reach the Government's target. The Government enjoyed a strong budgetary position, thanks to the fiscal reforms of recent years, particularly the VAT. However, the major Government failure to implement the ADP fully, and the continued sluggishness of private investment, meant that aggregate demand remained weak. Inflation declined to unprecedented low levels due to sharply lower rice prices, though non-food inflation was broadly unchanged. Readymade garments remained the most dynamic part of the industrial sector. The balance of payments also remained very strong; the decline in the current account deficit more than compensated for lower aid disbursements, thereby boosting external reserves to their highest level in two decades.

Poverty. The last Household Expenditure Survey, the core national data set for poverty analysis in Bangladesh, was conducted between September 1991 and August 1992. The analysis of the

---

[1] "Impact of the GATT Accord on Developing Countries," *Oxford Analytica*, December 22, 1993. The recent signing of the NAFTA Accord between the U.S., Mexico and Canada may also displace East Asian exports to the North American market, and induce them to divert this "lost" trade to Europe. This could in turn, displace South Asian exports into Europe. At the moment, a NAFTA-induced surge in European garment imports from East Asia -- with an associated displacement of South Asia's trade -- is prevented by the MFA, whose quota ceilings are binding for the East Asian exporters. The phasing out of the MFA may change this. See Raed Safdi and Alexander Yeats, "The North American Free Trade Agreement: Its Effect on South Asia," *Policy Research Working Papers*, No. WPS1119, The World Bank, March 1993.

incidence of poverty in 1991/92 based on this Government data suggest that poverty incidence was still high in both urban and rural areas at the start of the 1990s.[1] Measured in terms of the head-count index (the percentage of the population below the poverty line), rural poverty was 52.6 percent and urban poverty was 33.6 percent in 1991/92. Nationally, this amounted to a poverty incidence of 49.7 percent in 1991/92.

As discussed below, there has been a sharp decline in the price of rice during 1992/93, and this is likely to have had a substantial positive impact on poverty alleviation, since more than 70 percent of rural farm households are net consumers of rice. These developments are too new to have firm analyses and findings on their impact, but they are the subject of current research. Notwithstanding this most recent potential improvement in poverty, the still high incidence of poverty at the start of the 1990s strengthens the urgency of attaining faster economic growth beyond the 4 percent average of the 1980s. Accelerated reforms are needed that can yield GDP growth rates well beyond this average if there is to be a substantial reduction in poverty over the rest of this decade.

The Real Sector: Inadequate Growth

Growth Trends and its Sources. Real GDP grew in FY93 at an estimated 4.5 percent annually, as compared to 4.2 percent in FY92 (Table 1.3). This suggests a continuation of past trends, not insignificant in absolute terms, but clearly inadequate to deal with poverty. The lackluster growth in FY93 can be largely attributed to overall stagnation in the industrial sector (comprising manufacturing, construction, and utilities), where the growth rate increased only slightly, from 7.1 percent to 7.4 percent. The manufacturing sector itself grew somewhat faster (from 7.3 percent to 8.0 percent), with most of the growth coming from medium and large-scale enterprises. The service sector grew marginally from 4.8 percent in FY92 to 5.4 percent in FY93. Most of the services sector growth came from an expansion of public administration. Agriculture growth fell slightly to 1.9 percent in FY93, with the slower growth coming from the crops sector.

Agriculture continues to dominate the economy and determine the income and consumption level of the vast majority of the poor, producing about 36 percent of GDP and employing 60 percent of the labor force. Also, agriculture has the potential for greater total factor productivity growth and a significant impact on off-farm employment. This makes agriculture an essential element in Bangladesh's development strategy. Crop production dominates the sector, accounting for 71 percent of agricultural output and 24 percent of GDP. During the past two decades, the goal of achieving foodgrain self-sufficiency has governed agricultural development programs and policies. This goal has now been substantially achieved. In recent years, Bangladesh has produced sufficient rice to meet internal demand and has begun to export some fine rice. This is a watershed achievement that ten years ago would have been considered unattainable. Foodgrains production has increased from 15.3 million MT in FY83 to 19.7 million MT in FY93. Rice production has increased from 14.2 million MT to 18.5 million MT over the same period.

In FY93, overall foodgrain production grew by 2 percent, in large part due to a good aman crop whose output rose by 4.4 percent. Government domestic procurement of foodgrains fell from its level of 1 million MT in FY92 to 0.2 million MT. Foodgrain imports (commercial imports plus food aid) also declined from 1.6 million MT to 0.809 million MT. Distribution of foodgrains

---

[1] See Martin Ravallion and Binayak Sen, "Poverty in Bangladesh 1983-92," mimeo, World Bank, December 1993. The study, which is in progress, defines the poverty line in terms of the cost of a normative bundle of basic-needs goods, as compared to the "food-energy intake method" of setting poverty lines used by the Bangladesh Bureau of Statistics.

through the Public Distribution System dropped from 2.4 million MT. in FY92 to 1.1 million MT in FY93. Other major developments in the crop sector related to raw jute, whose production fell by 6.7 percent, as prices declined by 5 percent over FY93, following the sharp fall of 29 percent the previous year.

Table 1.3: Sectoral Sources of Growth FY73-93
(percent)

	FY73-80 (average)	FY81-90 (average)	FY88	FY89	FY90	FY91	FY92	FY93 (preli-minary)
GDP Growth Rate	4.9	4.8	2.9	2.5	6.6	3.4	4.2	4.5
Agriculture	2.4	3.0	-0.8	-1.1	10.0	1.6	2.2	1.9
Crops	3.0	3.5	-1.8	-1.9	12.1	1.2	1.7	0.9
Others	1.3	1.4	3.1	2.0	2.6	3.3	4.2	5.4
Industries	7.9	4.8	5.3	4.8	6.4	4.3	7.1	7.4
Manufacturing	7.8	2.6	0.6	2.8	7.3	2.4	7.3	8.0
Construction & Utilities	9.5	3.0	12.8	7.7	5.0	7.0	6.8	6.7
Services	7.4	6.5	5.3	4.7	4.0	4.6	4.8	5.4
Contribution to GDP Growth								
Agriculture	23.3	32.9	-10.6	-16.3	56.0	18.1	19.5	15.5
Industry	23.1	15.9	29.8	32.0	16.3	21.7	28.8	29.3
Manufacturing	16.2	9.9	2.2	10.9	10.8	6.9	17.0	18.0
Construction & Utilities	6.8	8.0	27.6	21.1	5.4	14.7	11.8	11.3
Services	53.6	51.2	80.8	84.3	27.6	60.2	51.7	55.2
Sectoral Share of GDP								
Agriculture	47.4	40.5	38.4	37.1	38.3	37.6	36.9	36.0
Industry	16.5	16.2	16.7	17.1	17.0	17.2	17.6	18.1
Manufacturing	12.0	10.1	9.8	9.8	9.9	9.8	10.1	10.4
Construction & Utilities	6.5	6.1	6.9	7.3	8.9	7.4	7.5	7.7
Services	36.1	43.3	44.9	45.9	44.7	45.2	45.5	45.9

Note: In constant FY85 prices.
Source: Bangladesh Bureau of Statistics and Staff estimates.

Rice prices declined sharply in FY93 (Figure 1.3). On average, nominal wholesale prices fell by 30 percent (24 percent in real terms) between April 1992 and March 1993, failing to peak before the start of the aman season. There also appears to have been a significant downward shift in the trend line after November 1992, as shown in Figure 1.3. The consensus appears to be that the price fall was precipitated by a combination of three reinforcing forces: *First*, the 1992 boro was a record harvest. Boro production amounted to 6.8 million MT, 7.6 percent or 0.5 million MT above production trends. *Second*, the 1992 boro season was also unusual in terms of record stock-piling by both non-millgate firms and millgate contractors. Apparently, non-millgate firms doubled their stocks compared to two years earlier, while millgate firms quintupled their stocks. Government procurement prices had steadily increased over the past five years. In previous years, the carryover of rice stocks had proved to be a lucrative investment; if prices dipped millers could withhold sales in anticipation of higher prices in the next procurement season. *Third*, in 1992 the Government abruptly suspended procurement early in the season due to overflowing public stocks and a shortage of warehouses space. When millers realized that procurement had been suspended indefinitely, they dumped their surplus stocks in panic, causing the first wave of the price fall. By the time the record aman harvest arrived, millers' working capital had been depleted by as much as 40 to 60 percent. The millers did not purchase paddy with the same gusto as they had in the last boro season. In addition, the Government stopped pre-financing paddy purchases. Thus, paddy purchases were reduced by 33 percent. Reduced paddy purchases along with a record aman harvest precipitated the second price fall.[1]

Figure 1.3: Declining Real Rice Prices a/

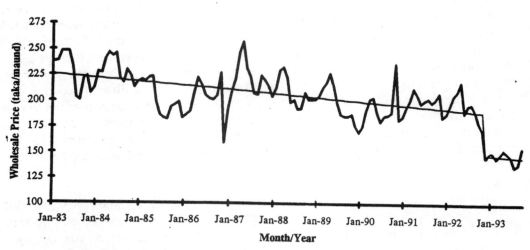

a/ In 1983 constant prices.
Source: Department of Agricultural Marketing.

The success in accelerating rice production is attributed largely to improved seed varieties and changes in the policy environment. Deregulation and liberalization have increased farmer access to improved technology, including minor irrigation equipment, fertilizers, power tillers, pesticides, and seeds. Rapid expansion of irrigation has enabled a shift from traditional rice varieties to HYVs. If this success is to be sustained, the emphasis on improving the provision of and access to agricultural inputs and services (with an increasing role for the private sector in these areas) must be maintained.

Having attained near self-sufficiency in rice, Bangladesh is now poised to enter a new phase of agricultural development. The opportunities facing the agricultural sector over the coming years are likely to be significantly different from those of the past two decades. The Government must now set new priorities and strategies for further developing the sector and inducing further increases in total factor productivity. Faster agricultural growth is an essential ingredient of the transition to a more rapid overall growth path; a stagnant agriculture would make it very difficult for the manufacturing sector to absorb the growing labor force. The *first* policy challenge is to sustain rice self-sufficiency while expanding into a more flexible and diverse agriculture. The current structure of agricultural production is not sustainable over the medium to long term. The pattern of agricultural growth over the past two decades suggests that virtually the entire growth in crop agriculture has been due to an increase in foodgrains (mainly rice and, to a smaller extent, wheat).[2] In the future, faster growth from the foodgrains part of the agricultural sector will depend heavily on the growth of domestic demand for

---

[1] Steven Haggblade and Mahfoozur Rahman, "The Laws of Gravity: A Study of Rice Price Behavior in the 1992 Boro Season," IFPRI, July 1993.

[2] See Wahiduddin Mahmud, "Agricultural Growth Strategy in Bangladesh: A Note," mimeo, The World Bank, November 1993.

rice and wheat, itself tied to the overall growth of the economy. Faster overall GDP growth approaching 7 percent will therefore make faster growth in agriculture also feasible. Faster agricultural growth will also depend on further growth in total factor productivity.

Second, agricultural growth will depend on the sector's ability to successfully diversify into other food and non-food crops, and to break into export markets. Diversification is essential for agriculture to continue to make significant contribution to GDP, particularly with limited opportunities and intense overseas competition for rice export. Much of the additional production may be expected to come in the form of higher value foods for cities and on-farm consumption. A recent study concluded that Bangladesh has the potential to shift out of rice into other food and cash crops.[1] Besides rice, the country seems to have a strong comparative advantage in the production of several food crops (potatoes, vegetables, bananas, and onions and other spices) and the principal cash crops (jute and cotton). The promotion of new agricultural activities must be market driven if diversification is to succeed. The evidence on crop output, however, suggests that farmers have in large part not yet taken advantage of these diversification possibilities. There is clearly a need to understand better why this is so, and what can be done to remove obstacles to crop diversification. A possible problem with adoption of such crops is that they require storage and transport infrastructure that is not yet substantively in place.

Third, the considerable scope for rural, off-farm employment and output growth is tied to a prior increase in farm incomes and rural aggregate demand. The connection between such growth in farm incomes and off-farm activities in Bangladesh also needs to be better understood, particularly against the recent experiences of other countries such as China.

Fourth, related to this prior necessity for growth in farm incomes, and despite the policy improvements of recent years, farmers still face a range of constraints to generating higher incomes per hectare. A concern commonly expressed is that farm size is too small in Bangladesh. However, China and Egypt also have levels of crop-land per capita comparable to Bangladesh, and yet show far higher average incomes per capita in agriculture. Furthermore, in comparisons with other densely populated but relatively better off Asian countries, Bangladesh shows comparatively lower yields per hectare for paddy, potatoes, wheat, pulses, and other crops, and comparatively low levels of input use, including irrigation, fertilizer, and pesticides. Thus, there is still room for increasing crop yields, and therefore farm incomes, in Bangladesh.

As a direct result of its topography, agricultural performance in Bangladesh is influenced to a large extent by water resource management and problems of flooding and drainage. While public investments are still needed for some types of irrigation and flood control, such investments need to be reoriented to focus largely on areas suitable for minor irrigation development. Efforts that have been initiated to introduce beneficiary participation in operations and maintenance of water control facilities, and to improve the functioning of completed schemes through more adequate maintenance, need to be enhanced. The poor project implementation performance of the Bangladesh Water Development Board is a constraint on agricultural performance. There is a need to introduce institutional adjustments in the water resource sector to overcome this problem. Some of the other constraints to higher farming intensity and higher yields are problems of poor rural infrastructure, weak rural institutions for formal credit, and low educational levels of the rural population.

---

[1] See Wahiduddin Mahmud, S. H. Rahman and S. Zohir, "Agricultural Growth through Crop Diversification in Bangladesh," mimeo, IFPRI-BIDS, May 1993.

The agricultural sector in Bangladesh clearly has a major potential for contributing to overall GDP growth and poverty alleviation. Many of the factors currently constraining growth in farm yields, incomes, diversification, and exports can be ameliorated through changes in the policy environment, investments in rural infrastructure, and technological change. Bangladesh has excellent soils, rechargeable aquifers easily tapped for irrigation, low-cost labor, and a climate that allows crops to be grown year-round. Taken together, these aspects point to the considerable potential for growth in farm and off-farm incomes in the future. There is a clear need to study and better understand how this potential can be realized.

In *manufacturing*, following the pattern established since the late 1980s, export-oriented industries remained the leading growth sectors. There was continuing strong production performance primarily in readymade garments (22 percent increase in the manufacturing production index for medium and large enterprises in FY93, see Statistical Appendix Table 8.1), and to a slightly smaller extent in leather (17 percent). However, among the other export-oriented manufacturing sectors, fish and shrimp output declined by 10 percent and jute bailing by 22 percent. Industrial chemicals (including fertilizers) and the pharmaceutical industry were the only domestic market-oriented sectors that registered strong production growth. The overall manufacturing production index increased 11 percent in FY93, as compared to 9 percent in FY92. The overall weakness of economic activity and investment was reflected in a 24 percent decline in cement production, and a 5 percent production decline in metal fabrications and machinery.

The growth rate in the *construction and utilities* sectors has continued to decline since FY91. The slowdown in construction is related to the sluggishness of the manufacturing sector and the overall weakness of economic activity. In the power sector, the lack of significant progress on reforming endemic institutional weaknesses and power wastage has limited the availability and disbursement of foreign aid linked to improvements in the efficiency of the sector. Similarly, institutional weaknesses in the state monopoly of the gas sector, a very substantial potential source of growth in Bangladesh, have dampened its recent expansion. The *services* sector grew at 5 percent, with public administration and defence registering the fastest growth.

Longer Term Changes in Economic Structure. Viewed in a longer-term perspective, these developments suggest the lingering legacy of the past. What is surprising is how little the structure of the economy and the sectoral composition of output, particularly from industry, has changed during the past decade. Though there are some questions about the data, the broad trends are clear. Agriculture's share declined from 57 percent of GDP in FY72 to 40 percent in FY81, to 38 percent in FY91, and to 36 percent in FY93. The share of industry, including manufacturing, construction and utilities, increased from about 12 percent of GDP in the early 1970s to 17 percent in FY81, stagnated at that level throughout the 1980s (17 percent in FY91), and was 18 percent in FY93. The services sector's share (including trade, transport, housing, Government, and banking) in GDP rose from 31 percent in FY73 to 43 percent in FY81, 45 percent in FY91, and 46 percent in FY93.

These long-term trends suggest four main conclusions, which further reinforce the need to focus on policies to generate faster manufacturing growth. *First*, the structural transformation of the economy slowed down considerably in the 1980s as compared to the previous decade, with almost complete stagnation in the GDP share of the industrial sector, as also in overall growth. *Second*, the decline in agriculture's share, much of which took place in the 1970s, was compensated mainly by a rise in the share of the services sector, and not of industry. *Third*, the stagnation in industry during the 1980s is of particular concern because of the poor performance of the manufacturing sector, usually the most dynamic part of a modern economy. The share of manufacturing in total industry declined from 65 percent to 55 percent between FY81 and FY91, with much of this being taken up by growth in construction and in the utility (power, gas, and water) sectors. *Fourth*, growth in the services sector in recent years suggests that its growth is now increasingly geared to faster growth in the industrial sector.

Sluggish Investment. The stagnation of GDP growth during FY93 was reflected in aggregate resource balances that show little or no dynamism, and testify to the persistent weakness of economic activity. There have been successful and important policy reforms in public resource management since FY90 that have raised domestic resources, curbed public consumption, and prioritized public expenditures in infrastructure and the social sectors. Bangladesh's long-term macroeconomic problems of relatively low domestic investment has interacted with these reforms to give rise to an aggregate demand problem. With both public and private investment remaining sluggish, these fiscal reforms have caused aggregate demand growth to fall behind the growth of gross national disposable income for the third year running since FY90. As a result, the reliance on foreign saving for investment has declined, but without significant increases in investment.

Gross domestic fixed investment rose slightly from 12.1 percent to 12.7 percent of GDP between FY92 and FY93, with two-thirds of this increase coming from the private sector (Table 1.4). This in itself is a welcome development, as private investment as a share of GDP has risen from its trough in recent years of 5.8 percent in FY91 to 7 percent in FY93. But public investment has stagnated at or below 5.7 percent of GDP since FY91, with the slight increase in FY93 just restoring it to this level after the decline in FY92 to 5.5 percent of GDP. Thus, the overall investment rate for the past seven years has remained between 12 and 13 percent of GDP, with a drop in FY91 to 11.5 percent (due to the cyclone and its impact on public infrastructure and private business expectations), and the very modest and gradual recovery since then to its level of 12.7 percent in FY93.

The reasons for sluggish public investment performance are by now well-known, but continue to be difficult to tackle. Despite the easy availability of domestic taka resources, a problem in the past, the introduction of improved guidelines on procurement, technical assistance, consultant recruitment, and periodic high-level reviews, the FY93 ADP expenditures remained well below expectations, coming in at only 10.4 percent higher than that achieved in FY92. As a result, for three years in a row, overall ADP performance has remained at or below 86 percent of the revised ADP.

Private sector investment has remained sluggish for reasons that have to do more with the business environment (Chapter II) and an apparent stalemate between borrowers and lenders in the financial sector (Chapter IV). Systemic problems in the financial sector are coming to the fore now, though even here, just as with local taka resources for the ADP, aggregate investible resources have not been a problem and credit supply has been plentiful. The demand for private credit has been low for a variety of complex and interrelated reasons, including high real interest rates; policy uncertainty for the private sector due to increased competition from import liberalization, doubts about the Government's commitment to reforms, new measures to enforce loan discipline; and a potentially small pool of credit-worthy borrowers with acceptable collateral. Low activity in SOEs -- the main clients of the NCBs and the denationalized commercial banks -- because of their own uncertain future restructuring and privatization prospects, have also dampened overall demand for investment funds. On the supply side, problematic portfolios and new prudential regulation for bad debt provisioning, collateral and capital adequacy have made bankers hesitant to lend.

Aggregate consumption as a percentage of GDP in FY93 fell slightly again, following a downward secular trend that has been evident since FY90. Gross domestic saving rose commensurately to 6.5 percent of GDP, an improvement as compared to the under 3 percent rate for most of the 1980s, which was amongst the lowest in the world. The average gross domestic saving rate in Bangladesh continues to be lower than those of India, Nepal, Pakistan, and much lower than those of Indonesia, the Philippines, and Thailand (Table 1.5). The continued strength of external workers' remittances edged the national saving rate upwards again in FY93 to 10.5 percent of GDP. The rise in gross national saving, brought about by the curb on public consumption as part of the fiscal reforms of the early 1990s, has replaced falling foreign saving virtually one-for-one over the past five years (Figure 1.4); national saving increased, and foreign saving declined by about 4.5 percent of GDP between FY89 and FY93. However, this declining reliance on foreign saving to fund domestic investment has not fundamentally altered the level of investment itself relative to GDP.

Table 1.4: Demand Linked Sources of Growth, FY88-93 a/

	FY88	FY89	FY90	FY91	FY92	FY93 Preliminary
	(percent of nominal GDP)					
Consumption	96.8	97.3	97.1	95.7	93.8	93.5
Private	85.1	83.6	83.1	81.9	80.0	79.7
Public	11.7	13.7	14.0	13.8	13.8	13.8
Gross fixed investment	12.4	12.9	12.8	11.5	12.1	12.7
Private	6.4	6.5	6.4	5.8	6.6	7.0
Public	6.0	6.4	6.4	5.7	5.5	5.7
Domestic demand	109.2	110.2	109.9	107.2	105.9	106.2
Net exports of goods and non-factor services	9.2	10.2	9.9	7.2	5.9	6.2
Exports	7.8	7.8	8.5	9.0	10.4	11.7
Imports	-17.0	-18.0	-18.4	-16.2	-16.3	-17.9
National saving	6.6	6.2	5.9	7.5	9.9	10.5
Private	5.5	5.2	5.3	6.6	7.3	7.5
Public	0.9	1.0	0.6	0.9	2.6	3.0
Domestic saving	3.2	2.7	2.9	4.3	6.2	6.5
Foreign saving	5.8	6.7	6.9	4.0	2.2	2.2
Net factor income and transfers from abroad	3.4	3.5	3.0	3.2	3.7	4.0
	(annual percentage change) b/					
Consumption	4.5	1.7	6.2	1.9	2.5	3.3
Private	4.1	-0.6	5.8	1.9	2.1	3.2
Public	7.0	18.4	8.6	1.6	4.8	3.7
Gross fixed investment	2.4	3.6	2.6	-9.1	8.7	8.8
Private	9.7	1.2	2.1	-8.1	17.4	9.1
Public	-4.5	6.2	3.2	-10.1	-0.3	8.5
Domestic demand	4.2	1.9	5.8	0.6	3.1	3.9
Net exports of goods and non-factor services	22.5	-4.7	-5.1	-38.4	-22.4	-10.0
Exports	6.8	10.0	8.9	5.1	13.0	20.6
Imports	13.8	3.0	2.7	-12.7	2.8	13.9
GDP at market prices	2.9	2.5	6.6	3.4	4.2	4.5
Net factor income and transfers from abroad	8.2	0.5	-14.0	4.1	19.9	11.3
Gross national disposable income	3.1	2.5	5.9	3.4	4.7	4.7

a/ In the national accounts, the public sector does not cover state-owned enterprises fully.
b/ Calculated at 1984/85 constant prices.
Source: Bangladesh Bureau of Statistics; and Staff estimates.

Table 1.5: Domestic Saving Rates in Selected Asian Countries
(percentage of GDP)

	1975/76-79/80	1980/81-84/85
Bangladesh	3.2	2.0
India	22.5	22.6
Indonesia	23.0	27.0
Nepal	12.1	7.9
Pakistan	7.7	4.8
Philippines	25.3	21.8
Thailand	23.1	19.1

Source: Asian Development Bank, "Financing Public Sector Development Expenditure in Selected Asian Developing Countries: An Overview," Manila, 1988.

Figure 1.4: Saving and Investment, FY85-93
(percent of GDP)

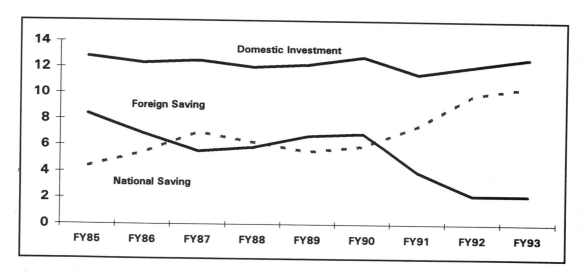

Note: FY93 is preliminary.
Source: Government of Bangladesh and Staff estimates.

Public Finance: Solid Gains from Stabilization

Strong Budgetary Position. Bangladesh's budgetary position continued to be sound in FY93 as the fiscal deficit remained just above 5 percent of GDP. This performance was partly due to effective macroeconomic management, reflected in rising revenues and tight control over current spending, and partly due to a disappointing rate of ADP implementation (see Section D). In addition to its negative impact on Bangladesh's long-term growth prospects, this situation has contributed to a short-run slowdown in economic activity. The impact of low public investment on aggregate demand was aggravated by the Government's continued borrowing from the non-bank public, offering private savers above-market interest rates on savings instruments, at a time when it was retiring its debt to the banking system. Preliminary data for the first four months of FY94 indicate a slow-down in revenue collections, especially from income taxes and the value added tax (VAT). This does not augur well for the success of the Government's efforts to increase public saving and improving the efficiency of the tax system over the medium term. More importantly, it highlights the twin policy challenges facing the Government on fiscal policy, where it must successfully tackle the current low aggregate demand by increasing ADP expenditures, as well as continue its efforts to increase resource mobilization through improved tax administration and coverage.

Continued Fiscal Stability. The Government's success at maintaining fiscal stability continued in FY93 (Table 1.6). Government revenues rose from 10.9 percent of GDP in FY92 to 11.7 percent in FY93. Current expenditures, at 8.6 percent of GDP, remained on target, and the food account deficit rose slightly. Thus, public saving rose from 2 percent of GDP in FY92 to 2.4 percent in FY93. In FY92, the Government was unable to translate higher public saving into a commensurate increase in much needed public investment through the ADP. The situation only improved marginally in FY93, as ADP expenditures (excluding self-financing) rose to 7.0 percent of GDP, as compared to 6.3 percent in FY92. This still remains low relative to the need for greater public investment in priority areas and the current resource availability. The overall fiscal deficit, at 5.4 percent of GDP, was marginally higher than its level in FY92.

The change in the structure of tax revenue away from distortionary customs duties, which started in FY91, accelerated in FY93 (Table 1.7). The share of trade taxes in total revenue fell from 36.5 percent in FY92 to 33.7 percent in FY93, reflecting progress in lowering import tariff. Lower tariff revenue was more than offset by improvements in VAT and direct tax performance. The extension of VAT to new sectors led to an increase in its share in tax revenue from 23.3 percent in FY92 to 41.9 percent in FY93. It should be noted, however, that this dramatic increase in VAT revenue occurred because many of the sectors that were covered under excise duty in FY92 were brought under VAT in FY93. Hence, changes in the sum of revenues from excise and VAT should provide a better measure of the net effect of VAT extension on the Government's revenues. The ratio of VAT plus excise revenue in total tax revenue rose from 41.1 percent in FY92 to 45.8 percent in FY93. Simultaneously, the share of revenue from income and profits taxes in total tax revenue, which was only 13.6 percent in FY90, rose from 16.1 percent in FY92 to 18.9 percent in FY93.

Table 1.6: Stable Fiscal Accounts
(percentage of GDP)

	FY89	FY90	FY91	FY92	FY93
Total Revenue	9.5	9.3	9.6	10.9	11.7
Current Spending	8.5	8.8	8.7	8.3	8.6
Food Account	0.6	1.2	0.9	0.6	0.7
Government Saving	0.4	-0.7	0.0	2.0	2.4
ADP ᵃ/	6.7	6.4	6.2	6.3	7.0
Other Capital Expenditure	0.9	0.7	0.6	0.6	0.8
Budget Deficit	-7.2	-7.7	-6.8	-5.0	-5.4

ᵃ/ Excluding self-financed projects.
Note: Figures may not add to total due to rounding.
Source: Finance Division, Ministry of Finance, and Staff estimates.

Table 1.7: The Changing Structure of Tax Revenues
(percent of total)

	FY90	FY91	FY92	FY93
Customs duties	37.4	36.2	36.5	33.7
Sales tax a/	11.0	12.1	-	-
Income and profits tax	13.6	17.3	16.1	18.9
Excise duties	28.8	26.0	17.8	3.9
VAT	-	-	23.3	41.9
Others	9.2	8.4	6.3	1.7
Total	100.0	100.0	100.0	100.0

a/ The sales tax was replaced by the VAT from FY92.
Source: National Board of Revenue.

While overall current expenditures of the Government were kept under control in FY93 (they rose by around 10 percent in nominal terms), shifts in their structure continued to occur. Two developments, one positive and the other negative, need to be highlighted. *First*, expenditures on operations and maintenance continued to grow sharply, increasing by 28 percent between FY92 and FY93. This is a highly positive indication of the Government's commitment to improving the quality of government services and creating a better link between the investment and recurrent budgets. *Second*, expenditures on wages and salaries also rose steeply by 19 percent. In FY93, this was offset by reductions in other items, especially "unallocated expenditures". A continued increase in the Government's wage bill is a disquieting development. It highlights the need for the Government to monitor closely its ability to control consumption spending over the medium term, particularly when it is not as strapped for domestic resources. It also suggests that the Government must sustain the political momentum required to keep this ability intact.

Impact of Fiscal Developments on Economic Activity. The failure to implement the planned FY93 ADP implied that the Government's strategy of using higher public investment as an instrument for achieving greater levels of economic activity and boosting aggregate demand did not have full play in FY93. This difficulty was not new, since FY92 had also witnessed a similar macroeconomic problem.

Table 1.8 shows that the Government has been retiring its debt to the banking system for the past two fiscal years, it repaid Tk 2.9 billion in FY92, and Tk 12.0 billion in FY93. This surprising, and under the circumstances undesirable, result has come about due to two factors. *First*, the inability to implement ADP projects fully has led to a lower than expected fiscal deficit, and this shortfall has not been offset by a one-for-one fall in aid disbursements. If the ADP had been executed as planned in the revised target, the budgetary deficit would have been around Tk 5.0 billion higher. *Second*, the Government sharply increased its borrowing from the non-bank public in FY93, although it did not need the additional financing. In FY93, borrowing from the non-bank public grew three times to Tk 11.7 billion from its level the previous year, with interest rates paid on this borrowing ranging between 12.75 percent and 18 percent, at a time when commercial banks were paying between 5 percent and 11 percent on fixed-term deposits based on maturity.

Table 1.8: Financing the Fiscal Deficit
(Taka billion)

	FY90	FY91	FY92	FY93
Fiscal Deficit	57.0	57.0	44.9	52.6
Net Foreign Financing	48.6	51.8	44.1	52.9
Net Domestic Financing	8.4	5.2	0.8	-0.3
Banking System	6.5	1.7	-2.9	-12.0
Other	1.9	3.5	3.7	11.7

Source: Finance Division, Ministry of Finance.

The Government has therefore transferred resources from the private sector to the banking system. This situation is problematic because the banks are unable to recycle these resources into new loans to finance private, productive activities. Bank lending rates remained high (partly because the high rates paid on Government savings certificates have precluded a major decline in deposit rates paid by banks), credit to the economy grew only slowly, and the banks remained highly liquid. The Government should give the highest priority to improved ADP implementation, and should lower interest rates on its saving certificates.

Slowdown in Revenue Collection In Early FY94? Preliminary data for the first four months of FY94 indicate that there has been a lower than expected revenue outcome (Table 1.9). Tax revenue during July-October 1993 was only Tk 26.3 billion, as compared to Tk 25.5 billion during the same period of FY92. Projecting tax revenue for the whole year on this basis yields a figure of Tk 92-95 billion, which is well below the Government's target of Tk 102 billion, and which would imply a decline in the tax to GDP ratio for the first time since FY90. It is particularly worrisome to note that the sum of revenue from VAT and excise duty in FY94, Tk 12.7 billion, is lower than the figure for the same period in FY93, Tk 12.9 billion (as excise has fallen by more than the VAT increase), and that revenue from income taxes has stagnated. Revenue from customs duties has increased despite the fact that tariffs have been reduced further in FY94, though it is not yet clear whether this is due to a slight pickup in economic activity (and hence in imports), the buoyancy of imports to the tariff cuts, or rising "tariff values" used by the Government for Customs assessment.

Table 1.9: Tax Revenues during July-October, FY92-94
(Taka billion)

	FY92	FY93	FY94
Total Tax Revenue	20.2	25.5	26.3
Direct taxes	2.4	3.6	3.6
VAT	5.1	10.8	12.3
Excise duties	4.1	2.1	0.4
Custom duties	8.3	8.5	9.6
Other	0.3	0.5	0.4

Source: National Board of Revenue.

This revenue shortfall, based as it is on the four month's performance, may not be cause for serious concern in the short run, since the Government is in any case facing difficulties implementing the ADP. However, action must be taken to improve revenue performance if the Government's medium-term objective of raising public saving and investment is to be achieved. Increases in tax revenue over the last two years have been mainly due to the introduction of VAT and its extension to new sectors. It seems that, for the time being at least, it will be more difficult to expand VAT further, to sectors such as retail trade, and coverage of agriculture is unlikely for the foreseeable future. The Government has expressed it desire to avoid increasing tax rates on the private sector in order to encourage investment, and plans to continue its efforts at trade liberalization through further tariff reductions. This implies that future increases in tax revenue will have to occur mainly through better administration. The Government needs to redouble its efforts in this area, with particular attention paid to improving the collection of domestic VAT and of direct taxes.

Money, Credit, and Prices: Record Low Inflation

Slow Credit Growth. Growth of money and credit continued to be slow in FY93, reflecting fiscal developments, low private sector demand, and weaknesses of the banking system. The inflation rate declined to 1.3 percent due to a sharp fall in food-grain prices, mainly rice. Nominal interest rates declined at more or less the same rate as inflation, and real lending rates remained very high at around 10 to 12 percent at NCBs. Faced with this situation, the Government took some measures aimed at reducing interest rates and encouraging, through moral suasion, the expansion of credit to the private sector, but with little success.

Fiscal developments implied that the Government was retiring its debt to the banking system. Thus, net credit to the Government, excluding bonds issued to recapitalize the NCBs, fell by 33.2 percent in FY93 to Tk 24.2 billion. Credit to the rest of the public sector continued growing at around 7 percent, which reflects the fact that the strong adjustment in central government finances was not matched by a similar adjustment in the public enterprise sector. Thus, total credit to the public sector only fell by 8.8 percent (Table 1.10), still representing around 30 percent of credit to the economy.

Table 1.10: The Evolution of Money and Credit Growth [a/]
(percent)

	FY89	FY90	FY91	FY92	FY93
Broad Money (M2) growth	16.3	16.9	12.1	14.1	10.5
Domestic credit growth	13.5	18.9	10.1	5.3	4.4
Public sector	-2.8	17.0	7.4	0.7	-8.8
Private sector	22.6	19.8	11.4	7.3 [b/]	11.3
M2/GDP	28.9	30.2	30.0	31.5	32.6

[a/] Data for FY92 and FY93 are adjusted for write-downs of industrial loans and recapitalization of nationalized commercial banks.
[b/] Agricultural loan write-offs led to a reduction in private sector credit.
Source: Bangladesh Bank.

A decline in Government's credit requirements is usually desirable as it implies that more resources are made available to finance private activities. However, such an increase in private sector credit is yet to materialize. In FY93, the growth rate of credit to the private sector was 11.3 percent which is more or less the same as the growth rate in FY91 and FY92, after adjusting for the write-off of agricultural debts. The failure of private sector credit to rise in response to the adjustment in public finances can be explained by factors affecting both the demand and supply of credit. On the demand side, private investment is still low as reforms aimed at encouraging private sector development are being implemented slowly. Thus, the private sector's credit needs are not rising. On the supply side, banks continue facing serious portfolio problems and are very cautious in their assessment of new loan applications. Moreover, they maintain high margins, to finance higher loan-loss provisions, which implies that lending rates have continued to be high, further discouraging new borrowers.

Money demand has remained fairly stable and the M2/GDP ratio rose slightly to 32.6 percent, which is consistent with an 10.5 percent growth in broad money. The rise in M2 and the modest increase in credit to the economy implied a slight decline in banks' excess reserves at Bangladesh Bank from their large build-up in FY92. But they also implied a significant increase in the banks' liquidity, as the growing shortage of government securities forced the banks to increasingly hold deposits at Bangladesh Bank to meet the statutory liquidity ratio, and the banks cash reserve ratio rose from 5 percent (the mandated minimum) in FY92 to 11 percent in FY93. Those cash reserves do not carry interest. Hence, the rise in liquidity has led to a further increase in banks' intermediation costs.

Record Low Inflation. The inflation rate fell to 1.3 percent in FY93. This has been mainly due to the decline in food prices by 1.1 percent (see Table 1.11). The fall in food prices is partly a reflection of Bangladesh's success at achieving rice self-sufficiency. Policy reforms in agriculture have led to a rapid increase in rice output which was not offset by higher demand. Prices of non-food items increased by 4.8 percent which is slightly above the price increase in FY92. The relative stability of non-food inflation at levels well below those that prevailed in the late 1980s is a reflection of the Government's sound fiscal and monetary policies. The sharp decline in inflation appears to be continuing in FY94. By end-November 1993, the annual inflation rate had fallen to -0.2 percent, as food prices fell by 3 percent and nonfood prices rose slowly at 3.4 percent per annum.

Faced with excess liquidity of the banking system and very low rates of inflation, the Government started taking measures to lower interest rates with the objective of stimulating investment and credit demand by the private sector. Thus, monetary policy was eased during FY93 through reductions of 2 percentage points in the Bank Rate to 6.5 percent, and of 1 to 1.5 percentage points in minimum deposit rates. However, these reductions were a case of too little too late, and the Government's policy of offering high interest rates on government saving certificates has undermined its attempts at lowering interest rates, as those certificates, whose real rates of return are currently above 10 percent, are directly competing with bank deposits. As a result, there has been very little change in real lending rates that continue to exceed 10 to 12 percent for most borrowers.

Bold action is needed now to stimulate private sector activity. The Government should seize the opportunity offered by a stable macroeconomic environment, and particularly low inflation, and fully liberalize interest rates by removing, or further lowering, the floor on deposit rates. Moreover, given that its fiscal situation is sound, there is no need for the Government to sell saving certificates at well above-market interest rates and cause disintermediation from the commercial banking system.

Table 1.11: The Evolution of Inflation, FY89-93 [a]
(percent per year)

	FY89	FY90	FY91	FY92	FY93
Overall Inflation	8.0	9.3	8.9	5.1	1.3
Food	5.7	7.1	6.9	5.5	-1.1
Nonfood	11.9	12.7	12.0	4.5	4.8
Fuel	10.5	8.5	40.2	6.7	4.6
Housing	11.7	11.7	7.3	3.0	6.0
Clothing	9.1	7.6	6.7	2.7	2.7
Others	14.0	18.4	1.8	4.2	4.2

[a] Calculated using the Dhaka Middle Class Cost of Living Index.
Source: Bangladesh Bureau of Statistics.

The External Sector: Mixed Developments

Strong Balance of Payments. Bangladesh's external position has continued to be very strong in FY93. Exports grew at 19.6 percent in nominal terms, led by garments and other non-traditional sectors. After stagnating in FY92, merchandise imports rose in FY93 by 11.8 percent, which could be a sign of an improving economy. Overseas workers' remittances continued growing, reaching $942 million in FY93. As a result, the current account deficit remained at 2.2 percent of GDP, its level in FY92, as compared to 6.9 percent in FY90. Although foreign aid disbursements fell by 6.2 percent, this was not sufficient to fully offset the improved current account, and reserves continued rising, reaching $2.2 billion (6.5 months of imports) by end-June 1993 (Table 1.12).

Table 1.12: Key Balance of Payments Statistics
(US$ million)

	FY89	FY90	FY91	FY92	FY93
Exports	1,286	1,524	1,718	1,993	2,383
Imports	3,375	3,759	3,470	3,463	3,986
Workers' Remittances	771	761	764	847	942
Current Account Bal.	-1,376	-1,541	-932	-516	-535
Aid Disbursements	1,668	1,810	1,732	1,691	1,587
Gross Reserves	962	585	966	1,679	2,197

Source: Bangladesh Bank.

As in FY92, the strong export performance in FY93 has been mainly due to the rapid expansion of exports of readymade garments, which reached $1,240 million. Receipts from exports of jute and jute products fell by around 5 percent to $358 million. Exports of frozen shrimp and frog legs, a potentially important foreign exchange earner, rose by 26.8 percent to $156 million. However, exports of leather goods, another potential growth sector, remained stagnant at $148 million.

Bangladesh is becoming increasingly dependant on garments exports (52 percent of total exports in FY93), which is rendering it more vulnerable to changes in the quota system in OECD countries and its eventual phasing out under the Uruguay GATT Agreement. More efforts at export diversification are urgently needed.

After three years of stagnation, imports rose in FY93. The main increase occurred in imports of textiles which are used as an input for garments production. In addition, imports of capital goods have risen by about 19 percent, which could be the first (albeit weak) sign of an investment pickup. Imports of other intermediate goods such as cement and fertilizers also appear to be rising slowly.

Preliminary data for FY94 indicate that the current account deficit, which had fallen from $1.5 billion in FY90 to around $0.5 billion in FY93 may have declined further. Merchandise exports only rose by 9.8 percent during the first quarter of FY94 compared to the same period in FY93. On the other hand, import growth appears to be accelerating to an annual rate of 16.9 percent. The increase in imports is a welcome development that may indicate an increase in economic activities. However, the lower export growth rate, if confirmed, would be worrying. The Government should redouble its efforts aimed at providing greater incentives for export diversification and growth (Chapter II).

D. INCREASING INVESTMENT: PUBLIC IMPLEMENTATION AND PRIVATE CREDIBILITY

Increasing investment from about 13 percent of GDP to over 18-20 percent is necessary if Bangladesh is to achieve the 7 percent growth rate required for a significant reduction in poverty. This must be the highest policy priority. Bangladesh is at a point of resource equilibrium that makes it possible, in the short- to medium-run, to use public resource management and trade and industrial policies more aggressively for the purposes of accelerating investment. The incentive framework for the private manufacturing sector can be decisively altered in favor of greater integration with world markets. With macroeconomic stability, this can be done without Bangladesh encountering significant inflationary pressures or external financing difficulties that have hamstrung other countries seeking faster growth.

The principal ingredients of the Government's successful macroeconomic stabilization -- a fundamental tax reform and tight controls on current spending -- have led, during the period FY90 through FY93, to a significant increase in public saving and to a virtually one-for-one substitution of foreign saving by national saving, but without any significant increase in investment. The restraint in consumption, especially public consumption, which has brought this about has been helpful in changing the situation that prevailed during much of the 1980s, when foreign aid was used to finance low priority public consumption.

It is important that these fundamental improvements in public resource management be sustained in order to facilitate medium-to-long term structural reforms in Bangladesh. However, the virtual stagnation in investment has implied that there has been a tighter squeeze in aggregate demand than originally envisaged. This inability to absorb resources is manifested (a) in foreign capital inflows adding to reserves to a point where they account for over six months of imports; and (b) in the Government's taka resources being used, not for high-priority spending, but to retire debt to the domestic banking system. It is clear that the Government must find ways of increasing aggregate demand through higher private and public investment if macroeconomic policy is to provide a stimulus to the economy.

This aggregate demand problem provides the backdrop for the discussion of two investment-related concerns: *first*, how to tackle improved implementation of the ADP; and *second*, how to ensure that the macroeconomic policy climate encourages greater private investment in internationally competitive, export-oriented manufacturing. The strongest possible efforts need to be made on both fronts. The continued emphasis on accelerated ADP implementation must be a top priority; so must ensuring that short- to medium-term macroeconomic policy supports greater private investment.

Increasing Public Investment: Accelerating ADP Implementation

A more rapid implementation of the ADP is the most effective direct instrument at the Government's disposal for stimulating investment, employment and economic growth. As noted above, the Government has made commendable progress in prioritizing its public expenditure program. As a result of these efforts, much unproductive current expenditure has been eliminated and the public investment program emphasizes programs in human resource development and physical infrastructure. However, the fundamental weakness of project implementation in implementing line ministries remains a problem. The lackluster ADP performance over the past three years, and commensurately, a ratio of public investment to GDP that has not yet reached 6 percent, is a matter of considerable and continuing concern. It represents a major failure of the political leadership and the civil service to take advantage of the current window of opportunity to promote growth and the resulting poverty alleviation. It is imperative that this performance improve as quickly as possible. Moreover, the fact that the ADP is well-prioritized implies that its execution would also improve the overall quality of such investment and growth. There is strong evidence to suggest that well-prioritized public investment has a significant crowding-in effect on private investment as well.[1]

ADP implementation was disappointingly low in FY93, and early indications for FY94 are not promising. The realized FY93 ADP was only Tk 70 billion, 80 percent of the original ADP (Tk 86.5 billion) and 85 percent of the "operational" target of Tk 80 billion. The real increase in ADP expenditures was only 5.5 percent and the ratio of public investment to GDP remained below 6 percent. If those trends continue, Bangladesh will not reach the target investment rate of 18-20 percent and a GDP growth rate of 7 percent, required to bring about a significant reduction in poverty. Remedial action by the Government is needed urgently to enhance implementation, while maintaining investment quality.

Quarterly Implementation Results for FY93. The Government intensified its project implementation efforts during the last quarter of FY92, and those actions continued to yield results in the first six months of FY93. Thus, the realized ADP during the first semester of FY93 was 36 percent higher than for the same period of FY92. Project aid disbursements were 25 percent higher and local expenditures rose by nearly 50 percent. The stage seemed set for the rapid expansion in public investment that Bangladesh clearly needs.

Unfortunately, the situation changed during the second half of FY93, as the Government's commitment to improved project implementation appeared to wane. High level meetings to review

---

[1] Sultan Hafeez Rahman, "Structural Adjustment and Macroeconomic Performance in Bangladesh in the 1980s," *Bangladesh Development Studies*, Vol. XX, June-September 1992, Nos. 2 and 3, pp. 89-125.

ADP execution, which highlighted to Government's commitment in this area and seemed quite effective, became less and less frequent and no action was taken to implement the procedural reforms introduced in FY92. The deterioration became more marked in the fourth quarter. Government efforts in FY92 had led to an improved implementation capacity, so that 52 percent of the ADP was spent during the last quarter. This acceleration of implementation efforts did not occur in FY93, and only 43 percent of ADP resources were spent during the last quarter (see Table 1.13). Comparing absolute implementation figures for the last quarters of FY93 and FY92 yields even more dramatic results (though it is likely that the quality of investment suffered at the end of FY92). Total ADP expenditures in the fourth quarter of FY93 were 11 percent lower than for the corresponding period of FY92, and expenditures of project aid were around 24 percent lower.

Table 1.13: The Quarterly Evolution of ADP Expenditures, FY90-93
(percent of total realized)

	Q 1	Q 2	Q 3	Q 4
FY90	13.3	22.0	21.8	42.9
FY91	15.3	21.7	25.8	37.2
FY92	7.4	21.5	19.0	52.1
FY93	11.3	24.8	21.3	42.6

Source: Implementation, Monitoring and Evaluation Division, Planning Ministry.

ADP Slow-down Continues in FY94. Data for the first six months of FY94 (Table 1.14) indicates a deterioration in performance over FY93. Although total ADP expenditures in nominal terms were some 6 percent higher during July-December 1993 than for the corresponding period of FY93, they are only 26 percent of the original ADP target, which is the lower than FY93 achievement. Hence, unless urgent action is taken by the Government, it is likely that ADP execution in FY94 will be just as poor, or poorer, than in FY93. This situation, unless corrected, sheds doubts on the Government's ability to implement its overall macroeconomic strategy to increase public investment in social and physical infrastructure.

Table 1.14: ADP Expenditures during July-December, FY93-94

	FY93	FY94
A. In Crores of Taka		
Total Expenditures	2,357	2,497
Taka Expenditures	1,078	1,189
Project Aid	1,279	1,308
B. In Percent of Initial Allocations		
Total Expenditures	27	26
Taka Expenditures	27	24
Project Aid	28	27

Source: Implementation, Monitoring and Evaluation Division, Planning Ministry.

Sectoral Performance. Table 1.15 shows the recent evolution of ADP expenditures in some key sectors. The main conclusion derived from this table is that project implementation capacity in the social sectors has improved significantly, a very positive development that augurs well for the Government's policy of emphasizing human development. The ADP realization rate, defined as the ratio of actual expenditures to initial allocations, for education increased from 56 percent and 61 percent in FY91 and FY92 to 89 percent in FY93. Actual expenditures rose three-fold over this period, from Tk 173 crores in FY91 to Tk 528 crores in FY93. Although the realization rate in the health sector has remained stable at around 80 percent, increased budgetary allocations implied that this rate is now consistent with much higher sectoral investment expenditures. ADP expenditures on health increased by 46 percent between FY91 and FY93. On the other hand, ADP allocations and expenditures on family welfare have stagnated over the last three years. Apart from the social sectors, power is another area that showed important improvement, with the realization rate increasing from 57 percent in FY91 to 87 percent and 80 percent in FY92 and FY93, which implied an increase in actual expenditures by 175 percent over that period.

Table 1.15: Sectoral ADP Realizations, FY91-93
(Taka crore)

	FY91	FY92	FY93
Education	173	299	528
Health	141	137	206
Family Welfare	310	271	283
Power	365	740	1,007
Self-financed	1,212	916	269
Agriculture	307	423	372
Rural Development	222	319	366
Transport	630	837	968
Industry	96	119	73

Source: Implementation, Monitoring and Evaluation Division, Planning Ministry.

Major shortfalls in the realization of the FY93 ADP occurred in the self-financed portion, and in agriculture, rural development and transport. The realization rate of the self-financed program fell from 144 percent in FY91 and 129 percent in FY92 to 74 percent in FY93. This implied a decline in realization figures from Tk 1,212 crores in FY91 to Tk 269 crores in FY93. The realization rate in the agriculture sector fell from 90 percent in FY92 to 76 percent in FY93, which implied a fall in public investment in that sector by about 12 percent. Similarly the realization rate in the area of rural development fell from 78 percent and 81 percent in FY91 and FY92 to 71 percent in FY93, although actual investment figures increased reflecting higher allocations. The transport sector's performance also appears to have worsened as its realization rate fell from 100 percent and 98 percent in FY91 and FY92 to 85 percent in FY93, although, once again, absolute investment figures rose reflecting higher allocations.[1] Finally, public investment in the industrial sector fell by around 40 percent between FY92 and FY93, which is a positive development consistent with the Government's policy of increased reliance on the private sector.

Ineffective Remedial Action. The Government has introduced several procedural changes during FY92 and FY93 that aim at improving project execution and aid utilization. However, those changes have not been fully implemented, which explains the disappointing ADP results. In particular, three unsuccessful attempts at procedural improvement warrant special mention. *First*, new

---

[1] Lagging ADP implementation in the transport sector can be a major bottleneck to expanding investment and growth. The evidence suggests that even a 0.6 percent increase in the public investment ratio in transport and telecommunications is associated with a 1 percent increase in the growth rate of GDP per capita. See William Easterly and Sergio Rebelo, "Fiscal policy and Economic Growth: An Empirical Investigation," paper for Conference on *How Do National Policies Affect Growth*, Feb. 8, 1993, The World Bank.

procurement guidelines that greatly simplify procedures and aim at expediting procurement decisions were adopted in May 1992. The Government also adopted a plan of action for implementing those guidelines, consisting of procurement training and monitoring of large procurement contracts by the Implementation, Monitoring and Evaluation Division (IMED). Little was done to implement those guidelines. It took the Government six months to distribute the new guidelines to project units. Procurement training consisted of one ineffective seminar that occurred 18 months after the guidelines were issued, and IMED is not monitoring procurement. As a result, little has changed. A review of procurement decisions during FY93 showed that on average they continued to take 8-34 months, and that the time limits set in the new guidelines are completely ignored.

Second, in an attempt to improve project management, the Government decided, in March 1992, that appointments of project directors and key project staff should be completed promptly, frequent transfers of project directors are to be avoided and the practice of hiring part-time project directors should be discontinued. This decision was conveyed to line ministries and executing agencies by a letter from the Minister of Planning. A review of the project management situation during FY93, indicated that these guidelines are not fully applied, nearly half of all projects surveyed were managed by a part-time director, and delays in hiring directors as well as their frequent transfer continue to be serious problems.

Third, in FY92 the Government increased financial authorities for contract awards and project expenditures. The objective of the reform is that relatively minor financial decisions should be taken at a lower level in order to expedite implementation. Once again those new financial limits are not fully applied. A review covering the General Education Project, Third Fisheries, Fourth Population and Health, and Forestry, indicated that decisions on contracts of less than Tk 5 crores, which under the new guidelines should be taken at the Directorate level, continue to be sent to the Ministries for approval.

Corrective Actions Urgently Needed. The failure to achieve a significant increase in public investment, despite a favorable budgetary outcome and a new procedural framework for project execution, is very disappointing. The Government must change this situation by acting immediately on three fronts: (a) high-level intervention is needed to ensure that procedural reforms are actually implemented; (b) selective administrative and civil service reforms should be expedited; and (iii) the private sector should be actively encouraged to take over projects that in the past were reserved for the Government and to play a greater role in executing ADP projects.

High-level interventions are necessary to ensure that reforms, particularly those affecting procurement and project management, are effectively implemented. IMED should be required to ensure that: (a) procurement training is undertaken; (b) the time taken to carry out large procurement is monitored and reported; and (c) it continues to closely monitor the largest projects and report on their status. Monthly meetings, to review ADP execution and the status of implementing procedural reforms, may be required to lend a sense of urgency, and to ensure that appropriate action is taken early enough in the fiscal year in response to emerging problems.

The experience of FY92 and FY93 clearly demonstrates that procedural reforms alone are insufficient to bring about a significant improvement in ADP implementation. Many of the obstacles to project execution are due to weaknesses in the civil service. Changes in the functioning of the bureaucracy, and its relationship with political decision makers, are required to ensure that decisions are taken at the right level, that decisions that could be taken by a single person are not passed on to a committee, and that officers are encouraged to take greater initiative. Therefore, it is essential that the Government give priority to implementing administrative reforms that would have a direct impact on the ADP, for example by expediting reforms of agencies that play an important part in project execution, and by assigning particularly capable civil servants to such agencies.

The Government should also try to increase investment in infrastructure by attracting private entrepreneurs, foreign and domestic, to areas such as power, telecommunications, gas and water supply. Different types of arrangements, e.g. direct ownership by the private sector or management contracts, could be tried (see Chapter III). Private investors do not face the same implementation constraints as the civil service. Hence, the move towards privatization could be exploited by the Government to increase the volume of investment in important sectors and expedite the implementation of key projects. It might also be useful to search for a means for the private sector to participate in the planning of the ADP, possibly through the establishment of a "round table" on the ADP.

Even for projects that continue to be owned and managed by public entities, new approaches, to make greater use of the private sector, should be envisioned. For example, since procurement continues to be the main source of delays in project execution -- because of the large number of steps in procurement processing, and the long processing time taken at various stages -- possibilities for combining as many components as possible within a small number of contract packages should be explored. This could entail combining design, supply of equipment/materials, installation/construction, supervision and commissioning. In some cases, it might be necessary to include maintenance (or management) after project completion as part of the contract, in order to make the contractor accountable for the quality and sustainability of the work. The gains from combining various types of procurement under one contract have been demonstrated in Bangladesh for the case of large civil works. Consideration should be given to extending it to other types of projects.

Increasing Private Investment: Macroeconomic Implications

The persistent sluggishness in public investment and Bangladesh's current low aggregate demand lend urgency to developing measures that can boost private investment and growth. Two priorities are considered here, and demand urgent attention: accelerated trade liberalization and its fiscal implications, and liberalized interest rates.

Accelerated Trade Liberalization

It is important for Bangladesh's economic future that private sector-led growth be competitive and outward-oriented. The Government's ongoing trade liberalization program has brought customs duties plus license fees on imports down to a weighted-by-imports rate of 30 percent in FY93. Further reform has taken place in FY94. The pace of reform, is, however, uneven and not strong enough to be viewed as credible by domestic and foreign private investors. Although the current account deficit has fallen from 6.9 percent to 2.2 percent between FY90 and FY93, this owes less to the buoyancy of exports, (except for garments, where the MFA quota system in importing countries is a significant factor) than to a compression of (non garments-related) imports for domestic consumption and investment. In the light of this situation, the Government should accelerate the removal of the remaining quantitative restrictions on imports and the reduction of tariffs across the board to levels -- of around 10 to 15 percent -- prevailing in internationally competitive developing countries.

Tax Revenue Implications. An important objection that could be raised to an accelerated pace of trade reforms than envisaged currently is its implications for tax revenue. Customs duties on imports accounted for 34 percent of tax revenue in FY93. While this share is expected to fall in FY94 and beyond as a result of the tariff liberalization, a more rapid implementation of tariff reductions may, depending on the buoyancy of imports, lead to a slowdown in the growth of public revenues in FY94 and FY95. As noted above, customs revenue during the first four months of FY94 was running higher than during the corresponding period in FY93.

In the context of faster tariff liberalization, the Government's current efforts to improve tax administration and collection (particularly for the VAT), would therefore become all the more important. As ADP implementation and private investment raise aggregate demand, imports will also increase, not least because of the high import intensity of investment. Therefore, making investment its foremost priority will also reduce possible losses of customs revenue from accelerated tariff liberalization. Accelerated tariff liberalization would also provide a quicker replacement of trade-distorting customs duties with trade-neutral VAT and income taxes.

Tariff liberalization, whether it is done decisively now or incrementally over a number of years, will inevitably present a potential short-run tradeoff with tax revenues. Furthermore, it should be recognized that the Government, despite its best efforts and the existence of a well-prioritized ADP over the past two years, has proved itself repeatedly unable to spend public revenues. Hence, an accelerated and decisive trade liberalization in the near future, and the underlying objective of accelerating structural adjustment, should not be held hostage to short-run revenue needs possibly geared to unrealistic targets for the ADP.

To complement tariff liberalization as a pre-commitment device, and to succeed in its export-oriented manufacturing growth strategy, it is also imperative that the Government ensure Bangladesh's export competitiveness against actual and potential competitors. This requires greater attention to domestic cost reducing measures, steps to link real wages with productivity, and a flexible exchange rate policy.

Liberalized Interest Rates

Notwithstanding recent reductions, lending rates of the commercial banks remain high in Bangladesh. They average 10 to 12 percent in real terms. Despite recent moves to relax the floors on deposit rates and associated reductions in such rates, they currently still remain in the range of 5-8 percent. The high spreads between deposit and lending rates reflect the deep-seated problems in the banking sector which, while very much the subject of the ongoing financial sector reform program, do not lend themselves to short-term solutions (see Chapter IV). However, even without changes in those spreads, more immediate action is possible with respect to the lowering of deposit rates in order to help bring about lower lending rates. Action should be taken to lower the average 12 to 13 percent rate being offered on the virtually risk-free postal and 5-year savings certificates. Such a policy might permit real lending rates to come down to around 6-7 percent, a move that would increase the demand for credit and provide a stimulus to private investment.

Given overlapping and complex weaknesses in the enabling environment for private sector development in Bangladesh, it is difficult to estimate by how much private investment would increase in response to a fall in lending rates. That investment will respond is clear from anecdotal evidence, surveys of business expectations, and empirical evidence in Bangladesh showing the relationship between investment and the real interest rate.[1] Therefore, it can reasonably be expected that declines in lending rates should provide a boost to private investment especially in export-oriented lines of activity.

---

[1] Sultan Hafeez Rahman, "Structural Adjustment and Macroeconomic Performance in Bangladesh in the 1980s.", *Bangladesh Development Studies*, Vol. XX, June-September 1992, Nos. 2 and 3, pp. 89-125.

In the past, the Government has opposed removing the floor on deposit rates and lowering deposit savings rates on the grounds that it needs to improve domestic saving performance. Thus, the Government has maintained that a fall in deposit rates and in returns to national savings schemes would have the undesirable effect of discouraging private saving in a country already characterized by a low domestic saving performance. (The latter has, however, shown significant improvement in recent years and is officially estimated as having risen from 2.9 percent of GDP in FY90 to 6.5 percent in FY93). This is a genuine concern. However, available evidence from many countries suggests that although the choice between financial and nonfinancial savings is affected by interest rates, total saving responds more strongly to income growth than to interest rates. This finding has been confirmed for Bangladesh as well.[1] Hence, inasmuch as the recommendation to move the interest rate structure downwards increases investment, employment and hence income, it should have a positive net effect on private saving.

E. PROSPECTIVE GROWTH AND AID DEVELOPMENTS

Accelerating Reforms for Rapid Growth

A transition to a higher GDP growth path of 6 to 7 percent per annum over the medium-term is critical to substantially alleviate poverty in Bangladesh. Macroeconomic stability provides an unprecedented window of opportunity for the Government to accelerate reforms aimed at reaching such a higher growth path, led by the private sector. The Government cannot afford to waste this opportunity. Stimulating private investment, and dramatically improving the effective implementation of the public investment program are the most important priorities. Only then would investment rise to the 18-20 percent levels relative to GDP that would make such growth feasible. This is discussed below as the *accelerated-reforms scenario*. The alternative is a *slow-reforms scenario*, under which the present pace of reforms would continue and investment levels would stagnate as they have done over the previous decade. GDP growth would then also stagnate around its long-term average of about 4 percent, and the number of absolute poor in Bangladesh would continue to increase. Such a slow-reforms scenario, and its resulting slow growth, would increasingly impose major social and political strains on Bangladesh. With slow GDP growth, rising numbers of absolute poor, low investment, and poor human and physical capital foundations to build on, Bangladesh would be confronted at the end of the 1990s with the sad fact of having lost another decade of development.

The Accelerated-Reforms Scenario. A transition to a faster GDP growth path will require a major investment effort in priority areas on the part of the public sector, and a robust private investment response to accelerated reforms over the medium term. It is also important to emphasize that the accelerated-reforms scenario is based on a policy package, with the growth effect of the entire package much greater than the sum of its parts. Accelerated ADP implementation is crucial to the accelerated-reforms scenario, since the burden of raising overall investment will fall initially on public investment. The accelerated-reforms scenario assumes that the Government would be able to bring the same high-level commitment and application to improving ADP implementation that it has brought to prioritizing the ADP. The objective would be to raise public investment from 5.8 percent of GDP in FY93 to above 8 percent over the medium term (Table 1.16). *Inter alia*, this would require developing (and then implementing) a consensus at the highest levels of Government to push much more firmly on procedural reforms and require tangible results from them, and to insist on strictly rational project

---

[1] See for example, Rahman (op. cit.).

personnel management. Also required would be substantive efforts to initiate relevant civil service reform where necessary for implementing the ADP, and to use the private sector to raise the overall ADP implementation capacity, for example, through the use of consulting firms in tendering and project supervision activities.

Table 1.16: Medium Term Growth Scenarios: Key Indicators
(in percent of GDP, unless noted otherwise)

	FY93 Actual	FY94	FY95	FY96	FY97	FY98	FY99	FY00	FY89-93 Average	FY94-98 Average	FY99-03 Average
					Projected						
Accelerated Reforms Scenario											
GDP growth rate	4.5	4.8	5.2	5.7	6.3	6.7	7.0	7.3	4.2	5.7	7.4
Gross fixed investment	12.7	13.8	15.4	17.0	18.1	18.7	19.2	19.3	12.3	16.6	19.3
Private	7.0	7.6	8.5	9.8	10.5	10.8	11.1	11.1	6.5	9.4	11.1
Public	5.7	6.2	6.9	7.2	7.6	7.9	8.1	8.2	5.8	7.2	8.2
National saving	10.5	12.0	12.9	13.9	14.3	14.4	14.4	14.5	7.9	13.4	14.6
Private	7.5	9.0	9.4	10.1	10.4	10.4	10.2	10.3	6.2	9.9	10.4
Public	3.0	3.0	3.5	3.8	3.9	4.0	4.2	4.2	1.6	3.6	4.2
Government budget											
Revenue	11.7	12.1	12.4	12.6	12.8	13.0	13.3	13.7	10.3	12.6	13.9
Expenditure	-17.1	-17.1	-17.7	-17.9	-18.3	-18.6	-18.9	-19.2	-16.6	-17.9	-19.5
Overall deficit	-5.4	-5.0	-5.3	-5.3	-5.5	-5.6	-5.6	-5.5	-6.3	-5.3	-5.6
External sector											
Current account balance	-2.2	-1.8	-2.5	-3.1	-3.8	-4.3	-4.8	-4.8	-4.4	-3.2	-4.7
Exports/GDP	9.6	10.3	11.0	11.6	12.1	12.5	13.0	13.5	7.7	11.5	14.0
Imports/GDP	-16.1	-16.7	-17.7	-18.9	-19.8	-20.6	-21.3	-21.5	-15.9	-18.7	-21.9
Reserves in months of imports	6.5	6.3	6.3	6.0	5.8	5.5	5.3	5.1	4.2	6.0	4.8
Slow Reform Scenario											
GDP growth rate	4.5	4.5	4.5	4.6	4.6	4.5	4.4	4.4	4.2	4.5	4.5
Gross fixed investment	12.7	13.0	13.5	13.8	13.5	13.4	13.2	13.4	12.3	13.4	13.5
Private	7.0	7.0	7.1	7.1	7.1	7.1	7.1	7.1	6.5	7.1	7.1
Public	5.8	6.0	6.4	6.7	6.4	6.3	6.1	6.3	5.8	6.4	6.3
National saving	10.5	10.9	11.5	11.8	11.5	11.3	11.1	11.1	7.9	11.4	11.3
Private	7.5	8.3	8.8	8.8	8.2	7.7	7.3	7.0	6.2	8.4	7.2
Public	3.0	2.6	2.7	3.0	3.3	3.6	3.8	4.1	1.6	3.0	4.1
Government budget											
Revenue	11.6	11.8	11.8	12.0	12.2	12.4	12.6	12.8	10.3	12.0	12.9
Expenditure	-16.9	-17.1	-17.5	-17.8	-17.9	-17.9	-18.0	-18.2	-16.6	-17.6	-18.4
Overall deficit	-5.3	-5.3	-5.7	-5.8	-5.7	-5.5	-5.4	-5.4	-6.3	-5.6	-5.5
External sector											
Current account balance	-2.2	-2.1	-2.0	-2.0	-2.0	-2.1	-2.1	-2.3	-4.4	-2.0	-2.2
Exports/GDP	9.6	9.8	10.3	10.5	10.6	10.7	10.7	10.8	7.7	10.4	10.9
Imports/GDP	-16.1	-16.2	-16.5	-16.7	-16.7	-16.9	-16.9	-17.1	-15.9	-16.6	-17.2
Reserves in months of imports	6.5	6.0	5.3	5.0	4.5	4.0	3.5	3.5	4.2	5.0	3.4

Source: Staff estimates.

A faster pace and greater effectiveness of structural reforms is necessary to stimulate private investment, to improve the environment for private sector activity, to integrate Bangladesh more closely with the world economy, and to enhance its competitiveness through faster trade liberalization. Accelerated reforms are also needed to deal with the problems of the state-owned enterprises, to restructure the infrastructure and utility sectors, to increase the efficiency, soundness, and competitiveness of the financial sector, and to make industrial labor markets more flexible. With faster and more effective reforms, the private sector would get clear signals that the reforms are credible, that they make a decisive break with the past, and are irreversible. After an initially slow response, private investment would be expected to gather strength, rising from its FY93 level of 7.0 percent of GDP to well over 10 percent over the medium-term (Table 1.16). This also assumes that the Government would move expeditiously on initiating new partnerships with the private sector (both foreign and domestic) in the important infrastructure and utility areas.

With total investment rising rapidly, GDP growth would accelerate, initially averaging about 5.7 percent per annum over FY94-98, but then growing much more rapidly to an average of 7.4 percent per annum over the next five years. Both exports and imports would rise rapidly with GDP growth. Exports would respond to structural adjustment in the form of accelerated trade liberalization, a flexible real exchange rate policy, and the effective facilitation of domestic and foreign investments. This response would be centered in export-oriented manufactures such as garments, processed agricultural products, and other labor-intensive subsectors in which Bangladesh would have a comparative advantage. Exports would rise from 9.6 percent of GDP to over 13 percent by the end of the decade. Rising imports, from 16 percent of GDP in FY93 to over 21 percent by the end of the decade, would be driven by accelerated and more effective import liberalization, increasing private and public investment demands for imports, the growing need for imports for processing and reexport, and the increase in economic activity as greater investment improves Bangladesh's aggregate demand problem. Assuming workers' remittances continue to grow, the current account deficit would increase from 2.2 percent of GDP to 4.8 percent by the end of the decade. The accelerated-reforms scenario assumes that there would be rising aid disbursements due to better ADP implementation, and a substantial increase in foreign direct investment due to large, lumpy investments in infrastructure and the utilities. These would nonetheless be more than offset by the strength of import demand, and external reserves would steadily decline to about 5 months of imports over the medium term.

Deeper improvements in tax administration and extending the domestic coverage of the VAT would likely make up for possible reductions in tariff revenue due to faster trade liberalization. Increasing revenue growth relative to GDP would continue, reaching 13 percent of GDP over the medium term. With rising capital expenditures in high priority areas such as SOE restructuring, infrastructure expansion and improvements, and the social sectors, but with the curbs on current expenditures still in place, the overall fiscal deficit relative to GDP would rise only marginally over the medium term, particularly as rapid GDP growth begins to yield even faster revenue growth through easier extensions of coverage. Credit for the private sector would be facilitated by improvements in intermediation quality as a result of privatization and greater competition in the financial sector. Public saving would increase as a result of better revenue performance, and private saving would respond to faster GDP growth. As a result, total national saving would increase from its FY93 level of 10.5 percent of GDP to 14.4 percent over the medium term.

Accelerated GDP growth in the 1990s would require that the almost stagnant structural transformation of the economy during the 1980s (see Section C) give way to clear shifts in the relative importance of agriculture, industry (particularly manufacturing), and services. The accelerated-reforms scenario assumes that agriculture growth would increase to 2.6 percent per year over the medium term, and then to 3 percent by 2000, from its current level of about 1.9 percent per annum (Table 1.17).

This significant increase would require a continuation of the already successful reforms in agriculture, increasing yields, higher cropping intensity, growth of total factor productivity, and diversification into higher value crops, (some for export) as a result of the approaching self-sufficiency in foodgrains.

Industry (including manufacturing, construction, mining, and the utilities) and the service sector would increasingly become the chief contributors to growth. This would be consistent with the structural transformation of the economy in response to accelerated reforms and the switching of private sector resources towards export-oriented manufacturing. The manufacturing sector's growth rate would rise from its FY93 level of 8 percent to over 11 percent over the medium term, thereby increasing its share in GDP from 9 percent to 12 percent. Demand links between manufacturing and services would be expected to become stronger, in part through improved financial services. Along with the manufacturing sector's growth therefore, the service sector's share would rise to almost 51 percent over the medium term.

Table 1.17: Projected Growth and Sectoral Composition of GDP
in the Accelerated-Reforms Scenario
(in percent)

	FY93 Actual	FY94	FY95	FY96	FY97	FY98	FY99	FY00	FY89-93 Average	FY94-98 Average	FY99-03 Average
					Projected						
Real growth rate											
Agriculture	1.9	2.0	2.6	2.7	2.8	2.9	3.0	3.0	2.9	2.6	3.0
Industry	7.4	8.6	8.8	9.1	9.8	10.1	10.4	10.6	6.0	9.3	11.0
Manufacturing	8.0	10.4	10.4	11.1	11.4	11.5	12.0	12.0	5.5	11.1	12.4
Other industry	6.7	6.3	6.6	6.4	7.5	8.2	8.0	8.5	6.6	7.0	8.7
Services	5.4	5.3	5.6	6.3	7.2	7.6	7.9	8.2	4.7	6.4	8.1
GDP	4.5	4.8	5.2	5.7	6.3	6.7	7.0	7.3	4.2	5.7	7.4
Sectoral Share [a]											
Agriculture	33.1	32.3	31.5	30.6	29.6	28.5	27.4	26.4	34.4	30.5	25.3
Industry	17.1	17.7	18.3	18.9	19.5	20.1	20.7	21.4	16.3	18.9	22.1
Manufacturing	9.4	9.9	10.4	10.9	11.5	12.0	12.5	13.1	9.0	10.9	13.7
Other industry	7.7	7.8	7.9	7.9	8.0	8.1	8.2	8.3	7.3	7.9	8.4
Services	49.8	50.0	50.3	50.5	51.0	51.4	51.8	52.3	49.2	50.6	52.5
GDP	100.0	100.0	100.0	100.0	100.0	100.0	100.0	100.0	100.0	100.0	100.0

[a] In constant FY93 prices.
Source: Staff estimates.

The Slow-Reforms Scenario. A slow-reforms scenario would be a stagnant growth scenario. It would also be the scenario that might obtain if the current sluggish pace of reforms does not quicken, and the status quo in critical areas such as finance, ADP implementation, and trade competitiveness is not broken. As Bangladesh's international competitors in South and East Asia accelerate policy reforms to take advantage of emerging and traditional markets overseas, Bangladesh would begin to lag behind. The potential loss of employment and income, despite the current window of opportunity offered by macroeconomic stability, would impose considerable development costs on Bangladesh. With slow structural reforms in the economy, particularly those aimed at enhancing the business environment and the confidence of the private sector, private investment, both domestic and foreign, would stagnate. The failure of the Government to resolve continuing problems in the implementation of the ADP would hamper public investment, and exacerbate the current problem of inadequate aggregate demand. If well implemented, a well-prioritized ADP could have a strong crowding-in effect on private investment. But slow ADP implementation instead would have an opposite, pernicious effect on private investment, thereby hampering the pace of private sector activity. As a result, the private sector would tend to prolong its investment pause. Under such a scenario, total investment relative to GDP would stagnate or increase marginally over its present level of about 13 percent (Table 1.16). Private investment would on average rise only slightly above its historical level of 6.5 percent of GDP.

Sluggish investment would mean that growth would also stagnate at 4 to 4.5 percent, suggesting a continuation of its average level over the past two decades. This would imply an increasing number of absolute poor in Bangladesh. Low investment levels would mean that import demand would remain sluggish. With slow structural adjustment and a continuing loss of competitiveness overseas, export growth would remain feeble, with exports rising only marginally above their present levels relative to GDP.

The current account deficit relative to GDP would on average remain lower than under accelerated reforms, in part because of depressed import demand for investment goods. The slow-reforms scenario assumes that aid requirements, and therefore aid disbursements, would decline commensurate with the slow implementation of the ADP and the inability of the Government to use domestic resources. As a result there would be a gradual worsening of the capital account, and combined with developments in the current account, this would eventually bring reserves down to below 4 months of imports.

The overall fiscal deficit would increase initially as the tax effort would not be strengthened. However, it would then more or less remain unchanged, since in the absence of vigorous ADP implementation expenditures would not increase substantially. Public saving would remain lower than under the accelerated reforms scenario.

Aid Issues

The longer term evolution of the structure of external aid to Bangladesh is closely tied to the pace and direction of economic reforms. The accelerated-reforms strategy would envisage increasing share of project aid over time, with parallel decreases in the shares of food aid and commodity aid, except to cushion unforeseen natural disasters or other exogenous shocks and for major externally-aided, structural adjustment programs. Already, as Bangladesh moves closer to sustainable food self-sufficiency, food aid requirements are tending to decline. This transition from a foodgrain deficit to a break-even or surplus position must be managed carefully. This section on foreign aid issues begins by examining some of the trends in food aid. It then reviews aid utilization in FY93.

Trends in Food Aid. During the past ten years, food aid relative to domestic foodgrain production has averaged around 8 percent. However, in recent years this ratio has fallen; by FY93 it had dropped to 4.6 percent. This is a significant development, and has involved both rapid increases in domestic output and declines in food aid.

Since the mid-1980s domestic rice production has increased by more than 20 percent. The trend growth rate of rice production between the late 1980s and early 1990s is estimated at between 2.6 to 3 percent per annum, greater than the population growth rate during the same period. Per capita foodgrain availability increased from 173 kg in 1983 to 184 kg in 1993, a 6 percent increase.

Food aid levels are declining as donors confront budgetary constraints in their own countries. A downward trend in food aid levels started in FY92. In FY93, food aid levels amounted to 716 thousand MT of wheat, a little more than half the amount in FY92. During the first half of FY94, food aid commitments were equivalent to US$32 million, as compared to US$60 million during the first half of FY93. These events herald a possible downward trend in food aid, though the changes are not likely to be of the same order of magnitude as occurred between FY92 and FY93. Donors were then responding to the Government's large food stock overhang and sharply reduced offtake. Furthermore, donors did not want to exacerbate the downward pressure on foodgrain prices that was observed between April 1992 and March 1993. Wholesale rice prices fell by as much as 30 percent in some production areas during this period. Wheat prices followed the same course; by June 1993 wheat prices had plummeted by 35 percent. Since then, wheat prices have recovered, although to a lower trend.

Although foodgrain prices in Bangladesh have recovered from last year's low levels, sustained large-scale inflows of food aid, particularly those intended for monetization,[1] may bring some downward pressure on prices. To illustrate the orders of magnitude involved, if rice production continues to grow at its current trend rate of 3 percent, and if GDP were to grow by, say, 4 percent annually, rice prices would need to fall by 20 to 25 percent to bring demand into line with the assumed increase in supply.[2] Such a drop in rice prices would have a strong disincentive effect on supply -- a 20 percent fall in the farmgate price of rice would reduce net returns to irrigated HYV rice by about 60 percent, with returns for some local varieties becoming insignificant or even negative. With a hypothetical 20 percent fall in the price of rice, and assuming a 1 percent annual increase in domestic wheat supply, demand substitution of rice for wheat would reduce the demand for wheat imports to about 500 thousand MT at current real prices by the year 2000.[3] If wheat aid was 1 million tons (approximately mid-way between the FY92 and the low FY93 levels), domestic wheat prices would also need to fall by about 20 percent to bring demand into line with the assumed level of supply. If imports continued at their FY92 level of 1.4 million tons, the necessary drop in wheat prices would be closer to 35 percent.

Besides donor concerns about downward pressure on prices, the need for food aid in normal years may be declining. Recent developments relating to the Government's food policy are partially responsible for this declining need. The Government has recently made efforts to rationalize its food operations and reduce procurement (Box 1.2). Despite these efforts, government stocks continued to rise in FY92-93 because reductions in procurement were not sufficient to offset reductions in offtake. Offtake in FY93 (1.1 million MT) was less than half of the offtake in FY92 (2.4 million MT). This sharp drop was initially caused by the abolition of the Palli rural rationing program, which accounted for 17 percent of the offtake from government stocks. A further decline of 40 percent in offtake resulted from the lack of sale from Government ration channels because domestic market prices fell below government ration prices.

By September 1993, the Government had reduced its stocks to about 800 thousand MT. However, three-quarters of its rice stocks were estimated to have exceeded the maximum safe shelf-life

---

[1] Monetized food aid provides the Government with counterpart funds for the ADP, non-monetized food aid primarily supports the Government's targeted poverty and relief programs.

[2] See Wahiduddin Mahmud, "Agricultural Growth Strategy in Bangladesh: A Note," mimeo, The World Bank November, 1993.

[3] For the cross-price elasticity of wheat demand with respect to rice price, see F. Goletti, "Food Consumption Parameters in Bangladesh," mimeo, International Food Policy Research Institute, Washington, D.C., April 1993.

by six months and were probably unfit for human consumption. A sizeable share of wheat stocks was also classified as unfit for human consumption. In the past, the offtake from Government stocks was always adequate to ensure the proper rotation of stocks. Therefore, the Government has not had to deal with the task of managing security stocks before. The Government has temporarily alleviated the problem of deteriorating stocks by selling them at discounted prices. As of end-November 1993, a total of 90 thousand MT of poor quality rice and 33 thousand MT of poor quality wheat had been sold. While the immediate problem of the disposal of the worst quality of rice stocks has been resolved, it is vital that stock management efforts be continued.

In reviewing these recent trends in food aid, it is important to point out the crucial role of food aid, through its non-monetized channel, in supporting the Government's targeted poverty and relief programs. Over the past four years, food aid has met, on average, 90 percent of the requirements of

---

BOX 1.2: RECENT GOVERNMENT EFFORTS TO STREAMLINE FOOD MANAGEMENT OPERATIONS

The Government is committed to reducing the cost of its food operations. The Government has eliminated the costly procurement practice of millgate contracting which pre-financed purchases from millers and paid above-market prices. In addition, the Government has lowered its procurement price for paddy to 200-210 taka/maund, and for milled rice to 310-325 taka/maund. The Government is now in the process of introducing a market-based system of procurement through open tenders. Moreover, in 1992 the Government removed import restrictions on wheat, thus allowing private wheat imports for the first time and eliminating its own need to import wheat commercially.

Most significantly, the Government eliminated in December 1991 the highly subsidized Palli rural rationing program (formally abolished in May 1992), which cost $60 million in subsidies each year. It is estimated that 70 percent of the foodgrains did not reach the intended beneficiaries of the program. Furthermore, transferring one taka of income to an eligible household participating in the rural rationing program cost an estimated Tk 6.55, compared to Tk 1.50 and Tk 1.20 in the VGD and RMP programs, respectively.[1] Since the rural rationing program accounted for 50 percent of public rice distribution, the Government was able to reduce its procurement of rice, helping to reduce the projected food account deficit in FY93 to two-fifths of what it was in FY92.

Despite these important reforms, the Government's food operations still do not have a clear strategy behind them:

- The Government lacks a clear role for its food operations in promoting national food security. Although public procurement of domestic rice was drastically reduced in FY92 and in the last boro season, it is still unclear whether these actions were part of a deliberate strategy to move away from price stabilization objectives and to limit domestic procurement for the purpose of targeted programs and maintaining an emergency security stock.

- The Government continues to subsidize foodgrain to relatively better-off groups through the OP, EP, SR and LE channels of the Public Food Distribution System. Offtake through these channels represents 23 percent of total foodgrain distribution. The savings from closing these channels could be used to expand programs that directly benefit the poor. If a subsidy to Government employees and the security forces is felt to be desirable, then it would be more efficient and transparent to provide this subsidy through the revenue budget instead of the food budget.

- There is no transparent policy determining the size of public food stocks. At the end of FY92, public warehouses were overflowing with 1.2 million MT of foodgrain of which a significant share was rapidly deteriorating (the Food Directorate's past stock disposal policy has been quite lax and not always based on a very effective application of the first-in first-out principle). A recent study estimates that an optimal stock level ranges somewhere between 1.4 million tons to 690 thousand tons, depending on food policy objectives.[2]

---

[1] "Options for Targeting Food Interventions in Bangladesh", The Working Group on Targeted Food Interventions, 1993.

[2] F. Goletti, R. Ahmed, and N. Chowdhury. "Optimal Stock for the Public Foodgrain Distribution System in Bangladesh," IFPRI Working Paper No.4, 1993.

Source: Staff analysis.

the Food for Work[1] (FFW) and Vulnerable Group Development (VGD) programs. FFW, VGD and the Rural Road Maintenance Program programs are currently the only safety net programs targeted at the rural poor, and are relatively cost effective. The FFW program reaches an estimated four million people by generating seasonal employment in exchange for food wages. The VGD program reaches 500 thousand destitute women in distressed areas--it has been shown to increase the incomes of poor households by over 19 percent, and to enhance calorie consumption at the household level.[2] Another factor to take into account in the context of food aid is the new Food for Education program, which is still in pilot form, but, if proved to be effective, could eventually increase the total programmed food distribution by almost 20 percent.

The reduction in food aid between FY92 and FY93 has meant that total distribution in FFW and VGD programs was reduced by 40 percent to 500 thousand MT. Changes in food aid levels should not be allowed to affect these relatively effective targeted safety programs. The Government and its food aid donors need to explore different options to ensure this. One option open to the Government in order to maintain and expand its targeted programs would be to use its own resources for local procurement of foodgrains. Another option would be for the Government to contract out the import and delivery of wheat at required sites. Other options for targeted safety net programs could include alternative cash-based programs. The donors could also increase food aid, or change its composition from monetized to non-monetized food aid.

Perhaps the least desirable of these options would be for the Government to revert back to high levels of domestic procurement. This would be potentially counterproductive, particularly if the Government re-introduces inefficient procurement practices such as the system of millgate contracting that was recently abolished. In addition, given the sizes of the foodgrain markets for wheat and rice, domestic procurement would have to be mostly rice. This has two drawbacks: from a nutritional viewpoint, rice is more expensive in terms of calories and protein provided per taka; from a targeting viewpoint, wheat is a better self-selecting commodity for targeted interventions because of its inferior good characteristics in Bangladesh, meaning that rice is preferred over wheat as income rises.

Aid Utilization and Capital Account Developments in FY93. Total aid disbursements during FY93 declined to $1.59 billion from $1.69 billion in FY92 (Table 1.18). This represents a 6 percent decline in FY93, following on previous declines of 2 percent in FY92 and 4 percent in FY91. This decline in FY93 was largely due to a near halving of food aid utilization, from $241 million in FY92 to $121 million in FY93; commodity and project aid disbursements remained largely unchanged from their FY92 levels. The disbursement of project and commodity aid during FY93 exceeded respective commitments, so that the total aid pipeline, which had opened at $5.98 billion in FY93, closed slightly lower at $5.31 billion.

Project aid disbursements increased by $30 million, or 3 percent over FY92, to $1.09 billion. Of this, 47 percent came from multilateral institutions. Despite improvements in recent years in procurement procedures, processing of project aid, and the Government's budgetary situation and local taka availability, project aid disbursements did not rise as much as expected due to the poor performance of the ADP (see Section D). Because of low commitments of project aid (in FY93 project aid commitments amounted to only $761 million, compared to an average of $1.09 billion during the

---

[1] Part of the wheat for Food for Work is monetized to pay for bridges, culverts, and compaction materials.

[2] Ahkter Ahmed, *Food Consumption and Nutritional Effects of Targeted Food Interventions in Bangladesh*, IFPRI, Washington, D.C., 1993. There is very little evidence to suggest that targeted food provision through FFW and VGD have a downward effect on wheat prices. See Hossain and Akash, *Rural Public Works in Relief and Development*, IFPRI, Washington, D.C., 1993.

Table 1.18: External Aid Commitments and Disbursements
(US$ million)

	FY81	FY82	FY83	FY84	FY85	FY86	FY87	FY88	FY89	FY90	FY91	FY92	FY93
OPENING AID PIPELINE													
Project Aid	2,003	2,444	3,044	3,374	3,644	4,061	4,633	4,390	4,699	4,601	5,239	4,847	5,260
Food Aid	50	59	49	42	60	195	324	207	299	232	204	119	104
Commodity Aid	399	361	454	477	592	375	460	609	452	500	478	408	616
Total	2,452	2,864	3,547	3,893	4,296	4,631	5,417	5,206	5,450	5,333	5,921	5,374	5,980
AID COMMITMENTS													
Project Aid	1,001	1,189	800	882	1,345	923	932	915	1,107	1,553	890	972	761
Food Aid	203	221	248	285	380	329	109	364	157	160	184	226	178
Commodity Aid	355	513	474	528	253	409	562	251	601	431	296	576	336
Total	1,559	1,923	1,522	1,695	1,977	1,661	1,603	1,530	1,864	2,144	1,370	1,774	1,275
Share of Non-Project Aid in Total (%)	36	38	47	48	32	44	42	40	41	28	35	45	40
AID DISBURSEMENTS													
Project Aid	560	589	470	553	591	710	967	831	904	1,165	1,056	1,064	1,094
Food Aid	194	231	255	276	244	203	225	300	226	188	268	241	121
Commodity Aid	392	420	452	439	432	393	403	509	538	457	408	386	372
Total	1,146	1,240	1,177	1,268	1,267	1,306	1,595	1,640	1,668	1,810	1,732	1,691	1,587
Project Aid Disbursement Ratio (%) [a]	28	24	15	16	16	18	21	19	19	25	20	22	21

[a] Disbursement as a ratio of opening pipeline.
Source: Economic Relations Division, Finance Ministry; Chairman's Report of the Bangladesh Aid Group Meetings.

past five years), and cancellation of existing slow and non-performing project components, the opening project aid pipeline for FY94 is estimated to have been $4.5 billion, down from $5.3 billion in FY93.

Commodity aid disbursements declined slightly by US$14 million to US$372 million in FY93. More than half of the total disbursement was from bilateral sources and in grant form. Although about $400 million of commodity aid was available from multilateral lenders, only a fifth of it was utilized. The slow disbursement of multilateral commodity aid was primarily due to slow implementation of the adjustment agenda supported by these credits, and the resulting long delays in tranche releases.

Food aid imports in FY93 amounted to 716 thousand MT of wheat, equivalent to a disbursement of US$121 million and a halving of the FY92 food aid utilization. Food aid commitments in FY93 also declined by 21 percent to US$178 million. Bangladesh did not utilize the available food aid, leaving 635 thousand MT of wheat in the food aid pipeline at the end of FY93.

Bangladesh's total external debt at the end of FY93 stood at around US$13.3 billion (54 percent of GDP), of which US$8.0 billion is owed to multilateral agencies, US$5.1 billion is owed to bilateral donors and the remainder is owed to private creditors. The debt includes a very high grant element as it is characterized by an average maturity of more than 35 years and an average interest rate of around 1.5 percent. The debt-service ratio in FY93 was around 12 percent, but is expected to decline to around 10 percent by 1995. Amortization on concessional debt rose from US$210 million in FY92 to US$264 million in FY93. Together with the decline in gross disbursements, this implied that net aid disbursements have declined from US$1.5 billion in FY92 to US$1.3 billion in FY93.

Despite the decline in aid flows, net capital inflows exceeded the current account deficit in FY93 and the balance of payments showed a positive overall balance of $518 million. Thus, foreign exchange reserves increased from $1.68 billion at the end of FY92 to S$2.19 billion at the end of FY93. This reserve level represents 6.5 months of FY93 imports. Bangladesh continues to accumulate international reserves. By end October 1993 gross reserves stood at US$2.35 billion. It is expected that the reserve level by end FY94 would exceed US$2.5 billion.

PROGRESS ON THE ADJUSTMENT AGENDA IN FY93-94

1.   Progress on the Government's reform agenda has been slow and uneven during FY93 and the early part of FY94. Increasing investment remains the highest short- to medium-term priority. This core medium-term priority should be supported by other elements of the reform agenda. To underscore these priorities, at the April 1993 Aid Group Meeting in Paris the Government reaffirmed its commitment to three priority areas for reform. The first two areas -- improving the enabling environment for the private sector and increasing public sector efficiency -- correspond to the main themes of this report. The third area -- enhancing the efficiency of human resource development programs -- addresses the longer-term issue of investing in people to ensure that they can take advantage of the opportunities made possible by faster growth, and to sustain such growth. Recent progress on the three elements of this reform agenda is discussed in this Annex.

A. The Policy Agenda: Promoting Faster Growth

2.   Strengthening the enabling environment for the private sector and improving public sector efficiency constitute a large and difficult growth agenda. Simultaneous progress on the reforms will strain the capabilities of the Government and its political commitment. However, the reforms form a package, with their combined effect likely to be greater than the sum of the parts. Thus, the importance of implementing them together cannot be overemphasized. Furthermore, while progress will not come easily, the current macroeconomic window of opportunity presents the best chances of achieving the accelerated pace of reforms that is necessary.

3.   Some progress has been achieved in all reform areas over the last year. However, reforms have proceeded slowly and hesitatingly, which explains the uncertain private sector response. Economic reforms are a process, not a set of discrete actions, and it is this process that has not yet reached critical mass in Bangladesh.

4.   Critics within and outside Bangladesh often prefer to view the agenda as driven by donor pressure rather than by domestic ownership of the reforms. These are important concerns. Yet, the agenda at its core closely mirrors the very objectives of governance based on which the Government of the Bangladesh National Party was elected in 1991 (Box A.1). As it crosses the halfway point in its first term of office, it may be appropriate for the Government and its political leadership to take stock of what has been achieved, and what must now be achieved over the remaining half of this term of office.

Strengthening the Enabling Environment for the Private Sector

5.   The Government has four short-term objectives in this area: deepening trade and industry reforms and making the reforms already underway more effective; initiating sustainable financial sector reforms; accelerating privatization of state-owned enterprises; and ensuring Bangladesh's export competitiveness. Some progress was made towards the first three objectives, particularly in the trade policy area, and to a lesser extent, on financial reforms and privatization. But even in these three areas, much more needs to be done. Very little was done to enhance export competitiveness, even though rapid growth of labor-intensive manufactured exports is a central part of the government's development strategy.

**Box A.1: Political Ownership of Reforms: Highlights from the 1991
Election Manifesto of the Bangladesh National party**

The present BNP Government took office in 1991. The following is the economic program component of the BNP pre-election manifesto as reported by BSS. There is a strong concordance between the Government's economic reform agenda and the pre-election manifesto of the BNP.

Economic Programs:

1. Adopting practical measures to realize the five basic needs of people - food, clothing, education, medicare and shelter.

2. Rapid industrialization through introduction of open and competitive market economy and providing facilities for investment by national and foreign entrepreneurs.

3. Creation of a strong economic infrastructure as a pre-condition for industrialization and overall economic prosperity.

4. Setting up small industries and other income generating projects for involving women in the overall development activities of the country and making them self-reliant.

5. Establishment of a modern children's hospital in each division on an urgent basis and adoption and implementation of special programs for health education and recreation facilities for children.

6. Creation of greater opportunities for employment through rapid industrialization by proportionate increase in financial allocations in the development of human resources and in education and health.

7. Give priority to the agricultural sector to make Bangladesh self-reliant in food. Increase facilities of loans on easy terms to the farmers and provide power connections for irrigation. Exempt loans and interests up to Tk. 5,000 for poor farmers. Reintroduce the program of canal digging and adopt practical methods for flood control.

8. Increase financial allocation for infrastructural development in the fields of roads, railway, river navigation, gas, electricity and telecommunication. Ensure implementation of Jamuna Multi-purpose and Meghna bridge projects.

9. Give priority to private sector, remove complications and impediments to healthy atmosphere for industry.

10. Adopt programs for implementation of priority projects under the Fourth Five-Year Plan by making maximum and best utilization of available resources. Give priority to financial allocation for poverty alleviation, agricultural, rural development, education, health and family planning. Adopt measures for control of population explosion.

11. Turn the national economic sectors like power, telephone, railway and industrial units into profitable bodies by restoring disciplined, skilled and dynamic management. Take measures for creation of competition and accountability through institutional changes.

12. Ensure positive results in the national economy by adopting firm but realistic measures to check inflation and stabilize commodity prices and to adopt administrative and legal methods for restoring discipline in banks and financial institutions.

13. Give priority to increasing the export of non-traditional items and limit the import of unnecessary or luxury items.

14. To pave the way for rapid industrialization though ensuring complete utilization of science and technology.

15. Adopt practical steps for solution of unemployment problems.

16. Ensure honorable place for women in every field of national development.

17. Provide incentives for savings in all fields, check unproductive expenditures and wastage.

18. Refuse to accept foreign aid or loans on such terms as are inconsistent with the national interest and demands, encourage foreign investment in priority projects.

19. Correct evaluation of the role of non-governmental organizations in development activities.

Source: *New Nation*, January 30, 1991.

6.   **Trade and Investment Liberalization**. The Government has taken several steps to make import liberalization and industrial de-regulation more effective, including: announcing its strategy of reducing effective protection over the medium term; continuing its efforts to lower and simplify tariffs; publishing a clear tariff schedule; strengthening the Tariff Commission; developing an action plan for legal reforms and a blueprint for de-regulation; and approving an action plan for implementing its export development strategy. Those efforts have helped improve the investment climate in Bangladesh, but the reforms have come too slowly to engender a strong private sector response. Serious consideration should be given to accelerating trade liberalization beyond the current phased plans, as discussed in Section D.

7.   Because of the complexity of the reform agenda, and because of uneven political commitment, there continues to be a large *effectiveness gap* between the Government's announced policies and actual implementation. Treatment of entrepreneurs by tax, customs and DEDO officials is yet to reflect the Government's new policies of liberalization and de-regulation. Tariff cuts have been accompanied by increases in assessed tariff values, especially affecting textiles and iron imports, which offset the reduction in duty; and undermine private sector confidence in the Government's policy. The action plan for implementing the export development strategy was only approved in October 1993. The Export Promotion Bureau (EPB), a key institution responsible for implementing the strategy, is considered to be too weak, and lacks the ability to carry out the often complex promotional activities specified in the plan.

8.   This effectiveness gap must be reduced. Four actions could help achieve this important objective. *First*, the Government should strengthen the institutions that deal with the private sector on a day-to-day basis; namely, the tax department, the DEDO office, the EPB and BOI. Those institutions need to be streamlined, their procedures simplified and their staff trained to deal with private investors in the new policy environment. *Second*, the use of "tariff values" should be discontinued. Tariffs should be assessed on the invoice value of imports. A system of pre-shipment inspection should be used to control fraud and simplify procedures. *Third*, procedures for duty drawback should be further simplified, and all duty drawbacks should be based on flat rates. *Fourth*, the Government should set up a formal mechanism for periodic consultation with the private sector, which could be modeled along the lines of "deliberation councils" used in some East Asian countries.[1] It should also seek to reduce the policy uncertainty generated by its uncoordinated, and sometimes contradictory, pronouncements and actions concerning the private sector.

9.   **International Competitiveness**. The Government's stated objective has been to enhance competitiveness through flexible management of the exchange rate and through steps to link real wages with productivity. Much better performance is needed in this key reform area, as discussed in Section C of Chapter I. The Government has agreed to a wage increase for public sector workers that does not take account of changes in productivity.

10.   The Government's export-oriented growth strategy, even if well-implemented, cannot succeed unless competitiveness improves. Hence, action in this area should be a priority. The Government needs to dovetail its flexible exchange rate policy with accelerated structural reforms, and ensure that it is consistent with a faster pace of trade liberalization and tariff reform aimed at boosting exports. Linking wages to productivity is a pre-requisite for success in developing labor-intensive exports. The Tripartite Committee, created in April 1993 to consider possibilities of linking wages to

---

[1] *The East Asian Miracle: Economic Growth and Public Policy* World Bank, 1993.

productivity, should be encouraged to complete its task, and should be given sufficient resources, including foreign technical assistance, to produce a high quality and realistic report as soon as possible.

11.   **Financial Sector Reforms**. This current round of financial sector reforms started in FY89. The Government has taken steps to strengthen financial laws and regulations. It passed the Financial Institutions Act, 1993. Amendments to the Negotiable Instruments Act are under consideration, and review of other laws, such as the Bankruptcy Act, are close to completion. Bangladesh Bank's ability to supervise commercial banks was strengthened, particularly by improving off-site supervision procedures and targeting on-site supervision more efficiently. The Government has started the process of privatizing Rupali Bank, and has completed the re-capitalization of NCBs. Problems caused by the outstanding debts of SOEs are being dealt with on a sectoral basis; a resolution of jute sector debts is to be started soon. Finally, the floor on savings and fixed-term deposits were lowered to 5 percent and 5.5 percent.

12.   Problems in the financial sector are a direct outcome of many years of misguided and rigid government and Bangladesh Bank regulations and directives, complicated by the breakdown of credit discipline. Actions taken so far have proven insufficient to deal with the legacy of the past. Efforts at debt recovery and bringing defaulters to justice have yielded fewer tangible results than expected. The spreads between lending and deposit rates continue to be too high, reflecting bank inefficiencies and the cost of non-performing loans. Excess liquidity held with Bangladesh Bank are a reflection of banks' weaknesses and their inability to direct resources to efficient private investment. NCB losses are high and their financial health, as well as those of the private banks, is fragile.

13.   Urgent action is needed to ensure that Bangladesh's financial system can mobilize savings and finance efficient investment within a competitive environment. Such action should include: further strengthening of Bangladesh Bank by reviewing all of its organization, management and staffing policies; taking concrete time-bound steps towards privatizing Rupali bank; increasing competition through entry of new banks and by ensuring that the two denationalized banks play a much larger competitive role in the sector; finding realistic solutions to the problem of bad debts; and liberalizing interest rates by removing or further reducing the floor on deposit rates.

14.   **Privatization**. A potentially adequate institutional framework for privatization is now more or less in place. The Privatization Board was given an autonomous body status finally in November 1993 (it was set up in early 1993), and its own budget. It has started recruiting local experts and foreign consultants. Privatization procedures have also improved, as the requirement that buyers keep all the staff of privatized units was dropped, the tendering system has been made more transparent and the terms of payment by private buyers have been made easier.

15.   However, cumulative delays have led to slower than expected progress at carrying out actual privatization. The Privatization Board has only tendered for five SOEs enterprises this year. The Textiles Ministry has succeeded in privatizing two out of ten mills slated for divestiture, and the first phase of privatization under the jute sector reform is just starting. This indicates that the Government's top priority in this area should continue to be to successfully complete privatization of the manufacturing units, and textile and jute mills already identified. Concomitantly, more efforts are needed to encourage private investment, domestic as well as foreign, in the power, gas and telecommunications sectors.

Increasing Public Sector Efficiency

16.　　　　Public sector efficiency has to improve to complement the efforts to raise public saving, to raise ADP investment in social and physical infrastructure, and to improve the quality of government services provided to the private sector. The Government's short- and medium-term objectives in this area are: improve the quality of public expenditures; continue the process of retrenching excess SOE employees; reduce SOE losses; and initiate broader reform of Bangladesh's administrative system. Progress has been achieved in the areas of public expenditures and retrenchment. However, the Government needs to redouble its efforts aimed at reforming public enterprises, especially BPDB, DESA, DWASA, and BWDB, and it should start taking concrete measures to enhance administrative efficiency.

17.　　　　**Public Expenditures.** Government action in this area involved project planning and approval, preparation of a Three Year Rolling Investment Plan (TYRIP), and improving allocations in the recurrent budget. New project preparation and approval guidelines were issued in June 1993. The objective of those guidelines is to expedite the preparation and approval process, while improving the quality of the project pipeline. The Government has also taken steps to enhance the quality of its TYRIP and link it to the budgetary process. Technical assistance for this to the Programming Division is now in place. The Planning Commission has decided to include an extra column in the TYRIP showing actual implementation during the preceding year, and to refrain from providing specific allocations to new projects when there are doubts about implementation capacity. It is expected that those changes would render the TYRIP and the ADP more realistic. On recurrent expenditures, the Government increased the allocation for operations and maintenance by more than 30 percent in the FY94 budget. However, there are doubts about the adequacy of allocations to specific sectors, particularly education and water.

18.　　　　The developments described above are encouraging, but more remains to be done. Improving planning and project approval processes will not yield results unless project implementation capacity in line ministries is strengthened. Moreover, appropriate measures need to be taken to ensure that the Programming Division's capacity to analyze projects and prepare the TYRIP and ADP will continue at its currently high level, even after its technical assistance program ends. In the area of recurrent expenditures, care needs to be taken to ensure that allocations for operations and maintenance are divided among concerned agencies in an efficient manner. Moreover, the Government needs to raise allocations for primary health and education, in a manner consistent with its policy favoring human development.

19.　　　　**Retrenchment.** The recent public sector wage increase, which will cost the six major public corporations around Tk 2.9 billion in FY94, will have a significant adverse effect on their financial position; and will make the task of restoring commercial viability more difficult. In this context, the public sector employee retrenchment program has taken on increasing importance. The program has led to the retrenchment of more than 20 thousand workers and staff in FY93; and it is expected to lead to the retrenchment of a similar number in FY94, with more than 15 thousand workers being retrenched from Bangladesh Railways and BJMC alone. In order to ensure adequate financing for severance pay, the Government has decided to double the Tk 3.0 billion allocation made in the original FY94 budget.

20.　　　　The Government's retrenchment program is proceeding well. The severance pay or "golden handshakes" currently used by the Government have been extremely effective in achieving desired staff reductions. It should now take stock of the lessons learned from this experience, and consider extending the program to cover more enterprises and Government departments. The Government is introducing a safety net and training system for displaced workers in the jute industry (see Chapter IV). It should consider extending it to other sectors that are being restructured. Dealing effectively with problems of worker separation requires linkages to labor market information systems, labor exchanges, and training programs.

21.   **SOE Reforms.** The Government's Railways Recovery Program is on track, and there are encouraging signs that actions to reduce systems losses of the Chittagong WASA are forthcoming. The Railways program is tackling the agency's deficit through reducing costs (including the wage bill), tariff adjustments, curbing ticketless traffic, and introducing a public service obligation policy for socially desirable but unremunerative services. Initial success at improving the Railways performance could be seen from the decline in its deficit from Tk 1.5 billion in FY91 to Tk 1.0 billion in FY93. Reforms of the Chittagong WASA are just starting. The inception report for a water management program has been prepared. A consumer survey is expected to be undertaken soon, and a computerized information system is under preparation.

22.   The pace of reforms in Power Development Board and DESA, Dhaka WASA, and BWDB has been disappointing. The Government must take strong action to improve the performance of those four entities, and stop the waste of public resources. Theft of electricity remains unacceptably high, as the combined systems loss of the two power companies in FY93 was at 36 percent and their collection to generation ratio is only 55 percent. Systems losses are also high in Dhaka's water sector. A still incomplete consumer survey for Dhaka WASA identified about 15,000 non-registered connections and 1,600 illegal connections. Moreover, the company's arrears situation has deteriorated. No action was taken to improve BWDB's organization. Key Board positions continue to be filled by acting appointees, without a clear mandate to implement reforms; and little effort was taken to ensure adequate funding for the sector's operations and maintenance.

23.   **Broader Administrative Reforms.** The Government needs to capitalize on the momentum gained through the on-going debate on civil service reforms. The Government has started a review of the machinery of government. Three activities are underway: first, an Administrative Reorganization Committee was appointed in August 1993. It was charged with a review of government organizations in order to recommend the necessary restructuring to modernize government and make it more efficient and cost effective. Second, a committee was created in the Ministry of Establishment to propose civil service reforms based on the UNDP's July 1993 report, the ODA-financed report of four government Ministries, and the USAID-financed Administrative Efficiency Study of 1989. Third, a Ministerial Commission has been created to propose concrete actions based on the work of the other Committees. The Government should ensure that these three initiatives yield their findings expeditiously, and pave the way for further action. The Government is yet to commence an overseas training program for the next generation of senior civil servants and a thorough review of personnel management practices in the civil service.

B. The Policy Agenda: Investing in Human Resources

24.   The Government's core agenda also emphasizes the importance of human development and poverty alleviation. Its short and medium-term objectives in this area include: carrying out an education sector review; studying and then implementing the structural re-organization of the Ministry of Health and Family Welfare; expanding social safety nets; implementing the new structure of elected local government; and strengthening the role of NGOs. Progress is being achieved in the areas of local

government, education and NGOs; but the Government should redouble its efforts aimed at restructuring the Ministry of Health and Family Welfare, and transferring food commodities from subsidized channels to channels that provide a safety net for the poor.

Enhancing Social Sector Efficiency

25.   **Education.** Reforms affecting the education sector are progressing relatively smoothly. An Education Expenditure Review has been initiated and should be completed by June 1995. The Government is giving top priority to extending the on-going reforms in primary education: it has increased recruitment of female teachers and girls' enrollment; approved the list of low-cost community schools to be built and has requested LGED to start construction; the experimental community schools program is meeting all quantitative targets; reconstruction of rural primary schools is proceeding ahead of schedule; and new curricula and textbooks have been introduced and distributed on time. Finally, on vocational and technical education the preparation of a possible project is being discussed with the donors.

26.   **Health and Family Welfare.** The Government recognizes that inadequate coordination between health and family planning is a serious problem affecting the quality of service and leading to under-utilization of field-level services. Yet, reforms in this area are occurring very slowly. In particular, a study of the structural reorganization of the Ministry of Health and Family Welfare -- with a view to integrating the two sets of services, strengthening supervision, improving cooperation between staff from the two ministries, and securing more community involvement -- is progressing very slowly. The consultants are yet to be chosen, and work has not started. Given the importance of this sector, the Government should expedite the processing of this study as a first step.

27.   **Safety Nets.** The Government has introduced a pilot Food For Education Program, which is expected to expand the social safety net and encourage school attendance by poor children. However, a large amount of the Government's food resources continue to be distributed through subsidized channels benefiting better-off groups, such as security forces and government workers. Government should reduce the size of those channels and use resources generated in this manner to expand the safety net programs, e.g. VGD and FFW. This reform has become particularly urgent, because food aid, which is the main resource used for the safety net, is declining. Hence, safety net programs are bound to suffer unless the Government carries out a major change in the way it allocates food resources. The Government is continuing to prepare a nutrition program.

Improving Government and Non-Government Delivery Platforms

28.   **Local Government.** The local government framework approved in 1992 consists of Union Parishads at the grass roots level and Zila Parishads at the district level. In addition, Thana (sub-district) Development Committees will act as coordinating units for development activities between the Union and Zila Parishads and the Central Government. Urban areas are divided into Pourashavas (municipalities), and the four major cities (Dhaka, Chittagong, Khulna and Rajshahi) are run by city corporations.

29.   This local government framework is expected to be in place before the end of FY94. Elections for the Union Parishads and Pourashavas were held in FY93. The Thana Development Committees were created in September 1993, and were functioning by December. Elections for the four city corporations took place in January 1994. Finally, it is expected that Parliament will pass

the act for Zila Parishads during its winter session, and that elections for this level of local government would take place in early 1994.

30.   As the new local government structure is being put in place, greater control over expenditures, especially in the areas of human development and poverty alleviation, should be given to elected local officials. Local government institutions will have to raise revenues to finance those expenditures. The Government should carefully consider increasing local revenue raising powers. In the past, this may have been a problem, as the natural tendency is to shun political controversy by taxing and collecting less. Hence, the Government may wish to consider providing local governments with incentives to improve their resource mobilization efforts, for example, by providing funds to match locally generated revenues.

31.   **NGOs.** The Government has taken two important steps aimed at improving the regulatory environment facing NGOs: a circular describing new regulations was issued and a booklet containing all laws and conditions affecting NGO operations in Bangladesh was distributed to ensure transparency. The Government should complement these positive developments by creating an institutional framework for regular dialogue between the Government and NGOs, similar to proposals for a deliberation council for private entrepreneurs.

PART II

REFORM PRIORITIES FOR
PRIVATE SECTOR MANUFACTURING GROWTH

CHAPTER II: REMOVING IMPEDIMENTS TO PRIVATE MANUFACTURING GROWTH

A. INTRODUCTION

Rapid, labor-intensive manufacturing growth is a central ingredient of any practical strategy to alleviate poverty through economic growth in Bangladesh. Limited prospects for domestic agricultural expansion forces growth to depend on industrial development, and the country's limited domestic market for manufactured goods forces it to depend largely on export. The domestic manufacturing sector must therefore be internationally competitive. The poor experience of Bangladesh with government control of industry (Chapter III) indicates that such industrialization must be led by the private sector. The Government's principal objective therefore must be to accelerate private sector reforms that can stimulate private investment to rise above 10 percent of GDP over the medium term.

Due to the two privatization phases during the 1975-83 period, the private sector now accounts for above 75 percent of manufacturing value added in Bangladesh. But, with the notable exception of the readymade garments industry (RMG), much of the existing manufacturing sector is characterized by an absence of robust growth, inflows of foreign capital or technologies, or sustained penetration of international markets. Instead, as discussed in Chapter I, manufacturing growth has been slow, its share of GDP has remained modest, private investment has stagnated, and Government interventions have continued. Furthermore, most firms have produced for the domestic market, capacity is under-utilized, protection levels still remain above internationally competitive norms, and rural industry is confined largely to handlooms and other cottage activities. These elements have come together in a characterization of Bangladesh as a "high-cost" economy in which transaction costs remain substantial relative to its neighbors and competitors.

At first sight, this poor performance of private manufacturing possibly bodes ill for the private sector's ability to become the engine of growth, and to engineer the rapid expansion of manufacturing jobs and net foreign exchange earnings that is essential for overall growth to alleviate poverty. However, as the RMG sector demonstrates, this lackluster private sector performance is due more to the continuing existence of policy, infrastructural, and factor market constraints, than to inherent weaknesses in the ability to invest or in entrepreneurial potential. These policy and institutional constraints can, and must be, eliminated. But they form a substantial reform agenda that must be tackled rapidly across a broad front if the private sector in Bangladesh is to grow faster.

In dealing with this reform agenda, the Government is once again faced with a choice between the high road of rapid, credible reforms that can forge a partnership with the private sector to boost its investment and growth over the medium term, or to continue on its present low road of gradual, incremental liberalization that will essentially maintain the status quo and the low growth equilibrium. The current window of opportunity offered by macroeconomic stability to make major microeconomic, structural reforms should not be wasted if Bangladesh wishes to enter a virtuous circle of growth, rising human capital investments, and productivity.

In considering the policy options for stimulating the private sector, three themes deserve attention and run through much of the discussion in this chapter. *First*, the principal aim of policy and institutional reforms must be to unfetter the private sector, to provide it with a level playing field, and to ensure that Government actions affecting the private sector are credible and irreversible. Only then will the private sector break out of its current "investment pause" (the period during which investors, due to policy uncertainties, would rather wait than invest). Getting over this pause is crucial, particularly against the backdrop of stagnant investment levels over much of the 1980s. This is a clear lesson provided by the success of the RMG sector. Where the institutional and regulatory framework is already in place, as was the case in Thailand in the mid-1980s, a relatively slow pace reforms may produce the required investment response (see Box 2.1). However, where this is not the case, and the reform effort is perceived to be fragile in the initial years, the depth and speed of the reform effort needed becomes greater, as happened in Mexico. Unfortunately, bureaucratic inertia and attitudes bred by the command economy in Bangladesh are changing slowly, and the different components of the Government often give mixed and confusing signals to the private sector about deregulation and its direction and speed.

Second, the Government must accelerate the implementation of both traditional reforms in trade and industrial policy, as well as the so-called "second generation" reforms for private sector development that have been important in East Asia. The latter include ensuring that the business environment is hospitable, deregulation and government actions are credible and effective, transactions can be transparent and predictable, and factor markets can meet the demands of the private sector. As the traditional reforms already underway in Bangladesh take root, the problems sought to be addressed by the second generation reforms are becoming more binding. These two approaches must be pursued together as a private sector development-cum-efficiency package, since they are mutually reinforcing, and delays in one impede the other.

Third, the spectacular success of RMG and the lack of dynamic growth in other parts of manufacturing suggest that the private sector's search for manufacturing growth should start from identifying products where there is a clear international demand for goods that Bangladesh can supply competitively. When such a base has been established, as in RMG, it would make sense to search upstream for production linkages and higher unit value addition. In many instances, industrial policy in Bangladesh has gone about attempting the reverse, protecting upstream industries in the hope that they will one day become internationally competitive themselves, or breed successful downstream industries that can export. As in the case of the textiles sector, this has usually failed to meet expectations.

The remainder of this introductory section briefly outlines some of the features of the slow growth of private manufacturing in Bangladesh. **Section B** discusses progress made on trade policy liberalization and the need for accelerated decontrol of the trade regime. **Section C** addresses the crucial need to enhance the environment for private investment in Bangladesh in a range of different areas, including investment deregulation, fiscal incentives, investment financing, exchange controls, and the legal framework. **Section D** presents the experience of the readymade garments industry and its spectacular growth in Bangladesh. It also discusses RMG-related prospects in silk and leather products. **Section E** illustrates the interaction between entrepreneurship and the policy framework in the case of the RMG, jute, and textiles industries.[1]

Some Features of Slow Private Manufacturing Growth in the 1980s

Total gross fixed investment declined strikingly from 16 percent of GDP in FY81 to below 12 percent in FY91; while the public share more or less stagnated, the private sector's share fell from 9.4 percent to 6 percent. Estimates of private manufacturing investment for the same period

---

[1] This Chapter draws on the preliminary findings of a forthcoming World Bank study on industrialization strategy in Bangladesh.

Box 2.1: Structural Adjustment and Private Investment in Mexico and Thailand

The contraction, pause, and recovery of private investment during adjustment is clearly evident in Mexico and Thailand during the 1980s (see box figure). On average in these two countries, the share of private investment in GDP rose by more than 2.5 percentage points between 1982-85 and 1986-90. In Mexico, however, the contraction of investment was sharper and the pause longer than in Thailand, reflecting the greater depth of the adjustment program needed and the time required to build a better business environment.

Following the discovery of oil in the 1970s, **Mexico** engaged in a cycle of fiscal expansion, currency appreciation, and debt accumulation that came to a sudden halt in 1982. In that year, the country embarked on a drastic program of demand restraint and real depreciation of the exchange rate. Beginning in 1985, policy reforms were deepened by trade reform, deregulation, and financial liberalization. Quotas were reduced from covering 100 percent of (non-oil) tradable goods production to less than 17 percent. Tariffs were substantially reduced. The tax system was reformed, regulations on domestic and foreign investments were phased out, and the financial system was liberalized.

Private capital formation in Mexico had started to decline in 1981, a trend that lasted until 1983, followed by an investment pause until 1987. Since 1988, a sustained increase in private investment has taken place. It took nearly six years for private investment to recover after the inception of the adjustment program in 1982. The long lag in the recovery of private investment in Mexico has been attributed to tight credit policies and high real interest rates, declining oil prices, considerable excess capacity, the perceived fragility of the reform effort in its initial years, debt overhang, and a drastic decline in public infrastructure investment. The acceleration in the recovery of private investment since 1988 reflects a gradual building up of confidence in the reform process, particularly associated with the success in bringing down inflation and the irreversibility of the trade policy reform. In addition, investment was boosted by the announcement of a debt reduction deal in the context of the Brady initiative in 1989, the acceleration of privatization and deregulation, and the initiative for a free trade agreement with the United States.

Thailand is a case study of investment response to gradual macroeconomic and structural reform. Thailand undertook structural reforms in the early 1980s in several areas: agriculture, energy, public enterprises, trade, and fiscal incentives to investment. In 1984, the exchange rate was devalued by 14 percent, supported by fiscal restraint, and noninflationary macroeconomic policy. Thailand's rate of GDP growth decelerated only mildly to 6.1 percent a year between 1982 and 1985. Growth resumed forcefully afterwards at an annual rate of 8.1 percent (1986-90). The entry of new firms seems to have been the most important source of expansion of output.

Private investment fell by nearly 3 percentage points of GDP between 1984 and 1986, but then recovered quite strongly. The gradual reforms undertaken by Thailand implied a less dramatic rupture with previous policies. This continuity helped to give the adjustment program credibility, reinforced by the stable macroeconomic framework.

The institutional and regulatory framework for investment was also important in explaining Thailand's relatively short investment pause and its strong investment recovery. The Thai government has long adopted a hands-off policy that minimized the regulatory barriers to the private sector. In particular, policy-induced barriers to entry are low, giving rise to the high rates of output expansion attributed to new entrants during the adjustment period. Under the adjustment program, the government rationalized and improved the universality and transparency of investment incentives, broadened the access of exporters to duty-free imports of intermediate goods, and streamlined the corporate business tax system. Thailand's more moderate adjustment also permitted the government to maintain relatively high levels of investment and maintenance in infrastructure.

Real private investment as a percentage of GDP in Mexico and Thailand, 1980-90

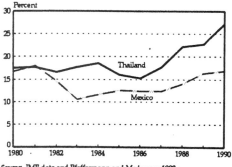

Source: IMF data and Pfeffermann and Madarassy 1992.

Source: *Adjustment Lending and Mobilization of Private and Public Resources for Growth, Policy & Research Series 22*, Country Economics Department, World Bank, 1992.

suggest a similar decline. As a result, the manufacturing sector's share *declined* from an average of 12 percent of GDP over the 1970s to 10 percent over the 1980s, a share that has remained remarkably unchanged over the past 13 years (Chapter I). Stagnation and decline in what typically should be the most dynamic part of a modern economy is the main cause of the persistently unsatisfactory GDP growth in Bangladesh.[1]

Five related elements appear to have combined over the 1980s to thwart the effective growth of the private manufacturing sector: high effective interest rates, and the problems linking the financial and industrial sectors; inward orientation and limited domestic markets; SOE domination and a poor appreciation of the role of technology; an industrial ethos that did not support orderly industrial exit; and falling product quality standards. The first of these elements has been the most important, and is treated in greater detail in Chapter IV. These elements have been reinforced by such policy factors as high protection levels, excessive and misguided regulation, *ad hoc* policymaking, and poor infrastructure.

High Interest Costs and Interlocking Problems of Finance and Industry. The cost of capital has remained very high, and it has been difficult to access for small manufacturing establishments. The result has been a non-supportive domestic financial system. The high cost of capital has contributed to the so-called "default culture", as businesses knowingly or unknowingly entered into debt contracts that could not be honored. With few apparent penalties for this, businesses have preferred to keep going rather than close down. This preference has often been induced by Government policy towards the "sick" industries, and enabled by an ineffective legal system. As a result, the financial system's resources have remained locked into loss-making enterprises. The outcome has been both a weak manufacturing sector and a weak financial system, mutually propping each other up. Direct Government ownership of both has blocked competition in either. This disorder has been partially responsible for preventing the development of a strong, export-oriented private manufacturing sector except in the case of RMG, where foreign financing has essentially bypassed the domestic financial sector. Small manufacturing enterprises have been particularly hamstrung by the inability of the financial system to support their operations. Official estimates show that more than 95 percent of total investment in the manufacturing sector in FY89-90 took place in large and medium-scale firms.

Inward Orientation. With the exception of RMG, the manufacturing sector has remained strongly oriented towards domestic markets and the processing of agricultural production for exports. The focus on internal markets has limited growth, since these markets are small and can only grow as rapidly as disposable income.

SOE Domination and the Role of Technology. The large manufacturing subsectors received remarkably little investment over the past decade, partly due to their public domination. SOEs invested little because it was believed that continuing small investments to improve operations were not necessary, a legacy of state planning that saw technology as a black box to be acquired and exploited, rather than as a process of continual improvement through management and worker cooperation.

---

[1] National income accounts probably understate value added originating in manufacturing: various estimates made in recent years suggest that larger establishments with 10 or more employees contribute substantially more than their component of manufacturing in the national accounts; less statistical work has been done on the small and household enterprises but what is available suggests that the national accounts underestimate this component also. There is no reason, however, to believe that the growth rate of manufacturing has been significantly greater than that of the rest of the economy in recent years. See "The Manufacturing Sector in Bangladesh: Structural Trends and Empirical Evidence," Report No. 10313-BD, February 27, 1992.

There was no particular subsector with a major share of value added that expanded investment rapidly and became an engine of growth. Both cotton textiles and jute manufactures have been mired in inefficiencies and Government interventions. In the case of cotton textiles oriented toward the domestic market, there was no reason to expand output because of market size; in the case of jute exports, pricing policy and labor settlements resulted in an industry that was unable and unwilling to raise productivity, since this would have required a more disciplined labor force and major investments.

Inadequate Scope for Industrial Exit. Dynamic industrial growth fueled by efficient manufacturing investment can only take place if enterprises are free to enter and exit. In Bangladesh, failing or sick enterprises have instead been able to command additional resources from the nationalized commercial banks (NCBs) and the Government to remain in business. The problem has been exacerbated to the extent that low private investment in manufacturing has been replaced by public sector or directed private sector investments, thus further reducing the incidence of exit. The absence of exit has therefore kept the quality of capital invested in manufacturing low.

Deteriorating Product Quality. The inward orientation of the manufacturing sector over the past two decades had the effect of degrading product quality. Low per capita incomes and a closed market encouraged firms to systematically lower quality, rather than raising it, in response to price competition. The pernicious effect of quality reduction has been threefold: (a) quality reduction ruled out exports as firms locked into domestic supply were in no position to adjust to quality sensitive international markets. This broke potential or actual links between domestic production and export; (b) enterprise "competition" through quality reductions pointed industrial engineering interests in the wrong direction, away from productivity enhancements and toward cost cutting by reducing quality; (c) the deliberate lowering of quality affected technology choices. Firms had no incentives for modernizing to produce output that was considered to be "too good" for the domestic market.

These broad lessons from the manufacturing sector's performance in the 1980s are now recognized by policymakers in Bangladesh, as evidenced by the underlying principles of the *Industrial Policy of 1991*. The Government's reform agenda aims to integrate Bangladesh firmly into world markets, and to enable its private sector to take unfettered decisions in a business-friendly environment in which it effectively faces world prices for its inputs. The implementation of this agenda has however been slow and uneven.

B. ACCELERATING TRADE LIBERALIZATION

The apparently easy option of promoting exports on the one hand, while protecting production for the domestic market on the other, is not available any longer, as countries across the world have found. Japan, the Republic of Korea, and Taiwan, China used such interventionist strategies for their export drive, but economies that lack their strong institutions have usually failed in similar efforts. If successful, such strategies also raise the specter of retaliation by developed countries. Instead, newly industrializing countries such as Malaysia, Indonesia and Thailand have combined trade liberalization with strengthened institutional and infrastructural support for exporters to achieve their export push (Box 2.2). In South Asia itself, major reforms are underway in the wake of this recognition.

Rapid progress on four groups of actions are required on trade policy to create a competitive export-oriented economy in Bangladesh: (a) removing the remaining non-tariff controls and streamlining import procedures; (b) fully implementing the next phase of the Government's scheduled tariff reform program no later than the FY95 Budget; (c) accelerating further progress during 1995-1997 towards a fairly uniform tariff structure with a low average that minimizes anti-export bias; and (d) removing export impediments, and improving the special incentives for exports designed to compensate for other policies that currently constrain export production.

BOX 2.2: EXPORT PUSH IN A CHANGING INTERNATIONAL TRADING ENVIRONMENT

What can Bangladesh learn from the export push regimes in East Asia? The northeastern economies--Japan, the Republic of Korea, and Taiwan, China--began their export drives decades ago by offsetting the protection of their domestic markets with highly targeted incentives to export. Such interventionist strategies are less viable today, when developed economies sometimes retaliate against allegedly unfair trade practices with import quotas and countervailing duties. Moreover, targeted market interventions have proven a particularly difficult and risky way of achieving economic goals, including export success. Economies that lack the unusually strong institutions of Northeast Asia have usually failed in such efforts.

In the past ten years, however, Southeast Asia's newly industrializing economies--Malaysia, indonesia, Thailand--have charted a new and promising approach to export push. Adapting to the changed global trading environment and their own institutional constraints, these three economies have promoted exports by combining liberalization of import restrictions with strengthened institutional and infrastructure support for exporters. Hence, these three economies are likely to be the more relevant model for countries hoping to export successfully in today's global economy.

These new tactics have not been confined to Southeast Asia. Indeed, as the northeast Asian economies have come under increasing pressure from trading partners they, too, have gradually shifted from high domestic protection and offsetting export incentives to more neutral trade regimes with broad institutional and infrastructure support for exports. Throughout East Asia, then, successful exporting economies are relying on pro-export institutional frameworks. Broadly consistent with the exporting economies growing obligations under international trade agreements, these frameworks include the following mechanisms for encouraging exports:

- **Widely available export credit**: All six economies have subsidized export financing, often through a central bank rediscount system. In most cases, bridge financing is extended to any firm with a confirmed export order as evidenced by a Letter of Credit; for many small and medium-scale enterprises, these bridge loans are their only access to formal-sector finance. Certain access to such credit encourages entrepreneurs to undertake new export ventures and helps them to penetrate foreign markets. Moreover, by using export performance as the yardstick for credit allocation, these programs engender stiff competition that reduces the scope for favoritism and corruption.

- **Access to imports at world prices**: Because gradual reductions in protection of domestic industry are slow to eliminate high-priced imports and the attendant negative impact on exports, East Asian governments have established a variety of institutions and mechanisms to give exporters access to imports at world prices. These include large free trade zones with their own extensive export-oriented infrastructure, smaller export processing zones, bonded warehouses, duty drawbacks and tariffs exemptions. Since the late 1980s, for example, major exporters in Indonesia have had unrestricted duty free access to imports.

- **Incentives for export-oriented foreign investors**: Southeast Asia's newly industrializing economies have been highly successful in wooing export-oriented foreign direct investment (FDI) by waving investment restrictions and offering special incentives. In Indonesia, the proportion of approved FDI going into export-producing enterprises increased from 38 percent in 1986 to 70 percent in 1991. In Thailand the proportion increased from 10 percent in 1971 to over 50 percent in 1988. In both economies, as well as in Malaysia, shifting the focus of foreign investment from import substitution to exports has been successful in generating much more exports and much more investment.

In each case, these export push incentives have been designed to offset lingering distortions dating from import substitution policy regimes. Combined with a strong commitment to an inexorable easing of import restrictions, they have demonstrated the governments' determination to prod firms, and eventually the entire economy, into becoming internationally competitive.

Source: *Adjustment in Africa*, Policy Research Report No. 2, Policy Research Department, The World Bank, 1993.

Freeing Up Imports: Eliminating Non-Tariff Barriers

Non-tariff barriers, including the combination of non-tariff import controls and inefficient import procedures, have traditionally been as important as fiscal measures in shielding Bangladesh from competitive international prices. Although intended to protect local industry, they raise input costs for other domestic producers, increasing their prices and causing them to demand more protection in turn. This vicious cycle has further oriented most of the manufacturing sector away from export. Good progress has been made in dismantling these controls, and the last steps now need to be taken to complete the task, and to address the issue of import clearance procedures.

Import Controls. The non-tariff barriers (NTBs) used include bans and restrictions imposed for either trade (i.e. protection) or non-trade (e.g. public safety) reasons, and discretionary permit requirements. The dismantling of the formal product controls has been addressed in a phased manner over recent years, to the point where a fairly small but difficult group of products remain to be addressed. A decade ago all imports to Bangladesh were subject to control, with a "positive list" attached to annual Import Policy Orders (IPO) listing those goods that could be imported. The liberalization process began in FY85 with the replacement of the positive list by lists containing goods subject to outright ban or some form of restriction, and eventually into a single "control list".

In subsequent years, the coverage of the control list has been gradually reduced. The most recent reductions made in October 1993 represent efforts to achieve the first stage of the Government's current goal of limiting restrictions for trade reasons to 39 headings, and then, at the second stage, eliminating this remainder. Currently, the 26 or so major controls clearly imposed primarily for protective and other trade reasons include 18 textile items. The trade-related items are due for removal by the end of FY94 to achieve the second stage of the Government's goal. In addition, several import controls whose justification is not trade related could be removed and replaced, if necessary, by other types of more appropriate regulation.

Onerous import permit requirements have also been removed. The last vestige of the permit system was eliminated in 1993; imports against direct payment by non-resident Bangladeshis may now occur without permit. The former requirement that all imports be made pursuant to prescribed entitlements in industrial or commercial "passbooks" was modified for industrial importers in 1992 to allow a lump sum value for all goods not on the control list. The Government has announced a further modification, eliminating the need for any prior entitlement for free imports. However, importers report that the announced liberalization has yet to be implemented at the ports.

The new 1993-95 IPO is more transparent than in the past, since the control list integrates all remaining items subject to a ban or restrictions (apart from certification, quarantine, and labelling requirements with wide coverage). This makes the IPO text itself purely explanatory, rather than adding extra controls, as it had done in the past.

Import Clearance Procedures. Import clearance procedures have been much discussed in recent years, but little improvement has been observed by either direct industrial importers or the commercial houses that provide import services for smaller manufacturers. Costly clearance delays, negotiation on valuation during Customs clearance, and harassment by port agencies beyond the control of Customs, continue to bedevil the import process. As the formal controls have declined, the cost of these procedural hurdles has become both more evident and more important in its effect on production and trade.

A major reform effort to streamline the onerous clearance and assessment procedures has yet to occur. Attempts to streamline port procedures, principally a voluntary preshipment inspection (PSI) scheme, have thus far been unsuccessful. The voluntary scheme was established in 1992 when the Government's objective of establishing a compulsory PSI scheme did not go through. The voluntary scheme has been little used during its first 18 months because PSI values did not automatically overrule Customs assessments. It is now being improved. Apart from goods with scheduled tariff values, invoiced values that are certified by PSI are now expected to prevail over values arbitrarily proposed by Customs assessors, effectively forcing a green channel approach. The Government hopes that this crucial change will increase the scheme's utilization, so that it may be continued as a fall-back in case a more thorough overhaul of the clearance system remains politically unacceptable. There has not been enough time to test the most recent modification to the voluntary PSI scheme. The modification could be further strengthened by requiring that PSI certified values dominate in all situations, even where tariff values exist. PSI is likely to achieve its twin objectives of enhancing revenue while expediting clearance only when it is compulsory, covers almost all types of imports, and delegates the primary tax assessment function to responsible offshore agents contracted by the Government.

Freeing Up Imports: Accelerating Tariff Reform

Nominal tariffs have come down over the part three years. However, the impact of tariff liberalization has been muted for two reasons. First, fixed tariff values in excess of world prices have been used for valuation purposes, and in many cases have boosted nominal protection significantly. Second, customs duty rates have not yet changed significantly for goods with high recorded import values as the Government has followed a pro-revenue stance in choosing items for tariff reductions.

Progress Made. Progress on tariff reform began in 1991. In its FY92 budget, the Government introduced value added taxation (VAT) to replace the import sales tax and most of the domestic excise duty. A standard rate of 15 percent was set, but a supplementary duty (SD) was also introduced to make the consumption tax rate higher on selected items. SD is imposed also on some intermediate goods (such as gas) for revenue reasons, implying a departure from the VAT. Although textiles and small-scale production were excluded from VAT coverage, this was still a large step towards trade neutrality and it established an alternative revenue instrument to allow subsequent tariff reduction. The FY92 budget also abolished the development surcharge and a regulatory duty, and added 10 percent to most customs duty (CD) rates under 100 percent to compensate for the resulting loss of revenue. The FY93 budget began to phase out end-user concession categories, further reduced high customs duty rates, and raised some very low duty rates.

The most recent FY94 budget reflects further efforts to reduce high duty rates and eliminate rate discrimination between end users and within similar product categories. There were reductions in customs duty rates for over a fifth of the 11,800 tariff lines. A few more CD exemptions were removed and several low rates raised, including for rice and wheat. Several categories were, however exempted from the VAT. The Finance Act of 1993 prevents the future restoration of very high rates, by revising the schedule of statutory rates of duty.

The progress on tariff liberalization can be seen from Table 2.1 in terms of nominal protection rates. The mean rate of nominal protection (unweighted) declined from 89 percent in FY91 to 50 percent in FY93, and further to 40 percent in FY94. The number of HS-8 codes with customs duty rates above 100 percent declined from 274 in FY91 to 17 in FY94. There has also been a significant reduction in dispersion, as measured by the coefficient of variation, though dispersion increased slightly in FY94. There has also been considerable compression of duty rates, with the number of rates declining from 18 in FY92 to 12 in FY94. Compression is also evident from the reduction in the number of HS-8 codes with duty rates of zero and duty rates above 100 percent. Finally, the impact of tariff liberalization can be seen in the reduction of the share of total customs duty revenue from goods with customs duty rates above 60 percent: this declined from 24.6 percent in FY92 to 10.1 percent in FY94. The mean import-weighted rates of nominal protection suggest that the tariff reform was slightly revenue reducing between FY92 and FY93, and will continue to be so in FY94 (based on FY93 import weights).

While the reduction in tariffs has been more significant in manufactured consumer goods than in intermediates and capital goods, rate escalation according to level of processing remains strong: the unweighted mean rate of protection is 57 percent for consumer goods. In contrast, tariff escalation is absent in the case of agricultural imports: their mean protection rate of 42 percent continues to be at par with manufacturing's 41 percent.

Table 2.1: Impact of Ongoing Tariff Reforms, FY91-94
(percent, unless otherwise noted)

	FY91	FY92	FY93	FY94
Nominal Protection Rate (% of assessed import value): a/				
Unweighted mean	89	59	50	39
Coefficient of variation	59	68	62	63
Import-weighted mean b/	42	40	30	28
No. of ad valorem customs duty rates	16	18	15	12
No. of HS-8 codes with:				
Customs duty = zero	346	376	323	308
Customs duty = 100%	2460	2315	768	39
Customs duty above 100%	274	249	46	17
Total import tax rate (% of assessed import value): c/				
Unweighted mean	91	84	72	58
Coeff. of variation	59	57	53	60
Import-weighted mean b/	44	59	45	43
Percentage share of customs revenue from goods with: b/ d/				
Customs duty = Zero-15%	8.7	13.0	19.1	21.9
Customs duty = 16-29%	29.0	11.9	0.0	0.0
Customs duty = 30-60%	35.0	50.4	63.2	68.1
Customs duty = 75-100%	6.4	16.8	16.9	9.6
Customs duty above 100%	20.9	7.8	0.8	0.5

a/ FY91 includes customs duty, development surcharge, license fee, advance income tax not refunded (est.), and sales tax minus domestic excise (est.). For FY92-FY94, sales tax is replaced by the protective impact of the VAT (for textiles), and allowance is made for the negative effect of supplementary duty.
b/ FY91 is weighted by CY91 imports; FY92 is weighted by FY92 imports; FY93 and FY94 are both weighted by FY93 imports.
c/ Including all taxes listed in footnote 1 plus the rest of sales tax, or VAT and SD.
d/ Ad valorem rated imports (i.e. excluding specific rated petroleum imports).
Source: National Board of Revenue and Staff estimates.

As tariff *rates* have declined, the importance of valuing goods at fixed standard tariff *values* (TVs) above international prices has increased sharply as a protective device. As Table 2.2 shows, for caustic soda (an important raw material for textile dyeing) the use of the tariff value raises the actual import tax rate to 150 percent, against an apparent import tax rate of 72 percent. Similarly on selected categories of steel billets, the actual nominal protection using the TV is 81 percent, against an apparent protection rate of 54 percent. The Operative Tariff Schedule for FY94 gives tariff values, often with multiple prices, for about 26 percent of the 11,800 tariff lines. The administrative process for setting and updating them is weak and has resulted in price overestimates. In response to public complaints, some TVs are being revised downward in line with world prices. In the absence of compulsory offshore preshipment inspection, the Government favors setting standard tariff values as a means of combatting under-invoicing and tariff evasion. TVs are a poor second-best in this regard, however, since they deal only with price, leaving quantity and quality aspects of shipments open to mis-declaration and informal negotiation between importers and Customs assessors. Moreover, they penalize honest importers who are able to obtain inputs or machinery on world markets at prices that are genuinely lower than the basis used by the authorities for prescribing TVs.

Table 2.2: The Protection-Increasing Impact of Tariff Values

		Apparent Tax Payment a/	Actual Tax Payment b/
Caustic Soda Solid (per metric ton)			
Average Invoice Value	$230.00		
Tariff Value	$480.00		
Customs Duty	45.00%	$ 103.50	$ 216.00
VAT	15.00%	50.03	104.40
Adv. Income Tax	2.50%	5.75	12.00
License Fees	2.50%	5.75	12.00
Total Duties & Taxes ($)		165.03	344.40
Apparent and Actual Import Tax on CD of 45.00%		71.75%	149.74%
Mild Steel Billets (per metric ton)			
Average Invoice Value	$235.00		
Tariff Value	$350.00		
Customs Duty	30.00%	$ 70.50	$ 105.00
VAT	15.00%	45.83	68.25
Adv. Income Tax	2.50%	5.88	8.75
License Fees	2.50%	5.88	8.75
Total Duties & Taxes ($)		128.08	190.75
Apparent and Actual Import Tax on CD of 30.00%		54.50%	81.17%

a/ Using invoice value.
b/ Using tariff value.
Source: Staff estimates.

As shown in Table 2.1, the unweighted average rate for all import taxes (customs duties, license fees, advance income tax, value-added tax, and supplementary duty) fell from 84 percent in FY92 to 72 percent in FY93, and to 58 percent in FY94, while their import weighted average fell from 59 percent in FY92 to 45 percent in FY93, and then to 43 percent in FY94. The tariff changes that have occurred so far appear to have had little negative effect on revenue receipts from import tax instruments (Table 2.3) for several reasons. *First*, CD rates have not changed significantly for goods with high recorded import value. For example, while the duty for machinery imports has declined to 7.5 percent, imported machinery spare parts (which are a large item in total imports) still carry a duty rate of 45 percent. *Second*, there has probably been a positive elasticity effect for some of those that have changed, i.e. lower rates may have encouraged higher volumes; this would offset the revenue reducing effect of tariff liberalization. *Third*, the trade neutral instruments yield a significant and increasing share of import taxation. Total import tax receipts in FY93 were Tk 43.7 billion compared with Tk 40.8 billion the previous year, attributable mainly to increases in VAT collection offsetting a modest CD decline. In the first quarter of FY94, the VAT was relatively unchanged while proceeds from the new CD schedule rose to Tk 9.6 billion, compared with Tk 8.7 billion in the previous July-September period.

Table 2.3: Import Tax Receipts, FY91-93
(billion taka and percent of total)

Revenue Source	FY91		FY92		FY93	
	Revenue	% of Total	Revenue	% of Total	Revenue	% of Total
Customs duty a/	29.74	73.6	25.92	63.5	25.27	57.8
VAT b/	7.98	19.7	11.96	29.3	14.89	34.1
Supplementary duty	-	-	0.22	0.5	0.21	0.5
License fee	1.2	3.0	1.21	3.0	1.55	3.5
Advance income tax	1.5	3.7	1.48	3.6	1.83	4.2
Total Receipts	40.42	100.0	40.79	100.0	43.69	100.0
Assessment Value of Imports	107.49		106.17		107.26	

a/ FY91 includes development surcharge and regulatory duty.
b/ Sales tax in FY91.
Source: National Board of Revenue and Staff estimates.

Accelerating the Outstanding Tariff Agenda. Before discussing the next steps that should be taken on tariff reform in the short to medium term, it is useful to place the progress made and the need for further reform, in a comparative light. Tariff data for Bangladesh, neighboring countries, and early-reforming countries are presented in Table 2.4. Although comparative data for the same year are not available for all countries, the data give an indication of the relatively large burden imposed by the present tariff regime on Bangladeshi consumers and manufacturers using imported inputs.

In terms of the restrictiveness of its tariff regime based on the most recent 1993 data, Bangladesh ranks second only to India among the South Asian countries. (Pakistan's 1991 average protection rate is higher, but it is undergoing rapid tariff liberalization, with a maximum rate now targeted at 50 percent). In India, the implementation of tariff reforms has been relatively rapid during the last two years. As a competitor in international markets, if India continues reforms at this pace, its example, and the depreciation of the Indian rupee that continued tariff reduction will create, will increase the pressure on Bangladesh to implement similar measures. The duty drawback system for exporters in Bangladesh does not reduce the cost of imported inputs to levels comparable to world prices, and thus will not be sufficient to offset the competitive pressure. In addition, the continuing reduction in rupee prices of India's imports will induce increased smuggling into Bangladesh, reducing tariff revenues.

Table 2.4: Cross-Country Comparison of Tariff Regimes

Country	Year	Maximum Tariff	Unweighted Average	Standard Deviation	Import Weighted Av.
South Asia					
Bangladesh	1993	302.5	51	32	31
	1991	510.5	82	45	-
India	1993	85	71	30	47
	1991	400	128	41	87
Pakistan	1991	425	66	40	42
Sri Lanka	1992	250	25	19	22
Nepal	1987	450	21	37	-
Intensive-Adjusting NICs					
Indonesia	1989	60	27	25	12
	1984	225	37	23	22
Mexico	1992	20	13	4.5	11
	1985	60	25	19	13
Turkey	1989	50			17
	1985	100		31	
Chile	1988	-	15	-	15

Source: L. Pritchett and G. Sethi, "Tariff Rates: What Do We Know? Why Do We Care?" mimeo, Policy Research Department, World Bank, 1993; GATT Trade Policy Review; World Bank data and Staff estimates.

Table 2.4 also includes data on the tariff regimes of Chile, Indonesia, Mexico, and Turkey, the countries which undertook intensive trade liberalization programs during the early and middle eighties. While it is difficult to establish an exact comparison between these countries and Bangladesh in terms of the stage of development, they are included in the cross-country comparisons to provide indicative targets for the Bangladeshi tariff reform. In all four countries, lower tariff rates and a more uniform tariff structure were achieved by the mid-eighties. Mexico and Chile have the lowest average tariff rates among developing countries. The success of the overall trade regimes of these countries is testimony to the appropriateness of the liberalization strategy that Bangladesh is in the process of implementing. It also indicates the considerable distance that still needs to be covered.

The Government has announced that its *short-term tariff agenda* is for the FY95 Budget to yield a maximum rate of nominal protection of 45 percent for final goods, with higher rates limited to products under time-bound agreements to be negotiated by the newly reorganized Tariff Commission. It would also complete the task which it set in 1991 to avoid discrimination against earlier stages of production by achieving the structure of 7.5, 15 and 30 percent nominal protection rates for raw materials and intermediates, eliminating user-differentiated rates for similar products, and minimizing zero-rating. These objectives are to be achieved by action on three fronts: (a) further reducing and consolidating CD rates and eliminating the permit/license fee; (b) ensuring that true world prices are used as the basis for assessment, rather than the present TVs; and (c) making the VAT/SD system fully trade-neutral. Each of these elements has difficulties to be overcome to complete this short-term agenda expeditiously.

Further progress on the CD schedule and the elimination of the licensing fee requires attention to both protection and revenue considerations. The reorganized Tariff Commission needs to rapidly undertake the analysis required to negotiate time-bound agreements on transitional adjustment assistance in the form of higher output or lower input CD rates. A particular difficulty may apply to reducing tariff protection for the textile industries, which are due to lose the benefits of both protective VAT and import bans at the same time; several parts of this subsector may be irretrievable and thus unlikely to qualify for continuing tariff protection under the time-bound agreement system. The normal tension between the revenue and protection functions of import taxation could dog attempts to reduce CD rates (e.g. from 45 percent to 15-30 percent for spare parts) and eliminate the license fee. The case of imported machinery spare parts is important to tackle because in the first wave of industrial restructuring, entrepreneurs are more likely to upgrade their machinery assets than to replace them with new machinery. Fortunately, as argued in Chapter I, current macroeconomic conditions and the Government's domestic resource position provide an adequate cushion for the possible reduction in customs duty revenues, depending on the buoyancy of imports. Improvements in VAT administration and coverage are important in this regard to ensure that this headroom for reducing CD rates remains available.

Tariff anomalies remain a significant problem. These are to be resolved by the restructured Tariff Commission. Since these arise partly from the contending objectives of tariff liberalization and revenue generation, there is a need for establishing a coordinating mechanism involving the Tariff Commission and NBR to resolve such conflicts.

As discussed above, the use of tariff values often cancels the effect of tariff reductions. To ensure that true world prices are used as the basis for assessment, TVs should be eliminated and the present combination of TVs and voluntary PSI should be replaced with the contracting of PSI agents to perform the assessment offshore for all or most imports.

Making the VAT/SD system fully trade-neutral requires greater efforts in three areas. *First*, the main removable departure from trade neutrality at present is the imposition of 15 percent VAT on all textile imports, but only 2.5 percent excise on equivalent domestic production. Recent studies on the textile subsector have produced no evidence that the subsector's necessary restructuring would be assisted by continuing this discrimination. In any case, if any additional protection could be justified for some branches of the subsector, it should be provided transparently through the choice of customs duty rates. *Second*, a more difficult problem to address is the VAT/SD exemption of cottage industry, and the substitution of a 2.5 percent turnover tax for small scale enterprises producing goods competing with imports that are subject to VAT. This situation should continue only as long as the VAT administration is still too underdeveloped to provide equal treatment. As with textiles, protection should be provided through customs duty, not manipulation of consumption tax instruments. The *third* departure works in the opposite direction, and would erode protection on many goods if the coverage of supplementary duty were expanded appropriately. It consists of the use of assessed import value alone as the base for calculating SD on imports, whereas SD on domestic production is levied on its ex-factory value, which notionally equates to import value plus customs duty and license fee.[1] This technical error should be corrected, with the affected CD rates lowered to offset the corrections.

The Government must make strong efforts to resolve the above issues before the FY95 Budget, to make room for further accelerated implementation of the *medium-term tariff agenda* and rate reductions by the end of FY95. To be internationally competitive, this implies tariff rates below 30 percent, with a high proportion set lower, and the continued absence of non-tariff barriers. An accelerated approach to such a target is to be preferred to a more leisurely pace of tariff reforms in order to obtain the benefits expected from trade liberalization. For several reasons, moving rapidly to such a regime from the expected FY95 structure should not be as difficult as resistance to the modest progress made so far might suggest.

The pattern of effective protection is very uneven, and the inefficiency of its implementation suggests that protection is often much lower than the tariff schedules indicate. For example, the effective protection rate in leather products for FY92 is estimated to be 67 percent, as compared to an average tariff in FY92 of 100 percent. For many producers, a low but well administered tariff may provide no less effective assistance than the present disorder which dissipates benefits in transactions costs, shares rent-seeking among various agents, and encourages smuggling at the expense of domestic industry.

The Government has asked the Tariff Commission to recommend time-bound levels of temporary protection for industries needing to adjust to low future protection. This transparent approach should facilitate the politically difficult decisions on what to protect, while shielding the Government from pressure to preserve protection at the expense of consumers. To ensure this, the Commission should be given as much autonomy as possible under the 1992 Act which reorganized it.

During the next year or so, firms facing sharply reduced protection will need to reorganize their operations. Within the community of medium- and large-scale enterprises, the example set by firms making an early adjustment that sensibly anticipates the new regime will be emulated by other firms. Even now, some entrepreneurs with comfortable domestic market operations are considering diversification into more efficient activities, including export production. Reducing protection for some industries will benefit others. Efficient industries will benefit in markets for scarce capital and skilled labor from the departure of inefficient import-competing firms. This will be reinforced by the commercialization and privatization of inefficient SOEs. The experience of other developing countries has shown that the reform process can be self-fulfilling.[2] If the Government's actions on tariff reform are credible and consistent, and if domestic and foreign investors believe that the low tariff regime is coming soon, they are likely to respond by establishing new activities to create the growth scenario within which difficult issues of closure and redundancy can be addressed more easily. As indicated in Chapter I, accelerated tariff reductions accompanied by an appropriate real depreciation of the taka in the context of structural adjustment would leave protection levels unchanged

---

[1] For example, with scheduled CD and SD rates of 75% and 25% respectively, the different basing of import and domestic SD reduces nominal protection from 75% to 60%. If that effect were intended it could be achieved more simply and transparently by reducing CD to 60% and applying SD to the CD-inclusive import value, in line with the procedure for the VAT.

[2] See G. Cordoba, "Ten Lessons From Mexico's Economic Reform" mimeo, March 1992. Mexico completed its trade liberalization within essentially a three-year period (1986-88), going from one of most closed to one of the more open economies of the world. Its experience suggests that the speed of trade reform is particularly useful for making liberalization irreversible. Credibility is important, and as in Mexico's case, a credible trade reform tends to be executed rapidly and is often concluded before the schedule laid out at the beginning. In Mexico's case, the propitious initial conditions included high foreign exchange reserves, a currency depreciating in real terms, and low aggregate demand so as to minimize any temporary import surge.

for import-substituting industries, while at the same time providing a major impetus to exporters and new firms entering the export industry.

In large measure, the rationale for continued protection is that it compensates for the high cost of doing business in Bangladesh, and to some extent, that private domestic entrepreneurs cannot perform better than SOEs. If the Government improves the business environment, some of the causes of entrepreneurs' excessive inward orientation would be removed. This should help sway domestic opinion towards assisting the Government fashion sound trade policy for outward-oriented growth.

Increasing the Effectiveness of Export Incentives

Explicit export bans or taxes, unlike other countries in the region, have been used only sparingly in Bangladesh, and much of the trade policy impediments to export have come from import barriers. Following the model of export push used by countries such as Malaysia, Indonesia, and Thailand (see Box 2.2), Bangladesh needs to combine import liberalization with the effective provision of institutional and infrastructural support for exporters and for foreign direct investment. Strenuous efforts need to be made to streamline the three principal export incentive schemes that are in place, and to ensure that they are made available to indirect exporters as well.

The progressive reduction of high protection against imports has somewhat increased access to imported inputs for export industries. Allowing the taka to depreciate modestly in nominal terms has also increased export earnings valued in local currency (although the effective pace of real depreciation is substantially less than that of several potential and actual competitors, as noted in Chapter I). Before the official and market exchange rates were unified in 1992, export sales using the official rate were subsidized through an "export promotion bonus" which reflected the official rate's margin from the more market-related secondary rate used for repatriating earnings of workers abroad.

The *Industrial Policy 1991* has the explicit goal of enhancing the environment for the growth of Bangladesh's export industry. In addition, the *Bangladesh Export Development Strategy, 1992-2000* was recently adopted to correct policy distortions and alleviate regulatory and infrastructural restrictions to private sector export production. The *Export Strategy* mandates improved and expanded rebates on taxes and duties on imported inputs for export production, technical and information service provision through the Export Promotion Bureau (EPB), grants and training for international marketing development, infrastructure investments and transfer of certification responsibilities to export agencies. The EPB's capacity to implement and monitor this strategy remains weak, however, and the Government needs to strengthen this capacity. Bangladesh's neighbors in the region, particularly India and Pakistan, are vigorously pursuing export incentive schemes and ensuring that they are effective. This makes it imperative that Bangladesh also provide the required institutional and policy support if it wants a successful export push.

Export production in Bangladesh has been assisted primarily by three instruments designed to offset impediments in the policy environment: the export processing zones (EPZ), the special bonded warehouse scheme, and the duty drawback scheme. The special bonded warehouse (SBW) scheme for producers who fully export their output has been a critical factor in the explosive development of the RMG sector and related international subcontracting. It has provided limited incentives for local sourcing (since the use of inland back-to-back letters of credit has made it available for producers of intermediates such as zippers and buttons). Until recently, however, the SBW scheme has also been limited in its coverage because it required back-to-back letters of credit, a method of financing imported raw materials which is not appropriate for many industries and which cannot be used by firms producing for both domestic and export markets. The result was that SBW has so far supported only RMG, hosiery and specialized textiles. Recent reforms allow other methods of financing, and firms using SBW facilities may now import up to a third of their annual requirements of raw materials. The Government also hoped to allow the import of machinery and spare parts under the SBW scheme, but this improvement has been delayed through an attempt to require a bank guarantee of payable duty.

The substantial increase in the use of the duty drawback scheme administered by DEDO is due to the rapid expansion of the range of products for which standard ("flat") rates are prescribed and codified, and the streamlining of procedures (including release of the duty rebate directly by the commercial bank involved), both facilitated by successful computerization of DEDO. Further increases in use of this scheme are expected, which will require continued or even increased efficiency in administration and DEDO's management capabilities.

The Chittagong EPZ exports mainly readymade garments; the recently opened Dhaka EPZ will be oriented toward high-technology industries. EPZ producers import raw materials and capital goods free of duty, retain foreign currency earnings, operate in a labor market free of unions, and are exempted from income tax for the first 10 years after opening. The EPZs are important in Bangladesh so as to provide a secure foothold for foreign direct investment. The first EPZ, established at Chittagong in 1984, increased export earnings from $34 million in FY90 to $127 million in FY93, despite the cyclone. Investment in that EPZ totalled over $100 million and value-added has averaged around 30-40 percent. While EPZs are clearly vital, investors still complain about lacking infrastructure and the need for simplified approval procedures for improvements.

Recent reforms aimed at export promotion have not been as effective as might have been hoped. The ban on re-export has been replaced by a set of restrictions which prevent most Bangladeshi entrepreneurs from undertaking trade among distribution centers. Only SBW licensees using back-to-back letters of credit are eligible, the price differential must be at least 15 percent, and each case must be approved by Commerce Ministry officials. Even with approval, difficulties have been reported in having import duties and taxes waived by Customs officials. The ban on consignment sales has been lifted only for perishable goods; for other manufactures consignments may only occur against confirmed letters of credit. This prevents trial shipments on a sale or return basis, a normal way to develop new markets and products. These restrictions, intended to prevent capital flight, are now not necessary when the taka has been made convertible on the current account.

The attempt to force SBW exporters to increase domestic value-added by limiting the proportion of export value that may be imported has been modified, but is not yet being implemented. This restriction particularly affects the RMG industry, for which the value-added requirement is 30 percent. This effectively prevents contractors from working with high value inputs. Potentially lucrative opportunities are lost for products which have low value-added on a per-unit basis, but, could yield substantial profits at high volumes of production. Such opportunities are also lost for products with value-added of less than 30 percent, but which would provide greater domestic value-added in absolute terms (for example, 10 percent of value-added on a $50 item is greater than 30 percent value-added on an $7 item).

Most of the improvements relating to SBW, DEDO or other impediments still leave restrictive clearance procedures to be administered by Customs, Chief Controller of Imports and Exports and the EPB, (even though EPB is supposed to be promotional). Other elements of the export control regime have not been improved. However, worse than the export controls contained in the biennial *Export Policy*, the Government occasionally imposes bans on an ad hoc basis; recent examples include exports of wet blue leather (ostensibly to encourage domestic finishing and crusting), and jute yarn export by mills that also produce other jute products. These ad hoc decisions create an atmosphere of uncertainty and a level of risk that is not consistent with stimulating investment in export-oriented industries by the private sector.

C. EFFECTIVE DEREGULATION FOR PRIVATE INVESTMENT

As the progress underway on trade liberalization begins to have effect, entrepreneurs will begin to investigate further ways to respond to the opening up of the economy. In so doing, domestic controls, incentives and other factors influencing the decision to invest will begin to gain in importance. With trade restrictions being removed, vestiges of past investment controls, inadequate tax policies, problems of private investment financing, remaining restrictions on access to foreign exchange, and the problems in the legal framework have now become the more binding impediments to private investment and expansion into export markets. The Government must act decisively and quickly to lower the costs of doing business imposed by such constraints, thereby enhancing the overall environment for private investment.[1] In solving these problems, as indeed in its entire interactions with the private sector, the Government needs to be extremely mindful of avoiding actions or pronouncements that might reduce the credibility of its reforms, and raise doubts about its commitment.

The pressures on the Government to remove these impediments is also likely to increase as the initial process of liberalization begins to gain impetus and critical mass. In many ways, with faster growth further progress in enhancing the business environment should become easier, since many of the present controls and incentives are mutually justifying in a interlocking web. It is difficult, for example, to give fully automatic access to investment incentives without first removing the trade controls to which the incentives are designed to provide an exception.

From Regulation to Effective Facilitation of Private Investment

The formal industrial policy of Bangladesh has been liberalized progressively since 1982 to make room for an increasing role for the private sector. The *New Industrial Policy* promulgated in that year to admit the joint role of private enterprise in developing the economy was followed in 1986 by a *Revised Industrial Policy* which further liberalized the environment. It was only in 1990, however, that serious efforts commenced to release private investment from bureaucratic control. The then Government was replaced before the new policy was promulgated, but an improved version was issued by the new Government as the *Industrial Policy 1991*, further revised in December 1992, along with a liberalized exchange control regime, a decision to end SOE presence in manufacturing, and a decision to convert the role of the Board of Investment (BOI) from regulation to facilitation of private investment. In terms of SOEs, particularly in manufacturing, Government actions still manifest a somewhat mixed commitment to relinquishing its investment. The Government is slowly pursuing a privatization program (see Chapter III).

Several features of the current policy should prove valuable for promoting private investment and making new private entry possible. Very few activities -- defense equipment

---

[1] A major source of high costs in Bangladesh is the weak and costly provision of infrastructure and utility services by the state-owned enterprises responsible for transport, telecommunications and utilities. Privatization, private provision, commercialization, and other reforms of infrastructure and utilities are discussed in **Chapter III**. Fundamental weaknesses in the financial sector, and labor market distortions, have also impeded manufacturing. The priorities for reform of financial and labor markets are discussed in **Chapter IV**.

production, international air transport, railway transport, security printing, forestry, and nuclear energy -- are now formally reserved for public investment. Power, telecommunications and domestic air transport were reserved until recently, but private investment is now possible and will occur in these sectors as their regulatory frameworks are clarified. The previously required sponsorship of ministries to facilitate private operations in their sectors has been largely abolished. Stock exchange listing of large companies is no longer compulsory. Procedures for obtaining work permits for expatriate staff have been eased. Since 1991, foreign-owned firms have been permitted outside EPZs and, in principle under the 1980 Foreign Private Investment (Protection and Promotion) Act, should receive equal treatment. Recent steps in this direction have comprised the elimination of required BOI permission for foreign firms to change their production capacity, and of the previously required Bangladesh Bank approval for dealing on the Stock Exchange. Foreign-owned firms also have been given access to the domestic banking system for working capital.

Other recent reforms have improved the environment for domestic as well as foreign investors. The first steps taken to transform BOI are to make registration automatic (and voluntary, unless tax incentives or facilitation services are needed); and eliminating tariff discrimination between industrial and commercial imports of machinery. These changes, while welcome, are too recent to provide experience of their efficacy. BOI continues to participate in some regulatory activities. In particular, it certifies industry eligibility to import materials subject to control, and to remit funds in excess of Bangladesh Bank norms for foreign loan servicing, royalties, dividends, and expatriate staff salaries. BOI's procedures continue to be identified by investors as a potential obstacle, but this is the fault of the exchange and import controls themselves, not BOI. The more important challenge facing that institution is to develop the capacity for delivering effective investor facilitation services, for promoting investment opportunities, and for helping the Government identify and remove impediments to greater private sector investment. BOI requires thorough reorganization to meet this challenge, and a plan to start this process appears to be nearing final approval.

Another potential problem -- breeding uncertainty for possible domestic and foreign investors -- lies in the provision of the *Industrial Policy 1991* for the Government to designate "regulated industries" for which it would frame rules to protect the environment, public health and the "national interest." Public health is commonly taken to refer to the existing regime for pharmaceuticals, but no formal identification of such industries has been issued and the "national interest" phrase has nowhere been defined. Transparent rules and a clear regulatory direction relating to the potential impact of each of the three categories are required.

Regulation for environmental purposes in particular remains opaque. The 1992 Environment Policy and Implementation Program did not identify regulated industries, and guidelines that are reported to have been drafted still await approval. BOI, Bangladesh Export Processing Zone Authority (BEPZA), and commercial banks refer some project proposals to the Environment Department for site clearance at their discretion. Although no list has been published, such clearances are reportedly required for all new projects in several industries: leather tanning, tobacco, industrial chemicals and spirits, cement, products based on industrial wastes, edible oil, and plastic sheets and bags. As well as being opaque, the clearance procedure appears to be cumbersome. Local authorities are also given a potentially useful, but currently ill-defined, role.

Both the free entry and exit of enterprises is crucial to bringing about a dynamic private sector. The importance of exit has been much less recognized in Bangladesh, even as slow progress has been made on deregulating investment entry. The availability and efficiency of investment will increase only if failing establishments are allowed to close. Without a clear exit policy, failing firms require resources to stay in business, reducing those available for otherwise stronger firms, increasing their input and thus output prices, and effectively precluding international competitiveness. The need for a clear exit policy cuts across both the private and SOE sectors; it also has ramifications for the financial sector and for labor markets. Preparation and approval of the proposed bankruptcy legislation must be accelerated in order to lay the foundation for orderly industrial exit.

Rationalizing Fiscal Incentives for Private Investment

Bangladesh offers a complex set of generous tax incentives for investment. This system has grown layer by layer, and now needs rationalization and improvements to ensure that both effective assistance and revenue objectives are well served.

The Corporate Tax System. Small improvements to corporate taxation have been made in the FY92-94 budgets but the outstanding agenda for tax reform -- to make the system effective as a revenue instrument while encouraging private sector development -- is large and difficult. In spite of some recent simplifications, Bangladesh retains a very complex tax system that would be difficult to manage even in a country with far superior accounting practices and tax administration. It features a still high nominal tax rate but low effective rates due to numerous general and industry specific provisions for reducing taxable income. These fall into four groups: special concessions for enterprises in EPZs; tax holidays outside the EPZs; other full or partial exemptions for certain activities; and an intricate array of investment and depreciation allowances. For firms not enjoying tax holidays, it also imposes double taxation of distributed income (dividends).

Several changes have been made in the basic *tax rate* on corporate income, including capital gains not reinvested. The current status and recent changes in income tax rates are summarized in Table 2.5. The statutory rates of corporate taxes are quite high in Bangladesh, suggesting the scope for noncompliance and tax avoidance. However, incentives such as tax holidays and accelerated depreciation reduce the effective tax rate at the margin. The corporate rates are also far above the maximum personal tax rate, which was lowered this year from 30 to 25 percent. The income of non-resident companies continues to be taxed at 30 percent. The share of corporate income tax is much higher than that of non-corporate tax, although it is declining, suggesting faster growth of the base for personal income tax.

The Government decided in 1991 to advance from 2000 to 1995 the deadline for reevaluating the *tax holiday scheme* which is available to new industrial companies located outside the EPZs. The duration of the tax holiday depends on location, ranging from 5 years in developed areas to 12 years in special economic zones. Eligibility conditions are general enough to ensure that very few firms in practice are ineligible. The decision to reevaluate the tax holiday scheme in 1995, with the idea that it would be abolished and replaced by alternatives such as accelerated depreciation allowances, is based on the recognition by the Government that tax holidays are a blunt instrument for promoting investment, and cost considerably in terms of lost revenues.

Table 2.5: Recent Changes in Income Tax Rates, FY91-94
(percent)

Taxpayer Group	FY91[a]	FY92	FY93	FY94
Industrial companies: publicly traded	46	45	40	40
Industrial companies: not publicly traded	52	50	45	40
Non-industrial companies: publicly traded	63	55	55	40
Non-industrial companies: not publicly traded	63	55	55	50
Banks, insurance, & financial institutions	63	55	55	50
Personal (maximum rate)	50	45	30	25

[a] The FY91 corporate tax rates include a 15 percent surcharge.
Source: Budget speeches for relevant years.

Generous tax treatment is afforded to *EPZ enterprises*, with income exempted for 10 years from the commencement of commercial production, including dividends from EPZ firms to non-resident shareholders. Such dividends continue to be exempt if they are re-invested in the same project in a prescribed manner. For 5 to 10 years after the expiry of this tax holiday, half of any income attributable to export sales continues to be exempted. For new plant or machinery in hi-technology electronic industries, a one year write-off is allowed during the holiday.

The standard *depreciation* allowance is calculated on a declining balance, historical-cost basis at a fixed percentage rate. The total amount is constrained by law not to exceed the original cost of the asset, excluding any grant, subsidy or rebate from the Government or other specified authority. The annual depreciation rates are 10, 20 and 30 percent for different categories of assets.

The treatment of *dividends* in the Bangladesh tax system falls somewhere between full double taxation and its avoidance through careful integration of corporate and personal taxation for investors. Most dividends are subject to both withholding tax (at the rate of 15 percent for corporate recipients and 10 percent for individuals) and income tax at the recipients' own marginal rates. These withholding taxes cannot be offset against other corporate tax liabilities.

Improving Fiscal Incentives. As the above summary indicates, the two salient features of the current Bangladesh tax system are its complexity and non-neutrality. Tax rates are quite high, but are riddled with exemptions. There are a large number of overlapping and potentially contradictory incentive schemes available, the full implications of which may not have been completely understood at the time they were introduced to promote one or another activity.

Tax systems in general reflect a compromise between a number of conflicting goals, not the least of which is the compromise between government revenue and incentives goals. The Government should continue to increase corporate tax revenues through improved administration; thus any reform to improve incentives must take revenue effects into account. A good corporate tax system for manufacturing sector growth should have a low total effective tax rate and depreciation allowances that mirror economic depreciation. Its more detailed design should incorporate four characteristics: buoyancy and elasticity with respect to revenue (while direct taxes on income are not likely to be the dominant source of revenue in Bangladesh, their contribution is important and likely to increase); neutrality (taxes should not distort investment decisions between different types of capital, between capital and labor, between debt and equity sources of finance, and between investments in different sectors of the economy); competitiveness (the tax structure must not deter foreign investment in Bangladesh); and simplicity, stability and transparency (the structure should be easy to understand, easy and efficient to administer, and easy for honest domestic and foreign firms to operate). Since simplicity and stability are important, such a system should be carefully designed, established, and then not changed. Initial steps towards its establishment are expected to occur in the FY95 Budget.

Financing for Private Investment

The failure of Bangladesh's financial institutions to develop a lending and investment environment in which the manufacturing sector could flourish has resulted in a continuous concern with the financial aspects of industrial projects, distracting enterprise management attention from production and marketing concerns. The manufacturing sector's needs were largely met by two development finance institutions (DFIs), term lending from NCBs, and a small capital market. They were joined in the 1980s by private banks. The rising volume of bad debt was largely ignored, in the belief that, as it was asset-based, and therefore, secure. Default was attributed to the bad behavior of businessmen, rather than to the policy environment. Chapter IV discusses the current problems that these policies in the financial sector have given rise to, and the urgent actions that are required to begin the process of bringing financial institutions back to health. This section briefly discusses foreign commercial financing of investment in Bangladesh.

Foreign Financing. In the absence of efficient domestic financial markets, manufacturing can be financed through the use of foreign funds in their four mains forms (other than donors' and multilateral banks' contributions for domestic intermediation). *First*, supplier credits have played the most significant role in Bangladesh over a long period, both on commercial terms and with aid donors' support. Commercial supplier credits have been available for some manufacturers subject to the rules of Bangladesh Bank with respect to down payment, interest rate and length of repayment. These rules were inappropriate to the risk environment in Bangladesh and have had a negative impact on the use of supplier credits. Recently they have been relaxed but are still fairly restrictive--maximum interest rate of LIBOR plus 4 percent, minimum repayment period of 7 years, and maximum down payment of 10 percent--and inconsistent with a liberalized foreign exchange policy. Within these rules, supplier credits may be contracted without case-by-case approval from the central bank, but BOI approval is required for any case that does not conform. *Second*, working capital is a newer but very significant form of foreign financing. It has been a major factor facilitating the development of the garment export trade, which is now using about US$500 million of such funds in the form of fabric supply.

Third, the potential for foreign portfolio investment has increased with the recent lifting of the regulations which governed these investments. In the current economic environment, however, little inflow is expected unless there is both an increase in market prices and implementation of stock market reforms (Chapter IV). Potentially, however, this is a very important source of funding in Bangladesh's capital scarce economy.

Finally, there has been some foreign direct investment, but its role has been limited, due initially to negative (and more recently to complex) Government regulations with negotiated rather than codified rules. While the atmosphere has improved over the past two years, a residual set of regulations and attitudes reflect adversely on Bangladesh as a site for international investment. There have been two important developments in recent years: KAFCO, the foreign financed fertilizer project represents an investment of the order of US$500 million for site preparation, factory construction and other infrastructure; and there has been significant investment by foreign companies in the Chittagong and the newly opened Dhaka EPZs. Together with financing for RMG working capital, these developments have meant that over the past three years there has been a major increase in foreign capital being used by the economy. So far its impact has mainly affected the garment industry, and in other areas the impact is just beginning to be felt.

Lifting Foreign Exchange Controls

Recent liberalization measures have resulted in a substantial reduction in the exchange controls on current account transactions for private manufacturing firms, yielding numerous improvements in foreign currency finance for the private sector. These include allowing non-residents to bring in funds to buy shares quoted on the Dhaka Stock Exchange; to remit dividends and sale proceeds, including capital gains, after withholding tax due on them, rather than requiring them to obtain tax clearance certificates; and to receive shares from Bangladeshi firms without central bank permission. Bangladeshis no longer need Bangladesh Bank's (BB) permission to have banks release funds for study abroad, and returning Bangladeshis who resume residence are allowed to operate foreign currency accounts. Foreign firms can now borrow in taka from domestic banks; and remittances for re-insurance premia, preshipment inspection fees, ship charter or purchase by private firms, surplus earnings of foreign airlines, shipping companies and couriers are all permitted. Banks may also issue guarantees and performance bonds on behalf of exporters.

Reforms Needed. Reforms are still inadequate in places, however, to provide appropriate economic signals and incentives. The restrictive new guidelines for supplier credits apply to other foreign borrowing as well, and reflect an unnecessary fear that such transactions may be used as a vehicle for capital flight. Other guidelines which, for the same reason may be exceeded only with BOI approval, cover the remittance of foreign nationals' salaries and savings, royalties and technical fees, and training abroad and foreign consultancy costs. BOI has established a new passbook system to monitor all utilization through the commercial banks in case its discretion is required, thereby perpetuating its regulatory role and reflecting a lingering control mentality. Back-to-back letters of credit to finance imported inputs for export production may now be opened without prior BB permission, but only by 100-percent exporting firms licensed as special bonded warehouses. Domestic firms wishing to enter export markets are denied this valuable facility. Once a firm is licensed as an SBW, however, it must always use back-to-back letters of credit and may not finance imports by any other means. This forcibly insulates the SBW-using firms from the domestic banking system.

Exporters can now retain proceeds in foreign currency, but only up to 5 percent for service exports and so-called low value added exports (garments, electronic goods, naphtha, furnace oil and bitumen), and 10 percent for other exports. This foreign exchange may only be used for the purchase of inputs or machinery or for business travel or trade fair costs. Such funds are not reconvertible if firms wish to use them for taka expenses. Another reform that has not gone far enough is the permission to make remittances or allow discounts from repatriated proceeds to meet short weight, quality and other claims on exporters; this is permitted only up to 10 percent of the proceeds or invoice value, which is inadequate.

Wholly or partly foreign-owned firms may now obtain short-term foreign currency loans from the domestic banking system. Foreign investors may not import against direct payment; instead they must bring in the funds and open letters of credit. Letters of credit are still required for all but a few types of imports. Annual entitlements of foreign exchange for travel purposes have increased, but still remain modest.

The various limitations that continue to be placed on foreign exchange transactions are not justified in an era of a partially convertible taka. The limits should be increased, or, preferably, abolished. Full liberalization of these aspects of the exchange control regime could appropriately occur in tandem with the final step in abolishing trade related non-tariff import controls by July 1994.

Towards a Well-Functioning Legal System

An accessible, and codified legal system, in which legal remedies are reasonably predictable and enforceable, can be an asset for private sector growth. Priority in terms of the private sector needs should be accorded to legal reforms that will protect private property, make contracts enforceable, facilitate the orderly exit of failed firms, clarify land titles, make audited accounts reliable, and encourage the use of modern technology in legal systems. Even if, as is the case in many successful developing countries, enterprises find ways to overcome inadequacies in the legal system, these efforts generally add to the costs of doing business.

Over the past two years, the Parliament has passed new laws covering commercial banks, capital markets, non-bank financial institutions, and the establishment of financial courts. Legislation is currently being developed with respect to the bankruptcy law. The new laws have not yet become fully effective, however, since implementing institutions are not yet functional and institutional shortcomings undermine statutory, as much as regulatory aspects, of the business environment. The Government has established a task force to formulate an action program for law reform, and has decided in principle to reestablish a permanent Law Reform Commission.

To strengthen contract law within the limits of court capacity, limits are needed on the adjournment and appeal processes, and outstanding awards should incur interest. The three statutes affecting land transfer and mortgaging also need to be modified to facilitate the processes of creating title and securing other interests at reasonable cost. These have become acute impediments to modern business dealings. False land titles abound, and mortgages are often unregistered to avoid the current high registration charges. Potential investors will look with care at laws concerning the structure and accountability of boards of directors and auditors, the protection of minority shareholders, and the issue of new stock within authorized capital. Such subjects would be appropriately covered in the revision underway of the 1913 Company Law, which needs to be given both direction and faster processing. Similar urgency applies to the laws to reorganize the Board of Investment, promote and protect foreign private investment, and modernize the bankruptcy legislation.

A new, comprehensive Labor Code is needed to integrate and modernize the Industrial Relations Ordinance, the Employment of Labor (Standing Orders) Act, and 45 other laws affecting employment and industrial relations (see Chapter IV). A Labor Law Commission, established in 1992, is expected to report shortly.

In order to make legal reforms effective, it will be important to focus attention eventually on improving the judicial process, including making the courts more functional. Procedural innovations that can be considered would include pre-trial conferences, broadened provisions for discovery, and mechanisms for ensuring that court orders are conveyed and executed. A Judicial Training Institute, complemented by the establishment of a Practicing Law Institute, would expand legal capacity.

D. THE READYMADE GARMENTS INDUSTRY

The readymade garments (RMG) industry is the manufacturing success story in Bangladesh. This section describes the growth of this sector, the policy environment that has sustained it, and the future development prospects of the sector.

The RMG sector is particularly interesting not just because it has been successful, but also because it is an example of how relatively modest changes in the policy environment, when other appropriate circumstances are also present, can lead to rapid success in an export-oriented industry. By way of illustrating this "RMG approach", the last part of this section also identifies the constraints on the development of two other sectors, silk, and leather garments and leather hides, where this RMG approach may be tried.

Readymade Garment Exports: Rapid Growth and Its Causes

The RMG industry was able to take off once two related adverse elements of the business environment -- difficulties in importing and financing raw materials -- were overcome through the offshore financing of world-priced inputs by back-to-back letters of credit (L/C) under the SBW scheme. This response was possible because other essential elements of this international industry could be brought together readily: the technology is simple and the plant cheap (sewing machines); a largely female labor force became available and was easily trained; the entrepreneurs appeared, initially foreign but soon nationals by the hundreds; and the need for export marketing was replaced by international subcontracting, with the buyers initiating orders along with providing raw materials and specifications. International buyers were initially attracted to Bangladesh by its favorable situation under the Multi Fibre Agreement. As a least developed country it could benefit from the quotas which otherwise limited the supply from more traditional garments producers such as Hong Kong and the Republic of Korea.

Spectacular Growth. The industry's development has been rapid (Table 2.6). Although a few units were registered with the Department of Textiles in the 1970s, the industry started at the end of that decade with the establishment of Daewoo-Desh, a joint South Korean-Bangladeshi venture which featured technical training abroad and other technology transfer. The 21 units which were registered by the newly formed Bangladesh Garment Manufacturers and Exporters Association (BGMEA) generated gross export sales of about US$10 million in FY83. Within just two more years garment exports soared to $116 million, 12 percent of the country's total FY85 export proceeds. Even more rapid growth occurred in the following two years, following the relocation to Bangladesh of quota-limited production growth from the Republic of Korea and also Sri Lanka. After slower growth in FY89 (when the Government and BGMEA attempted to stifle entry in response to the U.S. Government's application of its quota system to Bangladesh), a new phase of rapid expansion has occurred over the past few years. New registrations in 1992/93 alone totalled 420, and by September 1993 the total number of registered units had reached 1,630. The higher value added knitwear component of the industry is growing the fastest, now contributing a seventh of all RMG export proceeds. These reached $1.2 billion in FY93 or 52 percent of total exports, and are expected to continue to climb. Even when imported input costs are excluded, the net export value is substantial: $420 million in FY93 according to Bangladesh Bank calculations.

Favorable Industry Conditions. This international industry has a *prima facie* attribute, the need for low cost labor, that makes it broadly consistent with Bangladesh's comparative advantage. In addition, it has several special characteristics that help account for its spectacular rise, in effect, by side-stepping potential constraints on marketing, technology, financing, input supply, and labor. *First*, almost all of current production comprises cutting and making (and occasionally trimming) general and retail label garments for international subcontractors through about 250 buying houses, which place orders on behalf of their principals, arrange the supply of imported fabrics and monitor output quality. *Second*, the technology is uncomplicated, and designs and specifications are provided by the buyers. *Third*, most production capacity is located in Dhaka (80 percent) and Chittagong, and has simple factory space requirements; its only important utility need is electricity. *Fourth*, investment requirements are modest and working capital is largely financed offshore. Most firms are small or medium sized, with their respective fixed capital needs averaging Tk 7 million and Tk 18 million (US$175,000 and US$450,000); they can get into business quickly, avoiding costly gestation periods. *Fifth*, the difficulties other emerging export industries have experienced in obtaining world-priced raw materials have been by-passed by their supply and financing offshore, as well as by the inclusion of domestic producers of accessories and packaging in the SBW scheme's back-to-back L/C facility. *Finally*, the industry has been largely free of labor supply constraints (although this may now be changing), and entirely free of industrial strife; this has been due in large part to the coincidence of its rapid growth with the emergence of female participation in the urban industrial labor force (84 percent of RMG workers are female).

Table 2.6: Rapid Growth of the Readymade Garments Industry, 1982-93

| Year | BGMEA Regd. Unit | | Gross Exports (US$ million) | Export Quantity (mill. dozen) a/ | % of Total Exports |
	Year	Total			
1981/82	na	na	7.0	0.1	1.1
1982/83	21	21	10.8	0.2	1.6
1983/84	25	46	32.0	0.7	3.8
1984/85	134	180	116.0	2.8	12.3
1985/86	407	587	131.0	3.6	16.0
1986/87	14	601	299.0	8.3	27.8
1987/88	57	658	433.0	12.3	35.2
1988/89	54	712	471.0	13.7	36.6
1989/90	25	737	609.0	18.7	40.0
1990/91	43	780	736.0	28.0	42.8
1991/92	154	934	1,064.0	40.5	53.4
1992/93	420	1,354	1,240.5	46.2	52.0

a/ Quantity in harmonized units of equivalent dozens.
Source: BGMEA and Bangladesh Bureau of Statistics.

Crucial Policy Support. The special bonded warehouse (SBW) scheme is foremost among aspects of the policy and regulatory framework that have enabled RMG to grow rapidly. It has enabled: (a) many garment exporters to avoid the transactions cost of the alternative duty drawback scheme to ensure world-priced inputs; (b) Bangladeshi entrepreneurs to effectively access international capital markets for what otherwise would have been working capital requirements that the domestic banks would have found impossible to meet; and (c) some, albeit limited, domestic sourcing through the crucial inclusion of indirect exporters in the SBW scheme. But until recently the special requirements for SBW have also limited RMG's further and more beneficial development. It has partially reinforced RMG producers' reluctance (for quality reasons) to increase their industry's value added by using domestic fabric. It has also encouraged much of the industry to remain in the low-value end of the international market. This is more an outcome of the constraints placed on the SBW scheme in a possibly counterproductive attempt to use RMG's success as a vehicle for the textile subsector's recovery. As a policy instrument, the SBW scheme has also inevitably faced challenges from defenders of the traditionally protective regime, concerned about inevitable leakages of fabric and garments into the domestic market.

RMG's meteoric growth has been assisted by several other policy measures besides SBW. After SBW, *second* in importance has been the exemption of corporate taxation on export profits, although this has been weakened since 1992 by the imposition of advance income tax. *Third*, as an export-oriented industry, it has enjoyed a concessional duty rate of 7.5 percent on capital equipment imports for several years. This incentive has been improved recently by allowing SBW licensees to have their local banks guarantee the duty, with one-third liquidated when the equipment is installed and another third liquidated subsequently. However, this is still a more onerous duty regime than that available to EPZ firms, or to competitors in Hong Kong and elsewhere. *Fourth*, the industry was assisted (until the official exchange rate was unified with a secondary rate in 1992) by an Export Performance Benefit designed to close the margin between the official and market exchange rates. *Fifth*, the present quota allocation system has worked reasonably well, although quota reallocation toward the end of the quota year is sometimes inefficient and too delayed for RMG manufacturers to utilize the quotas before they expire. EPB remains too dependent on technical help from BGMEA in monitoring utilization. Quota management is crucial so as also to avoid over-supply of any category that can attract external penalties or embargo. The secondary market in quotas also works well, with quotas freely transferable to facilitate their utilization. The EPB plays only a minor role in this market, registering transfers when they occur but with no system for providing advance information on quota availability for transfer. *Finally*, and very importantly from the viewpoint of private sector development, the special status which the industry earned by its impressive early contribution to exports enabled the emergence of BGMEA as a strong industry association that could command the direct attention of the political establishment to ensure the availability of the above incentives.

The Role of MFA Quotas. It is often suggested that the industry's growth, and now its future health, depends on the favorable treatment which Bangladesh receives under the MFA, now expected to be phased out over the next 10 years under the Uruguay Round. The direction of RMG trade, and new developments such as the North American Free Trade Area (NAFTA), suggest that such caution is justified, and that the industry must become even more efficient to be able to compete in a post-MFA world.

During the 1980s, US importers actively pursued imports from Bangladesh; none of these were restricted until 1985, when quotas were placed only on a few popular items. Now, a large proportion (86 percent in 1992) of sales to North American markets are of products for which Bangladesh is subject to quotas. The quotas are not yet binding for about two thirds of the sales of such products. North American markets account for just over half of Bangladesh's RMG exports: 51 percent in FY92 compared with 80 percent of a much smaller total eight years earlier. The rest goes to West European markets in which Bangladesh still has unrestricted entry for all products, giving it an advantage over its competitors. Such sales have grown rapidly, especially since quotas have become more significant for Bangladesh in the US and Canada. Members of the European Community collectively account for 44 percent of RMG exports, led by Germany (13 percent). The potentially lucrative but difficult Japanese market, on the other hand, has been barely penetrated (0.2 percent). With the phasing out of the MFA over the long term, there could be an import surge into all these markets from the most efficient producers, at the cost of the less efficient ones. Over the medium term it is also possible that NAFTA may lead to a displacement of East Asian RMG imports into the U.S. and Canada. To the extent these exports by the more efficient East Asian producers are then diverted to the European Community, they may tend to displace Bangladesh's RMG exports into Europe.

Future Growth of RMG Exports

The further development of RMG may occur, as discussed below, in any or all of several directions.

More International Subcontracting. In the short to medium term, there appears to be no reason why the subcontracting industry should not continue to grow. There are some prerequisites for this, however. *First*, the favorable aspects of the policy environment need to be maintained; as noted earlier, these include more efficient customs management and further liberalization of the SBW scheme. *Second*, the industry's own efficiency can be improved to make it better able to face future competition. Although many firms use modern production technology, their workers' productivity is well below those of South Korea and Hong Kong, for example. An acute shortage of skilled labor has already emerged in contrast to the abundant supply of unskilled workers. Improved training facilities appear essential. A *third* critical factor is the need for even better management--with minimal if any political interference--of quota allocation, monitoring, and secondary market trading. Bureaucratic involvement is difficult to avoid, since quotas are awarded on a national basis and the alternative approach of leaving the task to the existing producers could reinforce some monopolistic tendencies. Fortunately, however, the industry is already large and entry easy enough for this risk to be smaller than the danger of excessive intervention. The current debate over the respective roles of BGMEA, the EPB, and other Governmental agencies purporting to champion new entrants should be resolved promptly so that agreed ground rules can facilitate unfettered growth.

A Move Up Market. Even without changing the subcontracting nature of the industry, there is scope for entering more profitable international garment markets. At present, Bangladesh has the lowest unit value among the top 10 exporters to the U.S. Apart from the silk and leather materials discussed below, Bangladesh exports could play a greater role in the fashion end of the cotton, synthetic, wool and other fabric-based apparel industry. This move has commenced, with the growth in export value at constant prices (averaging over 40 percent a year) exceeding the growth in volume (36 percent). It has been encouraged by the importing countries' use of import volume rather than value to define quotas, and the absence of quotas on higher value apparel items. For a substantial improvement to occur, however, entrepreneurs will need to respond to the long delayed implementation of the Government's policy of relaxing--or preferably removing--the domestic content requirement (expressed in proportional value added terms at 25 percent, and increased for wovens to 30 percent in 1992). This has discouraged moving to up-market fashion apparel and higher quality, since the domestic content requirement is most easily met by using cheaper imported fabrics that leave higher domestic labor shares of unit value.[1] The current IPO has finally relieved the requirement for woven items under quota worth more than $40 a dozen, but the half-hearted way in which this issue has been approached

---

[1] BGMEA cites the example of cotton shirts, with imported material at $1.91 a yard, meeting the local content requirement by earning local value added of $22 a dozen (31.13% of gross value), while shirts made of cotton denim, at $2.92 a yard, would fail to meet the requirement although earning more domestic content at $27 a dozen (28.07%).

illustrates the continuing preoccupation with propping up inefficient activities (existing fabric producers) at the expense of activities with more export and employment potential (up market RMG).

Beyond Subcontracting. While subcontracting should not be discouraged, a transition to greater control of marketing may be necessary for the industry's growth in the medium to long term as the quota system disappears. This is not possible in the meanwhile for that part of the trade which is under quotas, since these are controlled by foreign buyers. Their eventual abolition, and price and exchange rate considerations, could divert buyers to more traditional sources such as Hong Kong and Korea, or to potentially cheaper sources such as Vietnam, Nepal and perhaps Laos and Cambodia. Industry observers, however, tend to be optimistic about the ability of Bangladeshi entrepreneurs to make the transition. Indeed, a few are already finding and developing their own markets with little if any help from buying houses operating in Bangladesh. About 70 of the operating RMG units take some orders directly from foreign buyers. Many of these units are recent entrants, indicating a progressive trend in the industry's structure. BGMEA estimates that such sales now account for about 5 percent of the total, and producers may be responsible for materials procurement for another 5 percent. In addition, about two dozen of the present units are operated by joint venture companies, in which at least the foreign partner is likely to be directly linked to international buyers.

Increasing Value Added. Decreasing the dependence on imported cotton and synthetic fabric in RMG exports is often advocated as a means of helping the ailing domestic woven textiles industries. This development is yet to occur in any significant way for woven fabrics, but strong backward links are being developed in other respects. At present the RMG industry uses considerable domestic inputs in the form of *accessories* (buttons, zippers, labels, etc.) and *packaging* materials (cartons hangers and poly bags). Data on this trade are not available, but there about 25 factories making accessories and 30 others making hangers. Almost half the total output of the packaging industry is already dedicated to RMG export.

The knitted garments and hosiery subsector of RMG already has strong backward linkages in *knit fabric*. This segment only accounts for a seventh of garment exports, but it is becoming increasingly important. As of June 1993, the Department of Textiles (DOT) shows 206 knitting units registered as export-oriented, and 157 of them were integrated with RMG units. These unit supplied just over half of all RMG knit fabric requirements in 1993. While not yet highly competitive on price, local fabric suitable for knit garments is reported to be of good quality and more convenient to obtain since Customs procedures are avoided altogether.

The predominant raw material for RMG is *woven fabric*, most of which is now imported. The DOT has six spinning and 92 weaving units registered as export oriented (i.e., catering to RMG demand), but there is little evidence to suggest that these units are able to consistently supply significant quantities of cloth that would meet RMG quality standards. Besides the obvious domestic problems of quality, reliability of supply, and price, this has also to do with the subcontracting nature of RMG; risk averse foreign buyers and designers are less likely to specify domestic fabrics unless there are clear and proven cost advantages. Furthermore, the typical RMG requirement is for small batches of particular type of cloth, and this requires flexible production management and textile technology that is not easy to establish. Some other components of the textile subsector also have scope for growth or rejuvenation. As such, these developments would have to be based largely on the demands of export RMG units rather than domestic demand for cloth, and the restructured industries would need to be flexible and internationally competitive. If this can be so, they might be also able to export woven fabric directly, enabling scale economies to be achieved while meeting relatively small RMG requirements of particular types of cloth. This is most likely to occur if the Government replaces its present approach of forcing domestic value added by a systematic program to remove obstacles to exit, restructuring, and new investment in spinning, weaving and finishing industries.

Two other ways to enhance the value added of RMG exports from Bangladesh involve using different materials. First, it could compete successfully with countries such as China, Vietnam and Thailand for the export of silk garments and perhaps fabric (see below). This could be based on imported yarn (and even cloth for garments) until their domestic production can become competitive. Second, it could further develop the fledgling exports of leather garments, shoes and other products when the existing industry in wet blue, crust and finished leather is rationalized (see below). The potential development of these two industries could become increasingly important over the next decade.

Lessons from the RMG Experience

In the case of RMG, critical policy constraints were ameliorated and led to the growth of the sector. Without any improvements in the domestic financial sector, and without making any changes to Bangladesh's then high tariff walls, the sector grew because of the external financing through back-to-back letters of credit and the provision of special bonded warehouses to access inputs at international prices. This insulated the sector fairly effectively in a policy enclave. The other attendant conditions on the sector's success were simple technology, modest capital requirements, international subcontracting, and a non-unionized labor force that was predominantly female.[1] Within this policy enclave, the Government more or less let the sector alone, not regulating it while almost everything else in the manufacturing sector was heavily regulated. This experience reinforces the crucial importance of the effective deregulation of, and policy support for, the private sector.

The other major lesson to be learnt from the RMG experience is that the search for comparative advantage in manufactures in a country with a small domestic market such as Bangladesh's must start downstream. Exports prospects must be identified by first considering the possibility of establishing a firm export foothold, and only then seeking to move upstream to exploit backward linkages. As the discussion below shows, industrial policy has often sought to go the other way, and has failed. Had such misguided principles been applied to the RMG industry in the late 1970s, the consequences today would be hard to imagine. It is to Bangladesh's good fortune and the sagacity of the early RMG entrepreneurs that this did not happen.

Other RMG-Like Prospects: Silk and Leather

By way of illustrating the prospects for applying the RMG approach to other subsectors, this subsection highlights the problems and prospects for silk and leather. In considering these two sectors and the lessons enunciated above, it is of course important to note that the policy environment is now significantly liberalized relative to most of the early period in the RMG sector's growth. To that extent, the policy enclave approach may now be less effective than it was a decade ago. Nonetheless, as the discussion shows, specific ex ante opportunities for ameliorating policy constraints and lowering the cost of doing business may exist. These should be explored in conjunction with more fundamental restructuring that may be required.

---

[1] The RMG industry has, of course, been a success in many countries under similar enclave circumstances, for example, in Mauritius.

The Silk Industry

Bangladesh appears to have excellent potential for developing all stages of the silk industry, from mulberry to fashion garments. However, this is unlikely to occur without a significant change in the strategy for developing the industry. Here, as in RMG and some other industries with export potential, the search for comparative advantage should proceed upstream, from the advantage that may be revealed in export markets for the final product (in this case silk garments, initially under subcontracting arrangements, and perhaps also for handwoven silk fabric). Instead, public policy has focussed so far on promoting mulberry, cocoon, and raw silk production. Not only has this been ineffective in several respects; it has occurred with little regard to the competitiveness of downstream weaving and potential garment exports.

Silk Garments. A silk RMG export industry could be worth developing, even without seeking to first exploit the possibly greater potential for its backward links than may exist for cotton and synthetics garments. Bangladesh would not face any trade restrictions in world markets on silk garments, since there is little production in developed countries; now there is almost no chance of this since the Uruguay GATT Round has ruled out new quota restrictions. In addition, international demand for silk garments is growing fast, especially for medium grades. Bangladeshi entrepreneurs' performance so far in cotton and synthetic RMG has indicated their capability to perform efficiently as subcontractors, and move towards more entrepreneurial international marketing. The latter provides a good basis for a move into silk. A major advantage of such a move is the scope it creates for high value added in the future. The current difficulties noted below notwithstanding, silk weaving could become a significant supporting industry with high employment potential; this would provide more domestic value added -- much of it rurally located -- than is conceivable with cotton. Furthermore, the same may ultimately apply to the production of raw silk and yarn -- with an even stronger rural bent -- if the Government pursues a promotion program for mulberry, egg, cocoon, reeling and twisting based on removing, rather than creating or supporting, market imperfections. To capture the value added in both silk weaving and silk yarn, the Bangladesh Sericulture Board (BSB), and other public institutions established to support the rearing and weaving industries, need reorientation and closer cooperation with involved NGOs.

Silk Fabric. While domestic weaving may be initially unnecessary for successful export garments, it seems quite likely that an efficient silk weaving industry would emerge quickly in Bangladesh if it had access to world priced yarn. Raw silk and yarn production should be promoted too, so that value added could be increased eventually. But meanwhile, the potential of weaving should not be undermined by inappropriate means of encouraging its local content. Until an internationally competitive mulberry-silkworm-reeling agronomy emerges, the competitiveness of weaving should be facilitated by ensuring the availability of yarn for small scale weavers through import from Vietnam and other efficient producers. Thus, promotion of weaving should include the effective waiver or rebate of all taxes levied on yarn to be used for ultimate export. Since weavers cannot readily enrol in the SBW scheme, a component of the duty drawback scheme should be designed for them. A weaving industry successfully linked to a broad range of silk RMG export would also require new investment in semi-automatic looms, which can boost by at least four times the normal output of the pitlooms still predominately used in Bangladesh. The production of cloth suitable for silk RMG or direct export also requires (a) improved access to imported chemicals for dying and finishing; and (b) technical training in their use as well as in design for non-sari export market tastes. This applies to the finishing of handloom wovens as well as to the output of more automated weaving; small units would be particularly well served by process houses that could add value by providing such finishing services as padding, shrinking, decaterizing, calendaring and tamponing on an efficient scale. Private investment in such facilities should be encouraged.

Silk Yarn. Mulberry and the silkworms that thrive on it are well known to Bangladesh. By 1989/90 there were almost 7000 ha. under mulberry (mostly trees), over 1000 ha. of which were already productive. The planted area continues to grow with assistance from NGOs, especially the Bangladesh Rural Advancement Committee (BRAC), with a much greater suitable area remaining to be exploited. High yielding hybrid varieties of worm developed by the Bangladesh Sericulture Research and Training Institute (BSRTI) for rearing in non-traditional areas are beginning to displace current varieties. In spite of this progress, the present sericulture industry, could not support a major move into the international market for silk products. It may have been able to do so if it had developed in a free environment, but interventions so far to promote raw silk production have instead rendered it uncompetitive. Industry observers have identified several key problems, some of which remain to be solved: *First*, while balanced production of bush and tree leaf provides superior wormfeed, BSB initially concentrated for too long on promoting bush plantations, but recently has failed to promote them at all. *Second*, leaf yields remain low compared with neighboring countries due to lack of HYV plants, fertilization, and inadequate plant maintenance and irrigation. *Third*, cocoon yields are poor compared to China and India due again to lack of HYV varieties as well as deficient rearing and drying practices, and storage and transport facilities. *Fourth*, BSB's monopoly of the sale of eggs leaves open the possibility of mismanagement. *Finally*, mechanized reeling has expanded very slowly, and most existing mechanical units lack individual brake motion, halving the value of the yarn produced. Also, the absence of twisting facilities, except for one factory, precludes the domestic production of warp yarn. Each of these problems needs to be addressed if a competitive mulberry-silk industry is to develop.

The Leather Industry

Unlike silk, there is already a substantial domestic leather industry, part of which is export oriented. The latter includes some RMG, although that aspect is confined mainly to a small export trade in "Italian-made" garments for the U.S. market. Footwear is more important in terms of value added, accounting for just over US$4 million in exports in FY92. Small amounts are contributed by bags and gloves. Of far more significance at this stage are exports of crust and finished leather, earning US$144 million in FY92. These exports have not been growing, however, having reached that level in FY88, and then peaking at $179 million in FY90. The domestic market for leather, footwear, and other leather products is still more important than exports. Bangladesh produces between 2 and 3 percent of the world's leather. Most of the livestock base for this production is domestic, which the Food and Agricultural Organization estimates as comprising 1.8 percent of the world's cattle stock and 3.7 percent of the goat stock. The hides and skins have a good international reputation, but considerable value is lost through poor handling and transport practices.

In spite of its apparent importance and export experience, considerable effort may be required to convert the subsector into a strong export performer in the medium term. There are estimated to be over 200 tanneries altogether, 168 of which are registered with the Ministry of Industry. Only about 75 of them are operational (50 supply the domestic market), and the rest are debt-ridden and closed. Multiple problems face firms in this market, and some of them may be unable to service their heavy debt burdens.

Leather Enterprise Survey. Identifying priorities for private sector development and the growth of a particular industry should start from a systematic effort to learn what constraints firms perceive to be most binding. Without such an effort, the risk is great that a program of reform could be driven by preconceived views about the obstacles to a private supply response -- and thus fail to target the constraints most binding in practice. Surveys to elicit information directly from firms can show how regulatory, tax, and other measures work in practice, and the constraints that firms see as the most binding.[1] A 1993 survey[2] of the operating firms in the leather industry yielded the following conclusions.

The surveyed entrepreneurs identified the *high cost of capital* as a leading cause of unprofitability. Only the firms that can finance their working capital needs from retained earnings were making profits. There are only few such firms in an industry where working capital needs are at least four times the size of the initial capital investment. The leather industry provides a good example of the financing abuses and difficulties of exit discussed in this chapter. As many as 60 percent of the existing tanneries and other leather enterprises may be in considerable financial stress, and may need to close. Some now in financial difficulty were established before 1982 with inadequate project design; most, however, entered the industry between 1982 and 1989 with directed NCB and DFI credit. This credit continued to flow to borrowers with no net worth on the basis of overstated inventories of materials (akin to similar lending malpractices in the jute industry).

While SBWs are used for *import facilitation* in leather exports, entrepreneurs identified one of its unintended effects which effectively constrains greater exports of leather goods, and therefore greater value added. SBW is preferred over duty drawbacks because it works much better in practice than DEDO's operations. However, because SBW is restricted to 100-percent exporters, the largest and most technologically qualified tanneries have abandoned the domestic market for finished leather (where transactions costs are higher than for export) in order to use the SBW facility. Together with the high tariff on finished leather imports, this lack of high quality finished leather has deprived domestic leather goods makers of a reliable and price-competitive source of supply, accounting for the relatively low level of leather goods export. Domestic leather goods makers pay more for low quality finished leather in Bangladesh than their foreign competitors pay (f.o.b. Chittagong) to import higher quality finished Bangladeshi leather.

More generally, *raw material* supply constraints also affect the tanneries due to the high tariff on hides and skins and on wet-blue. This is felt by the industry to be the main cause of the grossly under-utilized tanning capacity. The tariff is prohibitive, and therefore yields almost no revenue for the Government at present. The high tariff also supports the rents earned from smuggling cattle and hides, a source on which the firms would prefer not to depend, and the higher prices obtained for domestic hides and skins. In spite of the drawback facility, the large working capital requirements implied by the tariff deter even export producers from importing. This may be resolved now as recent changes allow exporters to import hides and skins against a bank guarantee for the duty.

Export facilitation through the duty drawback scheme is reported to be abused by exporters, who may be shipping crust leather as finished leather in order to earn the higher flat rate rebate on the latter. These flat rates, amounting to 18-20 percent of f.o.b. value, apply regardless of quality or price of the chemicals used and of the resulting leather. These values have not been adjusted in three years despite inflation, other price changes and a significant tariff reduction. The entrepreneurs felt that the recent Indian and Pakistani devaluations had enabled those countries' leather industries to undersell Bangladeshi leather by about 20 percent.

---

[1] See Andrew Stone, "Listening to Firms: How to Use Firm-Level Surveys to Assess Constraints on Private Sector Development," DEC Working Paper Series No. 923, The World Bank, June 1992.

[2] The enterprise survey was conducted as part of a forthcoming World Bank Study on industrialization strategy in Bangladesh.

Many tanneries use inefficient (and often environmentally poor) *technology*. Entrepreneurs also pointed to the lack of well-trained *workers and technicians*, mainly due to political unrest in the University of Dhaka and its impact on its Leather Institute, and the moth-balling of the Leather Finishing Center shortly after it was built in 1987. The surveyed firms cited several *infrastructure* services as problems, with electricity supply being the most serious. Frequent power failures and voltage surges were a problem, as was the cost of power because the Government's order to eliminate peak rates for three-shift factories exporting most of their output was not being implemented. Transport and communications facilities were cited as secondary impediments.

Finally, on *foreign direct investment and marketing*, the entrepreneurs were keenly aware that Bangladesh was not able to attract investors who could assist their industry through the production of tanning chemicals and additional production of footwear for export. They were less worried about the absence of foreign buyers in the Bangladesh market, expecting that such buyers would appear as soon as Bangladesh had competitive leather goods to offer them.

E. ENTREPRENEURSHIP AND THE POLICY ENVIRONMENT

The availability and quality of entrepreneurship is fundamental to the strong development of the private manufacturing sector. The quality and prevalence of entrepreneurship has been much discussed with respect to Bangladesh's manufacturing development. An argument heard sometimes is that the country's political history, reinforced by the thrust of Government policy toward the private sector over the past two decades, has weakened the ability of society to produce entrepreneurship. Thus, the argument goes, only government intervention could create industrial development, either through continuing direct ownership or through fostering entrepreneurs who would first work under the direction and guidance of public institutions. This argument has clearly been shown to be false by the readymade garments industry.

In contrast to the outstanding success of the readymade garments industry, jute and textile manufacturers, on which policymakers had long pinned their hopes, have failed to meet expectations. These two experiences illustrate the interaction between private entrepreneurship and the policy environment in Bangladesh. They demonstrate that the entrepreneurial ability is there, but it needs support and a credible policy context. Where these conditions have existed, where the costs of doing business have been lowered, and where markets are promising, the private sector has responded, and it has flourished.

As discussed in Section D above, the **RMG sector** developed entirely in the private sector. The complicated questions for RMG, within the highly restrictive policy environment of the late 1970s, had to do with the financing of the imports of raw materials. Once this question was resolved, the essential entrepreneurial breakthrough, the entrepreneurs appeared, initially foreign but soon nationals by the hundreds, and the industry prospered.

In contrast to the RMG sector, the **jute sector** was built up over the 1950-1970 period with private mills largely owned by Pakistanis. The technology used was old and transferred from mills abroad. The management and labor skills built up over the period resulted in a reasonably efficient industry under heavy pressure from falling world prices. After Liberation in 1971, however, the mills were taken over and operated by the Government; management was not focussed on profits, subsidies were provided, overmanning became rampant, and investment was limited. In such an environment, entrepreneurship could not flourish. When portions of the industry were eventually privatized, the heritage of poor marketing policies, high wages compared to productivity, overmanning misunderstanding of the basis for managing working capital, and virtually no new investment, precluded effective entrepreneurship. In this case the technology was understood, but the available financing arrangements were not satisfactory, there was no shield from the pernicious effects of the policy environment, and the Government's intervention shifted the purpose of entrepreneurial activity away from efficient production to other goals. The integrated jute SOEs (integrating spinning and weaving, and in which the Government holds 43 percent ownership) continued to make losses. They now account for about a third of the operating firms, and bear debt equal to one fourth of debts of all the SOEs.

Finally, the **textile sector** has a complicated technology and was introduced prior to 1971 through Pakistan businessmen who established plants in Bangladesh. Following Independence and the nationalization of the enterprises, the civil service was not able to provide satisfactory managers and the profitability of the sector was destroyed by the poor management practices, high wages, and inadequate investment in plant and equipment. Subsequent privatization did not create an environment in which profitability was achievable.

These cases illustrate three discernible phases of entrepreneurial development in Bangladesh. The *first* round occurred before 1971; there emerged serious and successful businessmen, and fairly small enterprises, which grew up in a private sector environment. Most entrepreneurial development was in the hands of West Pakistanis. The *second* round followed Independence. After a period of nationalization, the objectives of government changed in the mid-1970s to include the private sector in manufacturing development. This was done, however, by the heavy-handed encouragement of investment by identifying permissible sectors, making directed capital available, providing protection through trade policies, and in many instances undertaking the purchase of output or supply of inputs. In effect, the Government removed the challenge and need to make profitability an important criteria of management. This round largely failed. The *third* round comprises the RMG entrepreneurs and emerged in the second half of the 1980s; here, once the production technology was revealed by the early entrants, there has been a steady flow of persons who entered this sector and exploited the high, available returns.

The failure of the second period (which is also reflected in the similarly unsatisfactory development of the principal term lenders to industry, the DFIs) was probably due to a number of phenomena: (a) excess capacity was created with no provision for exit; (b) interest rates were very high and debt-equity ratios rose substantially; (c) the size of individual investments was far greater than the managerial experience of the owners but, with no pool of experienced managers available, most owners preferred to retain family-management; (d) inadequate provision was made for the costs of technology transfer, since it was believed by planners that technology was simple to transfer and that no external assistance was needed; equipment suppliers reacted to this idea by fulfilling the expectations of the bureaucracy; (e) foreign investment was essentially prohibited until the mid-1980s; and (f) the lack of exit provisions, and the failure to move swiftly and decisively to recover loans, created and continually fortified the attitude that one could avoid repayment without legal or social insolvency.

The experience of these three subsectors in Bangladesh yields the basic conclusion that entrepreneurship is not a constraint on the development of manufacturing, except insofar as the Government creates conditions and circumstances that induce its failure. There is no shortage of persons who can undertake successfully the development of an export-oriented manufacturing sector when international demand exists. But this requires flexibility and independence that to date the Government has been reluctant to allow. Only increasing competition, not constraining it, can address the fears and the underlying attitudes, that without Government control, investment will not occur, economic power will be used to impoverish workers, and businessmen will continually collude against the interests of the general population. These attitudes are fortunately changing in Bangladesh. The process of entrepreneurial strengthening must be encouraged if there is to be significant manufacturing development to reverse the damage done to the sector in the 1970s and 1980s.

CHAPTER III: REFORMING STATE-OWNED ENTERPRISES

A. INTRODUCTION

State-owned enterprises represent the biggest public failure in Bangladesh. The fiscal burden and adverse economic impact of poorly managed state-owned enterprises (SOEs) are mounting rapidly. The gross FY93 losses of all SOEs including the railways, at about Tk 20 billion, amounted to a staggering 27 percent of the Annual Development Program, 45 percent of external project aid disbursements, and 2 percent of GDP. At this level, the Government could afford to finance a new infrastructure project of the size of the Jamuna Multi-purpose bridge every one and a half years entirely from domestic resources if the SOE losses could be eliminated. Because SOE losses have been largely financed by lending from the nationalized commercial banks, these losses have profoundly weakened the financial system, eroding portfolio quality and interest rate margins. Public failures raise private costs. Unreliable power supply, for example, induces private investments in standby generators, raising unit costs and creating significant idle capacity in such investments. On both public and private accounts, SOEs act as a strong impediment to faster, private-sector led growth in Bangladesh.

Tinkering at the margin will not cure the deep-seated woes of the SOE sector. Bangladesh cannot afford to wait any longer to experiment with such approaches. This Chapter deals with a three-pronged strategy for reform of the non-financial SOEs (financial SOEs are discussed in Chapter IV). *First*, there must be rapid, progressive privatization of selected SOEs, initially in manufacturing. *Second*, enterprises that are likely to remain in the SOE sector over the foreseeable future must be pushed to commercialize and face the market. *Third*, private sector entry must be facilitated, principally in the important utilities (power, gas, and water) and infrastructure (telecommunications and transport) sectors, so as to raise efficiency within the framework of public-private partnerships and a new regulatory environment. SOE performance is discussed in Section B, and the strategy in Section C. The three elements of the SOE strategy are discussed in Sections D, E, and F. SOEs in utilities and infrastructure constitute the bulk of total SOE assets. They account for the largest share of SOE losses, and have a direct impact on the competitiveness and efficiency of the private manufacturing sector. Given their importance and to illustrate these strategies, Section G discusses more detailed sector reform problems and priorities in power, gas, and telecommunications.

SOEs in Bangladesh date back to well before the liberation of 1971. A number of public enterprises producing paper, fertilizer, sugar, steel, machine tools, and docks and ship yards were run by the East Pakistan Industrial Development Corporation. A number of jute and cotton textile mills, engineering, chemical, leather, and food processing enterprises also operated in the private sector, but mostly under the ownership and management of West Pakistanis. After liberation, with the departure of these public and private sector owners, managers, and technicians, industrial activities came to a grinding halt. As a result, the Government took possession of all factories, banks and properties abandoned by the Pakistanis. In order to restructure the economy on socialistic patterns, Bangladeshi-owned factories, banks, and insurance companies were also nationalized. The large vacuum in management as a result of both actions was gradually filled, primarily by Bangladeshi bureaucrats returning from West Pakistan. However, within the next two years the Government came under heavy criticism for rampant corruption and inefficiencies in the SOEs. As a result, from 1975 onwards the grip on public control of industrial activities began to be slowly loosened.

Despite two successive rounds of divestitures in the mid-1970s and in the 1980s, some 225 non-financial SOEs (grouped under 39 corporations), four large commercial banks, three insurance corporations, two agri-banks, and three DFIs remain in operation in the state sector. SOEs account for

Table 3.1: Size and Importance of Non-Financial SOE Corporations, End-FY93
(Taka million)

Corporations a/		No of Firms	Assets	Sales	Number of Employees
Manufacturing/Industry					
BTMC	Textile Mills Corp.	42	18,084	5,067	23,262
BSEC	Steel & Engineering Corp.	20	26,069	4,251	12,217
BSFIC	Sugar & Food Industries Corp.	21	12,140	4,616	27,821
BCIC	Chemical Industries Corp.	23	133,701	17,188	27,067
BFIDC	Forest Industries Development Corp.	15	2,211	875	4,728
BJMC	Jute Mills Corp.	30	15,016	6,557	98,401
Power, Gas, Water					
BOGMC	Oil, Gas & Minerals Corp.	9	40,942	5,694	6,495
BPDB	Power Development Board	1	146,029	13,682	28,305
CWASA	Chittagong Water Supply & Sewerage Authority	1	1,417	163	820
DWASA	Dhaka Water Supply & Sewerage Authority	1	8,301	598	3,098
DESA	Dhaka Electricity Supply Authority	1	18,836	6,002	6,275
Transportation					
BSC	Shipping Corp.	1	5,238	1,971	795
BIWTC	Inland Water Transport Corp.	1	2,901	552	5,750
CPA	Chittagong Port Authority	1	11,595	1,638	8,139
MPA	Mongla Port Authority	1	5,136	370	1,990
BBC	Biman Corp.	1	7,817	7,952	5,578
BRTC	Road Transport Corp.	1	625	247	3,133
Trade/Commercial					
BPC	Petroleum Corp - units	8	24,612	59,919	3,056
BJC b/	Jute Corp.	1	1,864	570	350
TCB	Trading Corp. of Bangladesh	1	1,018	1,862	1,211
Agriculture					
BFDC	Fisheries Development Corp.	17	3,594	220	917
BADC	Agricultural Development Corp.	1	1,385	150	2,484
Construction					
CDA	Chittagong Development Authority	1	503	58	507
RAJUK	Rajdhani Unanayan Kartipakhya	1	5,466	19	734
KDA	Khulna Development Authority	1	305	29	218
RDA	Rajshahi Development Authority	1	270	22	77
Other/Service					
BFDC	Film Development Corporation	1	445	175	449
BFFWT	Freedom FightersWelfare Trust	4	1,609	554	2,417
BPRC	Parjaton Corp.	1	550	489	699
BCAA	Civil Aviation Authority	1	4,502	830	4,364
BSCIC	Small & Cottage Industries Corp.	1	2,617	147	1,545
BIWTA	Inland Water Transport Authority	1	3,195	491	3,956
REB	Rural Electrification Board	1	16,678	348	758
BEPZA	Export Processing Zone Authority	1	1,413	69	398
BHB	Handloom Board	1	377	21	240
BSB	Sericulture Board	1	45	37	1,071
BTB	Tea Board	1	91	49	319
BWDB	Bangladesh Water Dev. Board	1	1,065	510	4,768
SRTC	Sugarcane Research & Training Centre	1	69	33	478
	Total	215	527,731	144,025	294,890

a/ This list does not include Railways, Telephone and Telegraph, and financial SOEs.
b/ BJC was closed in FY93.
Source: Autonomous Bodies Wing, Ministry of Finance.

over 25 percent of total fixed capital formation, and 6 percent of GDP. SOEs dominate in capital-intensive sectors such as power, gas, water, railways, and telecommunication and in major banks and insurance companies. SOEs in the manufacturing sectors contribute about 23 percent of the sector's value added. Table 3.1 shows the assets, sales, and employment data of the non-financial SOE corporations. The SOE sector is important also because of its links to the banking system; some 90 percent of SOE financing has been borrowed from the nationalized banking system. With SOEs dominating the utility and infrastructure sectors, and large scale manufacturing such as jute and textiles, they have had far reaching consequences for the Government's finances and the prospects for industrial development of the country.[1]

B. SOE PERFORMANCE: MOUNTING COSTS

SOE financial losses have mounted consistently over the past decade. This represents the direct cost to the economy, and is most readily visible. As important, but harder to quantify, are the indirect costs on the growth of the industrial and agricultural sectors that poor service provision by SOEs has imposed. This is most apparent in the infrastructure and utility areas, as the more detailed discussion pertaining to these sectors in Section G shows. The intimate connection between the performance of the non-financial SOEs and the status of NCBs is highlighted in Chapter IV, as is the interaction between SOE employment policies and those in the private sector.

Worsening SOE Financial Performance

The long-term trend in profits of the SOE sector is one of deep decline. Starting from profits of Tk 1.3 billion in FY83, the SOE sector's overall returns fell to a net loss of Tk 16.3 billion in FY93. If the profits of the state petroleum and gas monopoly, BPC and BOGMC, are excluded, the FY93 loss would rise to Tk 17.1 billion, or 24 percent of the FY93 realized ADP of the Government, and 1.7 percent of GDP. And if the railway's losses are also included, the losses amount to 27 percent of the ADP and 2 percent of GDP. The biggest money-losers (Table 3.2) are the Bangladesh Power Development Board (Tk 7.8 billion loss in FY93), Bangladesh Jute Manufacturing Corporation (Tk 3.7 billion) and the now closed Bangladesh Jute Corporation (Tk 2.2 billion). The FY93 losses of the top ten amounted to Tk 18 billion. Of the other 39 corporations, about half show small profits. In FY93, the 39 corporations taken as a whole registered a negative return of 3.7 percent of capital employed. Had the corporations that incurred losses just broken even, the direct burden on public finances would have been some Tk 18.2 billion lower in FY93.

Underlying this worsening financial performance are deep-seated problems that afflict nearly all of the SOEs: lack of direction and autonomy, poor sector management, over-staffing and abuse of overtime, low productivity, rapid real wage growth, revenue pilferage, low prices, and rapid build-up of debt service obligations. Table 3.3 shows a snapshot, as of 1991, of the endemic problems in some of the largest SOEs and their large FY91-93 losses. The FY92 and FY93 losses show worsening financial performance in most cases, as their underlying problems have only exacerbated with the passage of time.

---

[1] This Chapter draws on the draft report, *Bangladesh: Privatization and Adjustment*, Report No. 12318-BD, The World Bank, February 1, 1994.

Table 3.2: Net Profits/Losses of Major SOE Corporations, FY92-93
(Taka million)

Corporation	FY92			FY93 (revised)			FY94 (budgeted)		
	Net Loss/ Profit	Capital employed (total assets)	Net Loss/ Profit as % of Cap. employed %	Net Loss/ Profit	Capital employed (total assets)	Net Loss/ Profit as % of Cap. employed %	Net Loss/ Profit	Capital employed (total assets)	Net Loss/ Profit as % of Cap. employed %
Manufacturing									
1. BTMC	-434.20	7190.80	-6.04	-959.29	7323.60	-13.10	-523.98	7494.60	-6.99
2. BSEC	-1068.50	14438.80	-7.40	-999.78	15117.90	-6.61	-609.08	15888.00	-3.83
3. BSFIC	-692.10	6370.60	-10.86	-924.05	6858.50	-13.47	-937.80	9112.70	-10.29
4. BCIC	-548.30	72658.00	-0.75	-65.97	75692.10	-0.09	-64.33	80227.00	-0.08
5. BFIDC	-142.40	1990.70	-7.15	21.31	2069.30	1.03	19.86	2143.30	0.93
6. BJMC	-3175.00	7056.10	-45.00	-3678.61	7540.60	-48.78	-2695.45	8804.20	-30.62
Power, Gas & Water									
7. BOGMC	509.54	28038.90	1.82	647.44	30096.40	2.15	727.14	33006.10	2.20
8. BPDB	-7749.20	139363.50	-5.56	-7847.49	146029.20	-5.37	-6530.47	153453.20	-4.26
9. DESA	-852.72	16152.00	-5.28	-842.25	18835.60	-4.47	-94.22	21521.00	-0.44
10. CWASA	-574.00	1417.80	-40.49	-46.31	1417.00	-3.27	-35.56	1433.00	-2.48
11. DWASA	4.57	6801.80	0.07	6.68	8300.90	0.08	3.33	9615.80	0.03
Transportation									
12. BSC	-541.88	5219.60	-10.38	37.59	5237.50	0.72	67.20	6155.10	1.09
13. BIWIC	-58.47	2758.30	-2.12	-46.79	28014.00	-0.17	58.04	2868.10	2.02
14. CPA	485.55	10850.50	4.47	100.00	11594.90	0.86	0.00	12233.70	0.00
15. MPA	196.52	4705.50	4.18	167.09	5135.90	3.25	172.69	5598.80	3.08
16. BBC	262.50	7922.30	3.31	194.29	7817.30	2.49	182.99	8267.70	2.21
17. BRTC	-237.12	736.00	-32.22	-297.76	625.10	-47.63	-192.85	590.30	-32.67
Trade									
18. BPC	4.55	9848.20	0.05	84.19	12365.20	0.68	94.31	13489.20	0.70
19. BJC a/	-1674.69	1707.50	-98.08	-2177.65	1863.90	-116.83	-2277.82	2036.00	-111.88
20. TCB	22.34	928.60	2.41	5.38	1018.10	0.53	5.19	1112.20	0.47
Agriculture									
21. BADC	-104.85	1591.00	-6.59	-221.30	1384.70	-15.98	-260.70	1144.00	-22.79
22. BFDC	-0.19	1817.80	-0.01	-6.42	1812.90	-0.35	11.56	1810.80	0.64
Construction Sector									
23. CDA	20.38	497.00	4.10	7.03	502.80	1.40	-0.05	554.10	-0.01
24. RAJUK	129.75	4729.60	2.74	51.78	5465.60	0.95	28.67	6111.20	0.47
25. KDA	6.97	246.10	2.83	5.43	305.50	1.78	6.42	420.10	1.53
26. RDA	0.33	235.70	0.14	5.24	2700.00	0.19	6.79	305.80	2.22
Service Sector									
27. BFFWT	4.89	1225.40	0.40	-17.75	1315.30	-1.35	12.57	1333.50	0.94
28. BFDC	-16.11	435.10	-3.70	-8.89	445.30	-2.00	-6.95	456.70	-1.52
29. BPRC	9.19	462.00	1.99	13.39	549.80	2.44	14.82	667.40	2.22
30. BCAA	325.94	3982.50	8.18	266.07	4501.80	5.91	277.14	4925.50	5.63
31. BIWTA	-8.91	2910.70	-0.31	-23.77	3195.40	-0.74	10.21	3620.60	0.28
32. BSCIC	-6.17	2495.60	-0.25	-7.16	2617.20	-0.27	-7.26	2915.10	-0.25
33. BEPZA	15.44	1078.10	1.43	16.95	1417.90	1.20	29.60	1617.00	1.83
34. BWDB	-32.54	1025.80	-3.17	39.14	1065.30	3.67	43.24	1101.50	3.93
35. REB	109.06	12641.20	0.86	186.52	16677.60	1.12	183.37	21088.40	0.87
36. BTB	7.77	89.70	8.66	0.23	90.80	0.25	-0.03	90.50	-0.03
37. BHB	-4.28	352.90	-1.21	-0.50	377.20	-0.13	0.00	402.30	0.00
38. BSB	-2.29	571.70	-0.40	-7.37	612.50	-1.20	-9.99	721.70	-1.38
39. SRTC	-0.49	71.30	-0.69	-4.15	69.90	-5.94	-1.22	73.20	-1.67
GRAND TOTAL	-15809.12	382614.70	-4.13	-16327.51	438060.50	-3.73	-12292.62	444409.40	-2.77

a/ BJC was closed in FY93.
Note: Acronyms are explained in Table 3.1.
Source: Monitoring Cell, Ministry of Finance •

Table 3.3: A Resume of Large SOE Problem Cases, FY91-93

Entity	Problems	Financial Results
Textile Mills Corp.	Low fixed prices, low capacity utilization, competition from smuggled cloth (through garment industry) and of yarn, overstaffing by more than 15%, wage costs absorb 95% of value added.	Net loss: FY91 Tk 574 million / FY92 Tk 434 million / FY93 Tk 959 million
Sugar & Food Industries Corporation	Reported net FY93 loss of Tk 0.9 billion; serious problem of overmanning (27,800 employees), employee costs were 141% of value added	Net loss: FY91 Tk 129 million / FY92 Tk 692 million / FY93 Tk 924 million
Dhaka Water and Sewerage Authority	System loss about 47%, problems of water unaccounted for similar to those in PDB, public taps run 24 hours a day, accounts receivables 5.9 months of total billings in FY93 (half due from Government and public corporations) tariff levels low, over-staffing by more than 30%: Performance improved in FY92/FY93, with tariff increases in both year.	Net loss: FY91 Tk 64 million / FY92 Tk 57 million / FY93 Tk 46 million
Inland Water Transport Corp.	Outdated fleet, high frequency of vessel disasters, fare pilferage and irregularities in collection system, low tariffs. Tariffs for ferry services increased 30% in July 1992. High operating costs due to high fuel costs and low utilization of vessels.	Net loss: FY91 Tk 37 million / FY92 Tk 59 million / FY93 Tk 47 million
Steel and Engineering Corp.	Markets for products drying up, competition from imports and domestic private sector, over-staffing by more than 10%.	Net loss: FY91 Tk 861 million / FY92 Tk 1.1 billion / FY93 Tk 1.0 billion
Oil, Gas and Minerals Corp.	Transmission and distribution lines developed but expected volumes of gas transmitted not realized, lumpy investment, heavy debt burden, insufficient prices for producers after 62% tax component, much layered procurement process lengthy, leading to project delays, weak sectoral planning.	Net profit: FY91 Tk 302 million / FY92 Tk 533 million / FY93 Tk 648 million
Railways	Losses stem from rate structure below operation cost, unremunerative local passenger trains, ticketless travelling, subsidized transport of essential goods and jute, free transport for some traffic, and excess staff. Major Railway Recovery Program (1992-97) is restructuring operations on commercial principles, reducing redundant labor, and increasing operational efficiency. Program is gathering momentum; railway losses reduced substantially in FY92, and further reduced in FY93.	Net loss: FY91 Tk 1.5 billion / FY92 Tk 1.1 billion / FY93 Tk 1.0 billion
Biman Airlines	Two ATP aircraft grounded for 8 months; $1 million paid by Biman for not taking delivery of third ATP aircraft, high purchase prices paid, domestic fares underpriced by about 30%, heavy debt service obligations.	Net loss: FY91 Tk 400 million / Net Profit: FY92 Tk 263 million / FY93 Tk 194 million
Jute Mills Corp.	Run-down equipment, over-priced raw material (raw jute) but stagnant export prices, restrictions on mill closure and on downsizing of capacity, heavy interest burden (Tk 700 million in FY92) on commercial bank debts, overstaffing by more than 25%, wage costs represent 166% of value added.	Net loss: FY91 Tk 2.5 billion / FY92 Tk 3.1 billion / FY93 Tk 3.7 billion
Power Development Board & Dhaka Electric Supply Authority	Revenues from 20-25% of power produced lost from collusion between employees and customers (improper billing, illegal connections, incorrect metering, and inadequate collections), high levels of accounts receivables (6.9 months), weak financial management and accounting, and strong trade union opposition to reform.	Net loss: FY91 Tk 2.8 billion / FY92 Tk 7.7 billion / FY93 Tk 7.8 billion
Shipping Corporation	Inefficient operation of fleet, stiff competition from foreign and domestic shipping lines, large amounts of accounts receivables, heavy debt service obligations (Tk 420 million a year).	Net loss: / Net Profit: FY91 Tk 527 million / FY92 Tk 542 million / FY93 Tk 38 million
Road Transportation Corp.	Ticketless travel, fare pilferage by crew and staff, operation of uneconomic routes as public service, costs of fuel, wages, tires and spares 25%-75% higher than in private sector, damage to buses during political disturbances.	Net loss: FY91 Tk 246 million / FY92 Tk 238 million / FY93 Tk 298 million

Source: Staff Analysis and Ministry of Finance.

An analysis of the financial data of the 39 non-financial SOE corporations for the past three years is presented in Table 3.4. Operating earnings (earnings before interest and taxes) have decreased further in FY92 and FY93. After applying the charges for interest expenses and modest income tax, net losses increased rapidly. The recent 17 percent pay raise granted to SOE workers is expected to add another Tk 30 billion to the net losses of the SOEs.

Table 3.4: Financial Performance of SOEs Corporations FY91-93 a/
(Taka crore)

	1990-91	1991-92	1992-93	1993-94 (budgeted)
Operating Income before interest & taxes	787.08	673.16	557.51	1032.62
Interest Expense	1076.48	1096.58	1211.97	1259.68
Income Tax	385.56	528.68	487.02	498.03
Net Profit/Loss	-674.96	-952.10	-1141.48	-725.09
Dividend	248.67	347.18	399.88	435.89
Depreciation	1080.17	1157.63	1228.92	1326.64
New Investment	4233.89	3281.87	2758.26	2589.42
Total Investment	41832.67	49772.73	52825.17	56461.87
Equity	9852.39	12858.13	11759.16	10965.74
Debt	31980.28	36914.60	41066.01	45496.13
Equity/Total Investment (%)	23.5	25.8	22.2	19.4
Dividend/Equity (%)	2.5	2.7	3.4	4.0
Interest Expense/Debt (%)	3.4	3.0	3.0	3.0
Depreciation/New Invest. (%)	25.5	25.3	44.6	0.51
Growth in Tot. Invest. (%)	-	19.00	6.10	6.90
Int.& Indirect Taxes Etc. Paid to GOB	330.24	417.09	623.81	651.17
Current Assets	11918.62	12412.08	13648.32	15025.58
Current Liabilities	12756.32	14055.30	17441.52	21018.44
Net Working Capital	-837.70	-1643.22	-3793.20	-5992.86

a/ List of SOEs in Table 3.2.
Source: Ministry of Finance; and Staff estimates.

The growth rate of new investment in SOEs declined to 6 percent per annum in FY93, from 19 percent in FY92. The real rate of growth of investment has been practically zero during the last two years. Depreciation allowances varied from one-quarter to one-half of new investment. SOEs as a whole had negative net working capital because of the huge losses incurred year after year. Equity as percent of total capital employed was 24 percent, 26 percent, 22 percent in FY91, FY92, and FY93, respectively. Notwithstanding the periodic conversions by the Government of the SOEs' outstanding debt into equity, the debt-equity ratio for SOEs as a whole has stood at about 75:25. Very high levels of debt thus characterize the SOEs' financial structure. This was funded by borrowing from the banking sector, some with government guarantees, as the nationalized commercial banks found SOEs to be ready clients. This has created a vicious cycle in which SOE losses have put into question the viability of the banking system. Total SOE debts to the nationalized commercial banks had grown to Tk 47 billion by end-June 1993. Furthermore, financing the losses of the SOEs has allowed NCBs to maintain rising portfolios of assets at high, but unrealizable, interest rates. Adding to the instability of SOE finances is the very high proportion of short-term liabilities which now account for almost one-half of total SOE debts. These loans in turn, threaten the financial viability of the NCBs due to the non-repayment of interest and principal. The rising debts of SOEs were funded at very low interest charges of around 3 percent, whereas nominal rates for commercial lending exceeded 16 percent until FY93. This suggests that the Government realized little or negligible amounts as interest payments on funds provided for investments in SOEs, and there were also delayed payments of taxes and duties to the Government by the SOEs.

A direct comparison of the financial profitability of private and public manufacturing enterprises shows the differences in their performance (Table 3.5). Only 43 percent of 159 SOEs included in the sample were found to be profitable, as compared to 74 percent of the private sector firms. In all the sampled industries, textiles, chemicals, food, and engineering, a higher proportion of private sector firms were profitable as compared to public sector firms.

Table 3.5: Profitability of Private Enterprises Compared with SOEs, 1989-91

Sectors	Private Enterprises			State Enterprises		
	Total Units	Profitable Units		Total Units	Profitable Units	
		Number	Percent		Number	Percent
Textile	19	10	53	42	9	20
Engineering	16	12	75	20	9	43
Food and allied activities	22	13	59	21	10	48
Pharmaceuticals & Chemicals	16	13	81	23	14	61
Miscellaneous	48	41	85	53	26	49
Total	121	89	74	159	68	43

Source: *Bangladesh: Privatization and Adjustment*, Report No. 12318-BD, World Bank, 1994.

Adverse Impact of SOE Performance on Industry

SOE losses have far-reaching fiscal consequences, not only because they burden the budget directly with periodic capital infusions from the Government, but also because of the write-offs and subsidies to the banking system for SOE bad debts. These bad debts, and the resulting poor quality NCB portfolios, have further weakened the ability of the banking system to finance the private sector's growth. Elimination of SOE losses could thus have a powerful impact on Bangladesh's public finance and growth prospects. In particular it would enable the Government to invest more on a priority basis in physical as well as social infrastructure, providing a better basis for the private sector to invest and operate efficiently in a competitive environment. While operations of these SOEs allowed a fraction of the labor force to enjoy significantly higher incomes, the Government suffered during the 1980s from shortages of domestic revenue to undertake foreign aid and loan financed projects included in its Five Year Plans. This reduced the rate of public investment in general, most importantly in infrastructure and human resources development, and increased dependence on external resources.

Public failures raise private costs. A significant impact of SOE operations and losses has been an upward shift in the structure of production costs in Bangladesh. For example, because of the problems in the Power Development Board (BPDB) and the Dhaka Electric Supply Authority (DESA), power failures are an endemic problem. Table 3.6 reports the results of a survey of 58 manufacturing industries in jute, textiles, pharmaceuticals, tanning and other sectors which had a total combined power loss of more than 20,000 hours during the first six months of 1993. As a result, the man-hour loss was 2.86 million hours and production loss was estimated at Tk 0.54 billion.

Table 3.6: Production Loss in Selected Industries due to Power Failures
(January-July 1993)

Sector	Total Period of Electricity Failure (Hours)	Man-hours Lost	Production Loss (in thousand Tk)
Jute	2,951	1,645,133	165,012
Textile	8,101	426,029	81,304
Pharmaceutical	880	67,118	163,255
Tanning	328	128,895	11,328
Cigarette	195	47,552	47,980
Tea	5,928	74,533	15,120
Food & Allied Industries	659	321,670	23,013
Glass	212	14,976	4,775
Paper	110	19,645	7,740
Ceramics	153	56,851	3,427
Others	493	61,271	17,095
TOTAL	20,011	2,863,672	540,050

Source: Metropolitan Chamber of Commerce and Industry Survey of 58 Manufacturing Industries, December 1993.

Furthermore, SOEs have had a major impact in terms of their own contribution to GDP and investment. SOEs account for a significant share of total fixed capital formation (over 25 percent) and 6 percent of GDP. Their contribution to value added in industry in FY92 was 14 percent, 8 percent in services, and insignificant in agriculture (Table 3.7). Their share in large scale manufacturing was 23 percent. SOEs dominate many important sectors: in the utilities (power, gas, water) they account for 71 percent of value added, nearly 100 percent in railway and communications, and 83 percent in banking and insurance. The concentration of SOEs in the capital intensive sectors explains their relatively high capital intensity.

To highlight the impact of poor SOEs performance, it is useful to show examples of some of the linkages these SOEs have with the rest of the economy as utilities and infrastructure firms, as manufacturing firms, and as trade and services providers. More detailed discussion of the low service penetration and service quality caused by SOE operations in the power, telecommunications, and gas sectors are discussed in Section G.

Utilities and Infrastructure. In the utilities and infrastructure sector, the largest money-losing SOEs are BPDB, DESA and Bangladesh Railways. Bangladesh has one of the lowest levels of power generation per capita (80 kWh) compared with the range of 200-350 kWh in Sri Lanka, India and Pakistan and about 800 kWh in Thailand. System losses in the power sector have recently ranged between 35-40 percent due to inefficiency, pilferage, and corrupt practices. Residential users are cross-subsidized by commercial and industrial users. Industrial users are also affected by high costs of getting power connections, power outages and fluctuating voltages. Many large and medium industries have bought diesel generators that have increased the unit cost of power.[1] Moreover, the Government has not invested sufficiently in the power sector to keep up with rising demand. More recently, power investment has been on hold with donors withholding lending to the sector pending corrective actions by the Government. Bangladesh Telephone and Telegraph Board (BTTB) is characterized by poor services and high costs, though the Government earns substantial revenues from BTTB even after its poor performance. Currently there are over a hundred thousand applicants waiting for telephone connections even at high deposit amount of Tk 20,000 per connection.

Table 3.7: SOE Contribution to GDP by Sector, FY92

	Contribution to GDP	Contribution of Public Sector Enterprises	% Contribution of Public Sector Enterprises
	Tk Million	Tk Million	%
Agriculture	315,723	294	0.1
Crops	228,620	259	
Forestry	31,005	Included in Manu.	
Livestock	27,376		
Fisheries	29,722	57	
Industry	150,168	21,505	14.3
Mining & Quarrying	120	-	
Manufacturing	82,571	-	
Large Scale	49,347	11,399	
Small Scale	33,224	-	
Construction	53,466	177	
Power, Gas, Water and Sanitary Services	14,011	9,929	
Services	436,396	33,170	7.6
Transport	102,456	3,084	
Trade Services	73,667	6,880	
Housing Services	79,066	143	
Public Admin. & Defence	42,375	7,185	
Banking & Insurance	17,793	14,768	
Professional & Misc. Services	121,060	1,110	
GDP at Market Prices a/	903,287	54,969	6.1

a/ GDP figure has been revised subsequently.

Sources: Bangladesh Bureau of Statistics and Budget of Autonomous Bodies, Monitoring Cell, Ministry of Finance, and Staff estimates.

Thus, not only have SOEs like BPDB, DESA and BTTB offered their products and services to their users, particularly industrial users, at high effective costs, but the expansion in these vital sectors has also been very slow. This has resulted in a substantial gap between the future supply and demand for these services which could hamper a faster rate of growth in economic activities and must be addressed as soon as possible through restructuring, rationalization, privatization and joint-venture arrangements.

---

[1] Experience in other countries suggests that the private, fall-back provision of electricity (captive generators), communications (radio equipment), water (captive boreholes), and transport services can add as much as an additional 10 percent to the total machinery and equipment budget for larger private firms that could utilize some economies of scale. For smaller firms, these costs could add up to as much as 25 percent (many small firms, of course, cannot afford the lumpy investment, and are left at the mercy of the public utilities). Since markets for onward sale of services are either thin or nonexistent, excess idle capacity -- above 75 percent -- is the norm for such fall-back investments. See K.S. Lee and A. Anas, "Impacts of Infrastructure Deficiencies on Nigerian Manufacturing: Private Alternatives and Policy Choices," INU Working Paper 98, World Bank, 1992.

Manufacturing. The poor performance of the manufacturing SOEs relative to their private counterparts has resulted in their dragging down the performance of the overall manufacturing sector, and is partly responsible for the poor performance and stagnation of the sector through much of the 1980s. Table 3.8 shows a comparison of SOE and private value added and fixed assets in eight selected manufacturing sectors. Even though the asset data are book values and therefore not entirely reliable, assuming similar asset vintages the evidence points to the considerably lower economic efficiency of SOE operations in most sectors. The ratio of value added to fixed assets in SOE is lower than in private firms by as much as 90 percent. A very rough idea of the potential SOE value added foregone in these subsectors due to their poor operations can be made by estimating their hypothetical value added as if they operated at or above the private sector's ratio of value added to fixed assets. Such a calculation suggests that SOE value added would be 18 percent higher for these sectors.

Table 3.8: Poor SOE Economic Performance in Manufacturing Relative to Private Sector, 1987-88
(Taka million)

	Total Fixed Assets	Value Added	VA/Fixed Assets
Food Manufacturing			
Government	1790	1964	1.10
Private	1431	1346	0.94
Textile Manufacturing			
Government	4435	5597	1.26
Private	3578	4251	1.19
Paper Products			
Government	2090	663	0.32
Private	123	82	0.67
Industrial Chemicals			
Government	12319	1704	0.14
Private	343	254	0.74
Other Chemicals			
Government	143	117	0.82
Private	212	327	1.54
Iron and Steel			
Government	404	333	0.82
Private	361	304	0.84
Fabricated Metal Products			
Government	523	100	0.19
Private	284	269	0.95
Non Electrical Machinery			
Government	1154	98	0.08
Private	172	142	0.83

Source: Bangladesh Bureau of Statistics: Report on Bangladesh Census of Manufacturing Industries 1987-88.

Public textile mills come under the Bangladesh Textile Mills Corporation (BTMC). A comparison of the productivity performance of the best and the worst public and private spinning and weaving mills shows that even with the newest and most modern private mills excluded, the best private mills performed better than the best public BTMC mills in terms of output per employee and spindle/loom productivity per shift. The worst private mills were not far behind the best public in spinning, and actually ahead of them in weaving (see Chapter II).

Poor SOE performance has raised costs for downstream producers which use SOE outputs as inputs for their production. Mills under BTMC produce yarn and cloth for mass consumption. Besides supplying yarn to weaving units, there is a large handloom industry that uses yarn for making clothes for rural consumption. Largely because of the poor quality and high price of yarn supplied from BTMC units, the handloom industry, which provided employment of over half a million in rural areas, is in decline. Cloth and yarn produced by BTMC units have remained stockpiled because of lack of buyers at high prices and poor quality (and the availability smuggled alternatives because of a high tariff on yarn). Handloom weavers have been impoverished by the low prices their products have fetched, leaving little or no profit.

BTMC's weaving capacity has also failed to supply quality fabrics to the readymade garments sector, which has almost entirely depended on imported fabrics for its fast growth in exports. Consequently, the readymade garments industry still provides only 25-35 percent value added. A dynamic and internationally competitive textile industry, supplying materials to the garments sector could have helped to increase value addition by another 5-25 percent in garment exports,[1] with increased domestic employment and higher net foreign exchange earnings. The domestic production of textiles is itself below domestic demand. This should not have been the case in Bangladesh with traditionally available skills in textiles if the textile sector had not become so deeply inefficient and uncompetitive.

Bangladesh Chemical Industries Corporation (BCIC) enterprises comprise three groups of SOEs: fertilizer factories, paper mills, and cement and chemicals. In terms of net fixed assets, BCIC is the largest manufacturing SOE, and has made substantial new investments during the past decade. BCIC has added four large natural gas-based fertilizer factories. Production of SOEs under the cement and chemical group is very small compared to the national requirement. Some fertilizer and newsprint is exported at below cost of production. Fertilizer is being produced from natural gas at about three-fourth of the economic cost of gas. BCIC has been covering its operating costs from its operating revenues, but large interest charges have turned the operating surpluses into losses. The fertilizer group has been earning some profit whereas the paper mills are losing money. Prices for paper and newsprint have been raised to cover rising costs, including costs of wastage and inefficiencies, and publishing costs are higher in Bangladesh than in the neighboring areas, including the Indian state of West Bengal.

Trade and Services. Another SOE, Bangladesh Agricultural Development Corporation (BADC) had a monopoly over distribution of fertilizer, and final prices paid by the farmer were much higher than the Government's subsidized prices. Hence although agricultural production increased with the use of fertilizer, farmers cost-price margins were squeezed by the public distribution system. The private sector now plays a major role in fertilizer distribution, retailing and imports. This move to privatize fertilizer sale has helped to increase use of fertilizer and employment of a much larger number of persons in rural areas.

---

[1] Textiles Working Paper, Background Paper No. 17 for the World Bank's forthcoming Industrialization Strategy Study on Bangladesh.

C. THE STRATEGY FOR REFORMING THE SOE SECTOR

Public investments can be conceptually divided into three categories: those that provide public services to the private sector (infrastructure and utilities); those that substitute for private productive activity (in manufacturing); and those that benefit the private sector directly, but with strong public externalities (such as health services). A strategy to deal with SOE problems arising from public investments of the first two kinds must rest on the fundamental goal of enhancing the role of competition for SOEs. A conceptual framework for making SOEs more competitive is shown in Box 3.1. The diagram unbundles the options for reforming SOEs as they relate to the nature of markets in which SOEs operate. The four options considered are for markets in which there is competition; where there can be competition for entry; in which larger monopolies can be split up into similar units; and the residual case of traditional SOE reforms such as commercialization. No single approach is likely to work in all circumstances, and policymakers may need to blend the available options to suit their objectives as well as the nature of markets in their efforts to deal with SOE problems.

Addressing the problems arising from public investments in state-owned enterprises in Bangladesh calls for a three-pronged strategy that is broadly consistent with the above framework and blends its elements. *First*, there needs to be a program of progressive, rapid privatization of SOEs. The SOEs to be privatized will initially be in the manufacturing sector. Most of the individual firms are smaller in size, but are a continuous drain on the fiscal and administrative resources of the Government. In view of their smaller size, they can be privatized more easily and quickly. Where there are serious problems of bad debts to the nationalized commercial banks (NCBs), as in the jute manufacturing industry, a thorough debt restructuring involving all three parties will be required. *Second*, there has to be a clearly formulated program of reform and commercialization for those SOEs that are likely to remain in the state sector for the foreseeable future. These are likely to be in infrastructure and utilities sectors, where the scale of operations and investments are large. The *third* prong is private sector participation and competition, again principally in infrastructure and utilities hitherto dominated by the Government. While expanding the area of private sector participation, this approach will simultaneously expose the remaining SOEs to competitive forces, prodding them to improve their performance.

Much of the planned privatization of SOE manufacturing units affects a comparatively small proportion of SOE assets. These are nonetheless very important because of the strong signal that their privatization will send to the private sector. Roughly 80 percent of SOE assets are in the utility and infrastructure sectors. These are not likely to be privatized in the foreseeable future. It is important to emphasize that to obtain much of the direct growth and efficiency impact of SOE reforms, the utility and infrastructure SOEs will need to be commercialized, and subjected to greater competition and various contracting-out arrangements. These arrangements will need to be established within a clear regulatory framework and an enabling environment. As difficult as privatization of the manufacturing SOEs may appear, it must be recognized that the larger agenda of dealing with the infrastructure and utility sector is even more important and needs urgent attention. The second element of the strategy to deal with SOEs is focussed on this priority, as is the third element. Both deserve the Government's concerted attention.

Though the three elements of this strategy are discussed separately here, it must be made clear that they are closely related in several ways. *First*, there is close interaction on the question of sequencing, i.e. whether to restructure the SOE before or after privatization. This is a hotly debated

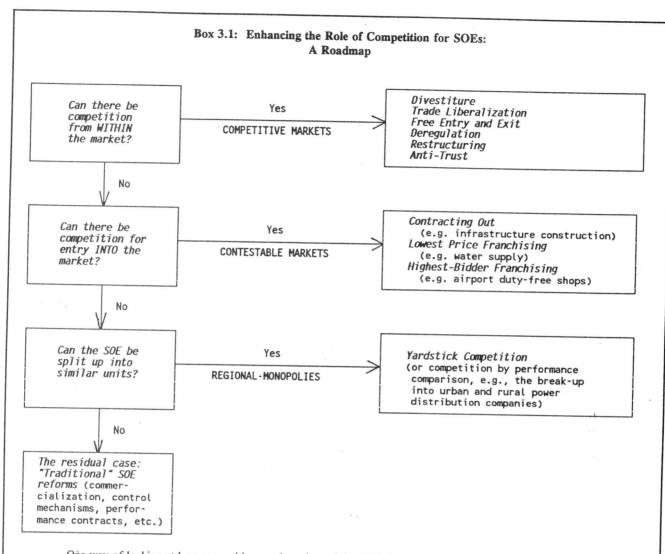

**Box 3.1: Enhancing the Role of Competition for SOEs:
A Roadmap**

One way of looking at how competition can be enhanced for SOEs is to unbundle SOE reforms into four stages. These four stages relate to the nature of markets in which SOEs operate, and whether or not there are natural monopoly elements in them.

Where the nature of markets is such that **free competition** is (or can be) possible, such as in manufacturing, divestiture of SOEs is the foremost option, accompanied by other policy reforms that provide an enabling environment for the privatized firms. Divestiture here may involve prior restructuring in some cases. For public utilities in particular, free competition may not be possible, and there the effort should be to seek **"contestable" markets**, in which there can be competition for new entry, and in which the subsequent threat of entry forces competitive behavior. The government can then choose the most competitive from among the bidders who want to enter the market. Where contestable markets are also not feasible for technological, political or other reasons, it is useful to think of splitting up the monopoly into comparable smaller **regional monopolies**. This would then entail using yardstick competition (under which the performance of comparable units can be judged against each other and against preannounced performance standards or yardsticks for the industry). Finally, this framework yields the large residual area of **traditional SOE reforms** such as commercialization, performance contracts, retrenchment, etc.

In practice, of course, there is considerable blending of these options. Often, there is need to adopt several different options simultaneously, such as the commercialization of an SOE as negotiations are underway for private entry through franchising or contracting out. The central message is that no single approach to SOE reform is likely to work under all circumstances. Policymakers need to carefully assess their objectives and the nature of markets in which SOEs function in dealing with SOE problems.

Source: Diagram adapted from Pankaj Tandon, "Product Market Aspects of Public Enterprise Reform," paper prepared for the World Bank Conference on the Changing Role of the State: Strategies for Reforming Public Enterprises, January 6-7, 1994, Washington, D.C.

issue in many countries, but evidence from an increasing number of privatization programs suggests that, in general, privatization should proceed first, since the Government does not have a comparative advantage in restructuring. Box 3.2 illustrates some useful decision rules for unbundling the complex decision problem on this issue. In the jute sector, the Government plans to restructure the debt of the jute mills before privatization because the debt overhang represents a major obstacle to the rationalization of the industry. *Second*, privatization of manufacturing SOEs will have an effect on the demand for better quality utility and infrastructure services, and therefore, on creating a constituency for reform. Once large manufacturing SOEs are in private hands, they are likely to add their weight to other vocal commercial customers demanding better quality services in, for example, telecommunications and transport. Evidence suggests that this has happened in Pakistan after the recent large privatizations.

Third, SOE reform and private entry are related because private entry within an appropriate regulatory environment will enhance competition (or quasi-competition, depending on the form of entry), and force even those SOEs remaining in state hands to commercialize more rapidly. This has happened to Indian Airlines, the erstwhile Indian domestic airline monopoly, once entry was made partially open. Indian Airlines' service performance on the trunk routes is improving after the explosive growth of alternative private carriers linking the major metropolitan centers. *Fourth*, the importance of choosing the appropriate regulatory environment cannot be overemphasized, since it links all three elements of the SOE strategy and affects the potential success of each. Box 3.3 presents some general, illustrative guidelines for making a transition to a new regulatory environment in South Asia, given the region's common characteristics of poverty, high population density, and weak regulatory and monitoring capacity. *Fifth*, economic growth and industrialization by themselves tend to create a more vocal and organized constituency for change, so that reforms dealing with SOEs that may have appeared unthinkable a decade ago may now appear quite realistic, or even conservative. This is particularly true if the reforms can very quickly make a difference in the quality and cost of service to those who might have not had any access to them in the past, such as telephone and other communications services.

D. PRIVATIZATION OF STATE-OWNED ENTERPRISES

Privatization, as an approach to addressing problems arising from SOE operations, began in Bangladesh as early as 1975. The first round of privatizations covered very small units that were initially taken over following the departure of the Pakistani owners. The Management Boards which ran these units were subject to rampant corruption, and the Government had perforce to sell these units as soon as the dust settled. The second phase of privatization (or denationalization) took place in the first half of the 1980s, and covered mostly jute and textile mills owned originally by Bangladeshi citizens prior to Independence. In these transfers, the Government retained the right to intervene in the conduct of the units if the new owners did not maintain these in operation, or failed in their contractual obligations. The second half of the 1980s saw further efforts to encourage the wider participation of investors in the privatization process. Accordingly, 34 percent of the shares of a few profitable manufacturing SOEs were sold to the public, and 15 percent were allocated for allotment to employees of each of the SOEs concerned. However, this program was not deemed to be a success. With the Government still retaining 51 percent of the shares, there was no significant improvement in operational efficiency. Overall, the divestiture of SOEs between the mid-seventies and the end of the eighties did

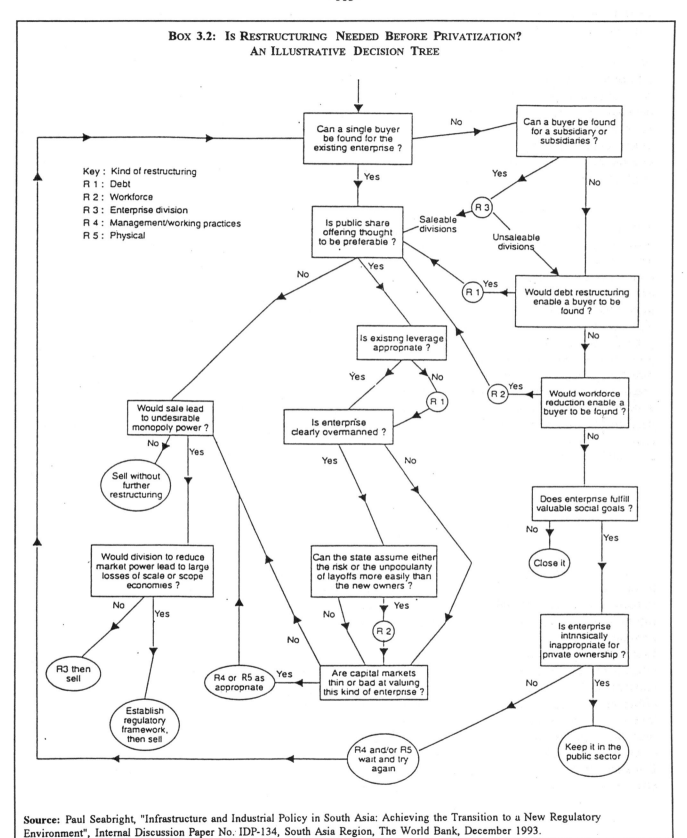

BOX 3.2: IS RESTRUCTURING NEEDED BEFORE PRIVATIZATION?
AN ILLUSTRATIVE DECISION TREE

Key : Kind of restructuring
R 1 : Debt
R 2 : Workforce
R 3 : Enterprise division
R 4 : Management/working practices
R 5 : Physical

Source: Paul Seabright, "Infrastructure and Industrial Policy in South Asia: Achieving the Transition to a New Regulatory Environment", Internal Discussion Paper No. IDP-134, South Asia Region, The World Bank, December 1993.

BOX 3.3: TOWARD A TRANSITION TO A NEW REGULATORY ENVIRONMENT: ILLUSTRATIVE GUIDELINES FOR MEDIUM-TERM INFRASTRUCTURE POLICYMAKING IN SOUTH ASIA

South Asia's Special Characteristics: South Asia has special features affecting infrastructure service delivery and regulation: pervasive poverty (networks are underdeveloped and externalities, relative to private benefits will be large); heavy dependence on agriculture (strong legacy of infrastructural subsidies designed to go hand-in-hand with the Green Revolution); high population density (infrastructural congestion severe, health externalities large); special form of its environmental externalities (pressure on forests from commercial logging and domestic fuel-wood harvesting, rather than acid rain).

Guidelines for Policy: S. Asian governments have limited information and capacity to regulate efficiently, and monitoring is hard. The following summarize desirable policies for such governments:

- ENCOURAGE COMPETITION, WHERE POSSIBLE, IN PREFERENCE TO REGULATION
- BASE POLICIES, WHERE POSSIBLE, ON SIMPLE RULES WHOSE APPLICATION CAN THEREBY BE MORE EASILY MONITORED
- USE STRUCTURAL REGULATION, WHICH NEEDS TO BE IMPLEMENTED ONLY OCCASIONALLY, IN PREFERENCE TO CONDUCT REGULATION, WHICH REQUIRES DETAILED INFORMATION AND CONTINUAL MONITORING
- DECENTRALIZE WHERE POSSIBLE TO FACILITATE COMPARISONS AND MAKE REGULATION MORE ACCOUNTABLE

Key lessons for short- to medium-term reforms: Applied to South Asia's situation, the guidelines suggest the following reforms:

Reform state-owned enterprises (SOEs)

- Increase prices when they are inefficiently low but ease the process where possible (e.g., more peak-load pricing);
- Rely more aggressively on the private sector to co-produce and to co-finance investments;
- Separate SOEs from government departments and grant public sector managers the freedom to pursue commercial goals; and
- Recognize the importance of the losers and gainers from reform, and use the political economy of implementation to improve the incentive to cooperate and to reduce the obstacles.

Assess the proper sequencing of privatization and restructuring

- In general, privatization should come first (the government has no comparative advantage in restructuring)
- In South Asia, government intervention and restructuring may be inevitable or desirable in some circumstances, including the following:
  - no buyer can be found;
  - existing debt level leads to a leverage problem;
  - overmanning, which the public sector can more easily reduce;
  - some units have a poor likelihood of being sold;
  - risk of monopoly power for the privatized firm;
  - need for political or logistical delays in privatization; and
  - problems of domestic capital market valuation

Reduce the complexity of private enterprise regulation (reduce barriers to entry, ease the access to scarce inputs)

More broadly:

- Privatize to improve production efficiency but also to improve the credibility of the government's commitment to stop interfering with production decisions;
- Promote yardstick competition (i.e., competition induced by comparing peer performance) and allow unit managers (rewarded according to their performance) more freedom to choose policies;
- Ensure that regulatory agencies have a degree of independence of the political process to ensure the credibility of the regulatory process; and
- Reassess the guidance provided by cost-benefit analysis when externalities and economies of scale matter (i.e., when simple rules such as "raise tariff to long run marginal cost" can lead to wrong policy conclusions).

Source: Adapted from Paul Seabright, "Infrastructure and Industrial Policy in South Asia: Achieving the Transition to a New Regulatory Environment," Internal Discussion Paper, No. IDP-134, South Asia Region, The World Bank, December 1993.

not materially change the role of SOEs in the economy, and, commensurately, made little contribution (less than Tk 2 billion) to the Government's capital receipts.

The growing disenchantment with the performance of SOEs and with the reform efforts to-date was reflected in the *Industrial Policy of 1991*, under which only air travel, railways, production and distribution of power, and defence industries were reserved for the public sector. SOEs in all other sectors were to be gradually privatized. Full foreign ownership of enterprises was also permitted. More recently, this policy has been liberalized further, and the Reserve List for the public sector has been narrowed down to allow private investment in the power, telecommunication, and domestic air transport sectors (Chapter II).

The Benefits of Privatization. Privatization is now a global phenomenon. With increasingly disappointing SOE performance in most countries around the world, more than 8,500 SOEs have been privatized in over 80 countries during the past 12 years. It has been increasingly realized that tinkering will not enhance performance in these enterprises, and they must change ownership in order to improve. More importantly perhaps, privatization is seen as a pre-commitment device for establishing a government's commitment to the efficient future management of the economy. Under such management investors would enjoy secure title to future projects if successful, combined with a price and regulatory system that ensures the coincidence of private and social project benefits.[1]

In Bangladesh, privatization is an important element of the Government's overall market-oriented adjustment strategy, with privatization and pro-market reforms mutually reinforcing one another. There are three potentially large benefits of privatization in Bangladesh: stemming the increasing losses of the SOEs; improving the efficiency and quality of services provided by SOEs; and signalling to the private sector the Government's commitment to the irreversibility of the pro-market reforms. *First*, with annual SOE losses nearing almost Tk 20 billion (US $500 million) in FY93, Bangladesh simply cannot afford to wait. There is now growing realization, not only in Government, but also among labor unions and the public, that privatization where possible is imperative.

Second, although it is the fiscal motive that had led many countries to privatize, the improvements in efficiency under private ownership need to be a central objective of any privatization exercise. International experience clearly suggests that privatization, when done right, works well. A recent two-year detailed study of 12 privatizations in the U.K., Malaysia, Mexico, and Chile suggests that divestiture was good for the economy as a whole, leading to higher productivity and faster growth.[2] After divestiture, Chile's telephone company doubled its capacity in four years, labor productivity increased in Malaysia's container terminal and Mexico's Aeromexico airlines, and a Chilean power distribution company reduced power theft substantially. When compensation payments were taken into account, in no case did privatization make workers worse off, and where workers shared in equity, they gained substantially. The study also pointed out that privatization is more likely to produce its benefits when the country has a market-friendly environment and a capacity to regulate.

---

[1] See David M. Newbery, "The Role of Public Enterprises in the National Economy," IPR45, Institute for Policy Reform, December 1992. This view is based on the notion that it is not the *extent* of state intervention, but its *quality* that matters. Why are both public and private enterprises in Korea so much more efficient than in many developing countries? This is because in Korea the Government was able to credibly commit itself to future actions that would support efficient private investment, and where necessary, public investment, and other agents responded appropriately. In the other countries, governments have not been able to commit, and have had to respond to the actions of private agents.

[2] See Ahmed Galal, Leroy Jones, Pankaj Tandon, and Ingo Vogelsang, *Welfare Consequences of Selling Public Enterprises*, World Bank, 1993.

Critics of privatization in Bangladesh often refer to drawbacks of the earlier privatization programs. Information on the performance the 500-odd small and medium industries divested since Independence remains limited. A survey by the Ministry of Industries in 1990 revealed that 49 percent of the divested units had closed down since divestiture. Critics of privatization cite this as evidence of failure. In a robust economy, closure cannot be taken to be a sign of potential weakness, since entry and exit are the very basis by which competition works. Thus, it is more plausible that closure of the privatized units represents a shift to a more efficient use of the physical assets, viz., land and factory buildings, of the privatized enterprises. Furthermore, the less-than-impressive performance of privatized enterprises in the 1980s does not, *per se*, constitute an argument against properly executed privatization. Rather it is evidence of poorly implemented past privatization. The evidence that does exist on performance of the private and public sector clearly demonstrates superior private performance. Listed companies on the Dhaka stock exchange significantly outperform the SOE sector in profitability terms. Further, the private sector on average uses fixed assets more efficiently than the public sector. Again, jute mills in the private sector have proved to be more efficient than those in the public sector.

Third, and very importantly, early privatization will help to improve the public credibility of the Government's commitment to stop interfering with production decisions in the future in which it would only be substituting for private activity. Evidence suggests that this effect of privatization is as (if not more) important as the improvement in production efficiency from privatization.[1] Raising the confidence of the private sector, by demonstrating the Government's commitment to increasing the private sector's role in the economy, is necessary for an increase in private manufacturing investment. Privatization can also mobilize local as well as foreign funds for investment and develop the capability of the stock market by increasing the number of equities listed. Privatization will help attract new technology and management techniques associated with foreign investment and joint ventures. Finally, privatization of certain parts of the utilities and infrastructure sector will improve the efficiency of services so that they become available on a timely, market-priced basis. However, it should be noted that privatization by itself will not improve the efficiency of privatized enterprises in the absence of market discipline. Where monopolies will have to continue, regulatory mechanisms will be required to provide yardstick competition (when performance of comparable units can be judged against each other and against preannounced norms) or other quasi-competitive mechanisms to ensure compliance with established competitive norms.

Current Privatization Efforts: Tardy Performance

Apart from the Government's policy statements on the sectors in which private investment will be permitted, the Government has yet to announce a comprehensive statement on privatization policy. While this may not be strictly necessary for moving ahead on privatization, the absence of such a statement creates uncertainty for both the private sector and the SOEs that may be slated for eventual privatization. Furthermore, it ignores the need to create a public constituency for privatization that can reduce opposition to the privatization process at each stage.

As it is, progress on privatization itself has been weak. In October 1991, the Government identified 40 industrial enterprises and 10 textile mills for the first phase of privatization (Table 3.9). At the April 1993 Aid Group Meeting the understanding reached was that in FY94 the Government

---

[1] See Newbery (op.cit.). New evidence and analysis on this will be available in a World Bank research study on SOE reforms; see the papers presented at the World Bank Working Conference on "The Changing Role of the State: Strategies for Reforming Public Enterprises," January 6-7, 1994, Washington, D.C.

would complete privatization of at least 50 percent of the 40 industrial units and of 24 textile mills, carry out the first phase of privatization under the jute sector reform program, and sign contracts for initial private investments in the power, gas and telecommunication sectors. The transfer of six units was completed by sale to a state-owned insurance company, and only three other units have so far been actually transferred to the private sector. Sale tenders for a further five units were approved by the Cabinet Committee on Finance and Economics in late 1993, but their transfer has not yet been completed, or is stalled in some cases. The Committee approved sale transactions for a further four units in March 1994.

The delay in gearing up the machinery for privatization is all the more troublesome because it has tended to erode, rather than build, confidence in the Government's commitment to the privatization process. Establishing this commitment is intended to be the major expected benefit of this first phase of privatization, paving the way for further accelerated reforms of the SOE sector. This is all the more important because the direct fiscal impact of this phase is likely to be small. The data on the manufacturing SOEs selected for the first phase of privatization, in Table 3.9, show that the combined FY91 losses of all 46 firms (excluding jute) chosen for privatization were only Tk 813 million. This represented 10 percent of the losses of the SOE sector as a whole. The combined assets of these firms represent only about 5 percent of total SOE assets.

The Government's jute sector adjustment plans are aimed at a major restructuring of the jute sector. With the inclusion of the jute privatization, there will be a significant reduction in SOE losses. With the expected divestiture of about a third of jute SOEs by the end of 1994, this would represent approximately another 9 percent of overall SOE gross losses, excluding petroleum.

Causes of Delay. There are three principal reasons for the slow progress on privatization. *First*, institutional problems and bureaucratic delays in changing the institutional arrangements for privatization, from the Inter-Ministerial Committee on Privatization to a properly constituted, autonomous Privatization Board, have wasted precious time. The lack of privatization expertise and teething problems in the Board have further slowed down the process. *Second*, no concerted efforts have been made to build a broad constituency for privatization comprising the public, the private sector, labor unions, and the SOEs themselves. In the absence of such a constituency, particularly one aimed at labor unions, it has been easy for minor complaints and valuation and liability problems to impede the privatization process. Without such a constituency, it has also not been easy to project the transparency of the process. *Third*, the poor financial condition of the majority of the SOEs identified for privatization has somewhat cooled the private sector's interest in the program. The Privatization Board did not start with a clear policy on when to restructure first or sell as is, though it now appears to be developing a pragmatic approach to this complex issue. In enterprises where negative net worth is clearly established, financial restructuring may be necessary (mainly through the Government absorbing some proportion of the outstanding liabilities), if the enterprise is to be sold. However, this assumes that the industry in which the enterprise operates is basically sound. If not, liquidation should be seriously considered.

There have also been concerns expressed in Bangladesh that the domestic capital market is too small to absorb the first phase of the privatization program of manufacturing SOEs. The World Bank study on Privatization and Adjustment in Bangladesh estimates that some Tk 32 billion (US $800 million) of local capital may be available over a 5-year period for the privatization program. This

Table 3.9: SOEs Slated for the First Stage of Privatization Announced in October 1991 a/
(Taka million)

	FY91 Profits/Losses	% of Total Op. Losses of all SOEs	FY91 Assets	% of Total Assets of all SOEs b/
Bangladesh Steel & Engineering Corp.				
1 Bangladesh Blade Factory Ltd	0.64		269.76	
2 Bangladesh Cycle Industries Ltd	-13.35		15.79	
3 Bangladesh Diesel Plant	-7.44		322.47	
4 Bangladesh Machine Tool Factory	-141.82		2,116.27	
5 Dhaka Steel Works Ltd (3 units)	-18.72		52.65	
6 General Electric Manufacturing	-47.78		957.20	
7 Metalex Corp Ltd	-17.49		868.00	
8 National Tubes Ltd	-23.78		817.47	
Sub - Total	-269.74	3.17%	5,419.61	1.32%
Bangladesh Sugar & Foods Ind Corp				
9 Amin Agency	-4.89		17.99	
10 Can Making & Tin Printing Plant	na		na	
11 Carew & Co. Ltd	-42.22		576.09	
12 Deshbandhu Sugar Mills Ltd	-33.29		167.47	
13 Kaliachapra Sugar Mills Ltd	-50.38		112.06	
14 Kustia Sugar Mills	-28.20		254.98	
15 Panchagar Sugar Mills	-13.23		333.74	
16 Rangpur Sugar Mills	-30.16		552.39	
17 Setabganj Sugar Mills	-9.75		453.39	
18 Shyampur Sugar Mills Ltd	-22.68		695.09	
19 Thakurgaon Sugar Mills	-12.17		554.58	
20 Zeal-Bangla Sugar Mills Ltd	-1.10		302.05	
Sub - Total	-248.07	2.91%	4,019.83	0.98%
Bangladesh Chemical Industries Corp				
21 Bang. Insulator & Sanitoryware	32.53		425.31	
22 Chittagong Chemical Complex	-19.35		310.79	
23 Chittagong Cement Clinker	74.13		378.37	
24 Chattak Cement Factory	48.52		1,107.49	
25 Dhaka Match Factory	n.a.		n.a.	
26 Eagle Box & Carton Manufacturing Co. Ltd	1.20		108.28	
27 Karnaphuli Rayon & Chemicals Ltd	67.11		2,023.81	
28 Khulna Hard Board Mills Ltd	3.23		57.72	
29 Kohinoor Battery Manufacturing Ltd	-53.33		108.61	
30 Kohinoor Chemical Co. Ltd	-66.61		386.96	
31 Lira Industrial Enterprises	4.63		92.76	
32 North Bengal Paper Mills	-120.02		671.68	
33 Potash Urea Fertilizer Factory	-25.31		1,719.17	
34 Sylhet Paper & Pulp Mills	-16.18		1,184.38	
35 Ujala Match Factory	-28.09		28.33	
36 Usmania Glass Sheet Factory Ltd	21.21		285.89	
Sub - Total	-76.33	0.90%	8,889.55	2.16%
Bangladesh Textile Mills Corporation				
37 Noakhali Textile Mills	-26.29		168.07	
38 Madaripur Textile Mills	-26.91		144.58	
39 Kishoreganj Textile Mills	-19.45		76.48	
40 Barisal Textile Mills	-31.53		93.69	
41 Kohinoor Spinning Mills	-19.87		79.68	
42 Bangladesh Textile Mills	-26.61		35.96	
43 Khulna Textile Mills	-17.78		20.08	
44 Sharmin Textile Mills	-27.97		82.46	
45 Dhaka Cotton Mills (National?)	-22.21		18.61	
46 Zofine Fabrics	-0.69		12.18	
Sub - Total	-219.31	2.57%	731.79	0.18%
Total (Except Jute)	-813.45	9.55%	19,060.78	4.63%
Bangladesh Jute Mills Corporation				
47-55 Nine Consolidated Units	-746.64	8.76%	4,484.46	1.09%
Total	-1,560.09	18.31%	23,545.24	5.72%

a/ Excludes four renationalized companies slated for privatization, namely Dosha Extraction, Bangladesh Oil Mills, National Ice Factory, and Star Roller Flour Mill.

b/ Excluding petroleum (BPC and BOGMC).

Source: Privatization Board, Government of Bangladesh.

estimate suggests that the required domestic absorptive capacity does exist for the manufacturing units. It further confirms that the real hurdle to expeditious privatization has been the weak institutional capacity of the Government.

This slow progress points to the need for clear direction that the Government should give to its privatization efforts, for reaffirmation at the highest levels of the value of privatization for the economy, and for strengthening the agencies charged with carrying out privatization in Bangladesh.

Strengthening the Privatization Board

Several different arrangements for implementing the privatization program have been tried in Bangladesh in the past, but without significant success. The earliest institutional setup during the 1970s was for the Cabinet to approve tender procedures, and implementation was placed in the hands of the Divestment Board of the Ministry of Industries. This led to complaints about the lack of transparency, and the inadequate performance of private enterprises was also often attributed to the way they were divested. Following the declaration of the *Industrial Policy of 1986*, the Government tried to remedy the above problems by creating two new institutions to accelerate the privatization program, an Executive Committee to function as an oversight body for the Divestment Board, and a Working Committee to assist in the review and implementation of divestiture. However, this failed to revive the lagging privatization program.

In 1991, the Government created the Inter-Ministerial Committee on Privatization (ICOP) with the responsibility of developing privatization policy as well as considering, approving, and monitoring specific privatization proposals of the various line ministries. Despite its best efforts ICOP failed, as it had no full-time members and no staff with the technical know-how to actually implement privatization, and was not given the mandate and autonomy to engage in actual transactions.

In early 1993 the Government replaced ICOP with a Privatization Board, a new apex agency created within the Cabinet Division, in which all privatization related activity was to be centralized. It was the setting up of the Board early in 1993 that had raised hopes at the April 1993 Aid Group Meeting in Paris that the first phase of the privatization would now move rapidly. However, the Board ran into a number of bureaucratic and administrative hurdles, partly related to the fact that it was granted autonomous status by the Government only in November 1993. The Board now has its own budget and full-time staff. The staff, under a chairman, consists of two full-time members, eight part time members, six directors and six deputy directors. The staff are to have working groups under their supervision. The Board also has the authority to recruit consultants, including financial advisors, industry experts, accountants, and lawyers.

Centralizing privatization in the Privatization Board was a step in the right direction. The experience of countries that have successfully privatized, such as Mexico, Argentina, Chile, and Pakistan, demonstrates that privatization should be centralized in one agency with overall authority for planning and executing the privatization program. Furthermore, the agency's secretariat should be flexible, and consist of a small number of technical staff who should anchor a much larger volume of work contracted out to technical experts on a need basis. This helps to keep decision-making relatively simple and expeditious, and at the same time makes it possible to tailor the depth and breadth of analysis required for particular transactions to their particular needs.

Having thus taken the first step, current arrangements for the Privatization Board need to be urgently reviewed in several respects to ensure that it can now carry out its tasks smoothly. *First*, care must be taken to ensure that the Board has the necessary authority and mandate to work closely with other parts of Government, the private sector, and potential buyers. The location of the Privatization Board in the Cabinet Division does not automatically vest it with the required authority or autonomy. Its leadership, its mandate, and the unqualified and active support at the highest levels of the Government are critical. Privatization invariably generates initial opposition from vested interests in the affected ministries, the SOEs, and elements of the private sector; it is best to anticipate this opposition rather than simply react to it. The Board needs autonomy for this.

Second, the Board should be given effective decision-making autonomy to manage, co-ordinate and implement the privatization program. It should have the authority to negotiate the final divestiture of small and medium enterprises, and should make recommendations to the Cabinet Committee on the sale of larger enterprises. These recommendations should be considered and decided upon expeditiously.

Third, it is of the utmost importance that the privatization program be transparent. The political economy of privatization in Bangladesh is complex. Unlike most other countries embarking on privatization, Bangladesh has a long history of privatization, and much of it is viewed in a mixed light by the public and by the interested development community. The Privatization Board should produce a set of operating guidelines that help to ensure that each divestiture adheres to a predictable, more or less standard procedure that is transparent and available for public scrutiny. Transparency should not, however, hamper the boldness of decision making in the Privatization Board, and should, on the contrary, facilitate decisions based on clear principles that can be widely understood.

Fourth, the Board needs to expand its immediate focus to also include the privatization of the more successful SOEs. Early, successful privatizations will be an important confidence-building step for the Board, for the private sector, and for the public.

Fifth, most of the detailed, technical work should be contracted out to private sector companies or advisors. The private sector could also be involved in the campaign for increasing public support. Private sector representation on the Board, or the use of a small advisory board consisting of respected business leaders and professionals, could be considered for this purpose. Due to the current inadequacy of domestic professional expertise (and experience) in privatization, external advisors will initially need to play a supportive role in carrying out the program. A program of technical assistance will thus need to be urgently put in place to provide operational and logistical support for the Board itself, and specific technical support for individual transactions.

Sixth, Government pay scales and rules, in respect of employment of consultants and tendering processes, are potentially a significant constraint to the effective operation of the Privatization Board. In hiring consultants, Government pay scales may not allow the employment of experts with the requisite experience. Similarly, Government rules severely limit effective publicity and advertising. It is essential therefore that the Board's activities be exempted from Government rules and regulations when they are judged, after due consideration, to be inappropriate. At the same time, care should be taken to ensure that Board's procedures permit adequate oversight of its activities.

Seventh, in the utility sector, particularly power and telecommunications, potential privatization may be highly complex. In these cases, the Government could consider establishing a separate institutional arrangement for each utility. These arrangements should benefit from the experience of operating the Privatization Board, and should closely coordinate with it.

Finally, the Board has an important role in coordinating external donors' supporting efforts related to privatization and in ensuring that their programs are consistent with the overall privatization objectives in Bangladesh.

Moving to a New Regulatory Environment

Successful privatization will need to be accompanied by a new and balanced regulatory environment in which competition can flourish. Evidence suggests that privatization works best when it is part of a larger program of reforms promoting efficiency.[1] This is particularly important in sectors where competition is likely to be weak, so that without proper regulation the expected benefits of privatization can be lost to society through private monopoly profits, or through externalities leading to environmental losses. Privatized enterprises should face credible competitive pressures and intelligent regulation to assure consumer protection and attention to safety and environmental standards.

At present there is no clear mechanism to ensure the regulation of monopoly power in the private sector. There is legislation (the Monopoly and Restrictive Trade Policies (Control and Prevention) Ordinance of 1970) on the statute books; but the law has not been made effective. The Ministry of Commerce has begun work on fair trade legislation, along with setting up an institutional structure to attain a number of regulatory objectives and make a transition to a new regulatory environment. Its objectives include measures to ensure that monopolistic and restrictive business practices do not impede or negate the realization of benefits that should arise from liberalization of trade and investment controls; to encourage and protect competition, and control concentration of capital and economic power; and to eliminate the disadvantage to trade and development that may arise from unfair trade practices. In pursuing the design of the appropriate regulatory framework, care must be taken not to lose sight of the as yet limited regulatory capabilities of the Government, the information needs of different regulatory options and the problem of inadequate information, and the difficulties of monitoring. Where institutional endowments for regulation are weak, as in Bangladesh, this would call for a simplified set of specific regulatory rules that can simultaneously provide commitment and promote efficiency.[2] Some of the illustrative principles presented above in Box 3.3 may be useful in this regard.

In balancing these objectives in the infrastructure and utility area, the Government will be faced with the choice of establishing a unique regime for each utility, or developing an overall framework which can apply to all utilities, or a combination of both. In the case of utilities where monopoly situations can arise in Bangladesh, consideration should be given to special sector procedures (see Section G). In each utility, the key regulatory issues should be identified and dealt with. A suitable model is the current work in the telecommunications sector where an appropriate regulatory regime has been identified. In the gas sector, the Petroleum Concessions Division, now part of Petrobangla, could conceivably be spun off to constitute the nucleus of a regulatory body. In some

---

[1] See Sunita Kikeri, John Nellis, and Mary Shirley, *Privatization: The Lessons of Experience*, The World Bank, June 1992.

[2] See Brian Levy and Pablo Spiller, "Regulations, Institutions, and Commitment in Telecommunications: A Comparative Analysis of Five Country Studies," mimeo, World Bank, April 1993.

other sectors, particularly in transport, regulatory bodies already exist, such as the Inland Water Transport Authority, Road Transport Authority and Civil Aviation Authority.

In formulating the appropriate regulatory regimes, Bangladesh can take guidance as well from international experience with utility regulation. There are four main regulatory options that have been applied in the regulation of utilities: the North American model which relies on a legal setting and procedures to determine the rules of the game and the appropriate tariff; the British model, whereby a separate regulatory body makes the key determinations; a license model, where the utility is granted a license to operate (the license defines the key regulatory issues); and a "light handed" approach which relies on a reasoned interpretation of broad principles. Given the current deficiencies in Bangladesh's legal system, the licensing option in conjunction with a regulatory body may be preferred regulatory model for utilities in Bangladesh. This is the approach envisaged in the telecommunications sector (Section G).

In the large utilities, i.e., power, telecommunications, and gas distribution and transmission, the broad outlines of the regulatory regime and the desirable long-run structure of the sector should be developed before substantial privatization (or private entry) proceeds. A piecemeal approach will not work, since once set, and once private entry (particularly foreign entry) takes place, the structure of the sector cannot be changed for a long time to come.

Outside the utility sector, the thrust of consumer protection should primarily come from competitive forces -- from competing domestic products and services as well as imports -- that will keep prices competitive and raise quality, rather than the mere strengthening of the Monopolies and Restrictive Trade Policies Ordinance. Such regulations, by introducing administrative discretion, often tend to have adverse effects on growth and competition. Similar regulations are being curtailed in other countries that are liberalizing their economies, and the Government should be cautious about reviving a regulatory regime which is being discarded elsewhere. However, when market failures are likely to occur because of externalities and the problems of asymmetric information between service providers and users, appropriate regulation will be called for.

E. IMPROVING THE EFFICIENCY OF STATE-OWNED ENTERPRISES

A number of key enterprises, particularly those in utilities and infrastructure, will remain in the state sector over the foreseeable future because of the slow pace of the privatization program, and the size and nature of their operations. It is important therefore to focus on improving their efficiency. These SOEs include power, gas, water, and telecommunications, whose efficient functioning is vital to development. This section discusses the approaches to improving efficiency in SOEs and subjecting them to greater competition. The discussion of private entry in the infrastructure and utility areas is contained in Section F.

Clarifying SOE Policy Direction. The uncertainties and delays surrounding the initial phase of the privatization program have resulted in a loss of direction for SOEs, which are uncertain about their own future, and are increasingly demoralized, further contributing to declining performance. It is important for both the public and private sectors that these uncertainties be dispelled as quickly as possible. The Government should clarify the broad contours of the transition path from the current situation to its objective of a largely private manufacturing sector, and public-private partnerships in the utilities and infrastructure areas. On this path, the reform priorities are likely to include: strengthening SOE oversight; commercialization and improving management autonomy; dealing with special SOE labor problems; reforming pricing policies; and enhancing competition and the scope for exit and entry.

Strengthening SOE Oversight. A process of SOE performance evaluation has been in place in Bangladesh since the early 1980s. In principle, the Monitoring Cell of the Ministry of Finance is expected to monitor SOE performance based on contracts with individual SOEs. These contracts include performance indicators and targets. However, enforcement of compliance with performance contracts calls for a strong SOE oversight body. In practice, the efficiency-based SOE indicators and targets are largely ignored, and the Monitoring Cell's activities are relegated more to reporting than genuine oversight. A major factor contributing to this ineffectiveness is the lack of a credible enforcement mechanism for the Cell to ensure target achievement. The Ministry of Finance should strengthen the existing system and give the Monitoring Cell a clear and strong mandate to evaluate SOEs and recommend action for non-compliance. This could be based on individual SOE corporate plans for the short term (one year), medium term (one to five years) and long term (over 5 years). An integral part of these plans should be loss reduction targets, rigorously enforced by hard budget constraints. The policy should make clear that failure to measure up to these targets would lead to divestiture of their activities. Genuine oversight will also require better data on SOE performance; for example, no data are available on the sources of bank financing and arrears. The latter are particularly important because increased profitability at the expense of arrears on interest would not amount to an improvement in performance.

Improving Management Autonomy and Corporatization. There has been a growing recognition within the Government that lack of management autonomy, as well as serious administrative, financial and legal obstacles, are affecting the operation of SOEs as commercial enterprises. SOE managers need to be given the authority to make independent decisions regarding investments, personnel and procurement. Accordingly, the *Industrial Policy of 1991* recommended that SOEs in the manufacturing area would be managed by boards of directors according to company law, and would enjoy autonomy in their management; sector corporations would be converted into holding corporations; and a major objective of industrial policy would be to improve the operational efficiency and economic viability of the SOEs. In addition, the Government recognized in the *1991 Policy* that there was surplus manpower in many SOEs that needed to be shed if they were to operate efficiently.

The Government subsequently requested technical assistance from the Asian Development Bank to study, diagnose and recommend measures to attain these objectives of the *Industrial Policy 1991*. The recently completed technical assistance report has recommended measures to give autonomy to SOE management in manufacturing by transforming them into limited companies under the Companies Act. Procedures have also been laid down for improving operating budgets and medium and long-term capital plans for SOEs. The ADB report proposes converting the SOE corporations in manufacturing into holding companies, to act as share holders and monitor performance of each SOE under it on behalf of the Government, and to be able to respond to potential privatization possibilities for the companies as per the Government's policy.

The ADB report has recommended contractual appointments for managing directors of the holding companies. Compensation for top managers is also to be linked with performance. Many countries (Korea, Indonesia and Pakistan) have established a linkage between performance and compensation with positive results. The chairmen and directors of holding corporations, and the boards of each of the individual SOEs, should have the powers to fix the salaries and wages of officers and workers according to their performance, unlike the current civil service terms and conditions. This would enable SOEs to attract and retain high quality staff.

The Government has accepted these restructuring proposals in principle, with the exception of the proposed delinking of pay from Government scales. However, there has been very little progress made in the implementation of these measures.

Addressing Special SOE Labor Problems. Labor issues are analyzed in Chapter IV. The discussion below is limited to the special problems that arise in SOEs. Prominent among the labor problem of SOEs are overstaffing, abuse of overtime, politicization and labor militancy, and schemes of remuneration which have little relationship to an SOE's productivity or ability to pay. Most of the major SOEs are characterized by a substantial degree of unionization of workers, with the largest concentration being in the jute and textile mills. Associated with this has been the politicization of the trade unions, with the main political parties setting up their own national-level labor organizations. A survey by the Directorate of Labor (DOL) found that during 1977-91 out of 796 industrial disputes, 300 cases (44 percent) were directly caused by political factors of extra-industrial origins. The unions have traditionally wielded considerable political clout, although in terms of political constituency SOE workers are only a very small fraction of the voters.

The strength of the unions is reflected in the remuneration and terms of employment SOE workers have been able to secure. Wages of SOE workers were recently increased by an average of 17 percent following a similar salary increase for Government civil servants in August 1991. This is expected to increase the wage bill in six major SOEs by Tk 2.9 billion, of which Tk 1.6 billion is due to retroactive payments. Despite mounting SOE losses, the average wage for SOE workers is around Tk 4,000 per month, which is more than twice the wage rate in unorganized labor markets and quadruple the average of the minimum wage in different subsectors.

Besides de-politicization of the labor unions, a key element of reform will be the need to move from the current centrally-determined wage structure of SOEs to one that is related to productivity and profitability of each enterprise's operations. It is the inflated wage and salary bill that renders most SOEs not viable. In several SOEs the cost of wages (including overtime) is more than their value added. Some of the more glaring examples are BJMC, BADC and BIWTC, where wages and salaries are more than 100 percent of value added. The importance of this cannot be overemphasized as the public sector has served as a trend-setter for wages in the private sector. Another special problem to be addressed is overstaffing. The problem is almost universal in all SOEs, but is particularly acute in the manufacturing sector, which accounts for about a third of total SOE employment. Overstaffing results from nepotism and corruption, together with the failure of many SOEs to restructure and reduce their labor force when production and services have declined, or where excess capacities have developed. Overstaffing has been variously estimated to range from 20 percent to as high as 50 percent in some SOEs. Overtime, which frequently is as much as 50 to 80 percent of wages, represents a flagrant abuse in the context of overstaffing. This position is untenable and a scaling down of total wage costs is necessary if SOEs are to work towards financial viability.

Staff rationalization (mostly voluntary separation) schemes are underway in a number of manufacturing sector enterprises. Some 20,000 employees were retrenched in FY93, to be followed by an additional 25,000 in FY94. To accommodate the program, the Government has increased its budget allocation from Tk 3 billion to Tk 6 billion in the current year. The World Bank's 1992 Jute Manufacturing Study suggested payments on separation of two months pay for each year of service, plus provident fund and interest due, the current legal requirement. The Government's jute adjustment program has adopted this principle, and workers will receive separation benefits ranging from Tk 100,000 to Tk 500,000 per worker. In the railways, separation payments have averaged about Tk 300,000 per worker. The principle of separation payments that has been developed so far, including the safety net and retraining arrangements, could be applied to other sectors as well with suitable modifications.

Reforming Pricing Policies. In Bangladesh, a principal problem for the SOEs' inability to generate surpluses for financing development and growth has been the pricing policies adopted by the Government, combined with high operating costs. Inappropriate pricing is particularly the case for railways and the rest of the transport sector, where prices have been kept below their long run marginal cost and subsidies are provided to consumers, even when there are no significant market failures or externalities. Such underpricing of SOE output is not the most efficient way for achieving equity goals. Typically, the beneficiaries of under-priced utilities are not the poor. Besides, it starves the SOEs of further developmental funds and their long run growth is adversely affected. In many other SOEs, cost reduction, rather than price increase, is the key issue. The use of cost-plus pricing rules does not create incentives for cost minimization for the SOEs. This is clearly the case when cost-plus rules are tailored to the costs of a specific SOE. It is better to use an average cost for the industry in setting a cost-plus formula.

Enhancing Competition and Scope for Exit and Entry. Another approach to improving SOE performance is to make SOEs operate in a more competitive environment. This should be approached in a variety of ways. For manufacturing, this could be achieved through trade liberalization, so that SOEs are subject to greater import competition. More importantly, they should also be subjected to greater domestic competition by providing a level playing field for the private sector in access to credit and Government contracts and by effectively liberalizing the procedures for private investment. By the same token barriers to exit need to be eliminated by allowing SOEs that are not viable to be sold or wound up. In these respects the Government has made some progress in creating a more competitive environment. Some public corporations such as BTMC and BSEC have allowed lay-offs in some of the enterprises under them. BTMC's textile mills were shut down prior to their offer for sale. This is an indication that SOEs can close down plants provided the Government institutes mechanisms to settle back-pay dues and employee compensation. Closing down of BJC by an Act of Parliament in FY93 is also an important example of the Government's emerging policy on exit of SOEs.

Some progress has been made in principle on private sector entry, though new entry has effectively only taken place in manufacturing. Excepting defence-related and communication industries and international air transport, there is no sector where entry by the private sector is now restricted (see Chapter II). New investments can be made in textiles, chemicals, engineering, electronics, leather, food processing, domestic telecommunication (cellular phones and rural telephones), tourism, agro-chemicals and pharmaceuticals. The Government has opened domestic air services to the private sector but only to destinations not covered by Biman. The Drug Policy of the past government is being revised to allow foreign firms to operate and export from Bangladesh. Progress has also been made in removing non-tariff barriers to trade, rationalizing tariff rates (though they still remain high), relaxing exchange controls on current account transactions, and preparing for reforms of business laws and the general legal framework. This has already opened opportunities for imports of some of the goods produced by SOEs which is creating competitive pressure to reduce prices (e.g., sugar, yarn, fertilizer, electrical goods, and chemicals). Private sector initiatives in the utilities and infrastructure sectors are discussed in the next section.

F. PRIVATE PARTICIPATION IN INFRASTRUCTURE AND UTILITIES

Privatization of state-owned manufacturing enterprises alone will not achieve the objectives of improvements in efficiency and reduction of the need for continuing state subsidies. These desired results will not occur unless the Government undertakes a deliberate policy of bringing the private sector to assume a greater role in the investment, operation and maintenance of the utilities and basic economic infrastructure.

Nearly all publicly supplied services that businesses need in Bangladesh, such as power, natural gas, telecommunications, transport and their associated facilities of roads and highways, ports and harbors, have sub-standard performance. Virtually all infrastructure has suffered from under-investment, inadequate attention paid to maintenance, and poor sector and operational management. As a result, the penetration of infrastructure and utility services remains among the lowest in the world (see Section G). Institutional weaknesses are also notable throughout the sector with transport, telecommunications and energy sectors the most affected. The poor financial practices of most of these agencies, evidenced by poor collection and accountability controls, accumulation of arrears and ageing accounts receivable, illustrate the problem. Increasing losses of the state-owned agencies obliges Government to provide direct budgetary subsidies or loans from NCBs, rarely repaid on schedule. There are also widespread corrupt practices involving customer evasion of legitimate charges, and frequent collusion between utility customers and meter readers and other billing and collection personnel.

Significant gains might be made by bringing in private managers and allowing such SOEs to operate like a private firm, even if ownership is not transferred. This would include management contracts and leases for existing units. These arrangements can facilitate later sale, particularly in Bangladesh, where capital markets and the domestic private sector's ability to purchase large SOEs outright may be weak, an unfavorable enabling environment in the past makes private investors reluctant to take on ownership of large assets in need of modernization, and where capacity to regulate is still weak. Concession arrangements, such as build-operate-own and build-operate-transfer, are appropriate for new facilities. Because the capital and technology requirements are likely to be beyond the capacity of the domestic market, foreign capital will be essential for such arrangements. Progress here will therefore depend crucially on how attractive Bangladesh is to foreign capital.

Management Contracts. Under management contracts, a government pays a private company a fee for managing the enterprises. Management contracts are usually less politically contentious than enterprise sales. In Bangladesh, the power sector provides an illustration of the potential for performance management contracts in improving the operation of existing power plants. An examination of plant operations over the last few years reveals the considerable benefits that can be gained if plant utilization and efficiencies can be improved to levels close to internationally acceptable norms. Instead of undertaking rehabilitation on a supply and install basis, performance contracts covering plant rehabilitation as well as management of operations for a limited period could be pursued. The bidders could be encouraged to introduce additional efficiency and operational enhancement techniques and equipment in return for a share of the profits gained from improved operations. This strategy is particularly advantageous as considerable new technology has now been developed in power generation, allowing smaller-scale plants and superior plant operation practices.

Management contracts are not devoid of problems, and though the concept is simple, they require a considerable effort to implement well. Where contractors do not assume risk, operating losses must be borne by the government, even though it has relinquished day-to-day control of the operation. Furthermore, management contracts are time-consuming to develop and can be expensive to implement. Unless proper legal safeguards are developed, and enforced by monitoring, there is a risk that the contractor may run down assets. Another drawback that must be guarded against is the tendency of management contractors to not provide adequate training for local counterparts. These risks can be reduced with properly drawn-up contracts. This will require strengthening the Government's capacity to negotiate, monitor and enforce contractual obligations.

Leases. Leases overcome some of the possible drawbacks to management contracts. The private party, which pays the government a fee for use of the assets, assumes the commercial risk of operation and maintenance, and thus has greater incentive to reduce costs and maintain the long-term value of the assets. Fees are usually linked to performance and revenues. Lease arrangements have been widely used in Africa, particularly in sectors where it is difficult to attract private investors. The contracted firm has usually been a joint venture, with the foreign partner bringing in essential technical and managerial expertise.

Concessions. When granted a concession, the holder has responsibility for capital expenditures and investments, and thus assumes the bulk of the risk. Concessions are therefore more desirable, but more complex to consummate than leases. This is because private financing tends to be weak in comparison to the size of the investment, particularly in sectors or countries where the political and economic risks are seen to be high. In such instances, the government might have to play a participating role with the private investor, sharing both the risk and the potential rewards. External agencies could participate to syndicate the financial package. Concessions have been successfully used in the recent privatizations of telecommunications and railways in Argentina. Venezuela plans to grant private firms concessions to operate and finance investments in ports and water supply.

Build-operate-own and build-operate-transfer (BOO, BOT) constitute one type of concessional arrangement that has come into prominent use recently: projects covered typically include bridges, power plants, ports, airports, trunk highways, and telephone systems. Under a BOO or BOT approach, the private sector project company, usually a foreign or joint-venture consortium of engineering, construction, and supply firms, will raise the bulk of the financing from commercial lenders, often supported by export credit guarantee agencies and bilateral and multilateral institutions. In return, the private investors seek guarantees and regulatory protection that attempt to minimize their risk. In a BOO contract, the company operates and owns the facility indefinitely. Under a BOT, a transfer to the government or possibly a local company is eventually made. The transfer date is such as to allow a period adequate for amortization of project financing and realization of a reasonable return, usually 10 to 35 years. In both BOO and BOT, the government usually signs with the project company certain concession and incentive agreements on the one hand, and, on the other, performance and delivery agreements to ensure high quality of service.

One advantage of BOO-BOT is that the country does not have to assume additional sovereign debt to finance the project. Another advantage is the greater likelihood -- especially if the concession agreement is awarded on an open competitive basis -- that the investors will utilize the most efficient technology. With performance parameters and cost containment built into the selection and award process, the public is also more likely to receive reliable services.

The examples of successful BOO and BOT projects in Asia are growing. In the Philippines a small turbine power plant was built under a BOT arrangement in Navotas, a suburb of Manila. The plant was built expeditiously and made a welcome contribution to reducing the power shortages in the Metropolitan Manila area. It has since then been followed up by a second, bigger plant. Malaysia first introduced BOO-BOT in projects with assured revenue earnings, such as the North South project. Based on this experience, BOO-BOT was adopted for less obvious areas such as the Ipoh Water Supply project. Although the Sri Lanka BOO-BOT program was not initiated until early 1993, a number of major projects are already under negotiation or being prepared for tender.

As BOO and BOT places heavy reliance on the foreign investor, the enabling environment must meet certain minimum criteria to be attractive for foreign investment. As most BOO-BOT projects last more than ten years, it is important to persuade the potential investor that the investment climate, and the enabling environment, will continue to be favorable over the long term. The importance of pre-commitment devices discussed earlier is relevant here. There should also be a reasonably assured demand for services. Finally, there needs to be a legal framework, both at the general business and specific entity level, that allows for BOO-BOT arrangements to take place, and supports such partnerships over the long project period envisaged.

The Government will have to work hard to attract concession arrangements. In Asia itself there are probably many viable infrastructure projects chasing too little money. Countries that do not have a strong track record with private foreign investment in infrastructure, or who do not yet have clear policy guidelines or incentive-based investment policy directives will be placed at a disadvantage in this competition. Bangladesh is currently in this disadvantaged position. Only through commitment, strong political support, and a long-term strategic plan will the opportunities develop for this type of investment. In some sectors, gas (through production sharing contracts) and telecommunications (operator licenses) for example, the medium- and long-run rewards are such that there will be several potential investors interested in Bangladesh. But in other sectors these investors may not be as forthcoming.

The Government's overall short-run objective should be to develop a suitable number of economically important candidates for BOO-BOT projects. The Government should first identify projects that have a strong demonstration potential and can be exemplary projects that would enhance the probability of attracting other private sector partnerships. Possible initial candidates include Petrobangla for development, exploration, and drilling contracts for gas under production sharing arrangements; contracting out opportunities for the Bangladesh Inland Water Transport Corporation (BIWTC), particularly existing operation and maintenance functions; similar opportunities for road transport; and opportunities for a new license to provide telecommunication services. As Bangladesh will be in competition with other Asian countries (notably India, Pakistan, Sri Lanka, Malaysia, China, Vietnam, the Philippines and Thailand) for attracting external private investment in economic infrastructure, there is an overall need for an effective marketing strategy to generate interest in Bangladesh and to increase the number of potential investors.

Institutional Framework for Concessions. The institutional arrangements for managing concessions, such as BOO-BOT or other private sector partnership projects, are as important as the selection and initial implementation processes. The Government's management of the concession will involve ensuring that appropriate regulatory disciplines are maintained, reviewing the terms of the concession to ensure the concessionaire maintains essential contractual obligations, negotiating the inevitable amendments that may arise in a concession, and managing the ownership change at the end of the concession period. BOO-BOT projects take place over a long period of time during which circumstances could change very much in the favor of the concessionaire. The concessionaires will inevitably be highly sophisticated and will be seeking to maximize their returns from investment. The Government must ensure that it has the capacity to negotiate and deal with these concessionaires before attempting any substantive BOO-BOT projects.

BOO-BOT projects can place significant demands on the Government as they are invariably complex in practice. In managing BOO-BOT the Government will need several kinds of expertise. It will need: (a) a financial monitoring and analytical capability; (b) technical and operational knowledge of each infrastructure sector; (c) regulatory and analytical capability; and (d) contractual legal support. The Privatization Board in close liaison with the line ministries and agencies, plus the Ministry of Finance are the appropriate coordinators of this expertise. They should maintain a financial monitoring and analytical capability. Technical and operational knowledge could be sourced from specialist international consultancies which are familiar with latest developments. The regulatory reviews should take place in the relevant line ministries, e.g., energy and transport. Legal support can be sourced from within the Board, the Law Ministry, and supplemented by outside expertise on a case by case basis.

G. REFORM PRIORITIES IN POWER, TELECOMMUNICATIONS, AND GAS

The Power Sector

The Case for Reform. The availability of an adequate, reliable and reasonably priced source of electricity is a prerequisite to Bangladesh's achieving its targeted growth of 6-7 percent per annum by the end of the decade. Bangladesh has two Government-owned and operated power utilities -- the Bangladesh Power Development Board (BPDB) and Dhaka Electric Supply Authority (DESA), established in 1990 (but operational in late 1991). In addition, rural electricity cooperatives (PBSs) operate under and are regulated by the Rural Electrification Board (REB). DESA (limited to Dhaka and its adjoining areas) and the PBSs handle only distribution; BPDB is responsible for all electricity generation and transmission; it also handles distribution in areas not covered by DESA or REB.

The installed generating capacity in Bangladesh has tripled between FY80 to FY93, from 822 MW to 2608 MW, and power generation has grown at about 11 percent p.a., compared to GDP growth of 4 percent per annum. Nonetheless, only about 12 percent of households are electrified and per capita generation in Bangladesh, at about 80 kWh p.a., is among the lowest in the world. Sri Lanka, India and Pakistan are in the range of 200-350 kWh and Thailand is about 800 kWh. About 26 percent of installed generating capacity (nearly 700 MW) is out of service awaiting major maintenance or rehabilitation, and the annual load factor, at about 58 percent, is low compared with good practice (60-65 percent) and with neighboring countries (e.g., India 62 percent, Pakistan 64 percent and Thailand 70 percent). Reliability of supply has also been a growing problem. The effective reserve margin of only 5 percent in recent years (good industry practice is 15-20 percent) has resulted in increased outages and forced users who cannot afford supply interruptions to rely on standby generators.

System losses have often exceeded 40 percent of gross generation, and cash collections have been less than 80 percent of current billings in recent years. BPDB and DESA's cash income has been less than half of the sales value of the power generated. While the situation improved somewhat in FY93, and the collection to generation ratio increased to 58 percent (36 percent system losses and 89 percent gross collections), their revenues foregone, due to the failure to bill or to collect, amounted to over Tk 5 billion (or a staggering 7 percent of the FY93 realized ADP of the Government). By contrast, in FY93 the rural PBSs sustained only 16 percent system losses, and recorded 101 percent collections and an 85 percent collection to import ratio. System losses in neighboring countries (e.g., Thailand 15 percent, Sri Lanka 17 percent, Pakistan 24 percent and India 28 percent) are also significantly less than those of BPDB and DESA. The ratio of consumers to employees for BPDB, at 41, is among the lowest in the world. Comparable figures are 50 for Pakistan, 61 for Sri Lanka, 65 for India and 107 for Thailand. For DESA, which is responsible only for distribution, the ratio of consumers to employees is 85, as compared with 163 for the PBSs.

Electricity tariffs for BPDB and DESA average Tk 2.27/kWh (US\$ 0.057/kWh), in line with or somewhat above those of its neighbors. While the PBSs set their own tariffs (Tk 2.53/kWh on average), GOB sets uniform tariffs for BPDB and DESA (accounting for nearly 90 percent of sales), with the result that political considerations often outweigh financial and economic requirements and cross-subsidies among consumers are common (including a subsidized rate to the PBSs). Nevertheless, the major contribution to the dismal financial performance of Bangladesh's power sector is BPDB and DESA's operating performance. DESA remains unable to collect sufficient revenues to cover even its operating expenses. Exchange rate losses on foreign loans (mostly government guaranteed bilateral and multilateral loans) also contribute to BPDB's financial woes. BPDB, Bangladesh's largest public sector enterprise in terms of capital employed, is therefore also the country's largest loss-maker.

Investment requirements for the power sector over the remainder of the decade are estimated to be about Tk 100 billion (1990 prices). Bangladesh is fortunate in having relatively low cost gas for power generation east of the Jamuna (provided GOB and Petrobangla can overcome the constraints on the gas sector's development). But the sector's continuing poor performance prompted IDA and other major donors to withdraw support from the sector in late 1990, eroding the possibility of foreign support of investment.

Directions for Reform. The Government owns, operates, and regulates the power sector in Bangladesh. This results in overlapping and unclear responsibilities with limited or no accountability. Deficiencies in the Government's sector management and in the institutional capacity of BPDB and DESA are the underlying causes of the power sector's poor performance. Weak management, strong unions, the shortage of trained manpower and the absence of competition have exacerbated institutional weaknesses. BPDP is vertically integrated, making it difficult to identify areas of, and responsibilities for, poor performance clearly.

The boards of BPDB, DESA and REB carry out the dual functions of oversight and operations, which is not conducive to accountability. For REB it is less of a problem in that it serves as a regulator for the PBSs, each of which is a cooperative with a board akin to a regular corporation. Since FY91, the PBSs have been setting individual annual performance targets with REB that have a direct impact on management and staff through salary adjustments based on performance. In addition, management and staff of the PBSs are not subject to Government salary scales and service rules; hence, there is an incentive to perform and services of poor performers can be terminated. BPDB and DESA also set annual performance targets with Government. However, implementation is ineffective, with limited monitoring and no direct impact on management or staff. BPDB and DESA managements' ability to improve the power sector's performance is severely limited by service rules which restrict lateral entry of qualified staff and rely on seniority as the primary criterion for promotion; salaries are set by the national Government pay scale and labor unions with strong political ties; and there are no management incentives to improve performance.

DESA's establishment in 1990 was a first step toward decentralizing BPDB's distribution function. In early 1992, the top management of BPDB and DESA undertook measures to establish staff discipline and accountability, particularly in the distribution function. These included introduction of an incentive/penalty scheme linked to performance of individual units in meeting system loss and collection targets, implementation of improved commercial operation procedures and first line supervision, and amendment of the Electricity Act of 1910 to provide for recourse against corrupt employees as well as consumers. Implementation has been mixed and the improvements in BPDB's and DESA's performance limited. The sustainability of these changes is uncertain.

The Government has recently established a system for demarcating distribution areas among the three entities; however, it is a somewhat mechanical system which fails to ensure least cost investments and viability of distribution units. The Government opened power generation to private investment in 1992, and there have been some expressions of interest and one memorandum of under-standing initialed.

In early 1993, the Government established an interministerial working group on the power sector under the Energy Secretary. The group's mandate grew to investigating measures to improve the existing public utilities and to attract private participation into the sector. The working group's recommendations have been assembled in a report that is now being considered by the Government. Several donors' renewed lending for power depends on the Government's formulating and initiating the implementation of a reform program addressing the sector's fundamental deficiencies and enabling sustained improvements in its performance. Without prejudging the working group's recommendations, the key elements of reform and various options which might be considered are outlined below.

Improving Power Sector Performance. The overriding reform objective is for the power sector to operate on a commercial basis without government subsidies (or at least with explicit and minimum subsidies) and provide adequate and reliable power supply to its consumers at competitive prices. This is likely to require breaking up the Government's monopoly of the power sector and introducing competition, setting up a transparent regulatory framework to deal with investors and to protect consumers, and encouraging private sector entry by creating an environment that allows it to compete on an equal basis. A firm political commitment to this reform, sufficient to allow focused implementation over a reasonably short time frame of 3-5 years, is the foremost condition for success.

There are three priorities for improving the power sector's performance over the medium-term: restructure the existing utilities; develop an appropriate regulatory framework to promote efficiency and competition; and attract private sector participation in power.

Existing Utilities. In Bangladesh, improving the performance and efficiency of the existing utilities (BPDB and DESA) is the first priority to reduce the drain on the national budget. A frequently used starting point in such a reform process is the unbundling of existing generation, transmission and distribution services which, in the short-run, facilitates performance evaluation and improves efficiency. A number of countries have initially established separate accounting units within the power utility, and commercialized them at a later stage. This process requires the concerned government to allow the operating entities significant managerial, commercial and financial autonomy while laying down the framework for accountability. The stage is then set for eventual privatization of the entities in phases.

The process of separating distribution from generation and transmission in Bangladesh was started with the formation of DESA to handle distribution in the Dhaka area (accounting for about 40 percent of generation). However, DESA's performance has shown little improvement since its start of operations, because no fundamental changes have been made in terms of its autonomy and accountability. Commercialization and corporatization of DESA, with clear demarcation of the roles and responsibilities of the Government (ownership), Board of Directors (policy and oversight) and management of the company (operations), would appear to be a priority; as the new company should have the same control as the private sector over the terms and conditions of employment, severance packages may also be needed for employees who are not hired by the new company. Separation of BPDB's remaining distribution functions from generation and transmission, and commercialization and corporatization of the resulting entities would follow. Consideration may also be given to separating generation and transmission, with the (longer term) possibility of several separate generating entities. This would facilitate private sector entry into generation through greater transparency in the publicly held transmission company and would enable competition among generators.

Rationalization of distribution areas among BPDB, DESA and REB/PBSs is a prerequisite to establishment of viable distribution entities and avoiding further duplication of investment between BPDB/DESA and REB/PBSs. As a first step which could be implemented immediately, BPDB and DESA should hand over those areas to REB/PBSs which are not viable units on their own and fall within existing REB/PBS areas. For the remaining areas, a rational division of operations would likely entail handing over the small supply units scattered throughout the country to REB/PBSs, as they have a proven capability in managing distribution operations in Bangladesh, and leaving the larger cities and towns and medium-sized units under BPDB (and DESA). Creation of several publicly held (corporatized) distribution companies out of the areas left under BPDB would generate yardstick competition (although they would not be directly competing with one another). Allowing generators to sell directly to large consumers would go one step further toward real competition. In increasing the role of REB/PBSs in distribution and enhancing the prospects of individual PBSs for financial viability, the need for subsidies, in the form of the bulk supply tariff, loan terms and deficit support during start-up years, should be reassessed and made explicit.

The strategy outlined above requires political commitment to overcome the opposition of entrenched interests; it also requires increased managerial capacity. Improvements in management could result from tapping into skills and incentives in the private sector, including equity participation arrangements (to rehabilitate, operate, and maintain facilities and franchise arrangements), management or performance contracts, and contracting out of services (e.g., meter reading, billing and collections). This would also help to develop new managers. A number of desirable reform features are already being practiced by the PBSs (e.g., separation of responsibilities between board and management, and linkage of management/staff salaries with performance). Cooperative arrangements with REB and the PBSs should be considered for transferring know-how in distribution operations to BPDB and DESA.

Transparent Regulatory Framework. As in most countries, separation of ownership and operation from regulation is needed in Bangladesh to introduce transparency, improve efficiency, promote competition and resolve conflicting interests. While it would be preferable for the regulatory body to be independent of the Ministry of Energy and Mineral Resources, establishment of a separate regulatory unit within or attached to the Ministry may be more feasible for the near term. The regulatory unit's primary objective should be to provide a level playing field for public and private power companies. Non-government representatives could be included on the regulatory body. The exact nature of regulation would depend upon the long-term structure and extent of competition envisaged in the sector, with regulation declining with increasing competition. This will require a long-term vision of the power sector's structure, and avoiding piecemeal regulation. Removing tariff setting from the political arena should be facilitated by requiring the regulatory unit to regulate tariffs using explicit economic and financial criteria, possibly including indexed rate regulation.

Potential for Private Sector Participation. Greater competition and private sector participation are critical to power sector reforms. Although government ownership may be the only politically feasible option currently, measures can be initiated now to allow private sector participation in the operation and management of generation, transmission and distribution facilities as discussed above, and equity participation, initially most likely in expansion of generation, but also possibly in franchising distribution areas. To attract private equity, the private sector must be assured of equitable access to and price of fuel (mainly gas), transparency in negotiations and adequate dispute resolution mechanisms. Once a detailed policy framework for private sector participation has been formulated, its public announcement, as has been done by India and Pakistan, may help in introducing competition in the industry and attracting foreign and domestic capital for investment in the power sector. Selling shares of existing companies to the public requires the companies to be well managed and earning a reasonable return on their assets.

The Telecommunications Sector

The Case for Reform. A key prerequisite for accelerated economic growth in Bangladesh is the availability of adequate telecommunications services. Bangladesh Telegraph and Telephone Board (BTTB), established in 1979 as a Government Board under the control of the Ministry of Post and Telecommunications (MOPT), is the monopoly provider of domestic and international telecommunications services in urban areas of Bangladesh. Rural services are currently provided to a very limited extent by both BTTB and Bangladesh Rural Telecommunications Authority (BRTA), a wholly privately-owned company, which is licensed to provide rural services to half of the 400 thanas. Hutchinson Bangladesh Telecom Limited (HBTL), a joint venture between a Bangladesh company and Hutchinson Telecom of Hong Kong, has a license for cellular radio services for the whole country. Based on both the Government's past efforts to involve private investors and the decision recently to remove the telecommunications sector from the Reserve List, the Government has indicated a willingness to introduce private sector participation in the telecommunications sector. However, there has been little progress in the absence of clear rules and procedures and BTTB's continuing role of service provision and self-regulation. Most importantly, BTTB lacks the motivation to offer reasonable terms for inter-connection to potential alternative providers because it would loosen its own monopoly.

Bangladesh's telephone penetration rate of two main lines per 1000 population is one of the lowest in the world. In the region, Pakistan's rate is 10, India and Sri Lanka have 7, and Nepal has 3.[1] Bangladesh's main telephone line growth has failed to keep pace with demand. During the 1988 to 1991 period, the main lines in service increased at a compound annual rate of about 6 percent, whereas the waiting list for telephone services grew at about 9 percent per annum. This has happened despite one of the highest installation charge for digital lines in the world, currently around US $500 per line. Based on BTTB's historical performance and recent estimates of demand projection by external sector consultants, there is a substantial and growing level of unmet demand. Without major sector reform, the gap between demand and supply is not expected to decline, and may increase, over the next ten years from its current level of about 270,000 lines. The situation may be somewhat ameliorated by the recent decision to add 130,000 digital lines, to be partially financed by issuing a Telecom Bond; however, this will take place within BTTB's existing monopoly with all its attendant problems, since the framework for private entry in not yet in place.

All current indicators of service quality are below international standards. It is estimated that successful call completion rates are around 30 percent, well below an acceptable target of 65 percent. Completion rates are higher in China (58 percent), Indonesia (40), Morocco (43), and the European Community (65). A recent small survey of business telephone users shows that there is widespread dissatisfaction with BTTB's overall performance (see Box 3.4). For medium to large business customers, the relative level of charges is not as important as obtaining the telephone

---

[1] *Asia-Pacific Telecommunication Indicators*, International Telecommunications Union, Geneva, May 1993.

connection itself and the subsequent quality of telephony service. Despite their relatively large potential revenue streams, almost 40 percent of business customers must wait for a period of twelve months for a new connection.

The telecommunications sector represents one of the best opportunities for Government to encourage significant private sector involvement because of its attractiveness in terms of growth and profitability. In addition, rapid reform in the telecommunications sector will serve as a model for reforms in other sectors, and also signal the Government's commitment to overall private sector-oriented reforms.

BOX 3.4: FINDINGS OF A SURVEY OF BUSINESS TELEPHONE USERS

1. The quality of BTTB's telephony services is poor, and in need of improvement. The time taken to install a line was stated to be anywhere from one month to over one year. A large majority of those surveyed claimed that calls were not completed on the first attempt, mainly due to wrong numbers or lines being engaged.

2. The speed of installation and repair depend on the specific private arrangements users have with BTTB staff, respondents frequently stated.

3. The majority of respondents emphasized that the relatively high level of charges was not so important as obtaining the connection itself and the subsequent quality of telephony service. However, price rises would not be acceptable without a major improvement in quality of service.

4. Respondents frequently cited the poor accuracy of phone bills.

5. Respondents wanted BTTB to focus its efforts on improving existing services rather than make new service offerings. They wanted BTTB to replace its existing analog exchanges with digital technology.

Source: Coopers & Lybrand, "Telecommunications Sector Reform Study," November 1992.

Constraints to Sector Development. The telecommunications sector's poor performance results from combination of factors: (i) a lack of clearly articulated Government regulatory policy for the sector; (ii) the absence of an effective regulatory structure; (iii) insufficient incentives for BTTB to strive for higher performance standards; (iv) inefficient BTTB management; (v) chronic under-investment in network facilities; and (vi) lack of competitive pressures and commercial incentives for good performance.

Telecommunications Sector Reform Program. In August 1992, an international consulting firm began a comprehensive reform study aimed at developing sector policy and regulation that would yield a sustained improvement in the sector. At the conclusion of each of the three phases of the study, workshops attended by all key stakeholders were held in Dhaka to deliberate on the findings and recommendations, and to build a consensus for sector reform. The result is an emerging sector reform agenda with three key guiding principles: promote new entry and competition in the sector; establish a transparent, predictable regulatory environment; and reform BTTB to enable it to compete in the new regulatory and competitive environment.

Promoting New Entry and Competition. The Government has taken initiatives in the past to promote private sector participation, in particular BRTA's rural franchise, HBTL's cellular license, and one additional rural franchise currently under negotiation. The centerpiece of the emerging policy agenda is the launching of a new majority privately-owned operator to compete with BTTB in the provision of basic services. The new operator will be authorized to install lines in those areas not already covered by rural franchises, and will be required to meet specific growth and service quality targets. The initiative will need to be supported by price rebalancing and adequate network interconnection and revenue settlement arrangements.

The new operating license should be awarded by competitive bidding to a consortium of domestic and foreign investors, led by a telecommunications network operator who has a proven international track record in the delivery of high quality services and who is required to inject equity in the new company. The award process could be completed within eighteen months once the policy agenda is approved by the Government. This approach is most likely to attract substantial investor interest because the new operator will operate in a reformed environment and will not have to deal with BTTB's endemic problems. Its dealings with BTTB would be limited to inter-connection and revenue settlement arrangements, clearly spelled out in the license of the new operator and regulated by a new regulatory body (see below). This approach is most likely to substantially improve sector performance and facilitate the flow of domestic and foreign private investment to the sector.

In addition, to meet growing demand, a wide range of other telecommunications market segments will be opened to competition. Specifically, provision of customer premises equipment, public payphones, and value added and data services will be liberalized. The granting of one or more additional licenses for cellular services to provide competition to HBTL is being considered by the Government.

New Regulatory Framework. The transition to an appropriate regulatory environment that is transparent and predictable is essential to promote competition, attract private sector investors, and ensure that operators make rational decisions about network and service development. The telecommunications strategy should include the establishment of Telecommunications Regulatory Board (TRB) as a statutory authority that is financially and operationally independent of the Ministry of Post and Telecommunications (MOPT), and responsible for administering most aspects of regulatory policy, including regulation of the radio spectrum. Setting up such a body, as experience from countries such as Argentina and Mexico shows, can be a long and complex process, particularly when the capacity and the information availability for regulation are low in Bangladesh. Thus, the regulation strategy should be, in the first instance, to amend the 1979 BTTB Ordinance to separate regulatory functions from operations, and to create a semi-autonomous regulatory group within MOPT with the power to license operators and otherwise regulate the sector; such plans could be completed within six months. In order to minimize the regulatory oversight by this transition regulatory group, while the TRB is being established, the licenses issued to the telecommunications operators should incorporate in detail the terms and conditions for operation, including the inter-connection obligations. Interim regulation would be focused mainly on technical matters and spectrum management.

Reform of BTTB. BTTB is an example of both poor sector and enterprise management. BTTB has poor scope for autonomous decision-making, which in turn reduces it accountability. All its revenues go directly to Government and it depends on Government's annual budgetary allocations for its operational and development needs, eroding accountability and responsibility in enterprise management and operations. In addition, Government procedures have contributed to delays in project approval and, at times, hindered long-term planning. BTTB is bound by civil service personnel procedures that limit its ability to attract and motivate high-caliber staff. Like many other Government agencies, BTTB's efficiency is adversely affected by a strong labor union and the severe problem of overmanning.

In order to substantially improve BTTB's performance, it would need to be transformed into a market-oriented commercial organization. The experience of other SOE sectors in Bangladesh, particularly power, jute, and textiles, suggest that reform from within by converting BTTB to a corporation or a public limited company will not work on its own unless it is faced with credible competition. To commercialize, BTTB needs to form a strategic alliance of its own with a leading foreign telecommunications firm (with substantial management control) in order to compete with the newly licensed second operator. The important first step in reforming BTTB would be to change its corporate status to a public limited company. However, there is strong labor union opposition to this move, and there will have to be greater political support for this conversion before such a strategic alliance can be formed. The introduction of competition through a new operator is expected to contribute some impetus for change from within BTTB, when such an option will become more feasible.

Status of Sector Reform Program. The Cabinet has approved in principle the amendment of the 1979 BTTB Ordinance to separate regulatory functions from operations. MOPT has completed the inter-ministerial consultations on a Telecommunications Policy Statement and will submit it to the Cabinet for approval by May 1994. In addition, MOPT is preparing the necessary technical assistance project documents in order to employ consultants to carry out a tariff study and a legal expert to help advise on inter-connection arrangements and drafting licenses as part of the follow up of the reform study.

Based on the experience of countries that have successfully implemented comprehensive telecommunication sector reform, it is evident that this will be a complex process and will require commitment as well as substantial expertise. In light of the increasing but still limited expertise within Bangladesh with comprehensive sector reform, it will be crucial for the Government to obtain the necessary expert assistance to ensure successful implementation.

The Gas Sector

Past Development and Performance. Natural gas is Bangladesh's only important indigenous commercial energy resource. To meet energy demand at least cost to the economy and reduce the country's dependence on imported oil, the Government has given high priority to the development of natural gas and natural gas liquids, and has allocated a significant share of public investment and external assistance to the development of supply capacity and delivery infrastructure. Gas was first discovered in Bangladesh in the mid-1950s by the international oil companies (IOCs). The two northern gas fields at Sylhet and Chattak were brought into production in 1960 to supply local industries in the Sylhet area on a small scale. The discovery of the main gas fields east of the Jamuna river followed in the 1960s when the IOCs found Kailashtilla, Titas, Rashidpur, Habiganj and Bakhrabad. The war of independence for Bangladesh intervened and caused the IOCs to withdraw. After Independence, efforts were made to continue exploration and develop the three fields at Titas, Habiganj and Bakhrabad which are closest to the main markets near Dhaka and Chittagong. By 1990, these three fields were supplying 93 percent of the gas used in Bangladesh.

The development of the gas fields in Bangladesh is still at a very early stage. There are presently 17 known gas fields; however, only the first round of appraisal drilling has been made, and only three fields -- Titas, Bakhrabad and Habiganj -- have sufficient wells and production data to allow reasonably accurate estimates to be made of gas reserves in place and recoverable. Because of this, gas reserve estimates have been made in a subjective fashion under several studies. The most conservative estimates puts the total gas reserve at 21 trillion cubic feet (TCF), of which 12.4 TCF is considered as recoverable. Five fields -- Kailashtilla, Rashidpur, Habiganj, Titas and Bakhrabad, account for two thirds of the known gas reserve.

While the current reserve estimates appear to be small, there is a significant potential for proving up new gas reserves in the numerous current field extensions as well as in the new prospects. The likelihood of significant increases in the reserve base over and above what is required to meet domestic demand indicates a strong potential for export. In fact, because the domestic market is relatively small, IOCs interested in Bangladesh would mostly aim at finding enough gas to build an export-oriented operation.

During the last two decades, the gas sector has undergone major expansion. Natural gas output increased from 11.5 billion cubic feet (BCF) in FY72 to 210 BCF in FY93, and now accounts for about 60 percent of the country's commercial energy supply, with the balance being met by imported oil and petroleum products (32 percent), coal (4 percent), and hydropower (4 percent). The availability of low-cost natural gas has been the driving force for the expansion of the power sector and the rapid development of the fertilizer industry in Bangladesh. Currently, about 90 percent of power generation is based on natural gas, and all of the agricultural sector's urea fertilizer requirements are met by local production. Power generation and fertilizer production account for about 43 percent and 34 percent, respectively, of the total gas consumption, with the remaining 23 percent accounted for by industrial, commercial and residential consumers.

The gas sector in Bangladesh is wholly dominated by Petrobangla, a group of eight state-owned Operating Companies (OCs) responsible for exploration, production and delivery of natural gas. By FY93, Petrobangla group had historically valued net fixed assets of Tk 14.4 billion, operating 27 wells with a combined production capacity of 660 million cubic feet per day, 1300 km of transmission lines and an extensive distribution network.

Unlike many other public enterprises, the gas sector has been a significant source of revenue for the Government Treasury. Through payment of VAT and supplementary (excise) duty (currently at a level equal to 62 percent of gross sales revenue), a 50 percent corporate tax and dividends, Petrobangla's contribution to the Government has been increasing steadily, from Tk 2.0 billion in FY86 to Tk 7.3 billion (US$183 million) in FY93, reflecting the results of a ten percent average annual increase achieved in the volume of gas sales and average gas tariff.

Notwithstanding its contribution to resource mobilization, there are serious performance shortfalls in the Petrobangla group. Despite substantial technical assistance provided by donors over the past decade, there has been a general lack of organized effort towards accumulation of technical know-how. As a result, the group has insufficient in-house capability to plan, design and supervise the sector's expansion program. Project preparation, design and engineering, as well as supervision of physical construction depends totally on foreign consultants. There have been many instances where a piecemeal approach to system planning, inadequacies in project design, lack of complementary investments, and neglect of supervision of consultants' work have contributed to long implementation delays, high investment costs, and idle assets. Gross inefficiency is also manifested in the drilling operation carried out by the Bangladesh Petroleum Exploration Company (BAPEX) which spent more than US$100 million in drilling 10 wells, of which 5 proved to be unsuccessful. The design of gas pipelines and refining facilities are complex. It is not necessary for Petrobangla to acquire such skills because gas entities worldwide employ specialized consultants for this purpose. It is more important that Petrobangla strengthen the necessary skills to supervise consultant work and increase its ability to evaluate their work expeditiously.

On the operational side, major inefficiencies exist in asset management and billing and collections, as evidenced by the virtual absence of proper reservoir management and maintenance, and high level of unaccounted sales in the non-bulk sales segment of the Titas franchise area. Over the 1968-93 period, annual system losses on average were estimated at around 4.5 percent of production; in FY93, the total system loss was about 7.8 percent, above 80 percent of it incurred by non-bulk industrial, commercial and domestic customers.

Sector inefficiencies result in direct costs due to ubiquitous implementation delays, inadequate coordination of design and thus redundancies in production, ex post modifications of facilities and lost revenues due to inadequate pipeline or processing interlinkages, and low capacity utilization. Implementation delays of three years in the Brahmaputra Basin project, for instance, are projected to add an additional 10 percent to its costs--US$5 million. The North-South pipeline added construction costs of US$14 million, and supervision costs of US$3.8 million, to the original construction contract costs of US$47.7 million for a one-year delay. Delays in the planning and contracting for the Ashuganj Natural Gas Liquid Plant are likely to add an additional 30 to 40 percent in the contract costs alone, without accounting for the associated production losses of the processing plant in Kailashtilla. Although gas development is likely to be concentrated in the north-eastern zone, gas demand will be mainly from the south. The existing gas networks for the north and south are not interlinked, and there is no provision to pipe surplus gas from the northern zone to the south, unless the Ashuganj-Bakhrabad (A-B) pipeline is built. Delays and uncertainties surrounding this pipeline could potentially impose heavy financial costs on the KAFCO fertilizer plant and the second unit of the Rowjan Power Station, which are under construction.

Several factors have contributed to the Petrobangla group's weak institutional capability and inadequate performance. *First*, since its inception, the Petrobangla group has been operated directly as a department of the Government. Besides tariff setting, many operational decisions are controlled by the Government. The group is governed by the Government salary scales and internal procedures, and requires approval from the Government agencies for investments, operating budgets, procurement and staffing. Operating budgets are not tied to annual and long term corporate plans, and there are no agreed sets of specific, annual and quantified performance targets for the group and individual OCs. Thus, the accountability of the group's management for performance is severely undermined. *Second*, the Government's excessive levy of excise duty on gas sales has resulted in OCs' profit margins that neither meet financial requirements nor reflect cost structures; this is the root cause of the group's low earning capacity and weak financial position. *Third*, being a state-owned monopoly on the one hand, and facing a state-owned monopsony on the other in terms of its sales, the group faces no competition and little consumer pressure and, therefore, has not been spurred to improve performance. *Fourth*, the role of the OCs in project implementation under Petrobangla's control has not been large. Increasing the OC's role would have several positive effects, including increasing the motivation for overall cost reductions and personnel training while the project is being implemented.

Accelerating Sector Development. Bangladesh's gas sector is now at a critical juncture. The sector has a large potential for increased contribution to the country's economic growth. However, to fully benefit from the country's hydrocarbon endowment, the Government needs to take rapid action to address the major constraints on the sector's development, i.e., Bangladesh's limited financial resources and technology limitations, and Petrobangla group's limited implementation capability. In the face of tighter external concessional aid and the Government's limited budgetary resources, the sector's future capital requirements far exceed what the Government can manage to allocate to it. Minimum investments required up to the year 1998 to balance supply and domestic demand are estimated at about US$800 million. This amount could increase significantly depending on the pace of the sector's future development.

In order to mobilize more capital required for achieving accelerated sector development and improve the performance of the existing sector entities, the Government has recognized the need to overhaul the prevailing sector arrangements. The main initiatives being considered by the Government relate to increasing private sector participation, particularly by international oil companies (IOCs), and commercializing or privatizing existing operations.

Private Sector Participation. Encouraged by the highly visible successes in attracting international private participation in their petroleum/gas sectors in other countries, the Government announced in July 1993 a new petroleum policy opening the gas sector for private participation. In September, the Government held a roundtable in Houston to promote participation of IOCs in upstream hydrocarbon exploration and production through production sharing contracts (PSC). The responses from the IOCs have been encouraging; several IOCs have signed memorandums of understanding with the Government, one contract for a off-shore prospect has been signed, and negotiations for two PSCs are expected to be completed by late February 1994. With its limited financial resources, Bangladesh would benefit immensely from the risk capital, management expertise, efficient operations, technical advances and global experience that IOCs could provide under favorable conditions. In order to facilitate and expedite the negotiation of these complex contracts, it is important that the Government coordinate its efforts among its various agencies. For example, the provision of a terminal facility to an IOC interested in export-sales may not be technically within the purview of Petrobangla, but should be coordinated internally by the Government.

Commercialization and Privatization of Petrobangla. There is a broad consensus at the Government level that privatization of the Petrobangla group would be an effective alternative to transform the individual OCs into efficient businesses. Yet, to make the eventual privatization offerings successful would require a wide range of readying steps. These include (a) letting OCs operate under private company law in form and substance with adequate managerial autonomy; (b) reforming gas tariffs to enable OCs to operate on a commercial basis; (c) decentralizing operational decision-making and developing competition in the sector. The last step could be carried out possibly through breaking up the monopoly power of the holding company, with each OC becoming an independent entity charged with being financially self-sufficient and placing its financial relationship with other OCs and the Government at arms length.

It is encouraging to note that the Government is planning to float a portion of its shareholding in two OCs -- Bangladesh Gas Fields Company Limited and Titas Gas Transmission and Distribution Company -- in the local capital market. Greater private sector participation will push Petrobangla to be more efficient. However, it needs to be emphasized that privatization is a complex process. Proper design and implementation of this process requires strong Government commitment and clear allocation of authority and resources to manage the process.

CHAPTER IV: REFORMING FINANCIAL AND LABOR MARKETS

A. INTRODUCTION

The smooth functioning of factor markets for capital and labor in Bangladesh is crucial for rapid export-oriented manufacturing growth led by the private sector. If these factor markets are uncompetitive, and prices (and therefore market supply and demand outcomes) are significantly distorted, resource allocation will suffer. Such distortions can arise from government policies and regulations, existing institutions, or market failures. They can significantly raise the costs of uncertainty for the private sector. On its path of accelerated reforms, the Government should do all it can to lower these uncertainty costs. Without appropriate resource allocation, private investment, employment and growth will suffer, undermining the Government's accelerated reform program.

Bangladesh's financial sector remains underdeveloped, uncompetitive, and oligopolistic **(Section B)**. Despite repeated attempts at reform, the quality of financial intermediation remains low. The sector is dominated by the nationalized commercial banks (NCBs) and market shares have stagnated. Real interest rates remain high despite low inflation. The NCBs suffer from poor portfolio quality, requiring extensive provisioning and therefore higher margins. The Government has recognized that fundamental reform to increase competition in the financial sector is now inevitable. This will involve rationalizing the structure of interest rates, privatizing the NCBs over time, resolving the emerging problems in private banks, enhancing the competitive posture of the denationalized banks, encouraging non-bank financial intermediaries, and permitting new banking entry. In moving to a new regulatory regime, the Government's ability to supervise banks will need to be greatly improved. It will also require parallel reforms in non-financial SOEs, whose bad debts are partly responsible for the financial sector's problems.

To be able to compete effectively on world markets where it has comparative advantage, Bangladesh needs flexible labor markets **(Section C)**. Inflexible wage determination mechanisms, poor labor-management relations, and misguided labor regulations are important causes of high private sector costs, and discourage private investment and employment creation. The availability of productive jobs with fair remuneration is for many in Bangladesh their only chance of escape from grinding poverty. The recent Wages and Productivity Commission awards, increasing SOE wages without any link to productivity and the firms' ability to pay, clearly indicates that the centralized system of setting wages is too politicized. A move to decentralized wage determination is required. Public wages importantly influence private sector wage outcomes. Proposals for a national minimum wage would further strengthen this link. The excessive and misguided involvement of the Government in labor markets is not conducive to the development of a flexible labor market that can generate rapid growth of employment and serve the needs of a dynamic, outward-oriented private sector. The reduction of the Government's role in industry through privatization and public-private partnership will help in this regard. A reduction of the Government's involvement will need to be accompanied by measures to strengthen desirable labor market institutions and appropriate safeguards for workers, including a safety net for workers displaced in the process of adjustment. It will also need increasing attention to the availability of labor with the appropriate skills required for labor-intensive growth led by an export push by the private sector.

B. REFORMING THE FINANCIAL SECTOR

Overview

Bangladesh has a small and undeveloped financial sector. It contributed 2.1 percent to GDP in 1989, declining to 1.8 percent by 1992; the sector is growing slower than GDP. In terms of the usual measure of financial deepening (M2/GDP), however, there was a small gain, from 29 percent in FY89 to 33 percent in FY93. As noted in Chapter I, Bangladesh suffers from low domestic saving and investment. While the saving rate has increased in recent years, the level (at 6.5 percent of GDP) is still very low in comparison with India, Sri Lanka and Pakistan. Although data are sketchy, financial savings in the form of bank deposits and other instruments may have increased their share of total savings. The gross domestic investment to GDP ratio has stagnated from 12.9 percent in 1989 to 12.7 percent in 1993, and remains extremely low relative to other country comparators and the investment requirements of 7 percent accelerated GDP growth in Bangladesh.

The health and efficiency of the financial sector are crucial to economic growth. It is the system by which a country's most profitable and efficient projects are systematically and continuously funded, and thus it is the mechanism which ensures that resources are directed to the most productive sources of future growth. The importance of financial institutions for rapid growth is undisputed. Comprehensive evidence from across 119 developed and developing countries over the 1960-1989 period provides compelling evidence that economic growth is dramatically dependent on financial sector size, private sector banks, credit to private enterprises, and interest rates.[1] The larger the financial sector in the context of the overall economy, the greater the share of lending by depository rather than central banks, and the greater the share of credit to the private rather than public sector, the greater is the rate of economic growth. These factors increase growth by raising both the amount and efficiency of investment.

The financial system not only transfers funds from savers to investors: it must be able to select projects which will yield the highest returns, agglomerate sufficient quantities of capital to fund the range of investment projects across economic activities, account for and price risk across assets, monitor performance, and enforce contracts.[2] To undertake this range of tasks, the sector requires highly skilled and knowledgeable staff; consistent, comprehensive and reliable information shared across financial institutions; and a history of competence and enforcement that both encourages savers to deposit and borrowers to repay. The most common role of government in successful financial systems has been to ensure that financial institutions serve these vital functions as efficiently as possible. This role has taken the form of regulation to monitor and enhance bank solvency and to limit financial sector instability.[3] Without these complementary roles, both the rate and efficiency of investment is severely eroded.

---

[1] Robert G. King and Ross Levine, "Financial Indicators and Growth in a Cross Section of Countries," *Policy Research Working Papers*, No. 819, The World Bank, January 1992.

[2] For a review of the range of demands on and requirements for financial system effectiveness, see Joseph E. Stiglitz, "The Role of the State in Financial Markets," *Proceedings of the World Bank Annual Conference on Development Economics 1993*, The World Bank.

[3] See *The East Asian Miracle: Economic Growth and Public Policy*, World Bank, 1993, p.276.

Bangladesh's continuing stagnation in investment and economic growth is related to the situation in its financial sector. The financial sector has the potential to contribute to economic and industrial growth by enhancing resource mobilization and improving resource allocation. At present, however, the sector's contribution to resource mobilization is modest and resource allocation is very poor. Non-performing assets constitute a majority of the portfolio of some NCBs and Government-owned development finance institutions (using prudential norms that are lenient by international standards). The biggest development finance institution has a very low collection ratio. A 1989 World Bank review of 33 small-scale industry credit projects that had closed over a fifteen-year period listed only one with a lower collection rate at completion than the three implemented in Bangladesh.[1] While the extent of bad debts in the nationalized commercial banks is not known with accuracy, they are believed to be substantial. If these bad loans are also bad investments, Bangladesh's capital/output ratio will have been adversely affected, lowering the rate of economic growth. If the annual impact of bad investments is compounded over the 23 years since independence, the overall effect on economic growth would be substantial. The main challenge for Bangladesh's financial system for the near future is to improve the quality of intermediation and resource allocation to contribute to a more rapid rate of economic growth and higher levels of saving and investment.

The major barrier to financial sector development has been the Government's ownership of the dominant financial institutions and its past interventions in credit allocation. Until the early 1980s, the Government owned, controlled and directed Bangladesh's financial system with the objective of allocating funds for sectors, projects and purposes of its choosing. Loan recovery was not emphasized because loans were collateralized and considered ultimately collectable. The quality of financial intermediation, judged by loan recovery rates, was poor. Bangladesh had virtually no private banking and the role of the private sector was considered secondary. In the early-1980s, the Government began to reform the financial sector. Interest rates on deposits were raised to provide a positive real return on deposits, private banks were allowed to enter, two Government-owned banks were denationalized--sold back to their former owners--and another nationalized bank was converted into a limited liability company and partially privatized. Based on reports prepared by a Government appointed commission and by the World Bank, the Government launched a reform program in 1989. Policy changes under this program, which are discussed below, have introduced flexibility in interest rates on deposits and loans and improved prudential regulations and supervision of banks. The impact on the quality of intermediation is, however, not known yet and a private industrialist still cannot obtain financing for a large project without having to approach a Government-owned commercial or development bank.

Financial Market Liberalization: Mixed Progress

Interest Rate Policy. Interest rate liberalization has proceeded apace since 1989 and reforms have been introduced without causing distress. The central bank, Bangladesh Bank, now specifies only the floor deposit interest rates for savings accounts and fixed deposits in banks and establishes interest rate bands for lending to agriculture, small scale industry and exports. In addition, the Government uses its moral-suasion to influence nationalized commercial bank interest rates. Deposit and lending interest rates are, however, high in real terms. The oligopolistic nature of the banking industry not only permits its dominant players (NCBs) to influence market interest rates, but the relatively high cost structure of NCBs influences high lending rates. Deposit interest rates at the

---

[1] "World Bank Lending for Small and Medium Enterprises: Fifteen Years of Experience," Industry and Energy Department Working Paper, Industry Series Paper No. 20, December 1989.

NCBs are high in real terms (Table 4.1) because Bangladesh Bank (BB) has not lowered floor deposit rates as rapidly as inflation has declined and competing instruments offered by the National Savings Directorate offer attractive returns. Lending interest rates are high in real terms because the NCBs have a high cost of funds and must cover high bad debt provisioning requirements and capital adequacy norms imposed by prudential regulations. The small domestic and foreign private banks, which are more efficient, have been sheltered under the oligopolistic market dominance of the nationalized and denationalized banks, enabling them to earn high margins. In this comfortable position, the private banks are apparently unwilling to undercut the NCBs. Thus, interest rates, though substantially liberalized, are not fully market determined because of structural reasons.

Table 4.1: High Real Interest Rates at Nationalized Commercial Banks
(percent per year)

	Deposits [a]		Term Loans	Working Capital	Commercial Loans
	Savings	1-yr Fixed			
March 1990	0.4	4.8	6.0	5.5	9.2
December 1990	-2.6	1.9	3.1	3.0	6.2
March 1991	-3.1	1.4	2.6	3.0	5.6
December 1991	5.0	9.1	12.1	10.8	14.7
March 1992	4.1	8.2	11.1	9.9	12.8
December 1992	3.8	6.3	10.7	11.7	13.6
March 1993	4.3	7.3	12.2	12.7	14.2
December 1993	6.2	8.2	12.8	14.3	16.0

[a] Floor rate.
Note: Deflated by Dhaka Middle Class CPI on a 12-month, point-to-point basis.
Source: Bangladesh Bank, Financial Sector Reform Program.

The Government also continues to introduce distortions in the interest rate structure by grossly mispricing some of its instruments and offering tax breaks on interest paid. For example, National Investment Bonds carry a higher interest rate than their risk and maturity warrant and savings certificates offer high after-tax yields to households. To avoid introducing distortions in market interest rates, the Government should not pay more or less than the appropriate market rate for its instruments, depending on their risk and maturity. Its instruments should be priced more rationally. Distorted and high real lending rates are bound to have had an adverse impact on private investment, and therefore on economic growth. All available surveys of private manufacturing enterprises consistently show that limited access to credit and its high cost are at the very top of their list of impediments to faster growth.[1] The enterprises also report that the effective cost of credit is usually even higher than the interest rate when bribes and delays are included.

---

[1] For example, limited access to credit was cited by respondents to three surveys as being the most important constraint they face. Their responses suggested that there was a significant gap between the interest rate and the effective cost of borrowing once delays and bribes were factored in. The three surveys were sponsored, respectively, by the Bangladesh Chamber of Commerce in 1991 (1200 establishments); by the World Bank in 1991 (107 firms); and by the Bangladesh Apex Agency in 1989 (500 entrepreneurs).

Directed and Subsidized Credit. Credit quantity targets for specific sectors or activities have been by and large eliminated. As part of the financial sector reform program, the Government agreed to provide interest rate subsidies to priority sectors from its own funds and in a transparent manner. BB refinance windows have been replaced by a single rediscount window which lends to eligible banks for any purpose at the same Bank Rate. BB still offers a Tk 1 billion facility to participating scheduled banks for term loans to small and cottage industries. Also, the Government has recently provided substantial funds to development financial institutions and the NCBs at subsidized rates to onlend to "sick" industries. Furthermore, the Government recently announced that banks would be asked to lend substantial resources from their own funds for industrial development. The Government has also made arbitrary remissions of interest and principal for sick industries. Thus, the Government's commitment to eliminating directed credit entirely is still uneven.

Because of perceived market failures, many governments, especially in South Asia, have intervened in credit markets to improve resource allocation. Generally these interventions have not been successful as the experience of India and Pakistan amply demonstrates. It is difficult to distinguish between market failure and projects with low returns, and the incentives in government-owned intermediaries are not conducive to profitable lending practices. The few success stories in directed and subsidized credit are where performance incentive difficulties have been overcome, such as in Korea and Japan. In these countries, directed and subsidized credit programs were structured very differently than in South Asia. *First*, the proportion of directed credit was small. *Second*, intermediaries used commercial criteria for selecting projects and borrowers. *Third*, the ability to export a sizeable proportion of output (often a critical test of efficiency) was an important determinant of access to special credit programs. *Fourth*, incentives within financial institutions, including government institutions, stressed professionalism and performance rather than acquiescence to political pressures. *Finally*, by promoting the development of private sector institutions, and involving them in priority programs, these economies developed a network of shared risks and shared monitoring--thus increasing the incentives for all institutions to finance profitable projects. The Government should resist reviving directed and subsidized credit programs unless it can assure similar conditions in Bangladesh.

Reserve Requirements. Reserve requirements are imposed on banking institutions based on deposit liabilities. For scheduled banks, they are currently 5 percent as cash reserve (down from 10 percent) and 15 percent as the statutory liquidity requirement (SLR). These reserve requirements are not a constraint on credit availability at present. However, in the absence of an adequate supply of eligible securities, the SLR has caused the banks to hold large excess cash deposits with BB. These deposits earn no interest, adding to the cost of funds for these banks. Reserve requirements are lower for agriculture banks, development banks and Islamic banks, providing them with some competitive advantage over scheduled banks. Insurance companies are subject to investment guidelines that restrict their portfolios to Government instruments.

Financial Institutions: Poor Performance

The formal financial sector in Bangladesh includes: (a) Bangladesh Bank as the central bank; (b) 22 commercial banks, including four nationalized commercial banks, two denationalized private banks, ten domestic private banks and six foreign private banks; (c) four Government-owned specialized banks, two of which have targeted the agricultural sector and the two others serve industry; (d) one Government-owned investment company; (e) four non-bank financial institutions; (f) two leasing companies; (g) two large Government-owned insurance companies (life and general) and several private insurance companies, including one foreign owned; and (h) the Dhaka Stock Exchange (DSE).

Bangladesh Bank. BB took over central banking functions from the State Bank of Pakistan at the end of 1971. The State Bank of Pakistan was itself formed in 1948 as an offshoot of the Reserve Bank of India. The modalities of BB's operations still owe much to its origins. The Bangladesh Banking Order of 1972 specifies BB's central banking responsibilities and gives it substantial powers to formulate and implement monetary and supervisory policies and to advise the Government on economic policy. The Banking Companies Act (1991) and Financial Institutions Act (1993) specify a wide range of prudential requirements and extend BB's powers to issuing directions to banks and financial institutions.

BB is in good financial condition and has no open or hidden losses. Its lending to the Government is not excessive. BB operates the country's payments system reasonably well, especially considering the poor transport and communications infrastructure. However, despite growing improvements in its screening of bank auditors, bank supervision capabilities, and staff training, BB suffers from its past image of a weak and ineffective organization, without much autonomy or authority. There is a strong need to continue to strengthen BB (see below), as it would otherwise not be capable of supervising an expanding and increasingly liberalized financial system.

Commercial Banks. As in other South Asian countries, commercial banks dominate the financial system of Bangladesh. Four nationalized commercial banks dominate the banking system with 63 percent of bank deposits and 53 percent of advances in 1993 (Table 4.2). These banks have lost market share between 1986 and 1993, in deposits from 69 percent to 63 percent and in advances from 56 percent to 53 percent. They continue, however, to exert oligopolistic market power over the banking system. NCBs have helped to further the Government's socioeconomic objectives by expanding their rural branch network and lending to agriculture, lending to small scale and cottage industries and funding SOEs. As discussed below, however, the combination of Government ownership and attempts to achieve these objectives have been at a high cost in bad loans.

Table 4.2: Deposits and Advances by Type of Bank
(Taka billion in 1989 constant prices)

	June 1986		June 1989			June 1992			June 1993		
	Tk billion	% share	Tk billion	% share	Growth Rate	Tk billion	% share	Growth Rate	Tk billion	% Share	Growth Rate
Deposits											
NCBs	102.82	69	115.97	64	4.0	141.04	65	6.7	155.37	63	10.2
Dom. Private Banks	29.17	20	42.66	24	14.0	54.96	25	8.9	61.74	27	21.4
Foreign Banks	9.35	6	13.69	8	15.9	11.27	5	-7.7	11.6	5	2.9
Specialized Banks	7.53	5	8.59	4	3.3	10.91	5	6.9	13.77	5	26.2
Advances											
NCBs	82.12	56	85.24	51	1.2	103.46	53	6.6	116.76	53	12.8
Dom. Private Banks	20.66	14	33.30	20	16.3	45.63	23	11.7	55.84	25	22.4
Foreign Banks	8.36	5	10.51	7	11.2	7.96	4	-10.1	9.42	4	18.3
Specialized Banks	36.14	24	37.81	22	1.8	39.36	20	-0.9	40.07	18	1.8

Source: Bangladesh Bank, Financial Sector Reform Program.

Domestic private banks, which include two denationalized banks, increased their market share between 1986 and 1993, in deposits from 20 percent to 27 percent and in advances from 14 percent to 25 percent. These banks expanded their network by 33 branches, comprising 85 percent of the 39 new branches created during FY92. The domestic private bank's growth is more impressive if data for the two denationalized banks is excluded. The denationalized banks share many of the same problems as NCBs. Domestic private banks offer higher interest rates to attract deposits and charge higher rates on loans (see below). Their service is considered better than NCBs and they have expanded into fee-based and international services. These banks compete for a limited number of creditworthy borrowers, but not with NCBs for priority or public sector lending. As BB's supervision improves, however, problems in the private banks are also emerging, including insider lending. They also face problems of capital adequacy. Foreign banks lost market share in deposits from 6 percent in 1986 to 5 percent in 1993 (Table 4.2), partly because of the failure of BCCI, and partly because they offer lower deposit rates. They cater to multinationals, international transactions and high net-worth individuals.

The Government and public sector accounted for 23 percent, and the private sector 77 percent of deposits in FY91, about the same distribution as in the previous year. The Government and public sector increased their share of bank credit from 31 percent in FY91 to 39 percent in FY93 (Table 4.3), reducing the private sector's share commensurately. If the government bonds issued to NCBs for recapitalization are excluded, over the medium term the share of public credit has remained more or less unchanged. The sectoral distribution of credit (Table 4.4) shows that the share of industry has stagnated completely since 1989 at around 27 percent; agriculture's share has also stagnated (the

Table 4.3: Public/Private Share of Commercial Bank Credit, FY89-93
(percent, end of period)

	FY89	FY90	FY91	FY92	FY93
Public Sector a/	24.3	23.4	30.8	31.5	38.8
Private Sector	75.7	76.6	69.2	68.5	61.2
Total	100.0	100.0	100.0	100.0	100.0

a/ Includes bonds issued by the Government to NCBs to recapitalize them.
Sources: Financial Sector Reform Project, Bangladesh Bank, and Staff estimates.

Table 4.4: Commercial Bank Lending: Sectoral Shifts and Growth, 1987-1993
(percent)

Sector	Dec. 1987	Dec. 1988	Dec. 1989	Dec. 1990	Dec. 1991	Dec. 1992	Mar. 1993
Agric. Forestry & Fishing	28.5	24.5	22.9	22.7	18.3	18.7	18.3
Industry	24.6	23.1	27.1	26.5	27.8	27.2	27.8
Construction	3.2	3.3	3.9	3.9	4.9	5.1	5.2
Transport & Communication	3.0	2.5	2.5	2.3	2.5	2.3	2.4
Trade	33.7	37.4	30.8	31.0	31.8	32.7	32.2
Working Capital	4.7	4.8	7.8	9.7	9.9	9.1	9.1
Others	4.3	4.4	5.0	3.9	4.8	4.8	5.3
Total	100.0	100.	100.0	100.0	100.0	100.0	100.0
Total Advances (Tk Million)							
Total nominal advances	128,344	152,362	183,718	210,457	219,105	249,099	255,458
Total real advances	104,404	114,762	126,605	133,160	131,924	144,815	147,765
Growth Rate (%)	1.0	9.9	10.3	5.2	-0.9	9.6	8.7 a/

a/ Annualized.
Source: Bangladesh Bank and Staff estimates.

decline in 1991 is due to agricultural loan forgiveness). Overall commercial bank advances actually declined in real terms in 1991, picking up in 1992, but then slowing down again in 1993.

The stagnation in credit to the industrial sector is worrisome for its impact on future economic growth. The standstill in lending is caused by complex factors affecting the supply and demand for funds. On the supply side, NCBs and the denationalized private banks have become hesitant to lend because: (a) prudential regulations governing asset classification, provisions for doubtful and bad debts, income recognition and capital adequacy have exposed their financial weakness; (b) they face an uncertain future which may include restructuring and privatization; (c) the development banks' long-term lending is stagnant and the commercial banks do not have the training or experience to make project loans or develop new products and services; and (d) large industrial projects are difficult to fund without consortium lending, with which the banks do not have much experience. As a result of this lending standstill, the banks have dealt with the resulting excess liquidity by retiring their liabilities with Bangladesh Bank and increasing their reserves above the statutory requirement.

The low demand for funds is a consequence of many complex and interrelated factors including: (a) low domestic demand growth because of the domestic absorption problem; (b) high real interest rates; (c) low activity in SOEs, among the main clients of NCBs and denationalized commercial banks, because of uncertainty surrounding future restructuring and privatization (NCB credit to the jute sector, which was almost 20 percent of annual credit to industry, has virtually ceased); (d) blacklisting of defaulting borrowers which may preclude many leading investors from access to credit; and (e) a dearth of creditworthy borrowers with acceptable collateral (some 3,000 small and medium scale sick industries have become uncreditworthy). More generally, as noted in Chapter II, weak private sector activity is also due to a range of problems that afflict the business environment. These include increased competitive pressure due to import liberalization and smuggling, high domestic wage structure due to public sector wage awards; Bangladesh's poor image as a foreign investment destination due to its inadequate infrastructure, labor and law and order problems, and weak implementation of rules covering foreign investment; and uncertainty about the Government's commitment to reform signalled by concessions to labor unions and slow privatization.

Bangladesh's larger commercial banks have performed poorly. All nationalized and denationalized banks are probably undercapitalized even under the current standard, which is somewhat lower than the minimum recommended by the Basle Committee. The Government recapitalized the NCBs to the tune of Tk 17.3 billion in 1992 and Tk 14.6 billion in November 1993. The series of recapitalizations have been necessary because the lax prudential standards have resulted in deferred and gradual recognition of losses and continued bad lending. In addition, previous recapitalizations did not cover bad jute loans. While estimates of bad debts are not definitive because of weak prudential standards and their yet uncertain implementation, they are likely to be substantial.

The high default rate among NCB borrowers has occurred because these banks have been poorly managed and have had little incentive to make good loans. Government direction and intervention has been rife. NCBs have had to make high-risk loans to priority sectors, new entrepreneurs, public corporations, 'sick' industries and borrowers with political influence. They have also had to endure loan forgiveness programs by the Government. Their own lending practices have not used commercial criteria; for example, they have used imprudently high debt to equity ratios as a basis for lending. They have also been lulled into a false sense of security because their lending has been collateralized and bad loans were masked by inadequate accounting practices. It is nearly impossible to foreclose on collateral and liquidate it. The recent legal reforms undertaken as part of the financial sector reforms have enabled the banks to obtain decrees in their favor from the Financial Loan Courts in their cases against defaulters. However, very little collateral has actually been liquidated because of weak legal enforcement mechanisms. These problems are being addressed through further legal reforms, including a new bankruptcy law, though these will have to be strengthened by substantial improvements in enforcement.

The two denationalized private commercial banks share many of the problems of NCBs. They have substantial bad loans inherited from the nationalized period. At the time of denationalization, the quality of their portfolio was possibly not fully disclosed to their former owners. Saddled with a bad portfolio and poor staff and lending practices, these banks have conducted their business as if they were still NCBs. Not surprisingly, they have not come up to normal commercial standards under the new and tighter supervision and prudential standards. Their net worth is likely to be seriously eroded, specially since they have not had the recapitalization support provided to NCBs.

On operational efficiency, the other domestic and foreign private banks have fared better than NCBs and the denationalized banks. Table 4.5 shows that the large private sector banks are more productive than NCBs: deposits and loans per employee at private banks are almost twice that at NCBs; private banks mobilize almost three times more deposits and loans per branch than do the NCBs. A commercial bank's cost structure is the most important determinant of its intermediation margins, and significant differences in margins indicate differences in efficiency. Table 4.6 shows the gross intermediation margin (which includes the interest margin and fee income) of NCBs and private banks. Margins at NCBs have been consistently lower than at private banks, and furthermore, have been declining since 1989. These differences are due to: their uncommercial approach to pricing loans, exacerbated by direct credit to jute and other sectors; their higher share of non-earning assets; and their lower fee income. Private banks are charging higher lending rates and earning more fee income, so that they can afford to pay slightly higher interest rates and still earn higher gross and profit margins. However, these data do not yet reflect the emerging problems with loan quality in domestic private banks as supervision and inspection improve, and their loan loss provisioning costs will also increase as a result.

Table 4.5: Poor Productivity of Nationalized Commercial Banks, 1989-92
(taka million)

Type of Bank	Deposits per Employee				Advances per Employee			
	1989	1990	1991	1992	1989	1990	1991	1992
NCBs	2.20	2.31	2.67	2.87	1.68	1.88	1.95	2.05
PSBs	3.94	4.09	4.51	4.97	3.25	3.33	3.80	3.75
	Deposits per Branch				Advances per Branch			
NCBs	38.06	40.64	47.41	50.52	29.11	33.10	34.60	36.06
PSBs	107.35	106.63	120.44	133.01	88.51	86.83	101.35	100.41

Note: NCB= Four Nationalized Commercial Bank; PSB = Four largest Sector Banks (Arab-Bangladesh, IFIC, City Bank, and National Bank)
Source: Annual Reports of various banks.

Table 4.6: Public vs. Private: Comparative Margins at Commercial Banks
(percent of average assets)

	Aggregate NCBs				Aggregate Private Banks			
	1989	1990	1991	1992	1989	1990	1991	1992
Interest Received	8.84	5.74	8.62	7.12	8.97	10.14	9.88	9.49
Interest Paid	7.47	7.37	7.23	6.59	7.95	8.06	8.06	7.75
Interest Margin	1.37	-1.63	1.39	0.53	1.02	2.08	1.82	1.74
Other Income	1.08	3.81	0.66	0.85	1.73	1.91	2.03	2.02
Gross Margin	2.45	2.18	2.05	1.38	2.74	3.98	3.86	3.76
Operating Cost	2.44	2.23	2.14	2.23	2.47	2.59	2.65	2.50
Staff Costs	1.75	1.59	1.53	1.65	1.16	1.23	1.23	1.21
Other Expenses	0.61	0.56	0.53	0.51	1.00	1.05	1.10	1.00
Depreciation	0.08	0.08	0.08	0.08	0.32	0.32	0.31	0.08
Profit (pre-tax) Margin	0.01	-0.05	-0.09	-0.86	0.27	1.39	1.21	1.25
(Taka Million)								
Total Yr-end Assets	160,804	177,485	200,620	215,644	22,393	24,810	29,462	32,746
Average Assets	141,717	169,145	189,053	208,132	20,749	23,601	27,136	31,104

Source: Bangladesh Bank and Staff estimates.

Specialized Banks. Two specialized banks serve industry and two serve agriculture. The industrial development banks -- Bangladesh Shilpa Rin Sangstha (BSRS) and Bangladesh Shilpa Bank (BSB) -- are publicly owned and severely troubled institutions that have been largely moribund for several years. They are among the worst performing banks in the World Bank's development bank project portfolio. Their main problems are political intervention and ineffective management. Prior to 1981, they served different markets. Industrial policy had called for enterprises with fixed assets greater than Tk 3 million to be in the public sector and BSRS was formed from three pre-independence financial institutions to lend to this market. BSB, the largest development bank with 1,000 employees, was formed by merging two other pre-independence institutions to serve mainly small private projects. Restraints on private sector activity were rolled back and, since 1982, there has been little new lending to the public sector. Thus, the two institutions differ little in clientele, lending objective or source of funds. In the past, these institutions relied largely on international credit lines and BB for funding, with their own fixed deposits accounting for 25 percent of total resources. But, for the last decade, foreign funding has ceased as BSB and BSRS failed to improve their performance. Domestic funding was also curtailed at the same time, but has periodically recommenced since 1989.

Bangladesh Krishi Bank and RAKUB, together with NCBs, serve the credit needs of agriculture. During the 1980s, a period of seriously deteriorating credit discipline, the Government directed these banks to expand their rural branch network and increase lending to agriculture. This expansion outstripped the institutions' ability to maintain the quality of its lending and recovery programs. Poor debt recovery was exacerbated by the involvement of local Government officials in borrower selection, mixed signals created by loan amnesty and interest remission programs and the use of credit for relief or patronage purposes. Many of the problems with agricultural credit can be attributed to lax credit discipline and political pressures.

Non-Bank Financial Institutions. Bangladesh has 17 general and five life insurance companies, including one foreign company. The insurance industry is dominated by two large wholly government owned corporations--Jiban Bima Corporation (JBC) for life insurance and Sadharan Bima Corporation (SBC) for general insurance. The insurance industry was nationalized until 1984, and until 1990, JBC and SBC had a monopoly over public sector business. In 1989, the latest data available, JBC accounted for 67 percent of life insurance assets, while SBC had 63 percent of general insurance assets. Both companies invest heavily in government securities, partially because of regulations on their investments and partially because of a lack of skills and understanding of risk management.

There are two private leasing companies started with investments from IFC and the Asian Development Bank. These companies are very successful and have expanded rapidly. Their collection rates and profitability are considerably better than banks. In many ways, the lease instrument is appropriate in Bangladesh's situation, especially for small-scale industry. Leasing does not have the onerous collateral requirements imposed by banks and repossession in cases of default is easier because the ownership remains with the lessor. Of course, the threat of repossession is no substitute for careful appraisal, supervision and monitoring.

Capital Market. Bangladesh's capital market is undeveloped. In particular, institutional capabilities are weak and the regulatory framework is fragmented and ineffectual. In 1993, legislation was passed to create a Securities and Exchange Commission and it has recently been constituted. Compared with other emerging markets in the region, the market is small in size and trading activity is thin. The Dhaka Stock Exchange (DSE), a self-regulated body, has 145 listed issues (135 equity, 4 debentures, and six closed-end mutual funds) with a market capitalization of about US$320 million in March 1993. Only about 25 to 35 issues are traded actively, with a daily turnover of US$20,000 and monthly turnover of 475,000 shares. DSE had 195 members in 1992, of which about 30 to 40 are active. The capital market has developed slowly because companies in need of finance could get cheap credit from NCBs and development banks, and investors can place funds in high yielding instruments which have much lower risk than equities.

The Investment Corporation of Bangladesh (ICB) is the largest single investor in the capital market. With majority Government ownership, it was created in 1976 to broaden the investment base and develop the capital market. To fulfill this objective, it was given preemptive rights to purchase shares being issued. ICB engages in underwriting securities and managing mutual funds. It also offers bridge finance, allowing ICB to defer initial public offerings until an enterprise has established a track record. Much of this activity was done in cooperation with development banks. Finally, ICB offers margin lending through its investor scheme to small investors, manages six closed-end mutual funds and one open-end fund. ICB has performed poorly and large segments of its loan portfolio are contaminated by arrears, resulting in a bad loan component of 40 percent. Recently, other private institutions have begun to underwrite issues. The Government is considering whether, with very firm financial management, ICB could be placed in a sound condition.

Problems for developing the stock market exist in the demand for securities and supply of securities. On the demand side, the main difficulty is that the Government offers riskless instruments with high after-tax returns, whereas equities offer lower returns, partly due to capital, dividend and interest tax arrangements, with higher risk. On the supply side, high stamp duties and government controls over instruments and their issue pricing have inhibited the supply of securities. Reforms underway will address many of these issues. There are 2,000 private companies in Bangladesh, providing ample scope for the stock market's expansion, if these distortions begin to be removed.

Finally, money markets have not developed in Bangladesh. There is virtually no inter-bank market. BB auctions 91-day bills but the buyers are mainly commercial banks which hold them to maturity to meet reserve requirements or manage their liquidity. Thus there is no secondary market in them. The Government has also issued longer maturity bonds but they are not traded. Debentures issued by autonomous bodies and corporations (housing and petroleum) are held by BB and the NCBs. Thus, there is again no secondary market. The Government's shift toward funding debt through savings certificates and away from Treasury bills has also reduced the prospects for a domestic money market. The development of a money market is important to establish a risk-free market interest rate as a benchmark for other interest rates.

Financial Instruments. Because its financial sector is relatively undeveloped, Bangladesh does not have a great variety of savings or lending instruments. By far the most important savings instruments are savings and fixed deposit accounts with banks and other financial institutions. By comparison, Government securities outstanding at the end of June 1992 amounted to less than 20 percent of bank deposits. Among Government securities outstanding, Treasury bills constituted about 49 percent, savings certificates 45 percent and bonds 6 percent. The value of equities and debentures was less than 5 percent of bank deposits, with debentures constituting a tiny part of capital market instruments. The noticeable features of these instruments are the high real interest rates and irrational risk-return profiles. Development banks have a sizeable stock of long-term loans outstanding, but net flow has been low for the past few years. Finally, leases have come into use in Bangladesh recently. Bank credit or long-term lending have not been successful in Bangladesh for the many complex reasons stated above. Given the relatively unreliable level of information available about financial institutions or borrowers in Bangladesh, this narrow range of instruments is appropriate. Insured bank deposits and cash credit, the main savings and loan instruments, tend to minimize information problems between borrowers and lenders.

Restoring Financial Institutions to Health

In spite of reforms implemented since 1989, and significant progress made in financial policy, Bangladesh's financial sector remains underdeveloped and continued reforms are needed along a broad front. The main issue is that the quality of financial intermediation remains poor. Almost all long-term lending to industry for several years appears to have been bad. The cost to the economy's growth has been enormous. Thus, improving the quality of intermediation dominates other important concerns such as resource mobilization and money and capital market development. Under present circumstances, additional resources at the disposal of NCBs would only result in more bad loans. Money and capital market development is contingent on the participation of healthy financial institutions and reputable firms in need of financing for expansion. A sound, efficient banking system, the main financier of industry, agriculture and trade, is essential for economic growth. Bankers' role in independently screening and monitoring investments and sharing risk, is crucial for the development of entrepreneurs and the economy.

Commercial Banks. There is ample evidence that the Government, like other South Asian governments, has not been successful in owning and managing banks. Politically motivated directed and subsidized lending has been rife and management accountability has been absent. Attempts at commercialization of government-owned banks in South Asia have not met with success. Countries similarly situated have implemented reforms gradually for many years to improve the performance of its banks, but they are still inefficient and provide poor service and are saddled with bad debts and inadequate capital. International experience suggests that developing a competitive, efficient banking system under government ownership is difficult at best. Thus, Bangladesh should privatize NCBs, allow new banks and financial institutions entry and permit the orderly exit of failed banks and financial institutions to develop a competitive, efficient private financial sector which can contribute fully to industrial and economic growth. Commercialization of the NCBs, while welcome, will not substitute for their ultimate privatization. As experience elsewhere shows, privatization works when done properly. The two banks privatized in Pakistan, Muslim Commercial Bank and Allied Bank, have performed very well (Box 4.1). They have outperformed public sector banks in deposit growth, controlling administrative expenses and the level of fee income generated. Furthermore, increased competition among banks in Pakistan has reduced bank spreads and intermediation costs for borrowers.

Box 4.1: Pakistan: The Benefits of Commercial Bank Privatization

In 1990, the government of Pakistan privatized two of the smallest nationalized commercial banks, Muslim Commercial Bank (MCB) and Allied Bank Limited (ABL). MCB was sold to a geographically and sectorally diverse group and ABL to its management and employees. These banks dramatically outperformed the remaining nationalized banks in terms of deposit growth, controlling administrative expenses and the level of fee income. Because of increased competition, the spreads of the remaining nationalized banks came down by 33 percent between 1990 and 1991. In 1992, MCB's deposits grew by 29 percent and since privatization, it has created 600 new jobs, inducted management experts and introduced modern technology. Between 1990 and 1992, MCB's deposits per employee increased by 82 percent, pre-tax profits per employee by 75 percent and pre-tax return on shareholder funds by 53 percent.

Source: Annual Reports of Muslim Commercial Bank and Staff interviews.

Rupali Bank, the partially privatized NCB, has been identified by the Government as a candidate for privatization. It should be privatized as soon as feasible. There appears to be some slippage in the progress toward this goal, and this needs to be rectified. The privatization strategy should minimize restructuring prior to privatization and fully disclose Rupali's condition to enable buyers to make informed bids. Restructuring prior to privatization could include a financial package to restore solvency and some downsizing of staff and branches that could be done quickly within a few months, leaving the main effort to the buyers' judgement and strategy. It may be advisable to amend the regulations restricting bank ownership by a group to 5 percent to interest buyers who can also manage the bank. Successful privatization will also require imposing a hard budget constraint on the SOEs, the main debtors of these banks--the major restructuring effort in the jute sector will assist in this regard. The privatization process should be transparent and utilize an auction to gain political support.

To reverse the public's poor perception of bank privatization, previous unsuccessful attempts (Box 4.2) should be rectified as a priority. The denationalized banks, Uttara Bank and Pubali Bank, have performed as badly as the NCBs. Uttara Bank and Pubali Bank need to be restructured urgently by the Government with BB's intervention and assistance. Restructuring could include a financial package to restore solvency, management and staff reorganization and branch closure. Where necessary, the problems in domestic private banks also need to be dealt with.

The Government should then build on the decisive, and hopefully successful, privatization of Rupali and interventions in Uttara, Pubali and other private banks, to privatize the remaining three, or at least two of the three, NCBs. As these banks are the biggest in Bangladesh in terms of branches, staff, deposits and assets, some phasing of privatization may be desirable for several reasons: (a) the Government's recapitalization obligations will be substantial; (b) finding sole buyers or a dominant buyer combined with widespread public ownership will not be easy, even if the banks are downsized or broken up; (c) pre- or post-privatization downsizing of branches and staff will be politically difficult and cannot be undertaken for all three simultaneously; and (d) the downsizing of their rural network has to be coordinated with a strategy for BKB and RAKUB, the specialized agriculture and rural credit banks (see below). In spite of these difficulties, decisive action to start preparation for privatizing these banks should be taken immediately, if only to remove the uncertainty surrounding their future.

Box 4.2: How Not to Privatize: The Poor Experience with Bank Privatization in Bangladesh

The privatization of two nationalized commercial banks (NCBs) in the early 1980's offers some interesting lessons in the pitfalls of implementing a policy of privatization. While the privatization of one bank (Rupali) was stalled after partial sale, the Government divested two other banks, Pubali and Uttara. The decision to divest these banks was related to the fact that their previous owners were Bangladeshi, and thus no legal entanglements were expected. The process of divestiture was, therefore, limited to negotiating only with the previous owners. However, to make it politically acceptable, a portion of the shares was reserved for the employees, and a small part for Government. The sale prices of Pubali and Uttara were fixed by Government on its "valuation" of net worth. Anxious not to miss a political window of opportunity, the Government skipped the essential task of properly evaluating asset values and restructuring finances where necessary. Even the asset valuation was reportedly unavailable to the prospective owners.

Almost a decade after privatization, the competitive position and operational efficiency of the two banks has hardly changed, no major management changes have occurred, redundant staff has not been shed, and the banks are suffering huge operating losses. In spite of the fact that both banks did not provide for classified loans, their combined loss in 1991 alone amounted to about Tk 243 million. A large part of the ongoing problems of the privatized banks can be traced to the history of mismanagement during the period of public sector management. Substantial advances--transferred during privatization as assets--have now turned out to be non-performing; overmanning continues under threat of militant unionism; and unprofitable branches cannot be closed as they serve the Government's social programs. While one bank is owed almost Tk 240 crore by Government-owned corporations (mainly textile mills) and on account of the recent Government agricultural loan forgiveness scheme, the other carries almost Tk 200 crore on account of the directed jute credits. Above all, the Government has not taken an evenhanded approach between NCBs and these private banks in meeting its debt obligations. In one case, whereas it compensated all the NCBs for its guaranteed debt for a closed out Government consumer corporation, it refused to pay the privatized bank, which had to ultimately seek a decree from the High Court. Another important aspect which has seriously undermined commercialization of these banks is the continuing lack of autonomy on staffing issues. The privatization terms not only bound the purchasers to abide by the service and employment rules agreed to by the Government in 1982, the banks were also required to follow strictly the frequent pay raises and annual bonuses awarded to public enterprises. In short, the basic ingredients for successful privatization--a healthy cash flow and managerial autonomy--were missing, thereby eliminating the possibility of any genuine commercialization.

With hindsight, three major lessons can be learned from the early experience with bank privatizations in Bangladesh. *First*, while change in ownership is a necessary condition, it is not a sufficient condition for successful privatization. There is a need to carefully develop a privatization strategy which includes a thorough ex-ante analysis of the financial and managerial aspects of the enterprises targeted for privatization. This must be done within an environment of strong banking supervision. *Second*, the failure to reap clear economic efficiency gains results in deepening public skepticism about the privatization process, and provides Government with a disincentive for further divestiture programs. *Third*, the choice of the sale strategy--public offering, wide ownership, as opposed to a closed deal--is also an important determinant of the ultimate success of the enterprise. In the case of the two banks, the mere transfer of shares to the previous owners did not precipitate major efficiency changes. The doubts surrounding the value of assets and the task of fixing responsibility for past debts has preoccupied the attention of the owners, to the detriment of introducing such changes.

Source: Staff analysis.

Development Banks. The specialized banks have performed even worse than the NCBs and long-term lending to industry is at a standstill. Thus, their situation should be resolved as quickly as possible. The Government has agreed to privatize BSRS and is prepared to make up for the bad debts in its portfolio. BSRS has reduced staff by 40 percent and has obtained a commercial banking license to attract buyers. Privatization has been delayed because of political resistance based on a misunderstanding of BSRS's market value. This resistance should be overcome so that the privatization proceeds. BSB, the larger industry bank, is probably in as bad shape financially as BSRS and still retains 1,000 poorly trained staff. Its management is ineffective and subject to political intervention. In addition, the Government has recently made Tk 1 billion available to BSB to fund risky rehabilitation projects. Damage control measures should be implemented immediately and options for its future should be explored.

With the low average collection rates from agricultural credit, BKB and RAKUB are not viable financial institutions. The experience of many developing countries suggests that the formal financial sector institutions are not successful lenders to agriculture and other rural borrowers. The lack of success is partly due to directed credit, subsidized interest rates and other policies. Research done by the World Bank on several countries, including India, suggests that the informal sector lenders are more successful in meeting rural non-farm and agricultural credit needs. While the interest rates they charge are higher than formal sector rates, their rates are generally not monopolistic. Rather, they incorporate fully the higher cost and risk of rural credit. An analysis of informal credit in rural areas should be made to ensure that those markets are competitive and the NCB rural network and BKB and RAKUB downsized accordingly. A much smaller network capable of charging market interest rates could be financially viable. This network could cooperate with the informal sector through an agency system to expand fund availability and ensure competition.

Finally, new banks and financial institutions should be allowed to enter if they fulfill stringent and transparent criteria. Apparently 47 applications for bank licenses have been received and 17 of these are considered serious, but no license has yet been granted. New entry and privatization will add to competitive pressures and bring down intermediation costs. In addition, new entrants may offer new instruments and services. The success of the two leasing companies started a few years ago has added an instrument appropriate for small scale industry development in Bangladesh.

Financial Regulation: Ongoing Need to Strengthen

Financial regulation needs urgent attention to ensure the safety of the financial system during the process of restoring the NCBs to health and as private banking expands through privatization and new entry. Prudential regulation and supervision should be upgraded, as should the capacity for enforcement. The legal system requires special attention to safeguard the interests of lenders and enable them to liquidate collateral in case of default. Finally, accounting and audit standards should be brought up to international levels to support prudential regulations and supervision and to protect lenders.

Bangladesh Bank. BB is the regulator and supervisor of the financial system and is faced with a multitude of difficult banking problems that it must tackle on a large scale. While its performance has improved in recent years, it still has some serious shortcomings. One priority would be to review the Bangladesh Banking Order to define BB's role and spell out its responsibilities and authority clearly. International experience suggests that, while there must be close coordination between fiscal and monetary policy management, central banks are more effective with a high degree of operational and legal autonomy. Because the key to more autonomy is improved performance, the current reform efforts should be strengthened urgently. BB's performance has been eroded by poor staff recruitment and promotion policies and management practices. Rationalizing the organization structure and reviewing personnel policies would be a good starting point. In addition, an early review of a few areas of potential risk such as monetary policy capacity, prudential regulation and supervision capability, foreign exchange operations, and deposit insurance would be valuable.

Prudential Regulations. Most countries have embraced a framework of prudential regulations under which banks are expected to operate. In Bangladesh, broad powers to regulate the banking system are contained in the Banking Companies Act (BCA), 1991 and its amendments in 1993. BCA and various BB circulars specify rules for (a) obtaining a banking license and expanding branch networks; (b) intervention in banks, suspension of business and winding up; (b) corporate governance, including insider lending; (d) prudential management including minimum capital, equity participation, lending exposure limits, income recognition, asset classification and provisioning; and (v) enforcement powers. These rules have certainly improved the financial sector's regulatory environment, but many are lax by international standards and need to be revised. For example, asset classification and provisioning rules have made the enormity of the bad debt problem transparent, but they are slack by international standards. Thus, loans overdue by one year are considered substandard in Bangladesh but bad by international standards. Many substandard loans are actually bad, but it takes years for them to be classified as doubtful and then bad. The cost of bad debts is deferred to the future and many pre-1989 bad debts are still not fully provided against. Thus, current borrowers pay high interest rates charged by banks to permit provisioning for bad loans made years ago. Quicker recognition of bad debts, more stringent provisioning requirements and a one-shot full recapitalization of NCBs accompanied by a major management restructuring should lead to lower lending interest rates and avoid a series of NCB recapitalizations spread over several years. The one-shot recapitalization would also make current NCB performance more transparent as the impact of poor lending in the past would have been removed.

Until recently, there were no regulations intended for non-bank financial institutions in Bangladesh. In 1989, Non-bank Financial Institutions Guidelines were issued by BB and the Financial Institutions Act was passed in 1993 to update the regulation and supervision of these institutions. Regulation of the capital market was spread over several pieces of legislation and implemented by at least four agencies. Currently an effort is being made to rationalize supervision of capital markets under the Securities and Exchange Commission.

While prudential regulations have been upgraded, much remains to be done to bring them up to international standards. The prudential ratios that need to be brought to international standards include capital adequacy, income recognition, asset classification and doubtful bad debt provisions, insider lending, banks' equity participation in other companies, lending exposure limits, and liquidity management. Currently, although BB has jurisdiction over issuing bank licenses and bank branching, in practice the Cabinet is consulted on most decisions. The application criteria and procedures for banks should be outlined in detail and applicants meeting those criteria should obtain licenses automatically. BB has powers to intervene in problem banks but the procedure is time consuming and inflexible and needs revision.

The regulation limiting bank ownership by one person or group to 5 percent may need to be relaxed, even though a waiver clause does exist. The regulation has been imposed to prevent the concentration of economic power, but may slow down the privatization of banks and the entry of new institutions. Investors prepared to risk substantial amounts of equity need to have management control. Concentration of economic power can be checked by increased competition and better supervision.

Supervision. The Banking Companies Act, 1991 and the Financial Institutions Act, 1993, provide BB with a sound legal basis for supervising banks and finance companies, permitting it to take all necessary measures to ensure the safety and soundness of the financial system. It conducted routine comprehensive inspections of 1,414 bank branches and special inspection of 382 branches in FY92. In addition, it conducted routine inspections of 35 branches of investment companies and special inspections of 16 branches in the same year. Recently, highly welcome efforts have been made to improve supervision. BB has shifted its focus of supervision back to banks as a whole rather than branches (required when new provisioning guidelines were introduced in 1989), improved its off-site surveillance and begun to use a bank rating system based on the U.S. CAMEL system. It is improving its capability by providing training and ensuring the selection of better external auditors. A set of common returns for all financial institutions is now in place for scheduled banks.

BB's supervision department has improved in recent years but is still diffuse and needs a tighter, simpler, more functional organization. BB's overall institutional weaknesses also impinge on its supervisory capability. Its inspection department and information systems for supervision are weak. Poor accounting policies, unspecialized staff, rigid promotion rules, and union problems have not helped. Supervisory staff should be specialists, their compensation and promotion should be based on merit. Supervision practices should be revised to assess the banks' activities and ability to identify, measure and control risks and optimize profits. Off-site surveillance reports should be rationalized and decreased in number.

BB has been reluctant in the past to take action, for political reasons, against banks known to be in bad financial condition except in the most egregious instances of fraud. BB should now intervene more aggressively in troubled banks to develop a sound private banking system and legal and political barriers to action should be dealt with expeditiously and firmly. Delays will prove costly for the Government, and ultimately for the economy.

Deposit Insurance. The Bank Deposit Insurance Ordinance was promulgated in 1984. Deposit insurance is provided for Tk 60,000 per depositor. Membership is mandatory for all banks and the low premium applies to all banks uniformly. The scheme is underfunded because of low premiums and lack of investment income and the premium funds are commingled with BB funds.

Legal Framework. The framework of business laws and legal procedures should facilitate transactions and the ability of contracting parties to enforce contracts in a timely and cost effective manner. Banks and other financial institutions have to be able to foreclose and liquidate collateral in the event of borrower default. Recently, several pieces of legislation were passed in Bangladesh to improve its legal framework for the financial system. Among these are the Banking Companies Act, Financial Loan Courts Act, Securities and Companies Commission Act, and the Financial Institutions Act. Bankruptcy legislation is under preparation. Gaps, however, still exist. The laws relating to contracts, negotiable instruments and statute of limitations need to be reviewed. The 21 special debt recovery courts issued 9,700 decrees in the first 13 months, and assisted in some out-of-court settlements, but the lengthy appeal process has stymied actual recovery. Some time limit should be placed on the appeals process and private foreclosure should be permitted to expedite liquidation of collateral. The jurisdiction of the Financial Loan Courts now needs to be logically extended by amending the law to include the implementation of its decrees. At the moment, implementation of Loan Court decrees is done under the Civil Procedure Code, which takes years and can afford the NCBs little hope of collecting on their collateral within any reasonable time frame. The special foreclosure powers given to development banks have not been used. Thus, much needs to be done to improve contract enforcement, especially to encourage private sector financial institution lending for industrial projects.

Accounting, Audit and Information Agencies. Finance is an information intensive industry that relies on accurate, timely and transparent information for its functioning and development. The Government has taken several steps to improve banks' accounting policies (mentioned above) and a

BB Accounting and Audit committee has formulated criteria for the selection of external auditors for banks and financial institutions. There is also a Standing Committee for reviewing bank and financial institution inspection reports. BB has recently established a credit information bureau to track borrowers and assist banks in risk management.

Among South Asian countries, Sri Lanka is the most advanced in adopting international accounting and audit standards. The Government of Sri Lanka is working with the accounting profession to require all large companies to adopt these standards and is establishing an Accounting Standards Board to monitor compliance. Bangladesh should consider following Sri Lanka's lead.

C. TOWARDS FLEXIBLE INDUSTRIAL LABOR MARKETS

There are powerful links between labor market policies and economic development in Bangladesh. The availability of productive job opportunities is the main route of escape from poverty for the poor whose only asset may be their labor. Both labor supply and demand are crucial, as is the functioning of labor markets.

The *supply* of efficient and competitive industrial labor is necessary for the success of Bangladesh's strategy of encouraging labor-intensive manufactured exports. As the experience of the high-performing East Asian economies demonstrates, motivated workers with the requisite training and skills are key to determining the economy's capacity to grow, compete, assimilate new technologies, and adapt in an open economic environment. Effective *demand* for both unskilled and skilled men and women in the work force depends on sound macroeconomic, technological and strategic policy choices. The interaction between supply and demand depends on well-functioning, flexible *labor markets* that efficiently allocate labor to emerging economic opportunities, link real wages to productivity, allow and encourage firms to restructure to remain competitive, foster labor-management cooperation, send appropriate signals about skill needs to workers, and strike a balance between employment generation and job security.

Excessive government intervention has prevented Bangladesh's labor markets from playing this role. Public wage policies and minimum wage regulations have allowed wages to increase faster than productivity, with a resulting serious loss of international competitiveness for public and private firms. Low productivity has also been caused by historically low levels of investment in plant and machinery. Labor legislation imposes high costs on firms needing to retrench workers in the process of adapting to changing world market conditions. There has been serious overmanning in most SOEs, a manifestation of the public consumption profligacy of the 1980s. This legacy is now posing sharp problems of SOE restructuring, privatization, and accelerated, pro-market reforms.

Over the past two decades, the Government's all pervasive role in the labor market has bred an excessive politicization of labor relations, and a deep distrust between labor and management. There has been no concerted effort in Bangladesh to understand and use the political economy of successful reforms in the context of labor markets. Experience on this has shown that to sustain and accelerate reforms, policymakers need to ensure that at most points during the reform process the potential winners outnumber the losers.[1] This requires using relevant institutions, such as trade unions,

---

[1] See Richard B. Freeman, "Labor Market Institutions: Help or Hindrance to Economic Development." *Proceedings of the Annual Conference on Development Economics 1992*, Supplement to the World Bank Economic Review and the World Bank Research Observer, The World Bank, 1993.

creatively and cooperatively. Instead, trade unions in Bangladesh have come to rely on general strikes and country-wide agitations to pressure the Government, because they have not had recourse to more conventional channels of direct industrial negotiations with employers. As a result, Bangladesh suffers from a poor image of industrial relations, thereby discouraging domestic and foreign investment, and hampering private sector development.

Bangladesh's labor force was estimated in 1989 at 50.7 million people, and is growing at around 3 percent per year. Internationally, it is more usual to measure the labor force from age 15 rather than 10, as is current practice in Bangladesh. The labor force of age 15 and above was 46.5 million people in 1989. Of this labor force, the sectoral distribution was as follows: agriculture was the largest employer (64 percent), then trade and services (15 percent), manufacturing (14 percent), construction and transport (4 percent) and other (2 percent). This labor force would be estimated at some 52 million people in 1993, with around 1.6 million workers entering the labor force every year. Providing productive employment for these new entrants into the labor is a colossal challenge.

Bangladesh's labor market is dominated by the informal sector. Of the total labor force in 1989, 45.8 percent were classified as unpaid family workers, 29.6 percent were classified as self-employed, 15.1 percent were classified as casual workers, and only 9.5 percent had regular full-time wage-employment. Hence, roughly 90 percent of Bangladesh's labor are working in the informal sector, or are hired as day-workers by formal sector firms. Yet, the rate of open unemployment has remained very low (1.0-1.8 percent) as sharing of low productivity work continues, implying a high rate of under-employment. Estimates of under-employment indicate that it was equivalent to a 26 percent open unemployment rate in 1993, and could rise to as much as 31 percent by the year 2000, unless policy reforms are implemented quickly.

The Government is the largest single employer in the formal sector. The civil service has around one million sanctioned positions. There were about 400 thousand contracted project workers, and some 200 thousand blue collar workers in SOEs. Of the formal sector employees in 1989, around 35 percent were employed by the Government. Hence, it is not surprising that Government wage and employment policies have an important impact on the formal private sector, especially in manufacturing.

In general, the level of education of the labor force in Bangladesh is not very high (Table 4.7). As would be expected, urban non-agricultural workers are more educated than the average for the labor force. Workers in manufacturing, finance, transport and communications, and trade, are, in general, also better educated in the urban areas. In urban manufacturing, 40 percent had education up to the 10th class, and 15 percent above that. While a labor force with large numbers of uneducated may be able to provide adequate skills for assembly-type productive activities that require mainly on-the-job training, it is clear that more sophisticated production processes will require workers with appropriate education and skill mixes as export-oriented, economic growth picks up. Thus, an increase in the general level of education is desirable for an export push, apart from its other social imperatives. As for specific higher skills, experience from many settings suggests that market provision is usually the best solution. If real wages are linked to productivity, i.e. if a worker who acquires skills becomes more productive than an unskilled worker, and real wages correctly reflect this productivity gain, then the worker would be willing to make an investment in skill training in view of higher future earnings. Under such circumstances, the worker should be able to purchase the appropriate training. For workers who are budget constrained, special credit programs for training could facilitate this. In contrast, highly-subsidized or free government training programs more often than not train people for the wrong type of skills, and do a poor job in terms of quality. This further emphasizes the fact that the link between wages and productivity is key: if a skilled worker does not receive an appropriate return, he will not invest in skill acquisition.

Table 4.7: Educational Level of the Workforce, 1989
(percent)

	No Education	Class 1-10	Class >10	Total
URBAN				
Manufacturing	46	40	15	100
Trade, Restaurants	26	52	21	100
Transport & Communications	53	35	13	100
Financial & Business Services	2	16	81	100
All Non-Agricultural Workers	35	38	27	100
NATIONAL				
Manufacturing	67	29	5	100
Trade, Restaurants	43	45	12	100
Transport & Communications	62	31	7	100
Financial & Business Services	9	20	71	100
All Non-Agricultural Workers	48	34	18	100
All Workers	64	29	7	100

Source: Bangladesh Bureau of Statistics, Labor Force Survey, 1989.

Reforms are needed to bring about significant change in the functioning of labor markets so that they can support accelerated growth of the private manufacturing sector in Bangladesh. Labor market reforms should be implemented to ensure that growth in the future will be labor-intensive. Government reforms should focus on both public sector wage policies, which affect overall wage levels in the economy and hence have an important impact on competitiveness and employment; and policies directly affecting private firms, particularly on minimum wage legislation, legislation on retrenchment, and policies affecting industrial relations.

Public Sector Wage Policies

Public sector wage policies have an important impact on the overall level of public expenditures; and hence on fiscal equilibrium. This is a powerful argument for ensuring that appropriate wage policies are in place. In Bangladesh, there is another reason why public wage policies have a significant impact on the economy. Public wages tend to lead private wages so that excessive increases in public sector wages could result in a generalized loss of competitiveness and a decline in private sector employment. Public workers represent around 35 percent of formal employment in Bangladesh. When they receive wage increases, pressures for similar increases for private workers mount, particularly, in sectors with a strong public presence, for example jute and textiles.[1]

Public sector wages are determined by National Wages and Productivity Commissions (NWPC), created by Government from time to time. The Commissions propose a uniform wage structure affecting all public sector workers. Commissions' recommendations have usually been based

---

[1] For example, in mid-January 1994 seven private jute mills in Khulna closed when workers demanded wages and allowances at par with new wage rates in public sector jute mills (under an agreement signed between public jute mill workers and the Government in July 1993). See "Workers' Action Leads to Closure of Jute Mills," *Morning Sun*, January 16, 1994.

on social and political considerations, with little regard to economic, particularly productivity issues. As a result, public sector wages have increased in real terms by 11-24 percent since the mid-eighties, at a time when productivity was declining and SOEs were making huge losses. Unrealistic public wage policies led to increases in private wages. This situation should not be allowed to continue, as it discourages the expansion of the labor-intensive manufacturing sector. Government should immediately take steps to institute a more de-centralized system of real wage determination, which would lead to a closer link between wages and productivity growth.

Drawbacks of the Present Wage Determination System. Even though there are some small differences, SOEs can be regarded as covered by a single set of uniform pay scales and allowances determined by Government on the recommendation of the NWPCs--four commissions have been established so far in 1973, 1977, 1985 and 1991. In the period between NWPCs, the Government provides workers with increases in the form of dearness allowances. The State-Owned Manufacturing Industries Workers (Terms and Conditions of Service) Ordinance of 1985 forbids collective bargaining on wages and allowances in SOEs. NWPCs include representatives of trade unions, employers and the Government. However, the tripartite nature of NWPCs does not amount to collective bargaining, because the Government retains the right to accept, reject or modify NWPC recommendations. For example, in July 1993 the Government announced a minimum basic wage for public workers of Tk 950 instead of the Tk 1,000 recommended by the NWPC. Rather than a form of collective bargaining, the NWPC represents a process of consultation in a system where pay and allowances are determined unilaterally by the employer--the Government.

This centralized wage setting system has led to a deterioration of industrial relations in the country, as it generates considerable pent-up pressures for a coordinated trade union response in a situation where there are no provisions for orderly, predictable collective bargaining. While the Government may take decisions unilaterally, it does so in a highly charged public arena of industrial and political pressures from trade unions. The Government is inevitably affected by these public pressures, which are expressed politically--on occasions even violently--because there are no arrangements for trade unions in the public sector to express themselves otherwise. The occasional opportunity to make a representation to a NWPC creates expectations that are subsequently rebuffed, as workers are unable to negotiate over the acceptance or implementation of the commission's recommendations. Such discussions as may take place are outside the Government's own policy on collective bargaining in the private sector, as they involve discussions with federations that are not collective bargaining agents (CBAs) and are therefore not required to accept the legal responsibilities incumbent on parties to collective bargaining.

The NWPCs have not functioned, and possibly cannot function, as Wages and Productivity Commissions. Given the constraints of a single wage structure for the entire public sector, they have only ended up as wages commissions, ignoring their productivity mandate. The existence of a single set of uniform pay and allowances means that it is virtually impossible to link the pay of individual enterprises or subsectors to their economic conditions, ability to pay and labor market circumstances. A uniform wage structure cannot provide sufficient flexibility to allow enterprises to adapt to changing conditions, or their own specific requirements. In particular, a uniform structure does not permit sufficiently flexible pay systems that can encourage productivity increases at the enterprise level.

Under the circumstances, it is not surprising that nearly all NWPCs have made their recommendations on the basis of social and political concerns with little or no reference to productivity. The wage increase awarded in 1993 on the basis of the recommendation of the 1991 NWPC provides a good example. Between 1986 (the preceding wage award) and 1993, the performance of the SOE sector deteriorated to the point where their annual losses imply a drain on public resources equivalent to one-fifth to a quarter of the realized ADP. Moreover, enterprises in key export sectors, such as jute, are facing a serious loss of competitiveness; and others in key infrastructure areas, such as power, are making huge systems losses primarily due to irregular practices. Yet, the process of wage determination led to real increases ranging between 11 percent and 24 percent, depending upon the grade (Table 4.8). The additional cost to those loss-making SOEs (Tk 3 billion in FY94) will ultimately have to be financed possibly either by the Treasury or by the banking system.

Table 4.8: Impact of 1993 Wage Award on SOE Worker Compensation
(Taka/month)

	Grade 1	Grade 8	Grade 16
A. In Nominal Terms			
FY86	1,029	1,419	2,018
FY93	1,924	2,910	4,214
Percent increase	87%	105%	109%
B. In 1986 Constant Takas a/			
FY86	1,029	1,419	2,018
FY93	1,143	1,729	2,503
Percent increase	11%	22%	24%

a/ Deflated by the Dhaka Middle Class CPI.
Source: Ministry of Labor and Manpower.

Public wage policies have also led to a loss of competitiveness in the private sector. In readymade garments, Bangladesh's fastest growing export, while the unit labor cost of producing a shirt in Bangladesh in the mid-1980s was lower than the cost in the U.S. (Table 4.9), it was double the unit labor cost in Sri Lanka, a major competitor and the appropriate comparator for Bangladesh. Furthermore, the unit labor cost in Bangladesh was 60 percent of Hong Kong's and 50 percent of Korea's, whereas it should have been much lower (Sri Lanka's was 30 and 28 percent, respectively) if Bangladesh is to be able to compete successfully in an eventual non-quota environment. While it is very likely that labor productivity in garments in Bangladesh has improved since the 1980s, the gap then was large enough to suggest that this could still be a matter of concern.

The jute sector, where SOEs play a major role, also provides a good example. The secular loss of competitiveness in the industry is partly responsible for the major restructuring of the sector that is now being started. Table 4.10 shows that unit labor costs, for all types of jute goods in private sector mills, have increased rapidly since the public sector wage awards in FY86. The increase in unit labor cost was not matched by an increase in export prices. As a result, the unit labor cost which represented 40.3 percent, 27.4 percent and 37.4 percent of export prices for hessian, sacking and CBC in FY86 rose to 78.4 percent, 66.5 percent and 58.6 percent in FY93. Private jute mills are making huge losses--Tk 20,647/ton of hessian, Tk 10,633/ton of sacking and Tk 16,888/ton of CBC--that are covered by borrowing from nationalized commercial banks. Hence, the rapid increase in their labor costs after 1991 cannot be justified by economic conditions.

Wages and Productivity in the Public Sector. There appears to be an emerging consensus in Bangladesh that public sector wages should somehow reflect changes in productivity. However, little has been done to implement reforms in this area. Two practical reasons are forwarded to explain the inaction. First, it is argued that it would be very difficult to arrive at a formula linking wages to value added, or any other measure of production, that would be transparent and yield politically acceptable results. Second, it is argued that labor productivity is often low due to reasons beyond workers' control--e.g poor management, over-staffing, low investment, power shortages, or lack of spare-parts. In those cases, it is felt that it would be unfair to penalize workers through lower wages.

Table 4.9: Unit Labor Cost of Producing a Shirt

	Person-hrs/ Shirt	Wage/hr (US$)	Unit Labor Cost (US$)
Bangladesh	1.870	0.15	0.281
Sri Lanka	0.400	0.35	0.140
NICs			
Hong Kong	0.329	1.40	0.461
Republic of Korea	0.346	1.53	0.529
Developed Country			
U.S.A.	0.233	7.53	1.757

Source: Mahmud Khan and Nuimuddin Chowdhury, "Trade, Industrialization and Employment," in *Bangladesh: Selected issues in Employment and Development*, ILO-ARTEP, New Delhi, 1986.

Table 4.10: Labor Costs and Export Prices in Private Sector Jute Mills
(Taka/MT)

	FY83	FY91	FY93	Annual Increase FY86-93
Hessian				
Unit Labor Cost	9,265	13,134	17,148	9.2%
Export Price	22,985	26,399	21,881	
Labor Cost/Exp. Price	40.3%	49.8%	78.4%	
Sacking				
Unit Labor Cost	4,719	7,528	10,065	11.4%
Export Price	17,246	14,587	15,142	
Labor Cost/Exp. Price	27.4%	51.6%	66.5%	
CBC				
Unit Labor Cost	7,542	11,139	15,274	10.6%
Export Price	20,148	23,735	26,084	
Labor Cost/Exp. Price	37.4%	46.9%	58.6%	

Source: Bangladesh Jute Mills Association.

Linking wages to productivity can be achieved without using a complicated formula. In fact, setting a mechanical formula for wage determination is probably not feasible or desirable, and a less interventionist approach may be easier to implement. Public sector wages could be linked to productivity if the system of wage determination is changed to allow for collective bargaining at a decentralized level; no formula or complicated analysis would be needed. Well-functioning labor markets all over the world ensure that wages do not increase at faster rates than productivity over an extended period of time, and that workers benefit from productivity improvements. This result is achieved through negotiations between labor and management, even though productivity may never be explicitly mentioned in such negotiations. The firm's ability to pay is considered to be an important factor in any collective bargaining situation, and a clear constraint on wage demands. Ability to pay, usually measured in terms of profits, is a good proxy for factor productivity. As the productivity of a firm's factors of production (mainly labor and capital) increases, its profits will rise and vice versa. Thus, wage discussions can be viewed as a way of allocating the firms' value added between labor and capital, which involves a judgement of the relative productivities of the two factors. For example, if productivity improvements are mainly due to new capital investments, the firm's depreciation and interest costs will rise and less of the increase will be available for wages than if the productivity improvement were only due to labor and no new investments had occurred.

Low labor productivity is often due to factors beyond workers' control. Nevertheless, it is impossible to continue raising wages over the long term without considering productivity changes, as firms will simply reach a point where they are unable to meet their wage bills. Bangladesh's public sector provides many examples of such situations; several SOEs' wage bills exceed their value added contribution to GDP. Most of the public industrial units have low productivity due to over-staffing, mismanagement and inappropriate government policies. Yet, wages continued rising for social and political reasons. Losses, which resulted from de-linking wages and productivity, were financed by the Budget and the NCBs. The objective of labor market reforms in a country like Bangladesh should be to create more productive employment and to ensure that most of the jobs created are sustainable over the long run. This objective cannot be achieved if real wages are de-linked from productivity.

Towards an Efficient System of Wage Determination. The present centralized system of wage determination needs to be replaced by one that allows for decentralized collective bargaining and differential wage awards that reflect productivity changes. Decentralization should subject public sector managers and employees to the constraints and discipline of market forces.

There are three essential features of a competitive market that can lead to efficient wage and employment decisions. *First*, enterprises should be profit seeking and self-reliant, and not receive government subsides. *Second*, they should be able to borrow to finance investment needs or working capital requirements, but are expected to repay their loans plus interest. *Third*, the enterprise should face domestic or international competition on the product market, and should not be able to unilaterally raise its prices to mask inefficiencies. In the case of a natural monopoly, as in power or urban water supply, output prices are regulated. The combination of these features is necessary to ensure that enterprises are staffed and operated efficiently, employing only that amount of labor necessary to produce the desired output level. Employees would be paid only the amount needed to recruit, retain and motivate a satisfactory work force.

The above three conditions are missing in most SOEs in Bangladesh. Hence, immediately moving to complete de-centralization may lead to difficult transition problems, as has happened in the East European economies. Management and labor may collude to increase the wage bill, strip assets, and raise enterprise losses even further. SOEs are not profit maximizing. They face a soft budget constraint and finance losses through government subsidies or borrowing from NCBs, which they often do not repay. In some cases, they have high tariff protection that allows them to raise product prices. Thus, those enterprises are not under pressure to contain their wage bill, and leaving employment and wage decisions entirely to their managers and staff can lead to perverse results.

Over the medium-term, the solution is to change the environment within which SOEs operate and then completely decentralize wage decisions. In most cases a change in environment will automatically occur through privatization. For SOEs that remain in the public domain, management must face a hard budget constraint. A system of appropriate incentives needs to be introduced before employment and wage decisions are left entirely at the discretion of SOE management and staff.

Regulations Affecting Private Enterprises

In addition to public sector wage policies, Government policies have an important impact on the level of employment and competitiveness of private firms through minimum wage regulations, regulations affecting their ability to retrench workers, and regulations affecting the quality of industrial relations. Current legislation gives firms considerable flexibility, in principle, to restructure themselves by retrenching or laying-off workers. However, it imposes an extremely high cost on restructuring firms which may render them uncompetitive. Several well publicized general strikes, accompanied by country-wide labor agitations, have done serious damage to the image of industrial relations in Bangladesh. Thus, poor industrial relations, together with the law-and-order problems associated with it, are often cited as an important deterrent to the expansion of private investment.

Minimum Wage Regulations. Under the Minimum Wage Ordinance 1961, the National Minimum Wages Board (NMWB) has the duty to recommend minimum wages for sectors or groups of workers referred to it by Government. The idea is that minimum wages would be set for industries that do not have adequate machinery for the effective regulation of wages, i.e. well-functioning collective bargaining procedures. Currently there are 38 sectors covered by minimum wages, and adjustments to those sectoral minima are made very infrequently (usually every 5-10 years). The Board often recommends three different minima for unskilled, semi-skilled and skilled workers; and in some cases a fourth minimum is specified for highly-skilled workers. There is some evidence to suggest that minimum wages are binding, i.e., formal, recorded employment is affected by the minimum wage.[1] Minimum wages also lead to informal employment arrangements that circumvent the law, and are, therefore, not recorded in the employment statistics.

The latest NWPC recommended in 1993 that the present system be changed, and that sectoral minimum wages be replaced by a *national* minimum wage of Tk 900/month. This recommendation has not been implemented. If this recommendation were to be adopted it would imply a major change in the philosophy of government intervention in this area. Instead of intervening only to protect workers in situations where normal labor market mechanisms are not functioning properly, under this proposal the Government would intervene in all sectors regardless of the efficiency with which collective bargaining is carried out. Clearly, this recommendation, motivated by a desire to ensure a minimum subsistence level of wages, will conflict with the broad objectives of maintaining employment opportunities and enhancing competitiveness. Moreover, it could create serious problems as it does not cover workers who really need protection; would generate serious enforcement problems; would impose undue increases in costs on some of the economically weaker sectors; and would create a focus for labor management disputes at the national level.

---

[1] K. Anderson, N. Hossain and G.S. Sahota, "The Effect of Laws and Labor Practices on Employment and Industrialization in Bangladesh," *Bangladesh Development Studies*, Vol. XIX, March-June, 1991.

The coverage of the proposed national minimum wage will be limited to already privileged workers. The proposal is intended to apply to all workers in industry in the private sector employed in establishments with ten or more employees. That is, this minimum wage would cover 3-3.5 million workers in the formal private sector, while 41-43 million informal sector and day laborers will continue to have no protection whatsoever. Wages in the informal sector tend to be a small fraction of formal wages, and informal sector workers do not enjoy job security and other benefits that are available to their formal sector colleagues. Hence, the NWPC's proposal is not for a truly national minimum wage, and the proposal cannot achieve its objective of providing a safety net for the lowest income groups. Moreover, it should be noted that the objective of ensuring a minimum level of earning can conflict with the desire of increasing employment as rising labor costs may discourage some firms from expanding.

There is a widespread agreement that the system of enforcement of existing minimum wage provisions in Bangladesh is seriously defective; and hence the national minimum proposed by the NWPC may be unenforceable. In a recent survey covering 166 industrial enterprises, only 47 percent of the sample stated that they adhere to minimum wage regulations. The remaining 53 percent apparently do not concern themselves with this issue, and more than likely enter into contractual arrangements that effectively bypass the minimum wage law and are not recorded in the official statistics. Laws that are not implemented bring the legal process into disrepute and impose unnecessary costs (in the form of rents) on economic agents. The existence of minimum wage provisions can be expected to have some effect even if they are not enforced. Outside investors may expect them to be enforced and base their investment decisions on labor costs based on minimum wage provisions. If a "national" minimum wage were introduced, the question of enforcement will become even more problematic than it is now.

There is always a tradeoff between extending the coverage of minimum wage regulations and the sustainable minimum level. The broader the coverage and the larger the number of additional establishments and workers brought in, the lower would be the viable level of the national minimum wage, if undue increases in costs are not to be imposed on some of the economically weaker sectors currently excluded from Wage Orders. The NWPC proposal of a Tk 900/month minimum wage would impose important increases in costs even on some firms that are currently covered by sectoral minimum wages. For example, it would imply that minimum wages in tea gardens would more than double, that minimum wages in garments would increase by 44 percent and that minimum wages in glass and silicate would rise by 43 percent.

The proposal for a national minimum wage would make the wage determination process even more politicized. If a national minimum wage were established there will, naturally, be periodic pressures to revise it upwards. The existence of a national minimum wage would provide a focus for political pressures, particularly from trade unions with relatively weak collective bargaining strength. It is likely that political parties will also seek the opportunity to gain political advantage by calling for an increase in the national minimum wage. Such politicization would not help achieve wage levels consistent with employment generation and competitiveness. Moreover, it would lead to a further deterioration in industrial relations.

Regulations Affecting Firm Restructuring. Labor market flexibility, which mainly refers to the ability to lay-off or retrench workers, is essential for industrial competitiveness and growth. Economies are continuously subject to the strains of restructuring. In particular, firms operating in the international market must always search for ways of reducing costs and becoming more competitive. Cost reductions often involve retrenching workers, who would eventually find new jobs in an expanding economy.

Bangladesh's labor laws offer sufficient flexibility to firms, but impose a relatively high cost of restructuring. The Employment of Labor (Standing Orders) Act, 1965, allows employers to terminate employment provided they give the worker 120 days' notice or payment in lieu, and a gratuity equal to one month's basic wages (plus any dearness allowance) for each completed year of service. This clearly permits dismissals or retrenchment on grounds of redundancy. Moreover, workers can be laid-off provided they are paid half of the total of basic wage plus dearness allowance, and the full amount of housing allowance, if any, that would have been payable to them had they not been laid off. Employers also contribute 8.3 percent of workers' salaries to a Provident Fund. By an executive order, the gratuity for retrenched and retiring workers from SOEs was raised to two months' pay per year of service. Recently, the contribution to provident fund was also raised for SOE workers to 10 percent. These increases have a spillover effect in the private sector.

These high costs of restructuring put Bangladesh firms at a disadvantage vs. international competitors, and may discourage them from expanding employment when demand for their product is rising. The gratuity and provident fund contribution imply that the total cost of retrenchment in Bangladesh is 25 percent of basic pay plus dearness allowance for each year of service. This is high by international standards. In Sri Lanka, employers are required to make a contribution of 12 percent of the employees' wage to the provident fund, and an additional 3 percent to the employees' trust fund. Gratuity payable to workers who have worked for a minimum period of 5 years is half a month's pay per year of service. These termination benefits in Sri Lanka add up to only 19 percent of wages per year of service. In Turkey, the gratuity is equal to one month's wages for each year of service, half of that provided by Bangladesh for SOE workers.

It is very difficult to consider reductions in retrenchment costs borne by employers without the introduction of alternative safety net protection for displaced workers, which will have to be financed by the Government. The Government should consider lowering the gratuity over the medium-term to comparable levels that prevail in other countries (in Bangladesh itself it was one month per year of service in the mid-eighties), but simultaneously introduce alternative safety net programs for workers to protect them after restructuring and to render this change socially acceptable. Under its jute adjustment program, the Government has prepared a social safety net program for retrenched workers (Box 4.3), and the experience gained from this should help to extend the safety net to other sectors.

Regulations Affecting Industrial Relations. Harmonious labor-management relations can contribute to faster and more competitive industrial growth, as it enables employers and labor to strike a balance between the need of the enterprise to be competitive and the workers' aspirations for wage growth. This can lead to better motivation and the acceptance of short-term sacrifices to achieve medium-term benefits. The system of industrial relations in Bangladesh does not generally succeed in achieving this cooperation, and many entrepreneurs consider poor industrial relations, and law and order problems linked to it, to be a key factor discouraging them from investing and expanding their operations.

The labor movement in Bangladesh is characterized by a large number of unions, a small percentage of unionized workers, and a division at the national level into many labor federations associated with different political parties. The number of trade unions has been increasing steadily since independence, reaching 4,065 registered unions in 1992 with a total membership of around 1.6 million workers. That is, only 3.5 percent of the total labor force and 33 percent of the formal sector workers belong to labor unions, and the average size of a union is only 400 members. The unions are organized at the national level into 23 federations, 14 of those federations are associated with 11 political parties.

According to data provided by the Directorate of Labor, there were only 11 industrial disputes in 1992, they were all for economic reasons, and they led to a loss in production valued at only Tk 86 million. However, this data does not show the overall picture of disruptions caused by politicization, as it concerns only disputes arising under the Industrial Relations Ordinance (IRO), it does not include those growing number of strikes which take place outside the framework of the Industrial Relations Ordinance. For example, there were several well-publicized cases of disruptions, (due to inter-union rivalries) that are not captured by this data. Moreover, this information is inconsistent with industrial surveys which indicate that labor unrest and law and order problems are considered to be a serious deterrent to private sector development.

Box 4.3: Safety Net for Retrenched Workers in the Bangladesh Jute Industry, 1994-96

The Government has prepared a safety net program for retrenched workers in the jute industry that includes separation benefits and retraining. Under the current legislation, employees in the public sector are entitled to receive separation benefits of two months of basic wages for every year in service. In the jute mills, the separation benefits would vary from Tk 100,000 (US$2,600) to Tk 500,000 (US$13,000) depending on the number of years in service and the nature of employment. Employees who decide to leave the mills which are scheduled for privatization, and employees whose services are not required by the new mill owners, will also be eligible for these benefits.

Approximately 16,000 employees are expected to be retrenched as a result of the closure and downsizing of public sector mills during FY93-95. A program, to be implemented over a three-year period beginning in January 1994, has been developed to retrain them for alternative employment. The program will rely on existing NGO and Government-sponsored training systems. The chosen NGO would set up a Jute Training Resource Center (JTRC) in Dhaka and Khulna. The program would involve employee counseling within the mills and various options for retraining through JTRC.

Upon the completion of counseling, each employee would apply to JTRC for retraining. JTRC, in turn, would coordinate with the selected training organizations to arrange the training programs. The following is a brief description of the training options:

(a) Option 1 - No Services Required. If desired, the individual employee may choose to take full separation benefits and retire or seek other employment outside the sector. It is expected that at least 50 percent of the retrenched workers would take this option.

(b) Option 2 - Skill Training. Under this option, the employee would take full separation benefits and also participate in a 3-4 month skill training program and seek employment outside of the jute sector with newly acquired skills. When the participant chooses this option, he would be provided with a list of about 20 training courses for his selection. He would be required to pay Tk 4,000 (US$100) toward the cost of training prior to participating in the training course. It is estimated that this option could accommodate at least 5,000 employees (31%). The Government will be under no obligation to guarantee employment to the workers participating in the training program.

(c) Option 3 - Self-Employment Training. In this option, the employee would take the full separation benefit and also participate in a six-week self-employment course to assist him in planning for self-employment. The employee would be required to pay Tk 4,000 (US$100) of the cost of training prior to participating in the training course. The course would be conducted by the JTRC. During the course, the affected employee would also be assisted in the preparation of simple business plans and would receive some training in basic management, finance, accounting and sales, etc.

Source: Staff analysis.

Trade union multiplicity and politicization, which are manifestations of the same phenomenon, are not conducive to sound industrial relations. The importance of SOEs in industry, and the direct involvement of Government in their management through civil servants is one of the causes of this unhealthy phenomenon. Because of the centralization of managerial authority in the public sector, trade unions are unable to pursue their objectives (e.g. wage improvements) through the normal machinery of industrial relations. Under these circumstances, it is quite natural that trade unions become dependent on political parties in trying to achieve their objectives. Thus, the plurality of political parties is reflected in the structure of the trade union movement. Moreover, the efficiency of different political parties in satisfying union demands explains the fact that the unions affiliated with the ruling political party of the time tend to dominate the trade union movement. The National Labor Law Commission is examining the factors relating to union multiplicity.

So long as industrial relations at the plant level involve Government (rather than management) and unions as the main actors, the work place will continue to be the scene of proxy wars among different political parties through their respective unions. Privatization would help resolve this problem, as it would imply that a smaller proportion of the labor force would be directly affected by Government labor market activities. Similarly, measures to de-centralize the wage determination process for those enterprises that will remain in the public domain would help further de-politicize industrial relations.

Strengthening the position of CBAs would also help improve industrial relations, because inter-union rivalries mostly result from attacks launched by minority unions on the position of the CBA. This could be achieved through amendments to the IRO. The IRO provides that a CBA remains in that position for two years following its designation, and that it will have the exclusive right to undertake collective bargaining, represent workers in any proceedings and declare strikes. In theory, therefore, there are no means available under the law for other trade unions to challenge the CBA during those two years. The fact that CBAs nevertheless come under attack, often through violent means, seems to point to the need for further tightening of the law with the aim of providing them with enhanced protection. This could be achieved by introducing two changes to the IRO. First, the list of unfair labor practices on the part of employers could be expanded to include employers' acquiescence in dealing with trade unions which are not CBAs, on matters on which the CBAs only are entitled to negotiate. In many cases of inter-union rivalries, management, usually for political reasons, sides with the challenging union and fails to protect the CBA and maintain established industrial relations. Second, the list of unfair labor practices on the part of workers could also include non-CBA unions pressuring employers to deal with them on matters reserved for the CBA. It would also be desirable to make clear in the IRO that a non-CBA trade union has the right to represent its members only in individual grievances, which should be settled without resort to industrial action. Appropriate penalties for failure to abide by those regulations should be specified and enforced.

Bangladesh has tried to promote better labor-management relations by fiat, without much success. The IRO provides for the establishment of a "Participation Committee", consisting of management and labor representatives, in every firm employing 50 or more workers. The objective of those committees was defined in very general terms with a view to promoting better labor-management relations. Very few such committees actually operate, and hence this provision did not succeed in promoting cooperation at the plant level. Neither the unions nor management were interested in the success of those committees. CBAs are suspicious that the committee would encroach on their exclusive right to represent workers. Employers are wary that unions would use the committee to interfere with their managerial prerogatives, and that CBAs would dominate the committees and use them as another channel to pursue their demands.

The Government has also tried to promote tripartite consultations at the national level, but its efforts have not improved industrial relations. The Tripartite Consultative Committee (TCC) and the Tripartite Productivity Committee (TPC) are national organizations that aim at increasing labor-management cooperation. However, those institutions are not contributing effectively to the creation of consensus or to the diffusion of tension. Apparently, this failure is mainly due to the dominance of Government in those institutions. For example, representatives of public sector corporations, who are civil servants, sit as employers in the TCC. Thus, little dialogue between private employers and trade unions actually takes place in these fora.

As a result of the ineffectiveness of the established machinery for tripartite consultation, the alliance of the main national trade union federations (SKOP) has, for the past decade, sought to negotiate with Government directly outside the existing legal framework. In order to force Government to accept negotiations or agree to concessions, SKOP has often resorted to well-publicized general strikes accompanied by country-wide agitations, resulting in significant economic losses and serious damage to the image of industrial relations in Bangladesh.

This state of affairs needs to be changed. In spite of past failures, the Government should renew its efforts to promote cooperation and consultation, focussing mainly at the enterprise level. Joint consultation is best promoted as a voluntary exercise based on collective bargaining. In this case, it would function as an extension of collective bargaining to new subjects such as work organization and quality control. Normally the parties to joint consultation are the same as those who have signed the collective agreement: the CBA and the employer. Joint consultation established voluntarily by collective agreements would be more acceptable to employers and unions than that established under legislative compulsion. Their participation in formulating the consultative machinery would reduce their fear of losing certain prerogatives.

Government should play a promotional and supportive role. Existing tripartite organizations, particularly the TPC, could become more instrumental for the promotion of joint consultation if they became genuinely tripartite; that is, if the representation and role of private employers and unions is increased and that of government officials and public sector corporation managers reduced. The role of the National Productivity Organization (NPO) could be expanded to include support to voluntary consultations at the plant level. It could provide advice and training to employers and unions on ways of promoting consultation. However, for the NPO to succeed in this mission it will need to be staffed by experts in industrial relations, productivity and enterprise management.

An efficient system for settling labor disputes is a pre-requisite for harmonious industrial relations. The existing framework in Bangladesh is generally regarded as ineffective; because conciliation rarely succeeds in resolving disputes and the labor courts are extremely slow. Between 1987 and 1991, conciliation was able to settle only 3 labor disputes that had led to work stoppage, which is in sharp contrast with the situation prevailing in most other countries where the vast majority of industrial disputes are settled through conciliation. The ineffectiveness of conciliation is due to the pervasive role that Government plays in the labor market (which implies that most disputes require a political solution), as well as to the relatively low status given to conciliators. The performance of the adjudication machinery before the labor courts is also far from satisfactory. On average, labor courts receive between 5 and 6 thousand cases every year, but they only adjudicate 2-3 thousand. Thus, the number of labor disputes pending before the courts is increasing rapidly by more than 3 thousand a year (Table 4.11). This situation is clearly untenable.

Government should take steps to improve the efficiency of conciliation and the labor courts. In order to improve conciliation Government must, as much as possible, leave employers and trade unions to settle their differences with minimal political intervention. Parties to industrial disputes should be encouraged to request the assistance of conciliators rather than seek political solutions. Concomitantly, efforts should be made to strengthen the Directorate of Labor, which is responsible for conciliation services, and raise the quality and status of conciliators. Delays in Labor Courts are due to

Table 4.11: The Number of Cases Handled by Labor Courts

Year	No. Received	No. Disposed	Increase in Unresolved Cases
1986	5,256	1,641	3,615
1987	5,732	2,038	3,694
1988	5,538	1,663	3,875
1989	5,338	1,988	3,350
1990	5,499	1,758	3,741
1991	5,264	2,364	2,900

Source: Employers' Association, Dhaka.

lengthy procedures, and the ability of any party to the dispute to postpone action by simply failing to attend the proceedings. The Government should consider simplifying procedures as much as possible with the objective of expediting the resolution of pending cases.

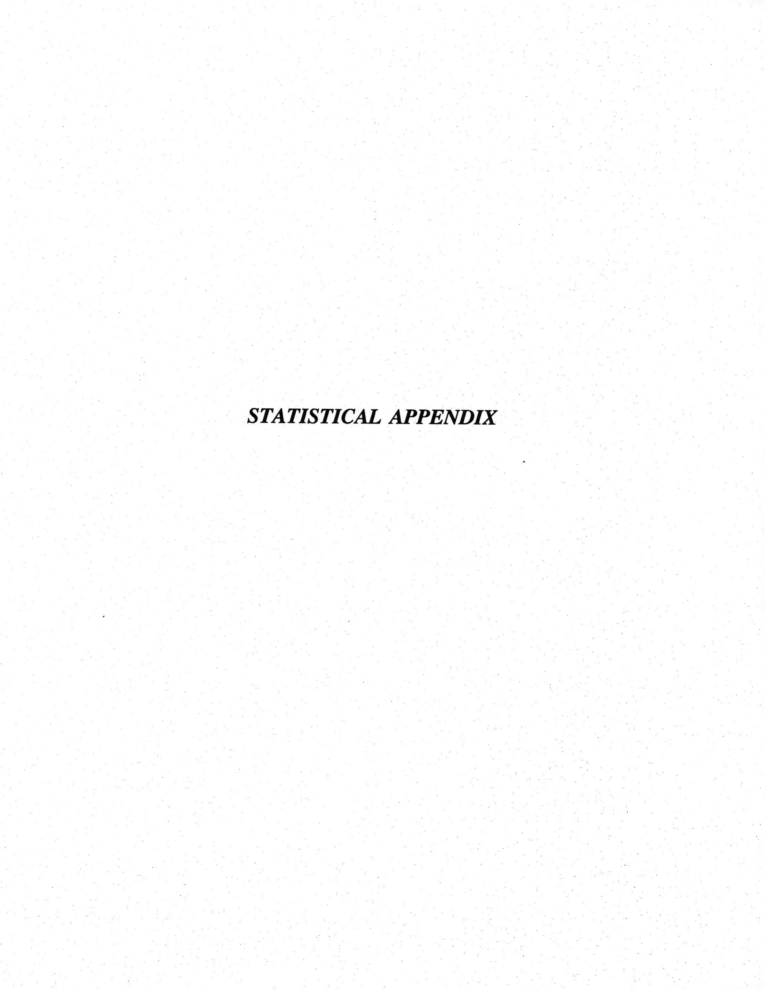

STATISTICAL APPENDIX

STATISTICAL APPENDIX

Table 1.1
BANGLADESH POPULATION PROJECTIONS ('000)
Projection with NRR = 1 by 2010

AGE GROUP	1990	1995	2000	2005	2010	2015	2020	2025
TOTAL M+F	108275	119401	130512	141306	151211	160787	170385	179659
MALES								
0-4	8287	8092	8161	8059	7665	7665	7874	7945
5-9	8146	7978	7847	7968	7914	7542	7556	7778
10-14	7378	8045	7891	7776	7909	7862	7497	7517
15-19	6283	7276	7944	7804	7702	7841	7801	7445
20-24	5242	6149	7132	7804	7683	7593	7742	7713
25-29	4331	5099	5993	6972	7652	7547	7473	7634
30-34	3665	4202	4957	5846	6826	7508	7420	7361
35-39	2626	3544	4072	4821	5706	6679	7363	7291
40-44	2161	2522	3414	3936	4679	5553	6515	7199
45-49	1827	2056	2405	3269	3784	4511	5369	6315
50-54	1541	1713	1931	2267	3094	3594	4298	5131
55-59	1304	1409	1568	1775	2094	2870	3347	4019
60-64	1037	1146	1241	1387	1579	1872	2581	3027
65-69	753	857	950	1034	1164	1335	1595	2216
70-74	513	567	648	723	793	902	1046	1263
75+	580	575	611	684	774	874	1007	1184
TOTAL	55676	61230	66765	72154	77018	81749	84686	91040
FEMALES								
0-4	8027	7844	7900	7789	7398	7388	7580	7638
5-9	7746	7747	7627	7733	7669	7296	7298	7500
10-14	6894	7646	7663	7561	7682	7623	7257	7265
15-19	6033	6784	7542	7576	7492	7619	7569	7212
20-24	4968	5886	6639	7407	7465	7394	7532	7493
25-29	4107	4813	5725	6486	7268	7339	7284	7435
30-34	3440	3966	4667	5579	6349	7131	7217	7177
35-39	2486	3313	3835	4535	5446	6213	6994	7094
40-44	2055	2385	3192	3712	4411	5310	6073	6852
45-49	1756	1962	2286	3073	3590	4276	5162	5918
50-54	1464	1657	1858	2176	2940	3445	4117	4984
55-59	1177	1355	1540	1737	2045	2775	3265	3917
60-64	910	1052	1219	1396	1586	1878	2563	3033
65-69	645	771	898	1049	1214	1391	1662	2287
70-74	432	501	604	711	842	986	1145	1385
75+	458	488	553	663	799	973	1182	1427
TOTAL	52599	58171	63748	69182	74193	79308	83899	88619

	1990	1995	2000	2005	2010	2015	2020	2025
Birth Rate		31.4	28.3	25.2	22	20.5	19.7	18.7
Death Rate		11.2	9.9	8.9	8.1	7.9	7.9	8.0
Rate of Nat'l. Inc.		2.02	1.84	1.63	1.39	1.25	1.17	1.07
Net Migration Rate		-0.6	-0.6	-0.4	-0.3	-0.2	-0.1	-0.1
Growth Rate		1.96	1.78	1.59	1.36	1.23	1.16	1.06
Total Fertility		4.000	3.391	2.874	2.436	2.280	2.258	2.236
NRR		1.572	1.382	1.212	1.058	1.000	1.000	1.000
e(0) - Both Sexes		55.48	57.62	59.89	62.19	63.37	64.58	65.83
e(15) - Both Sexes		49.92	50.63	51.56	52.65	53.43	54.24	55.07
IMR - Both Sexes		90.9	77.5	64.9	53.8	49.2	44.7	40.1
q(5) - Both Sexes		0.129	0.108	0.0885	0.0711	0.0651	0.0591	0.0530
Dep. Ratio	85.4	74.3	64.9	57.8	52.1	47.6	44.8	44.6

Source: World Bank.

Table 1.2
POPULATION BENCHMARKS BY DISTRICT
(thousands)

Division District	1961 Census	1974 Census	1981 Census					1974-to-1981 Growth Rat	1991 Census a/				
			Total	Male	Female	Households	Average HH Size		Total	Male	Female	Households	Average HH Size
Rajshahi	11850	17332	21087	10789	10298	3716	5.7	2.8	26668	13642	13026	5053	5.3
Dinajpur	1710	2571	3198	1647	1551	580	5.5	3.2	4044	2080	1964	777	5.2
Rangpur	3796	5447	6490	3325	3165	1196	5.4	2.5	8155	4155	4000	1594	5.1
Bogra	1574	2231	2718	1384	1334	489	5.6	2.9	3460	1776	1684	685	5.0
Rajshahi	2811	4268	5263	2677	2586	894	5.9	3.0	6705	3417	3288	1241	5.4
Pabna	1959	2815	3418	1756	1662	557	6.1	2.8	4305	2214	2091	756	5.7
Khulna	10067	14195	17150	8831	8319	2884	5.9	2.7	20804	10645	10159	3807	5.5
Kushtia	1166	1884	2273	1167	1106	359	6.3	2.7	2865	1475	1391	521	5.5
Jessore	2190	3327	4016	2069	1947	633	6.3	2.7	5006	2568	2438	887	5.6
Khulna	2449	3557	4353	2264	2089	741	5.9	2.7	5279	2711	2568	974	5.4
Barisal	3068	3928	4668	2398	2270	830	5.6	2.7	4092	2077	2015	771	5.3
Patuakhali	1194	1499	1840	933	907	321	5.7	2.7	3580	1814	1766	654	5.5
Dhaka	15294	21317	26249	13632	12616	4643	5.7	3	33593	17460	16133	6377	5.3
Jamalpur	1449	2059	2445	1241	1204	452	5.4	2.5	3085	1578	1507	643	4.8
Mymensing	4083	5508	6543	3355	3188	1208	5.4	2.5	8035	4090	3945	1565	5.1
Tangail	1487	2078	2444	1243	1200	420	5.8	2.3	3044	1545	1500	586	5.2
Dhaka	5096	7612	10049	5376	4673	1705	5.9	4.0	13817	7397	6420	2544	5.4
Faridpur	3179	4060	4768	2417	2351	858	5.6	2.3	5612	2850	2762	1039	5.4
Chittagong	13630	18635	22565	11597	10968	3892	5.8	2.8	28811	14752	14059	4950	5.8
Sylhet	3490	4759	5650	2897	2753	966	5.8	2.5	7052	3588	3464	1184	6.0
Comilla	4389	5819	6880	3481	3399	1203	5.7	2.4	8652	4361	4291	1485	5.8
Noakhali	2383	3234	3813	1899	1914	680	5.6	2.4	4884	2435	2449	853	5.7
Chittagong	2983	4315	5476	2913	2563	906	6.0	3.5	7195	3814	3381	1225	5.9
Chittagong	385	508	746	407	339	137	5.4	5.6	1028	554	473	202	5.1
TOTAL	50841	71479	87051	44849	42201	15135	5.8	2.9	109877	56500	53377	20187	5.4

Note: Data shown represent actual census results, not adjusted for probable undercounting.
The adjusted 1981 Census estimate of total population is 89,940,000 for the Census date of March 8, 1981.

a/ District wise population of Bangladesh (adjusted). Supplement No. 1 to the Preliminary Report on Population Census, June 1992.
Source: Bangladesh Bureau of Statistics.

Table 1.3
VITAL POPULATION STATISTICS

	1981	1982	1983	1984	1985	1986	1987	1988	1989	1990	1991	1992
CRUDE DEATH RATE [per thousand]												
National	11.5	12.2	12.3	12.3	12.0	11.9	11.5	11.3	11.4	11.3	11.0	11.0
Rural	12.2	12.8	13.2	12.9	12.9	12.3	11.8	11.8	12.0	11.8	11.5	11.3
Urban	7.2	6.9	7.5	8.5	8.3	8.4	7.6	7.4	7.3	7.9	7.3	7.5
INFANT MORTALITY RATES [per thousand]												
National	111.5	121.9	117.5	121.8	112.0	116.0	113.0	110.0	98.0	94.0	90.6	88.0
Rural	112.5	123.2	120.8	122.0	113.0	118.0	115.0	112.0	105.0	97.0	94.4	91.0
Urban	99.4	103.0	98.8	119.5	99.0	101.0	95.0	91.0	84.0	71.0	69.3	65.0
Male	113.4	124.1	118.8	113.5	114.2	122.0	120.0	116.0	102.0	98.0	94.4	90.0
Female	109.4	119.4	116.0	109.3	109.0	111.0	105.0	105.0	95.0	91.6	86.8	86.0
LIFE EXPECTANCY AT BIRTH [years]												
National	54.8	54.5	53.9	54.8	55.1	55.2	56.4	56.0	56.0	56.0	56.1	56.3
Rural	54.3	53.9	53.1	54.4	54.7	54.8	56.1	55.4	55.0	55.4	55.8	56.0
Urban	60.1	60.6	60.3	58.7	60.1	58.8	60.0	60.9	61.0	60.5	60.0	60.5
Male	55.3	54.4	54.2	54.9	55.7	55.2	55.6	57.0	56.0	56.3	56.5	56.8
Female	54.4	54.8	53.6	54.7	54.6	55.9	54.9	56.0	55.6	55.6	55.6	55.9
CRUDE BIRTH RATE [per thousand]												
National	34.6	34.8	35.0	34.8	34.6	34.4	33.3	33.2	33.0	32.8	31.7	31.4
Rural	35.7	36.9	36.4	36.1	35.3	35.4	34.6	34.5	34.2	34.3	32.9	32.2
Urban	24.8	22.9	27.1	25.0	28.0	25.9	24.8	24.9	24.3	24.6	23.9	23.7
FFERTILITY RATE [per woman]												
National	5.04	5.21	5.07	4.83	4.71	4.70	4.41	4.43	4.24	4.33	4.23	4.18
Rural	5.28	5.50	5.36	5.08	4.91	4.89	4.64	4.59	4.58	4.57	4.48	4.33
Urban	3.20	3.01	3.45	3.10	3.52	3.26	3.05	2.84	2.92	2.95	2.88	2.88

Source: Bangladesh Bureau of Statistics.

Table 1.4
COMPARISON OF CHILD NUTRITIONAL STATUS RESULTS FROM THREE NATIONAL SURVEYS

Indicator	INFS, 1975-76	INFS, 1981-82	BBS, 1985-86	HKI,1982-83	HKI, AUGUST 1990	BBS, 1985-86	BBS 1989-90	BBS 1992
Chronic malnutrition a/	73.7%	57.3%	(Weighted) 56.1% (National) 57.6% (Rural) 44.2% (Urban)	42.00% (Rural) - -	49.5% (National) 48.8% (Rural) 51.2% (Urban)	(Weighted) 56.1% (National) 57.6% (Rural) 44.2% (Urban)	(Weighted) 51.1% (National) 52.2% (Rural) 44.3% (Urban)	(Weighted) 45.7% (National) 46.8% (Rural) 37.5% (Urban)
Acute malnutrition a/	21.6%	20.0%	(Weighted) 8.1% (National) 8.2% (Rural) 6.9% (Urban)	6.0% (Rural) -	11.3% (National) 10.9% (Rural) 12.1% (Urban)	(Weighted) 8.1% (National) 8.2% (Rural) 6.9% (Urban)	(Weighted) 8.6% (National) 8.8% (Rural) 7.3% (Urban)	(Weighted) 7.0% (National) 7.2% (Rural) 5.5% (Urban)
Definitions of:								
Chronic malnutrition	< 90% median height for age	< 90% median height for age	< 90% median height for age	< 90% median height for age	< 90% median height for age	< 90% median height for age	< 90% median height for age	< 90% median height for age
Acute malnutrition	< 80% median weight for height	< 80% median weight for height	< 80% median weight for height	< 80% median weight for height also 2sd from median heightfor age & weight for height.	< 80% median weight for height	< 80% median weight for height	< 80% median weight for height	< 80% median weight for height
Actual sample size	430 cross-sectional	510 cross-sectional	3283 urban and rural cross-sectional; four data collection periods	Rural sub-set 2800 cross sectional.	1900 urban and 4590 rural children b/	3283 urban and rural cross-sectional; four data collection periods.	2356 urban and rural cross-sectional; four data collection periods	2110 urban & rural N.A.
Age range	0-59 months	0-59 months	6-71 months	3-71 months.	6-59 months	6-71 months	6-71 months	N.A.
Reference standard used	Harvard	Harvard	NCHS	NCHS	NCHS	NCHS	NCHS	NCHS
Population covered	Rural	Rural	Urban and rural	Urban and rural	Urban slum and rural	Urban and Rural	Urban and rural	Urban and rural

INFS = Institute of Nutrition and Food Sciences, Dhaka University.
BBS = Bangladesh Bureau of Statistics, National Nutrition Survey and Household
        Expenditure Survey.
HKI = Helen Keller International
a/ Shows percent rate among total population.
b/ Urban areas include urban slums only and rural areas include disaster prone areas only.
Note: The INFS surveys used the Harvard Standard as the international reference
        standard for comparison of child growth data while BBS used NCHS reference.
        Some variation in nutritional status would be accounted for by the different
        standards used. Random variation due to small sample sizes used by INFS are more
        likely to account for the differences in nutritional status found by the
        three surveys. The BBS survey sample was divided into four data collection
        periods over a year's time while INFS surveys collected data once during

Source: Bangladesh Bureau of Statistics.

Table 1.5
HEALTH STATISTICS

	1981	1982	1983	1984	1985	1986	1987	1988	1989	1990	1991
Hospitals (number)											
Government	512	544	560	568	596	600	608	608	608	608	610
Private	164	164	164	164	164	164	267	267	267	267	280
Hospital Beds (number)	23792	23907	25057	26641	27645	28077	33138	33334	33376	33376	34353
Government Dispensaries & Hospitals	19021	19136	20286	21870	22874	23306	26575	26871	26913	26913	27111
Private	4771	4771	4771	4771	4771	4771	6563	6463	6463	6463	7242
Registered Doctors (number)	10065	10333	11496	13500	14591	16090	16929	17475	18323	19387	21004
Registered Nurses & Midwives (number)	5975	7434	8588	9650	10817	12111	12837	13944	15091	15036	17368
Public Expenditure (Tk million) a/											
Revenue	932	1052	1382	1820	1920	2483	2985	3211	3600	3950	4308
ADP	742	808	1134	1293	908	1058	1102	3144	2310	3028	5267
Total Expenditures as % of GDP a/	0.63	0.64	0.72	0.75	0.61	0.67	0.69	0.96	0.90	0.95	1.30
Per Capita Expenditure (Tk) a/	18.28	20.31	26.29	31.38	27.81	34.02	38.34	59.62	54.17	62.47	65.71

a/ Fiscal year data , revised estimate.

Source: Bangladesh Bureau of Statistics.

Table 1.6
FAMILY PLANNING STATISTICS
[thousands]

	1980/81	1981/82	1982/83	1983/84	1984/85	1985/86	1986/87	1987/88	1988/89	1989/90	1990/91	1991/92	1992/93
Voluntary Sterilizations													
Tubectomies	232.50	235.08	274.84	336.50	232.39	116.42	140.63	97.17	130.94	141.95	97.40	92.13	63.20
Vasectomies	26.30	67.82	88.32	215.67	259.21	151.13	209.93	99.89	100.03	83.11	67.90	69.15	50.46
Total	258.79	302.91	363.16	552.17	491.60	267.55	350.56	197.06	230.97	225.06	165.30	161.28	113.66
Delivery of Contraceptive Devices													
IUDs	41.60	83.67	117.74	303.34	432.45	367.67	420.34	379.13	361.70	365.62	274.23	269.57	261.77
Pills (cycles)	8238	7751	8258	9726	11553	12137	15023	19100	24620	34346	42704	46629	63920
Condoms (doz.)	87112	93230	116821	131096	151940	135907	149236	166436	181976	198023	133798	159514	224134
EMKO	60.79	63.55	69.63	64.25	71.98	46.42	39.31	14.78	10.12	4.03	4.67	2.17	0.77
Injections	112.01	81.07	72.70	122.46	165.93	216.49	314.75	392.00	604.70	1257.58	1689.11	2254.78	2561.16
Foam tablets	5011	4126	5404	4385	3222	3125	3463	3890	4100	1547	25174	9258	1778
COUPLE-YEARS OF PROTECTION [thousands]													
By Sterilization a/													
Tubectomies	522	705	909	1155	1272	1261	1276	1245	1252	1269	1240	1208	1150
Vasectomies	319	355	408	583	784	857	981	983	984	969	940	915	874
Total	841	1060	1317	1738	2055	2118	2257	2228	2236	2238	2179	2123	2024
With Contraceptive Devices b/													
IUDs c/	122	169	236	469	760	900	1050	1114	1142	1165	1090	1032	984
Pills	543	517	551	648	770	809	1002	1273	1641	2290	2847	3109	4261
Condoms	581	622	779	874	1013	906	995	1108	1213	1320	892	1063	1494
EMKO	15	16	17	16	18	12	10	4	3	1	1	1	0
Injections	28	20	18	31	41	54	79	97	150	314	422	564	640
Foam tablets	33	28	36	29	21	21	23	26	27	10	168	62	12
Total	1322	1371	1637	2067	2625	2702	3159	3622	4175	5099	5420	5830	7392
Total	2130	2404	2918	3775	4680	4820	5416	5850	6411	7337	7599	7953	9416
Married Females Aged 15-49 d/	16097	16629	17179	17746	18332	18937	19562	20208	20875	21565	19946	20590	-
Apparent Contraceptive Rate e/	13.2	14.5	17.0	21.3	25.5	25.5	27.7	28.9	30.7	34.0	38.1	38.6	-

a/ Cumulative, assuming year-to-year carry-over of 90%.
b/ Assuming one couple-year of protection per 15 cycles of pills, 150 condoms or foam tablets, or 4 doses of injectables or vials of EMKO.
c/ Cumulative, assuming year-to-year carry-over of 70%.
d/ Staff estimates based on age-specific marriage rates from 1981 census.
e/ Couple-years of protection per married female aged 15-49.

Sources: MIS, Directorate of Family Planning, Bangladesh Bureau of Statistics, and staff estimates.

Table 1.7

DISTRIBUTION OF POPULATION BY ECONOMIC ACTIVITIES

(in million)

	1984/85			1985/86			1989		
	Male	Female	Total	Male	Female	Total	Male	Female	Total
1. National									
Population aged 10 years and above	34.30	33.10	67.40	36.00	34.40	70.40	36.70	34.10	70.80
Economic participation:									
Civilian labor force	26.80	2.70	29.50	27.60	3.20	30.80	29.80	20.90	50.70
- Employed	26.40	2.60	29.00	27.40	3.10	30.50	29.40	20.70	50.10
- Unemployed	0.40	0.20	0.60	0.20	0.10	0.30	0.40	0.20	0.60
Other	7.50	30.20	37.80	8.40	31.00	39.20	6.80	13.30	21.10
- Household work	0.10	24.70	24.80	0.00	24.90	24.90	..	..	..
- Inactive	7.40	5.50	13.00	8.40	6.10	14.30	..	..	..
2. Rural									
Population aged 10 years and above	29.40	29.00	58.40	30.70	30.00	60.70	31.00	28.90	59.90
Economic participation:									
Civilian labor force	23.20	2.20	25.40	23.60	2.60	26.20	25.60	19.50	45.10
- Employed	22.90	2.10	25.00	23.40	2.50	25.90	25.30	19.30	44.60
- Unemployed	0.30	0.10	0.40	0.20	0.10	0.30	0.30	0.20	0.50
Other	6.40	26.70	33.00	6.90	27.50	34.30	5.40	9.40	14.80
- Household work	0.10	22.10	22.20	0.00	22.40	22.40	..	..	..
- Inactive	6.30	4.60	10.80	6.90	5.10	11.90	..	..	..
3. Urban									
Population aged 10 years and above	4.90	3.90	8.80	5.40	4.20	9.60	5.80	5.10	10.90
Economic participation:									
Civilian labor force	3.70	0.40	4.10	4.00	0.60	4.70	4.20	1.50	5.70
- Employed	3.60	0.40	4.00	4.00	0.60	4.60	4.10	1.40	5.50
- Unemployed	0.10	0.00	0.10	0.00	0.00	0.10	0.10	0.10	0.20
Other	1.20	3.40	4.70	1.30	3.60	4.90	1.60	3.60	5.20
- Household work	0.00	2.50	2.50	0.00	2.50	2.50	..	..	..
- Inactive	1.20	0.90	2.20	1.30	1.10	2.40	..	..	..

.. Not available separately.

Source: LFS 1984/85, 1985/86 and 1989, BBS.

Table 1.8
EMPLOYMENT BY OCCUPATION AND BY SEX a/
(thousands)

Occupation	1983/84			1984/85			1985/86			1989		
	Male	Female	Total	Male	Female	Total	Male	Female	Total	Male	Female	Total
Professional & Technical	623	78	701	554	82	636	878	112	990	1129	340	1469
Administrative	182	3	185	218	4	222	281	4	285	149	8	157
Clerical	639	40	679	810	139	949	816	101	917	897	74	971
Sales	2876	134	3010	3246	112	3358	3417	128	3545	3584	122	3706
Services	916	117	2033	781	1151	1932	769	1215	1984	783	679	1462
Agriculture, Forestry, Fishery	16213	216	16429	16474	238	16712	17123	355	17478	18251	18755	37006
Production & Transport	3795	771	4566	4116	763	4879	3966	1109	5075	4589	781	5370
NEC	303	69	372	231	58	289	194	94	288	4	3	7
Total	25547	2428	27975	26430	2547	28977	27444	3118	30562	29386	20762	50148

a/ Labor force includes population above 10 years of age.

Source: LFS 1983/84, 1984/85, 1985/86 and 1989 BBS.

Table 1.9

INCOME DISTRIBUTION AND POVERTY INDICATORS

		1973/74	1981/82	1983/84	1985/86	1988/89
I. Income Distribution:						
Percent of income accruing to:						
Bottom 40%	- Rural	19.10	18.82	19.24	19.95	18.02
	Urban	17.80	16.07	17.84	19.20	17.52
	National	18.30	17.36	18.95	19.35	17.53
Lower middle 40%	- Rural	38.40	38.77	38.06	36.21	-
	Urban	38.00	36.02	37.91	37.87	-
	National	-	37.32	37.67	35.80	-
Upper middle 15%	- Rural	26.50	25.64	24.56	23.71	-
	Urban	26.60	27.01	27.79	26.10	-
	National		26.37	25.09	24.67	-
Top 5%	- Rural	16.00	16.78	18.14	21.36	19.81
	Urban	18.60	20.89	16.93	18.04	20.02
	National	16.40	18.95	18.30	21.35	20.51
Gini Coefficient	- Rural	0.35	0.36	0.35	0.36	0.37
	Urban	0.38	0.41	0.37	0.37	0.38
	National	0.36	0.39	0.36	0.37	0.38
II. Poverty Incidence:						
Percent of population with daily calorie intake per person below:						
2122 calories	- Rural	83	74	57	51	48
	Urban	81	66	66	56	44
	National	92	73	58	52	47
1805 calories	- Rural	44	52	38	22	30
	Urban	29	31	35	19	21
	National	48	50	38	22	27
Numbers of people with daily calorie intake per person below (millions):						
2122 calories	- Rural	57.4	60.9	47.0	44.2	40.5
	Urban	5.6	6.4	7.1	7.0	10.8
	National	63.0	67.3	54.1	51.2	51.3
1805 calories	- Rural	30.7	43.1	31.3	19.1	24.9
	Urban	2.0	3.0	3.8	2.4	5.0
	National	32.7	46.1	35.1	21.5	29.9
Total population	- Rural	61.7	82.3	82.5	86.6	84.4 a/
	Urban	6.9	9.7	10.7	12.5	24.5 a/
	National	68.6	92.0	93.2	99.1	108.9 a/

a/ The derived total population is inconsistent with those in the HES (FY89, p.47) which
 indicate a total population of 104 million of which 90.8 million in rural and
 13.2 in urban. The latter will, however, result in poverty incidence indicators
 substantially different from the HES estimates.

Source: BBS, Household Expenditure Surveys.

Table 1.10
SCHOOL ATTENDANCE AND ADULT LITERACY RATE, 1991

	Age Group			
	5-9	10-14	15-19	20-24

A. School Attendance a/

BANGLADESH
Both	41.0	54.2	28.4	9.9
Male	42.3	56.0	35.8	16.6
Female	40.0	52.3	20.7	4.1

RURAL
Both	39.2	52.1	25.5	7.8
Male	40.6	54.0	33.8	14.4
Female	37.7	49.8	17.0	2.5

URBAN
Both	49.9	62.8	38.2	16.3
Male	50.8	64.0	42.6	22.5
Female	48.9	61.4	33.6	9.7

B. Adult Literacy Rate

National	35.32
Rural	31.12
Urban	54.43
Male	44.31
Female	18.57

a/ School attendance of population 5-24 years of age.
Source: Bangladesh Bureau of Statistics.

Table 2.1
GROSS DOMESTIC PRODUCT AT CURRENT PRICES
(Taka Million)

	1982/83	1983/84	1984/85	1985/86	1986/87	1987/88	1988/89	1989/90	1990/91	1991/92	1992/93
Agriculture	116418	148403	169970	188382	219761	231623	245392	271790	300596	312438	321088
Crops	95071	120009	135031	139489	164975	167646	176467	194211	217823	222451	224850
Forestry	7665	10947	10948	18981	20544	25374	24187	26529	28639	31005	32442
Livestock	6741	8053	11785	15401	16222	17875	21266	25300	26564	28115	30347
Fisheries	6941	9394	12206	14511	18020	20728	23472	25750	27570	30867	33449
Industry	49403	57771	64982	72337	80019	89639	101593	116529	131375	150306	165226
Mining and Quarrying a/	3	4	4	3	4	3	4	89	112	134	141
Manufacturing	32760	37733	40112	43563	47631	50437	55608	64506	72801	82571	91030
Large Scale	16808	20543	21282	23380	26911	28517	31414	37565	42259	49347	56126
Small Scale	15952	17190	18830	20183	20720	21920	24194	26941	30542	33224	34904
Construction	15028	18095	22518	26058	28839	34602	39262	43110	47261	53590	57166
Power, Gas Water and Sanitary Services	1612	1939	2348	2713	3545	4597	6719	8824	11201	14011	16889
Services	127606	146342	171981	205508	239421	275874	312613	349252	402421	443758	482490
Transport, Storage and	39866	41797	45655	54605	61901	65945	71774	75061	97697	108672	113395
Trade Services	26950	30813	38816	41505	45883	50396	55015	61583	68279	73766	78575
Housing Services	22257	28558	32444	37066	40988	49982	59866	66358	73867	79055	87209
Public Admn. & Defense	8733	8934	13235	17366	20867	24735	29203	32764	38191	43406	49020
Banking and Insurance	4341	5152	6889	8935	10116	11435	13126	15110	16299	17793	19426
Professional and Misc. Services	25459	31088	34942	46031	59666	73381	83629	98376	108088	121066	134865
GDP at Market Prices	293427	352516	406933	466227	539201	597136	659598	737571	834392	906502	968804
Growth Rate (%)	12.71	20.14	15.44	14.57	15.65	10.74	10.46	11.82	13.13	8.64	6.87
Indirect Taxes - Subsidies	..	..	21794	25516	30082	32695	37601	41807	50070	57492	66212
GDP at Factor Cost	..	..	385139	440711	509119	564441	621997	695764	784322	849010	902592

a/ Due to variation in coverage, the figures may not be comparable for the previous period.
Note: FY93 Figures are preliminary.
Source: Bangladesh Bureau of Statistics.

Table 2.2
GROSS DOMESTIC PRODUCT AT CONSTANT (1984/85) PRICES
(Taka Million)

	1982/83	1983/84	1984/85	1985/86	1986/87	1987/88	1988/89	1989/90	1990/91	1991/92	1992/93
Agriculture	160278	168264	169970	175549	176250	174901	173037	190354	193421	197662	201364
Crops	127784	133921	135031	139599	139596	137119	134509	150828	152575	155101	156526
Forestry	10791	11801	10948	11413	11168	12038	12309	12586	12845	13147	13536
Livestock	10006	10507	11785	12131	12801	12922	13348	13805	14102	14615	15522
Fisheries	11697	12035	12206	12406	12685	12822	12871	13135	13899	14799	15780
Industry	56696	63049	64982	66709	72093	75902	79568	84632	88294	94558	101580
Mining and Quarrying a/	3	4	4	3	4	2	3	66	80	94	95
Manufacturing	37921	40765	40112	41156	44403	44682	45927	49256	50423	54117	58435
Large Scale	19537	22134	21282	22088	25087	25263	25945	28095	29269	32342	36029
Small Scale	18384	18631	18830	19068	19316	19419	19982	20561	21154	21775	22406
Construction	16711	20072	22518	22908	24469	27475	28816	29749	31087	32471	34094
Power, Gas Water and Sanitary Services	2061	2208	2348	2642	3217	3743	4822	5561	6704	7876	8956
Services	156442	160225	171981	182335	194004	204332	213998	222541	232727	243969	257176
Transport, Storage and	41742	43508	45655	47115	52341	54293	56611	59024	60840	63349	66383
Trade Services	36692	36093	38816	39389	40394	41675	43663	44965	46707	48561	50940
Housing Services	30489	31413	32444	33435	34534	35645	36811	38030	39316	40656	42187
Public Admn. & Defense	10726	9984	13235	15944	17191	18553	19839	20363	22334	24184	26256
Banking and Insurance	5551	5867	6889	8700	9180	9312	9417	9523	9755	10002	10302
Professional and Misc. Services	31242	33360	34942	37752	40364	44854	47657	50636	53775	57217	61108
GDP at Market Prices	373416	391538	406933	424593	442347	455135	466603	497527	514442	536189	560120
Growth Rate (%)	4.7	4.9	3.9	4.3	4.2	2.9	2.5	6.6	3.4	4.23	4.46
Indirect Taxes - Subsidies	..	..	21794	23496	24657	24958	26667	28200	30907	34019	37518
GDP at Factor Cost	..	..	385139	401097	417690	430177	439936	469327	483535	502170	522602

a/ Due to variation in coverage, the figures may not be comparable for the previous period.
Note: FY93 Figures are preliminary.
Source: Bangladesh Bureau of Statistics.

Table 2.3
GROSS DOMESTIC PRODUCT, SECTORAL DEFLATORS
1984/85 = 100

	1982/83	1983/84	1984/85	1985/86	1986/87	1987/88	1988/89	1989/90	1990/91	1991/92	1992/93
Agriculture	72.64	88.20	100.00	107.31	124.69	132.43	141.81	142.78	155.41	158.07	159.46
Crops	74.40	89.61	100.00	99.92	118.18	122.26	131.19	128.76	142.76	143.42	143.65
Forestry	71.03	92.76	100.00	166.31	183.95	210.78	196.50	210.78	222.96	235.83	239.67
Livestock	67.37	76.64	100.00	126.96	126.72	138.33	159.32	183.27	188.37	192.37	195.51
Fisheries	59.34	78.06	100.00	116.97	142.06	161.66	182.36	196.04	198.36	208.57	211.97
Industry	87.14	91.63	100.00	108.44	110.99	118.10	127.68	137.69	148.79	158.96	162.66
Mining and Quarrying	100.00	100.00	100.00	100.00	100.00	150.00	133.33	134.85	140.00	142.55	148.42
Manufacturing	86.39	92.56	100.00	105.85	107.27	112.88	121.08	130.96	144.38	152.58	155.78
Large Scale	86.03	92.81	100.00	105.85	107.27	112.88	121.08	133.71	144.38	152.58	155.78
Small Scale	86.77	92.27	100.00	105.85	107.27	112.88	121.08	131.03	144.38	152.58	155.78
Construction	89.93	90.15	100.00	113.75	117.86	125.94	136.25	144.91	152.03	165.04	167.67
Power, Gas Water and Sanitary Services	78.21	87.82	100.00	102.69	110.20	122.82	139.34	158.68	167.08	177.89	188.58
Services	81.57	91.34	100.00	112.71	123.41	135.01	146.08	156.94	172.92	181.89	187.61
Transport, Storage and	95.51	96.07	100.00	115.90	118.26	121.46	126.78	127.17	160.58	171.54	170.82
Trade Services	73.45	85.37	100.00	105.37	113.59	120.93	126.00	136.96	146.19	151.90	154.25
Housing Services	73.00	90.91	100.00	110.86	118.69	140.22	162.63	174.49	187.88	194.45	206.72
Public Admn. & Defense	81.42	89.48	100.00	108.92	121.38	133.32	147.20	160.90	171.00	179.48	186.70
Banking and Insurance	78.20	87.81	100.00	102.70	110.20	122.80	139.39	158.67	167.08	177.89	188.57
Professional and Misc. Services	81.49	93.19	100.00	121.93	147.82	163.60	175.48	194.28	201.00	211.59	220.70
GDP at Market Price	78.58	90.03	100.00	109.81	121.90	131.20	141.36	148.25	162.19	169.06	172.96
Growth Rate (%)	7.7	14.6	11.1	9.8	11.0	7.6	7.7	4.9	9.4	4.2	2.3

Source: Bangladesh Bureau of Statistics.

Table 2.4
GDP GROWTH AT CONSTANT (1984/85) PRICES
(In Percentage)

	1982/83	1983/84	1984/85	1985/86	1986/87	1987/88	1988/89	1989/90	1990/91	1991/92	1992/93
Agriculture	4.42	4.98	1.01	3.28	0.40	-0.77	-1.07	7.70	1.61	2.19	1.87
Crops	4.17	4.80	0.83	3.38	0.00	-1.77	-1.90	9.16	1.16	1.66	0.92
Forestry	6.11	9.36	-7.23	4.25	-2.15	7.79	2.25	2.25	2.06	2.35	2.96
Livestock	2.73	5.01	12.16	2.94	5.52	0.95	3.30	3.42	2.15	3.64	6.21
Fisheries	7.19	2.89	1.42	1.64	2.25	1.08	0.38	2.05	5.82	6.48	6.63
Industry	1.47	11.21	3.07	2.66	8.07	5.28	4.83	6.36	4.33	7.09	7.43
Mining and Quarrying a/	..	..	..	..	..	..	..	..	..	..	..
Manufacturing	1.89	7.50	-1.60	2.60	7.89	0.63	2.79	7.25	2.37	7.33	7.98
Large Scale	2.60	13.29	-3.85	3.79	13.58	0.70	2.70	8.29	4.18	10.50	11.40
Small Scale	1.15	1.34	1.07	1.26	1.30	0.53	2.90	2.90	2.88	2.94	2.90
Construction	-3.43	20.11	12.19	1.73	6.81	12.28	4.88	3.24	4.50	4.45	5.00
Power, Gas Water and Sanitary Services	53.01	7.13	6.34	12.52	21.76	16.35	28.83	15.33	20.55	17.48	13.71
Services	6.17	2.42	7.34	6.02	6.40	5.32	4.73	3.99	4.58	4.83	5.41
Transport, Storage and	7.21	4.23	4.93	3.20	11.09	3.73	4.27	4.26	3.08	4.12	4.79
Trade Services	5.24	-1.63	7.54	1.48	2.55	3.17	4.77	2.98	3.87	3.97	4.90
Housing Services	3.08	3.03	3.28	3.05	3.29	3.22	3.27	3.31	3.38	3.41	3.77
Public Admn. & Defense	22.47	-6.92	32.56	20.47	7.82	7.92	6.93	2.64	9.68	8.28	8.57
Banking and Insurance	-5.68	5.69	17.42	26.29	5.52	1.44	1.13	1.13	2.44	2.53	3.00
Professional and Misc. Services	6.53	6.78	4.74	8.04	6.92	11.12	6.25	6.25	6.20	6.40	6.80
GDP at Constant Market Prices	4.68	4.85	3.93	4.34	4.18	2.89	2.52	6.63	3.40	4.23	4.46

a/ Due to variation in coverage, the figures may not be comparable for the previous period.
Note: FY93 Figures are preliminary.
Source: Derived from Table 2.2.

Table 2.5
GROSS DOMESTIC PRODUCT BY EXPENDITURE IN CURRENT PRICES
(Taka Million)

	1985/86	1986/87	1987/88	1988/89	1989/90	1990/91	1991/92	1992/93
Net Resources a/	512371	587472	652301	727201	810691	894159	960014	1028558
Consumption b/	455104	519895	580444	646493	716264	798204	850163	905511
Private b/	417021	479741	531889	584063	613046	683472	725226	771624
Public c/	38083	40154	48555	62430	103218	114732	124937	133887
Investment c/	57267	67577	71857	80708	94427	95955	109851	123047
Private b/	29229	33404	38290	42891	47275	48562	60063	67455
Public c/	28038	34173	33567	37817	47152	47393	49788	55592
Resource Balance	46144	48271	55165	67603	73120	59767	53512	59754
Exports of goods and NFS, fob d/	31168	39843	46438	51361	62683	75347	94110	113743
Imports of goods and NFS, c&f d/	77312	88115	101603	118964	135803	135114	147622	173498
Gross Domestic Product, at market prices c/	466227	539201	597136	659598	737571	834392	906502	968804
Net factor income from abroad d/	14271	18669	20466	23381	22363	26522	33810	38822
Gross National Product, at market prices	480498	557870	617602	682979	759934	860914	940312	1007626
Net Indirect taxes	25516	30082	32695	37601	41807	50070	57492	65078
Gross National Product, at factor cost	454982	527788	584907	645378	718127	810844	882820	942548
Gross Domestic Savings e/	11123	19306	16692	13105	21307	36188	56339	63293
Gross National Savings f/	25393	37975	37158	36486	43671	62710	90149	102115
Foreign Savings g/	31874	29602	34698	44222	50749	33245	19702	20932

------------ (As Percentage of GDP)------------

MEMO ITEMS								
Consumption	97.61	96.42	97.20	98.01	97.11	95.66	93.79	93.47
Private	89.45	88.97	89.07	88.55	83.12	81.91	80.00	79.65
Public	8.17	7.45	8.13	9.46	13.99	13.75	13.78	13.82
Investment	12.28	12.53	12.03	12.24	12.80	11.50	12.12	12.70
Private	6.27	6.20	6.41	6.50	6.41	5.82	6.63	6.96
Public	6.01	6.34	5.62	5.73	6.39	5.68	5.49	5.74
Exports of goods and NFS, fob	6.69	7.39	7.78	7.79	8.50	9.03	10.38	11.74
Imports of goods and NFS, c&f	16.58	16.34	17.01	18.04	18.41	16.19	16.28	17.91
Gross Domestic Savings	2.39	3.58	2.80	1.99	2.89	4.34	6.21	6.53
Gross National Savings	5.45	7.04	6.22	5.53	5.92	7.52	9.94	10.54
Foreign Savings	6.84	5.49	5.81	6.70	6.88	3.98	2.17	2.16

a/ GDPmkt + Resource Balance.
b/ Derived as residual.
c/ BBS data
d/ From Balance of Payments Table 3.1, converted into Taka by using average exchange rate.
e/ GDP (mp)-Consumption = GDI-Net Imports.
f/ GDS + Net Factor Income from Abroad.
g/ Current Account Deficit of the Balance of Payments.
Note: FY93 figures are preliminary.

Source: BBS and Staff Estimates.

Table 3.1
BALANCE OF PAYMENTS
(US$ millions)

	1985/86	1986/87	1987/88	1988/89	1989/90	1990/91	1991/92	1992/93
Merchandise exports, fob	819	1074	1231	1286	1524	1718	1993	2383
Merchandise imports, fob/c&f a/	-2364	-2620	-2986	-3375	-3759	-3470	-3463	-3986
Trade Balance	-1545	-1546	-1755	-2089	-2235	-1752	-1470	-1603
Non-factor services, net	1	-30	-11	-14	15	76	67	76
Receipts	224	227	255	312	379	395	474	523
Other transport	23	22	27	32	36	34	37	38
Travel	18	14	10	17	20	17	25	32
Government services, n.e.i.	32	29	39	51	92	96	78	99
Other	150	162	179	212	232	247	334	354
Payments	-223	-256	-266	-326	-365	-318	-406	-447
Other transport	-39	-43	-41	-52	-63	-73	-102	-107
Travel	-53	-48	-77	-114	-112	-61	-109	-126
Government services, n.e.i.	-84	-110	-106	-115	-138	-141	-142	-149
Other	-47	-55	-41	-46	-52	-44	-53	-65
Investment income, net	-109	-122	-133	-109	-123	-102	-89	-73
Receipts	36	35	55	79	67	65	91	94
Interest on reserves	31	30	41	67	41	52	61	49
Other interest & investment income	5	5	14	11	26	13	30	45
Payments	-145	-157	-188	-187	-190	-168	-180	-167
Interest on external public M&LT debt	-73	-82	-123	-139	-131	-129	-137	-144
IMF service charges	-38	-39	-39	-43	-48	-33	-35	-11
Other interest & investment income	-35	-36	-26	-5	-10	-5	-7	-12
Private unrequited transfers, net	586	731	788	836	802	846	975	1065
Receipts	586	731	788	836	802	846	975	1065
Workers Remittances	555	696	737	771	761	764	848	942
Others	31	35	51	65	41	82	127	123
Payments	0	0	0	0	0	0	0	0
Current Account Balance	-1067	-966	-1111	-1376	-1541	-932	-516	-535
Amortization of public M&LT debt	-117	-154	-166	-170	-186	-197	-210	-239
IMF transactions, net	-28	134	-18	68	-164	4	85	2
Aid disbursements, total	1306	1595	1640	1669	1810	1733	1611	1675
Other long-term capital, net	-5	-7	-7	44	0	1	0	6
Direct & portfolio investment, net	-5	2	3	2	3	2	10	16
Subscriptions to int'l non-monetary orgs	0	-3	-2	0	0	-1	0	-1
Other, net	0	-7	-8	42	-3	0	-10	-9
Short-term capital, net	10	-140	-160	-139	-131	-144	-106	-271
Resident official sector, net	3	-10	-5	4	0	0	-1	1
Deposit money banks, net	2	-70	-97	-144	-38	-40	-18	-3
Other, net	6	-60	-57	-	-93	-104	-87	-269
Liabilities constituting foreign authorities reserves, net	0	-40	-40	-	-	0	0	0
Food borrowing, net	-69	-96	6	43	-21	-21	-19	-8
Gross	13	0	39	55	0	0	0	0
Amortization	-82	-96	-33	-12	-21	-21	-19	-8
Errors & ommissions, net b/	70	-69	-2	-72	-144	-62	-103	-112
Change in reserves c/ (- = increase)	-100	-257	-144	-66	377	-381	-742	-518
MEMORANDUM ITEMS:								
Reserve level, end of June (US$ m)	495	752	897	962	585	966	1679	2197
- Reserves, excluding gold (US$ m)	479	729	873	941	565	943	1657	2171
- Gold, national valuation (US$ m)	17	23	24	21	20	23	22	26
Average annual exchange rate (Tk/US$)	29.8861	30.6347	31.2460	31.1430	32.9323	35.6670	38.1520	39.1395

-- = not available separately.
a/ Merchandise imports are reported on a mixed valuation basis, partly fob and partly cif.
b/ 7% on average level of reserves.
c/ Including valuation changes other than those of reserves.
d/ Including changes in the valuation of reserves.
Note: 1993 Figures are preliminary estimates.
Source: Bangladesh Bank.

- 185 -

Table 3.2
BALANCE OF PAYMENTS - REQUIREMENTS AND SOURCES FORMAT
(US$ millions)

	1982/83	1983/84	1984/85	1985/86	1986/87	1987/88	1988/89	1989/90	1990/91	1991/92	1992/93
FOREIGN EXCHANGE REQUIREMENTS											
CURRENT ACCOUNT											
Merchandise imports	2309	2353	2647	2364	2620	2986	3375	3759	3470	3463	3986
Payments on investments	135	121	148	145	157	188	187	190	168	180	167
Non-factor services	208	191	217	223	256	266	326	365	318	406	446
Subtotal	2652	2665	3011	2732	3033	3440	3889	4313	3956	4049	4599
CAPITAL ACCOUNT											
Public M&LT debt amortization	74	72	110	117	154	166	170	186	197	210	239
Food loan amortization	0	60	99	82	96	33	12	21	21	19	8
Long-term capital, net	0	8	3	5	7	7	-44	0	-11	0	-6
Short-term capital, net	36	-65	35	-10	140	160	139	131	136	106	272
Subtotal	110	75	247	194	397	365	278	338	343	335	513
TOTAL REQUIREMENTS	2762	2740	3258	2926	3430	3805	4166	4651	4299	4384	5112
FOREIGN EXCHANGE SOURCES											
CURRENT ACCOUNT											
Merchandise exports	686	811	934	819	1074	1231	1286	1524	1718	1993	2383
Remittances	628	627	476	586	731	788	836	802	846	975	1065
Investment income	27	57	58	36	35	55	79	67	65	91	94
Non-factor services	203	222	228	224	227	255	312	379	395	474	523
Subtotal	1544	1717	1697	1665	2067	2329	2513	2772	3024	3533	4065
CAPITAL ACCOUNT											
Aid disbursements	1346	1268	1267	1306	1595	1640	1669	1810	1733	1611	1675
IMF transactions, net	47	19	-7	-28	134	-18	68	-164	4	85	2
Food borrowing, gross	0	51	190	13	0	39	55	0	0	0	0
Other	-6	-96	-30	0	-40	-40	0	0	0	0	0
Subtotal	1386	1242	1420	1291	1689	1621	1792	1646	1737	1696	1677
TOTAL SOURCES	2930	2959	3117	2956	3756	3950	4304	4418	4760	5229	5742
Increase in gross reserves	235	160	-146	100	257	144	66	-377	399	742	519
Errors and omissions	-67	37	5	-70	69	2	72	144	63	103	111

Source: Bangladesh Bank.

Table 3.3
VALUE OF TOTAL EXPORTS BY COMMODITY
(US$ million)

	1982/83	1983/84	1984/85	1985/86	1986/87	1987/88	1988/89	1989/90	1990/91	1991/92	1992/93
Primary Commodities											
Raw jute	110	117	151	124	104	81	97	125	104	85	74
Frozen shrimps, fish & froglegs	72	95	87	115	136	140	141	138	142	131	165
Other fish products	2	2	2	5	4	5	7	8	6	4	9
Tea	47	69	61	33	30	39	40	39	43	32	41
Spices, incl. tamarind & sesame	0	1	0	0	0	0	0	-	-	0	-
Fruits & vegetables	0	3	4	15	18	16	10	9	6	6	9
Tobacco	2	3	3	1	1	1	2	1	2	2	2
Betel leaves	1	1	1	4	3	2	1	0	1	1	2
Raw cotton	0	0	0	0	0	0	1	-	-	0	-
Crude fertilizers	0	0	0	0	1	2	1	1	0	1	2
Oil cake	0	0	0	0	0	0	0	-	-	-	-
Wheat & rice bran	2	3	3	0	0	0	0	-	-	-	-
Rice	0	0	0	0	0	0	0	-	-	-	-
Animal casings	0	0	0	0	0	0	0	0	0	0	0
Lizard skins	0	1	1	1	0	0	0	-	-	-	-
Tortoise & turtle meat & shells	1	1	1	1	1	2	1	0	0	0	2
Bees wax	0	0	0	0	0	0	0	-	-	0	-
Manufactured Goods											
Jute Manufactures	305	336	358	294	275	265	243	331	285	179	195
Jute specialty products	12	21	32	1	27	36	37	-	73	123	97
Textiles, incl. silk & silk waste	1	0	0	0	1	1	2	-	0	0	29
Readymade garments	11	32	116	131	299	434	471	609	736	1064	1240
Cotton yarn & thread waste	0	0	0	0	0	0	0	0	-	-	-
Handicrafts	2	2	2	2	4	4	4	5	5	9	5
Pottery & coir products	0	0	0	0	0	0	0	-	-	0	-
Wood & furniture components	0	0	0	0	0	0	0	-	-	-	0
Bamboo & bamboo products	1	0	1	0	0	0	0	0	0	1	0
Leather & leather products	58	85	70	61	135	147	137	179	137	149	151
Sugar	0	0	0	0	0	0	0	-	-	-	-
Molasses	1	0	0	0	0	1	1	-	0	0	0
Pulp	0	0	0	0	0	0	0	0	-	-	-
Newsprint	4	7	9	7	8	7	4	3	4	1	1
Paper	0	2	2	0	2	5	3	1	-	5	2
Hardboard & particle board	0	0	0	0	0	0	0	-	-	-	-
Cellophane	0	0	0	0	0	0	-	-	1	-	-
Rayon	0	0	0	0	0	0	0	-	0	-	0
Pharmaceuticals & crude drugs	1	0	0	0	0	0	0	0	1	1	2
Glycerine	1	1	1	1	1	1	1	1	0	0	0
Urea	10	10	5	3	4	25	53	17	36	21	51
Naphtha	19	23	21	14	10	8	12	8	14	3	15
Furnace oil	8	0	0	0	2	4	4	9	19	5	21
Bitumen	4	3	0	0	0	0	0	-	-	-	0
Wire & cables	0	1	1	0	0	0	3	8	2	0	0
All others a/	8	3	9	5	7	8	10	31	100	169	263
TOTAL	687	823	940	819	1074	1232	1286	1524	1718	1993	2383

a/   Includes items for which details are not shown or available separately.
-   = Negligible or not available.

Source: Bangladesh Export Promotion Bureau.

Table 3.4.
QUANTITY AND VALUE OF TRADITIONAL GOODS EXPORTS

		1981/82	1982/83	1983/84	1984/85	1985/86	1986/87	1987/88	1988/89	1989/90	1990/91	1991/92	1992/93
Raw Jute													
	Value (mill US$)	101.69	110.00	117.19	150.81	123.89	104.00	80.53	97.27	124.62	104.21	85.5	74.3
	Quantity (000 bales)	1911.37	2246	1902	2408	2301	2241	1345	1617	2064	1360	1394	1356
	Unit price (US$/bale)	53.20	48.98	61.62	62.63	53.84	46.41	59.87	60.15	60.38	76.63	61.33	54.84
Hessian	Quantity (000 M.T.)	188.56	224.60	214.10	184.64	151.37	204.50	198.70	100.70	-	-	91.19	101.51
Sacking	Quantity (000 M.T.)	292.91	195.96	162.23	176.95	242.49	194.49	178.70	155.60	-	-	190.62	185.20
Carpet-backing	Quantity (000 M.T.)	54.31	90.75	94.20	72.60	69.74	72.18	71.10	31.60	-	-	62.50	29.18
Carpets	Quantity (000 M.T.)	0.22	0.70	0.24	-	-	-	-	-	-	-	-	-
Others/discrepancy	Quantity (000 M.T.)	1.35	-3.01	37.23	10.00	10.20	17.50	16.50	145.10	-	-	146.83	187.32
Total Jute Manufactures													
	Value (mill US$)	283.50	306.00	336.12	357.72	294.32	274.73	265.01	243.34	328.05	284.79	178.87	195.35
	Quantity (000 M.T.)	537.36	509.00	508.00	440.00	467.60	479.90	465.00	433.00	510.00	505.00	346.00	315.90
	Unit price (US$/M.T.)	527.59	601.18	661.64	813.00	629.42	572.47	569.91	561.99	643.24	563.94	516.97	618.4
Jute Speciality Products													
	Value (mill US$)	8.04	12.00	20.05	32.08	0.86	26.81	36.30	36.52	-	73.00	122.77	97.02
	Quantity (000 M.T.)	13.20	22.00	30.00	35.15	1.01	-	60.00	64.00	-	-	145.14	187.32
	Unit price (US$/M.T.)	608.71	545.45	668.23	912.61	846.69	-	605.00	570.63	-	-	845.87	517.93
Tea													
	Value (mill US$)	37.94	46.00	68.90	61.02	32.70	29.66	38.80	39.83	39.48	43.21	32.43	41.14
	Quantity (mill lbs)	69.04	67.65	67.65	56.53	65.76	47.10	60.48	55.24	66.98	58.26	52.09	72.23
	Unit price (US$/000lbs)	549.50	680.00	1018.48	1079.33	497.24	629.70	641.53	721.01	589.43	741.68	622.58	569.61
Leather and Leather Products a/													
	Value (mill US$)	63.08	58.00	85.26	69.80	60.73	134.82	147.17	136.98	178.89	134.29	144.46	147.91
	Quantity (mill sq ft)	87.28	93.89	102.91	81.75	71.52	137.46	118.21	127.56	157.22	101.36	119.55	138.63
	Unit price (US$/000 sq ft)	722.76	617.74	828.50	853.81	849.13	980.79	1244.99	1073.85	1137.83	1324.88	1208.36	1066.94
Total Value, Traditional Exports		494.248	532	627.515	671.427	512.494	570.02	567.81	553.94	671.04	639.5	564.0	555.7
In Constant FY81 Prices		612186	621963	611759	504.6	562.6	625.6	567.3	572.9	641.4	550.1	542.2	571.7

- = Not available seperately.

a/ Excludes hides and skins, but includes leather goods.

Source: Bangladesh Export Promotion Bureau and Bangladesh Tea Board.

Table 3.5
QUANTITY AND VALUE OF NON-TRADITIONAL EXPORTS

	1983/84	1984/85	1985/86	1986/87	1987/88	1988/89	1989/90	1990/91	1991/92	1992/93
Frozen Shrimps, Froglegs and Fish										
Value (mill US$)	95.00	86.85	114.70	134.16	139.65	141.38	137.89	141.80	130.53	165.33
Quantity ('000 lbs))	38.46	38.24	47.16	45.58	48.33	45.19	47.88	52.92	44.32	48.35
Unit price (US$/lb)	2.47	2.27	2.43	2.94	2.89	3.13	2.88	2.68	2.95	3.42
Other fish products and preparations a/										
Value ('000 US$)	2186	2450	5420	4020	5210	6550	7600	5590	4080	9360
Quantity (mt)	..	..	..	..	..	..	1439	1621	972	1879
Unit Price (US$/kg)	..	..	..	..	..	..	5	3	4	5
Newsprint										
Value (mill US$)	6.54	8.50	7.34	7.65	7.06	4.29	3.00	3.99	0.89	0.73
Quantity (000 tons)	14.00	18.00	16.00	19.00	13.95	7.70	4.67	8.71	1.55	1.34
Unit price (US$/ton)	467.14	472.11	458.75	402.63	506.09	557.14	641.85	458.36	574.19	545.18
Paper										
Value ('000 US$)	2560	1586	..	..	4500	3120	678	..	4640	1740
Quantity (000 tons)	2371	2453	..	..	5948	3756	620	..	..	2117
Unit price (US$/ton)	1079.71	646.56	..	..	756.56	830.67	1093.55	..	..	822
Naptha										
Value (mill US$)	26.00	20.68	13.91	10.24	8.08	11.94	7.92	13.68	2.99	15.25
Quantity (000 MT)	100.70	89.00	80.00	77.77	65.00	69.00	58.63	54.54	17.87	125.71
Unit price (US$/MT)	258.19	232.33	173.88	131.67	124.31	173.04	134.99	250.83	167.37	121.31
Furnace Oil										
Value (mill US$)	..	..	..	..	3.68	4.01	8.93	18.77	5.34	21.42
Quantity (000 MT)	..	..	..	..	39.00	54.00	111.67	159.44	73.35	248.55
Unit price (US$/MT)	..	..	..	..	94.36	74.26	80.00	117.73	72.80	86.18
Bitumen										
Value ('000 US$)	3120	106	50	440	220	100	..	..	..	130
Quantity (MT)	13000	459	209	2008	1000	500	..	..	..	800
Unit price (US$/MT)	240.00	230.94	239.23	219.12	220.00	200.00	..	..	..	163
Urea										
Value (mill US$)	9.73	4.79	2.57	4.18	24.93	53.37	17.04	36.30	21.35	51.18
Quantity (000 tons)	61.00	26.30	20.50	35.00	223.46	465.00	116.59	289.91	195.97	427.51
Unit price (US$/ton)	159.54	182.13	125.37	119.43	111.56	114.77	146.17	125.21	108.94	119.72
Garments										
Value (mill US$)	31.57	116.20	131.48	298.67	433.92	471.09	609.00	735.63	1064.00	1240.48
Total Non-traditional Exports (mill US$) b/	194.49	263.00	306.43	504.48	663.40	731.92	852.66	1145.44	1429.00	1827.14
In constant prices of FY81 ('000 US$)	202.26	317.52	379.37	539.30	524.78	572.73	618.21	823.10	936.19	1341.80
Total Exports ('000 US$) b/	822.00	934.44	819.20	1073.77	1231.20	1285.92	1523.70	1717.55	1993.09	2382.89
in constant prices of FY81 ('000 US$)	814.02	832.24	944.68	1143.86	1098.03	1145.72	1259.58	1373.19	1478.41	1913.50

.. = not available separately.
a/ Includes dried and salted fish and fish products, sharkfins, and fishmaws.
b/ Includes other items not shown above.
Source: Export Promotion Bureau.

Table 3.6
QUANTITY AND VALUE OF MAJOR IMPORT COMMODITIES

	1983/84	1984/85	1985/86	1986/87	1987/88	1988/89	1989/90	1990/91	1991/92	1992/93
Major Primary Goods (mill.US$)	**758**	**836**	**449**	**469**	**752**	**610**	**585**	**636**	**497**	**406**
Rice /a(mill. US $)										
Value (mill. US$)	56	176	8	50	150	17	102	4	5	7
Quantity ('000,long tons)	179	690	39	261	671	60	300	11	42	19
Unit Price /a (US$)	313	255	205	190	224	283	340	355	119	343
Wheat /a										
Value (mill. US$)	342	322	212	223	339	357	241	327	250	140
Quantity ('000,long tons)	1877	1899	1164	1508	2342	2077	1234	1566	1440	810
Unit Price /a (US$/long ton)	182	170	182	148	145	172	195	209	174	85
Oilseeds										
Value (mill. US$)	2	6	0	25	39	11	14	1	19	35
Quantity ('000,mt tons)	5	20	0	116	148	42	50	2	25	-
Unit Price (US$/mt ton)	370	300	250	216	264	262	274	350	760	-
Crude Petroleum										
Value (mill. US$)	233	226	177	126	136	132	123	212	152	142
Quantity ('000 tons)	1004	985	1008	1000	988	1096	1008	1182	1018	1124
Unit Price (US$/ton)	232	229	176	126	138	120	122	179	149	126
Raw Cotton										
Value (mill. US$)	125	106	52	45	88	93	105	93	71	82
Quantity ('000 bales)	388	305	181	205	267	349	375	250	284	
Unit Price (US$/bale)	322	348	285	220	330	266	280	370	250	
Major Intermediate Goods (mill US$)	**369**	**433**	**517**	**357**	**476**	**563**	**567**	**689**	**597**	**718**
Edible Oil a/										
Value (mill. US$)	87	103	136	115	176	170	200	208	141	152
Quantity ('000 tons)	100	136	272	283	382	408	425	500	325	
Unit Price (US$/ton)	870	757	498	406	461	417	471	415	434	
Petroleum Products b/										
Value (mill. US$)	122	133	165	104	136	153	174	207	168	162
Quantity ('000 tons)	464	570	805	732	790	926	973	711	825	807
Unit Price (US$/ton)	263	233	205	142	172	165	179	291	204	200
Fertilizer a/										
Value (mill. US$)	75	137	108	25	46	108	46	91	117	131
Quantity ('000,long tons)	356	666	640	145	277	535	227	457	590	
Unit Price (US$/long ton)	211	206	169	172	166	202	203	198	198	
Cement										
Value (mill. US$)	37	26	57	64	67	83	83	106	106	115
Quantity ('000, mt.tons)	748	588	1333	1601	1563	1893	1500	1800	1650	
Unit Price (US$/ton)	49	44	43	40	43	44	55	59	64	
Staple Fibres										
Value (mill. US$)	9	3	1	7	7	9	10	6	15	31
Quantity ('000 bales)	27	10	3	29	24	24	25	15	38	
Unit Price (US$/bale)	333	300	333	241	292	375	400	400	400	
Yarn										
Value (mill. US$)	39	31	50	42	44	40	54	72	50	127
Quantity (million .lbs)	37	26	56	39	38	37	45	60	40	
Unit Price (US cents/.lb)	105	119	89	108	116	108	120	120	125	
Capital Goods (mill. US$)	**616**	**691**	**1003**	**856**	**1090**	**1070**	**1296**	**1231**	**1284**	**1246**
Others (mill. US$) c/	**610**	**687**	**396**	**939**	**668**	**1132**	**1311**	**914**	**1085**	**1616**
TOTAL IMPORTS (mill.US$)	**2353**	**2647**	**2364**	**2620**	**2986**	**3375**	**3759**	**3470**	**3463**	**3986**

a/ As a large portion of imports is financed on a grant basis, unit prices are often available for accounting purposes only.
b/ Includes petroleum products imported by BPC from its refining operations in Singapore as well as imports of non-fuel petroleum products.
c/ Consumer and other intermediate goods not seperately shown.

Note: 1 bale of raw cotton = 500 lbs; 1 bale of polyester = 618 lbs; 1 bale of viscose - 441 lbs; 1 bale of yarn = 400 lbs.
Source: Planning Commission.

Table 3.7
IMPORTS AND EXPORTS VOLUME AND PRICE INDICES AND TERMS OF TRADE
(1980/81 = 100)

	1983/84	1984/85	1985/86	1986/87	1987/88	1988/89	1989/90	1990/91	1991/92
IMPORTS									
Rice									
Value Index	138.61	435.64	19.80	122.52	371.29	42.08	252.48	9.65	12.38
Volume Index	216.18	833.33	47.10	315.22	810.39	72.46	362.32	13.29	50.72
Unit Price Index	64.12	52.28	42.04	38.87	45.82	58.07	69.68	72.66	24.40
Wheat									
Value Index	162.89	153.36	100.97	106.21	161.46	170.03	114.78	155.89	119.07
Volume Index	192.20	194.45	119.19	154.41	239.81	212.68	126.36	160.35	147.45
Unit Price Index	84.75	78.87	84.72	68.78	67.33	79.95	90.84	97.22	80.75
Edible Oil									
Value Index	94.56	111.95	147.28	125.00	191.30	184.78	217.38	225.54	153.26
Volume Index	70.92	96.45	192.91	200.71	270.92	289.36	301.42	354.61	230.50
Unit Price Index	133.33	116.07	76.35	62.28	70.61	63.86	72.12	63.60	66.49
Oilseeds									
Value Index	18.19	54.58	0.91	227.40	354.74	100.05	124.61	6.37	172.82
Volume Index	18.17	67.31	1.35	390.38	498.06	141.34	168.27	6.73	84.13
Unit Price Index	100.11	81.09	67.57	58.25	71.22	70.79	74.06	94.60	205.42
Crude Petroleum									
Value Index	67.81	65.78	51.51	36.67	39.58	38.36	35.80	61.59	44.24
Volume Index	76.95	75.49	77.26	76.64	75.72	84.00	77.26	90.59	78.02
Unit Price Index	88.13	87.13	66.68	47.85	52.27	45.67	46.34	67.98	56.70
Petroleum Products									
Value Index	76.34	83.22	103.25	65.08	85.10	95.74	108.88	129.34	105.12
Volume Index	88.57	108.81	153.67	139.73	150.80	176.77	185.74	135.72	157.49
Unit Price Index	86.19	76.48	67.19	46.57	56.43	54.16	58.62	95.29	66.75
Fertilizer									
Value Index	72.12	131.73	103.85	24.04	44.23	103.85	44.23	87.02	112.50
Volume Index	101.64	190.15	182.72	41.40	79.09	152.75	64.81	130.48	168.45
Unit Price Index	70.95	69.28	56.83	58.07	55.93	67.99	68.25	66.69	66.79
Cement									
Value Index	112.92	79.35	173.96	195.32	204.48	253.31	253.31	324.12	323.51
Volume Index	167.71	131.84	298.88	358.97	350.45	424.44	336.32	403.59	369.96
Unit Price Index	67.33	60.19	58.20	54.41	58.35	59.68	75.32	80.31	87.44
Raw Cotton									
Value Index	115.74	98.15	47.78	41.67	81.48	86.11	97.22	85.65	65.74
Volume Index	151.56	119.14	70.70	80.08	104.30	136.33	146.48	97.66	110.94
Unit Price Index	76.37	82.38	67.58	52.03	78.12	63.16	66.37	87.70	59.26
Total a/									
Current Price Index	92.89	104.50	93.33	103.43	117.88	133.24	148.40	136.99	136.72
Constant Price Index	104.24	123.76	108.52	118.41	133.49	138.29	142.49	126.09	126.86
Unit Price Index	89.12	84.44	86.00	87.35	88.31	96.35	104.15	108.65	107.77

a/ Includes items not shown above.   Continued

Table 3.7 (Continued)
IMPORTS AND EXPORTS VOLUME AND PRICE INDICES AND TERMS OF TRADE
(1980/81 = 100)

	1983/84	1984/85	1985/86	1986/87	1987/88	1988/89	1989/90	1990/91	1991/92
EXPORTS									
Raw Jute									
Value Index	98.59	126.88	104.23	87.49	67.75	81.83	104.84	87.67	71.92
Volume Index	97.84	2.43	118.37	115.28	69.19	83.18	106.18	69.96	71.70
Unit Price Index	100.77	175.17	88.05	75.90	97.92	98.38	98.74	125.32	100.31
Jute Goods									
Value Index	94.14	100.19	82.43	76.95	74.23	68.16	91.88	79.77	50.10
Volume Index	101.31	87.75	93.25	95.71	92.73	86.35	101.71	100.71	69.00
Unit Price Index	32.92	114.18	88.40	80.40	80.04	78.93	90.34	79.20	72.61
Tea									
Value Index	169.40	150.02	80.60	72.92	95.40	97.93	97.07	106.24	79.74
Volume Index	103.01	86.08	100.13	71.72	92.09	84.11	101.99	88.71	73.31
Unit Price Index	164.46	174.28	80.50	101.68	103.59	116.43	95.18	119.76	100.53
Leather									
Value Index	150.42	123.14	107.14	237.85	259.64	241.66	315.60	236.92	254.86
Volume Index	127.67	101.12	88.73	170.53	146.65	158.25	195.05	125.75	148.31
Unit Price Index	117.82	121.42	120.75	139.48	177.05	152.16	131.81	188.40	171.84
Frozen Shrimps, Froglegs and Fish									
Value Index	237.80	217.38	287.11	340.93	349.56	353.89	345.03	354.94	319.45
Volume Index	232.37	231.03	284.92	275.37	291.99	273.02	289.27	319.72	257.49
Unit Price Index	102.49	94.23	100.92	122.13	119.90	129.82	119.50	111.18	122.21
Naphtha									
Value Index	87.12	69.28	46.61	34.31	27.07	40.01	26.52	45.84	27.91
Volume Index	86.54	76.48	68.75	66.78	55.75	59.30	50.39	46.87	78.39
Unit Price Index	100.67	90.59	67.80	51.34	48.47	67.47	52.63	97.80	35.61
Total a/									
Value Index	115.66	131.48	115.24	151.09	173.24	180.94	214.40	241.67	280.44
Volume Index	114.17	110.32	122.12	149.31	160.43	171.39	185.80	198.20	224.42
Unit Price Index	101.31	119.19	94.37	101.00	107.99	105.57	115.39	121.93	124.97
TERMS OF TRADE INDEX									
Export Price Index	101.31	119.19	94.37	101.00	107.99	105.57	115.39	121.93	124.97
Import Price Index	112.05	140.29	107.80	114.46	123.19	108.95	109.78	111.73	112.53
TOT	90.41	84.96	87.54	88.24	87.66	96.90	105.11	109.13	111.05
Annual Charge %	16.19	25.21	-23.16	6.17	7.62	-11.59	0.76	1.78	0.72

Source: Bangladesh Export Promotion and Planning Commission.

Table 3.8
TOTAL IMPORT FINANCING
(US$ million)

Year	Cash	Barter	Special Trade	WES a/	Loans & Grants	Total
1972/73	396.3	49.4	-	-	541.0	986.7
1973/74	397.3	64.0	-	-	392.9	854.2
1974/75	273.7	62.0	3.0	41.2	810.7	1190.6
1975/76	430.1	23.7	5.2	40.4	786.5	1285.9
1976/77	307.2	28.8	2.7	56.2	449.9	844.8
1977/78	497.3	48.6	2.6	88.1	794.7	1431.3
1978/79	442.6	73.7	2.9	116.1	1005.6	1640.9
1979/80	901.7	75.4	3.5	177.4	1181.2	2339.2
1980/81	1056.3	96.6	2.7	334.3	1178.9	2668.8
1981/82	976.9	100.6	4.1	342.2	1262.9	2686.7
1982/83	489.9	49.9	10.6	479.2	1287.1	2316.7
1983/84	637.4	75.3	7.2	494.8	1138.1	2352.8
1984/85	735.2	63.9	6.8	695.8	1145.8	2647.5
1985/86	649.3	85.1	33.1	676.2	920.3	2364.0
1986/87	366.4	79.0	27.4	879.1	1268.5	2620.4
1987/88	443.9	84.7	43.0	1090.2	1324.2	2986.0
1988/89	422.7	90.9	90.9	1435.3	1160.2	3200.0
1989/90	568.9	63.2	55.2	1797.9	1273.5	3758.7
1990/91	485.0	72.0	36.0	1505.0	1372.0	3470.0
1991/92	782.0	26.4	15.0	1426.5	1213.5	3463.4
1992/93	2515.8	17.6	6.3	173.1	1273.1	3985.9

a/ Wage Earners Scheme.

  1993 figures are preliminary estimates.

Note: Data reflect payments rather than commodity arrivals.

  Valuation for commodities financed under loans and grants is on a
  mixed fob/cif basis, depending on the terms of the respective aid
  agreements; all other categories reflect cif valuation.

Source: Bangladesh Bank, Statistics Department.

Table 3.9
AID PIPELINE
(US$ million)

	1983/84	1984/85	1985/86	1986/87	1987/88	1988/89	1989/90	1990/91	1991/92	1992/93
FOOD AID										
Opening pipeline	41.8	60.4	194.4	323.8	207.4	299.3	231.7	230.9	119.2	104.0
Commitments	285.2	380.2	329.6	109.0	364.0	157.0	159.7	183.8	226.0	177.7
Disbursements	276.4	244.5	202.8	225.4	300.5	226.9	187.5	268.6	241.2	121.0
Closing pipeline	50.5	196.1	323.8	207.4	299.3	231.7	203.9	119.2	104.0	164.5
Pledges	219.0	246.0	235.0	222.0	226.0	214.0	183.0	156.0	188.1	216.3
COMMODITY AID										
Opening pipeline	476.7	591.7	374.7	460.4	609.1	451.5	499.6	478.5	408.2	615.8
Commitments	528.2	251.8	408.9	562.1	251.2	601.3	430.7	295.9	575.7	336.1
Disbursements	439.2	431.6	393.4	402.5	509.4	537.7	456.7	408.1	386.0	372.1
Closing pipeline	565.7	362.8	460.4	620.0	451.5	499.6	467.3	408.2	615.8	638.8
Pledges	488.0	523.0	437.0	559.0	564.0	585.0	590.0	553.0	462.7	409.5
PROJECT AID										
Opening pipeline	3374.1	3644.5	4061.8	4633.2	4390.1	4699.0	4601.2	5238.7	4846.7	5260.0
Commitments	881.7	1339.6	922.9	932.2	914.5	1115.1	1553.3	890.6	972.4	760.7
Disbursements	552.8	590.9	709.8	967.2	830.5	903.9	1165.4	1055.9	984.2	1181.9
Closing pipeline	3703.0	4063.1	4633.2	4598.2	4699.0	4910.2	4943.0	4847.0	5118.8	4710.0
Pledges	913.0	932.0	999.0	1126.0	1233.0	1257.0	1423.0	1087.0	1463.0	1544.2
TOTAL										
Opening pipeline	3892.6	4296.6	4630.9	5417.5	5206.6	5449.8	5332.5	5948.1	5374.1	5979.8
Commitments	1695.0	1971.5	1661.4	1603.3	1529.7	1873.4	2143.7	1370.3	1774.1	1274.5
Disbursements	1268.4	1267.0	1305.9	1595.2	1640.4	1668.5	1809.6	1732.6	1611.5	1675.0
Closing pipeline	4319.2	4622.0	5417.5	5425.6	5449.8	5641.5	5614.2	5374.4	5838.6	5513.3
Pledges	1620.0	1701.0	1671.0	1907.0	2023.0	2056.0	2196.0	1796.0	2113.8	2170.0
Ratio of Actual Commitments										
to Pledges (%)	104.6	115.9	99.4	84.1	75.6	91.1	97.6	76.3	83.9	58.7

Commodity aid includes cash aid, and project aid includes technical assistance.
Discrepencies between closing pipeline in one year and opening pipeline in the next
year result from adjustments for currency revaluations, aid cancellations, and
reclassifications.

Source: Economic Relations Division.

Table 3.10
COMMITMENTS AND DISBURSEMENTS OF AID BY TYPE OF AID
(US$ million)

	1982/83	1983/84	1984/85	1985/86	1986/87	1987/88	1988/89	1989/90	1990/91	1991/92	1992/93
COMMITMENTS											
Food Aid	248.4	285.2	380.2	329.6	109.0	364.1	157.0	159.7	183.8	226.0	177.7
Grants	248.4	271.8	380.2	329.6	109.0	364.1	157.0	159.7	183.8	226.0	177.7
Loans	-	13.4	-	-	-	-	-	-	-	-	-
Commodity Aid	474.4	528.2	253.1	408.9	562.1	251.2	601.3	430.7	295.9	575.7	336.1
Grants	268.1	240.4	152.6	225.9	206.1	138.5	188.1	178.6	104.5	184.8	231.5
Loans	206.3	287.8	100.5	183.0	356.0	112.7	413.2	252.1	191.4	390.9	104.6
Project Aid	799.8	881.7	1344.6	922.9	932.2	914.5	1115.1	1584.6	890.6	972.4	760.7
Grants	320.2	346.3	347.5	609.9	578.6	378.3	316.0	546.4	196.7	688.0	325.3
Loans	479.6	535.4	997.1	313.0	353.6	536.2	799.1	1038.2	693.9	284.4	435.4
TOTAL	1522.6	1695.1	1977.9	1661.4	1603.3	1529.8	1873.4	2175.0	1370.3	1774.1	1274.5
DISBURSEMENTS											
Food Aid	255.4	276.4	244.5	202.8	225.4	300.5	226.9	187.5	268.6	241.2	121.0
Grants	221.0	263.0	242.0	202.8	225.4	300.5	226.9	187.5	268.6	241.2	121.0
Loans	34.4	13.4	2.5	-	-	-	-	-	-	-	-
Commodity Aid	452.0	439.2	431.6	393.0	402.5	509.4	537.7	456.7	408.1	386.0	372.1
Grants	244.5	244.4	243.9	256.0	176.0	170.7	164.0	135.7	246.2	192.0	207.8
Loans	207.5	194.8	187.7	137.0	226.5	338.7	373.7	321.0	161.9	194.0	164.3
Project Aid	469.9	552.8	590.9	709.8	967.2	830.5	903.9	1165.4	1055.9	1064.0	1094.0
Grants	121.9	226.4	214.9	503.8	255.5	352.6	282.0	442.7	316.7	484.0	328.0
Loans	348.0	326.4	376.0	206.0	711.7	477.9	621.9	722.7	739.2	580.0	766.0
TOTAL	1177.3	1268.4	1267.0	1305.6	1595.1	1640.4	1668.5	1809.6	1732.6	1691.2	1587.1
Memo Items:											
Grants											
Commitments	836.7	858.5	880.3	1165.4	893.7	880.9	661.1	884.7	485.0	1098.8	734.5
Disbursements	587.4	733.8	700.8	962.6	656.9	823.8	672.9	765.9	831.5	917.2	656.8
Loans											
Commitments	685.9	836.6	1097.6	496.0	709.6	648.9	1212.3	1290.3	885.3	675.3	540.0
Disbursements	589.9	534.6	566.2	343.0	938.2	816.6	995.6	1043.7	901.1	774.0	930.3

Source: Economic Relations Division.

Table 3.11
AVERAGE EXCHANGE RATES
(Period averages; Taka per US$)

	1982/83	1983/84	1984/85	1985/86	1986/87	1987/88	1988/89	1989/90	1990/91	1991/92	1992/93
QUARTERLY AVERAGES											
PRINCIPAL RATE a/											
July-September	22.4187	24.5393	25.2823	26.6890	30.3000	31.0000	31.8902	32.2700	35.3550	36.779	39.000
October-December	23.6330	24.9723	25.8510	30.1740	30.5250	31.0857	32.1570	32.2700	35.7310	38.026	39.000
January-March	24.5000	25.0827	26.2380	30.5030	30.8000	31.3976	32.2700	32.7580	35.7900	38.803	39.600
April-June	24.5000	25.2000	26.8780	30.3000	30.9140	31.5000	32.2700	34.4310	35.7900	39.000	39.815
SECONDARY RATE b/											
July-September	22.8800	26.3200	27.9000	32.5900	33.1500	33.0000	32.9000	32.9250	36.0660	37.494	-
October-December	24.4000	27.4000	25.8000	33.4500	33.1500	32.9000	32.9100	32.9250	36.4460	38.536	-
January-March	24.7900	27.4600	30.4500	33.2000	33.0000	32.9000	32.9100	33.4220	36.5050		-
April-June	26.2200	27.9400	31.3000	33.2000	33.0000	32.9000	32.9100	35.1260	36.5050	-	-
FISCAL YEAR AVERAGES c/											
Principal Rate	23.7629	24.9486	26.0620	29.8861	30.6347	31.2458	32.1468	32.9323	35.6670	38.152	39.534
Secondary Rate	24.5725	27.2800	28.8625	33.1100	33.0750	32.9250	32.9075	33.5990	36.3810	-	-

a/ Unweighted averages of monthly exchange rates shown. The rates are period averages of the market rate (IFS, line rf), which are cross rates based on a fixed relationship to the Pound Sterling since January 1972.
b/ Unweighted averages of end period monthly data. As of January 1992, secondary rate has been abolished.
c/ Unweighted averages of quarterly exchange rates shown.
Source: International Financial Statistics and Statistics Department, Bangladesh Bank.

Table 3.12

Real Exchange Rate Index
(Base 1988 = 100)

Year	RER
1987	101.0
1988	100.0
1989	106.0
1990	99.7
1991	96.3
1992	89.7

Source: IMF.

Table 4.1

EXTERNAL PUBLIC DEBT OUTSTANDING INCLUDING UNDISBURSED AS OF JUNE 30, 1993
Includes only debt committed for a period up to June 30, 1993
(in thousand of US Dollars)

	DEBT OUTSTANDING		
	Disbursed	Undisbursed	Total
CREDITOR TYPE: SUPPLIERS CREDITS			
CREDITOR COUNTRY			
CHINA	4,275	298	4,515
FRANCE	1,858	-	1,858
HUNGARY	3,634	-	3,634
INDIA	1,812	370	2,182
PAKISTAN	1,751	-	1,751
ROMANIA	2,733	-	2,733
USSR	100,504	5,059	100,504
YUGOSLAVIA	1,047	-	1,047
TOTAL SUPPLIERS CREDITS	117,556	668	118,224
CREDITOR TYPE: FINANCIAL INSTITUTIONS			
CREDITOR COUNTRY			
FRANCE	-	-	-
TOTAL FINANCIAL INSTITUTIONS	-	-	-
CREDITOR TYPE: MULTILATERIAL LOANS			
CREDITOR COUNTRY			
ASIAN DEVELOPMENT BANK	2,943,045	1,135,530	4,078,574
EEC	45,540	-	45,540
IBRD	60,611	-	60,611
IDA	4,738,742	1,522,633	6,261,375
INTERNATIONAL FUND ARG (FAD)	152,163	48,283	200,401
ISLAMIC DEVELOPMENT BANK	23,159	14,555	37,714
OPEC, SPECIAL FUND	65,372	23,522	88,894
TOTAL MULTILATERAL LOANS	8,028,632	2,744,478	10,773,109

Continued

Table 4.1 (Continued)
EXTERNAL PUBLIC DEBT OUTSTANDING INCLUDING UNDISBURSED AS OF JUNE 30, 1993
Includes only debt committed for a period up to June 30, 1993
(in thousand of US Dollars)

	DEBT OUTSTANDING		
	Disbursed	Undisbursed	Total
CREDITOR TYPE: BILATERAL LOANS			
CREDITOR COUNTRY			
INDIA	8,974	2,105	11,079
IRAN	8,759	-	8,759
IRAQ	5,012	-	5,012
JAPAN	3,591,006	227,335	3,818,341
KOREA, REPUBLIC OF	1,220	-	1,220
KUWAIT	83,661	7,598	91,259
NETHERLANDS	16,971	2,640	19,557
PAKISTAN	-	32,200	32,200
POLAND	1,052	-	1,052
ROMAINA	3,652	17,493	21,145
SAUDI ARABIA	103,035	4,005	107,040
SWITZERLAND	4,724	-	4,724
TURKEY	725	-	725
UNITED ARAB EMIRATES	45,679	-	45,679
UNITED STATES	990,202	103,280	1,093,482
USSR	25,069	-	25,069
YUGOSLAVIA	12,873	-	12,873
TOTAL BILATERAL LOANS	5,140,000	519,774	5,660,463
CREDITOR TYPE: EXPORT CREDITS			
CREDITOR COUNTRY			
AUSTRIA	2,416	-	2,416
FRANCE	1,149	-	1,149
INDIA	47	-	47
NETHERLANDS	2,755	-	2,755
UNITED KINGDOM	1,041	-	1,041
USSR	148	-	148
MULTIPLE LENDERS	37,583	2,879	40,417
TOTAL EXPORT CREDITS	45,093	2,879	47,972
TOTAL EXTERNAL DEBT	13,331,971	3,267,797	16,599,768
CREDITOR TYPE			
SUPPLIERS CREDITS	117,556	668	118,224
FINANCIAL INSTITUTIONS	-	-	-
MULTILATERAL LOANS	8,028,632	2,744,478	10,773,109
BILATERAL LOANS	5,140,690	519,774	5,660,463
EXPORT CREDITS	45,093	2,879	47,972
TOTAL EXTERNAL DEBT	13,331,971	3,267,797	16,599,768

NOTE: (1) Only debts with an original or extended maturity of over one year are included in this table.
(2) Debt outstanding includes principal in arrears but excludes interest in arrears.
(3) Figures are preliminary.

Source: World Bank.

TABLE 4.2
BANGLADESH: SERVICE PAYMENTS, COMMITMENTS, DISBURSEMENTS, AND OUTSTANDING AMOUNTS OF EXTERNAL PUBLIC DEBT
PROJECTIONS BASED ON DEBT OUTSTANDING INCLUDING UNDISBURSED AS OF JUN 30, 1993
INCLUDES ONLY DEBT COMMITTED - JUNE 30, 1993
DEBT REPAYABLE IN FOREIGN CURRENCY AND GOODS
(IN THOUSANDS OF U.S. DOLLARS)

DATE	DEBT OUTSTANDING AT END OF PERIOD		TRANSACTIONS DURING PERIOD					OTHER CHANGES	
					SERVICE PAYMENTS				
	DISBURSED ONLY	INCLUDING UNDISBURSED	COMMITMENTS	DISBURSEMENTS	PRINCIPAL	INTEREST	TOTAL	CANCELLATIONS *	ADJUSTMENT **
	(1)	(2)	(3)	(4)	(5)	(6)	(7)	(8)	(9)
198506	5,415,390	8,750,696	1,079,191	621,803	105,621	76,867	182,488	133,269	-
198606	6,852,578	10,692,206	1,003,762	777,404	144,858	103,570	248,429	92,841	1,175,447
198706	7,968,131	11,671,176	795,285	1,020,263	145,111	121,970	267,081	170,049	498,845
198806	8,917,613	12,509,354	865,423	906,239	192,587	144,258	336,846	159,730	325,071
198906	9,624,904	13,204,771	1,262,539	974,249	192,965	140,477	333,442	161,278	-212,878
199006	10,500,439	14,352,362	1,341,515	1,099,754	225,661	144,549	370,209	96,728	128,465
199106	11,322,769	15,164,800	1,160,633	1,026,220	333,281	150,270	483,551	153,028	138,922
199206	12,190,266	16,369,355	831,219	720,383	314,689	156,587	471,276	352,638	962,377
199306	13,331,971	16,599,768	527,502	1,006,341	264,060	148,306	412,366	404,118	371,379
			*** THE FOLLOWING FIGURES ARE PROJECTED ***						
199406	14,085,742	16,111,150	---	1,065,522	299,176	179,912	479,088	176,868	-12,574
199506	14,616,360	15,790,979	---	850,709	320,174	181,492	501,666	---	3
199606	14,803,187	15,447,021	---	530,708	343,962	180,416	524,378	---	5
199706	14,708,367	15,085,835	---	346,379	361,202	177,284	538,486	---	15
199806	14,595,740	14,710,701	---	102,514	375,143	172,954	548,097	---	10
199906	14,273,007	14,308,071	---	79,899	402,632	167,408	570,039	---	1
200006	13,861,700	14,067,217	---	29,639	440,061	161,145	602,006	---	8
200106	13,402,339	13,404,312	---	3,458	462,908	154,069	616,977	---	3
200206	12,918,539	12,919,094	---	1,416	485,220	147,006	632,225	---	2
200306	12,414,401	12,414,434	---	522	504,662	139,882	644,545	---	2
200406	11,893,624	11,893,658	---	---	520,778	132,617	653,396	---	1
200506	11,374,553	11,374,587	---	---	519,072	125,327	644,399	---	0
200606	10,842,503	10,842,537	---	---	532,049	118,383	650,431	---	0
200706	10,318,082	10,318,116	---	---	524,422	111,610	636,032	---	0
200806	9,789,507	9,789,541	---	---	528,574	104,940	633,514	---	0
200906	9,252,840	9,252,873	---	---	536,665	98,295	634,960	---	-1
201006	8,726,205	8,726,239	---	---	526,636	91,882	618,518	---	1

* Includes Writeoffs; Projected amounts in this column are amounts excluded from projections due to unknown terms.

** This column shows the amount of arithmetic imbalance in the amount outstanding including undisbursed from one period to the next. The most common causes of imbalances are changes in exchange rates and transfers of debts from one category to another in the table.

Note: Figures are preliminary.

Source: World Bank.

Table 5.1
REVISED BUDGET SUMMARY
(Tk crore)

	1983/84	1984/85	1985/86	1986/87	1987/88	1988/89	1989/1990	1990/91	1991/92	1992/93
A. REVENUE SURPLUS	530	547	652	760	416	-348	38	513	1617	2550
Receipts	3033	3477	4073	4716	5146	5822	6778	7823	9517	11060
Expenditues	-2503	-2930	-3421	-3956	-4730	-6170	-6740	-7310	-7900	-8510
B. FOREIGN FLOWS	3483	3307	4018	4372	5086	4885	5545	6103	6039	6365
C. NET DOMESTIC CAPITAL										
Domestic Loans & Advances	-109	248	-252	-173	-400	-521	-499	-557	-539	15
Net Public Accounts	167	148	160	160	183	223	260	549	677	260
Total Net Domestic Capital	58	-100	-92	-13	-217	-298	-239	-8	138	275
D. EXTRA-BUDGETARY RESOURCES & DEFICIT FINANCING	106	479	5	-166	355	955	882	383	362	0
TOTAL RESOURCES AVAILABLE	4177	4233	4583	4953	5640	5194	6226	6991	8156	9190
E-USE OF RESOURCES										
ADP	3433	3508	4096	4513	4651	4595	5103	6121	7150	8121
Non-ADP Projects	210	207	144	92	70	98	106	125	138	117
Food Account	535	518	344	349	919	501	1018	744	868	924
Food-for-Work	198	216	348	326	400	526	471	510	564	418
Net Food Outlay	337	302	-4	23	519	-25	547	234	304	506
Others	0	0	0	0	0	0	0	0	0	28

Source: Ministry of Finance.

Table 5.2
CURRENT BUDGET: REVISED ESTIMATES
(Tk crore)

	1983/84 Revised Budget	1984/85 Revised Budget	1985/86 Revised Budget	1986/87 Revised Budget	1987/88 Revised Budget	1988/89 Revised Budget	1989/90 Revised Budget	1990/91 Revised Budget	1991/92 Revised Budget	1992/93 Revised Budget
REVENUE										
Tax Revenue	2410	2807	3242	3788	4307	4833	5712	6312	7661	8934
Production, consumption and distribution taxes	2020	2355	2710	3156	3503	3950	4610	5085	6166	6962
(Custom duties)	1000	1120	1338	1550	1618	1820	2167	2328	2820	2835
(Sales taxes)	345	410	461	550	525	540	531	823	0	0
(Excise duties)	600	750	772	900	1172	1400	1700	1713	1360	320
(Value Added tax)									1675	2500
(Stamp taxes)	75	110	125	140	170	170	177	187	251	312
(Motor vehicle taxes)	0	10	14	16	20	20	35	35	40	50
(Supplementary tax)	0	0	0	0	0	0	0	0	20	945
Taxes on income	331	390	460	550	664	750	875	1071	1300	1720
Land revenue tax a/	33	40	51	56	89	85	114	60	85	100
Other taxes and duties b/	26	22	21	28	49	48	113	96	110	152
Non-Tax Revenue	623	670	831	929	839	989	1067	1511	1856	2126
Nationalized sector	123	283	362	349	215	255	178	439	701	789
(Industries)	30	60	85	92	80	70	50	276	381	360
(Banks)	93	223	277	257	135	185	128	163	320	429
(Other public sector c/)	0	0	0	0	0	0	0	0	0	0
Interest receipts	102	140	233	200	225	220	345	300	300	350
Registration fees	30	40	43	65	60	63	70	70	80	96
Forest	29	36	50	51	50	60	20	25	30	40
Railways	154	-30	-53	-104	-149	-150	-139	-149	-126	-100
Post Office & T&T (net)	-13	8	0	9	37	78	53	220	254	295
Other d/	0	193	196	359	401	463				
Total Curent Revenue	3033	3477	4073	4716	5146	5822	6779	7823	9517	11060
EXPENDITURES										
General Services	1015	1108	1367	1722	2003	2241	2592	2583	2936	3547
- General administration	329	382	404	567	692	694	826	914	1081	1263
- Justice and police	185	220	348	302	348	378	451	451	509	740
- Defense	491	493	596	829	934	1139	1279	1180	1301	1494
- Scientific departments	10	13	19	24	29	30	36	38	44	49
Social Services	677	904	923	1414	1705	2079	2084	2241	2389	2831
- Education	365	493	600	747	820	949	1094	1182	1382	1674
- Health & population planning	129	160	113	275	305	321	367	387	431	516
- Social welfare	183	251	210	392	580	809	623	672	577	640
Economic Services	324	199	247	304	357	411	460	492	570	674
- Agriculture	80	109	95	174	196	234	256	283	300	346
- Manufacturing & Construction	6	8	64	20	22	23	28	26	29	33
- Transport & Communication	214	51	55	64	86	98	113	118	167	209
- Others	24	31	33	46	53	56	63	66	74	86
Debt Service	274	318	428	445	590	733	662	854	1108	1025
- Domestic								417	634	550
- External								437	473	475
Food Subsidy e/	160	250	141	50	0	627	631	373	344	153
Other Subsidy e/	53	15	0	19	65	79	310	397	245	134
Contingency	0	136	315	2	10	0	1	370	308	146
Total Current Expenditures	2503	2930	3421	3956	4730	6170	6740	7310	7900	8510

a/ Tax levied on land holdings. It was virtually abolished in FY74 together with the imposition of the Agriculture income tax but reinstated in 1976/77.

b/ Includes electricity duties, estate duty on agricultural land, taxes on immovable property, gift taxes, capital gains tax, tool taxes, betterment tax on commercial establishments and other levies.

c/ Includes receipts from nationalized insurance, other industrial operations and disinvestment of industrial units. For 1973/74 these are included under industries above.

d/ Receipts of various government departments, especially under general administration, social economic agriculture and other services etc.

e/ There has been a change in the definition of subsidy, especially during FY93. FY93 figures therefore, are not fully comparable to the previous years' figures.

Source: Ministry of Finance.

Table 5.3
ACTUAL INCOME AND EXPENDITURE OF THE CENTRAL GOVERNMENT
Taka billion

	FY84	FY85	FY86	FY87	FY88	FY89	FY90	FY91	FY92	FY93
Total Revenue	28.60	35.93	42.28	48.00	53.29	62.66	68.90	80.00	98.89	112.34
Tax	23.70	28.87	32.98	38.77	42.63	49.56	57.30	65.20	79.51	90.52
Non-tax	4.90	7.06	9.30	9.23	10.66	13.10	11.60	14.80	19.38	21.82
Total expenditure	-60.65	-65.89	-77.47	-93.03	-95.90	-110.11	-214.00	-137.00	-143.81	164.07
Current expenditure a/	-23.03	-26.61	-34.97	-41.59	-48.19	-56.08	-64.70	-72.30	-75.64	-83.54
Food account deficit	-3.80	-4.26	-1.68	-0.13	-5.64	-3.93	-8.80	-7.40	-5.75	-4.62
of which: foodstock change	(0.27)	(1.96)	(0.27)	(0.12)	(5.10)	(-2.34)	(2.9)	(1.38)	(2.25)	(-) d/
Annual Development Program (ADP)	-30.11	-30.40	-36.50	-46.30	-37.98	-44.17	-47.20	-52.00	-57.01	-66.90
Other capital expenditure and net lending b/	-3.71	-0.06	-4.32	-5.01	-4.09	-5.93	-5.20	-5.30	-5.41	-9.01
Overall budget deficit	-32.05	-29.96	-35.19	-45.03	-42.61	-47.45	-57.00	-57.00	-44.92	-51.73
Excluding foodgrain stocking	-31.78	-28.00	-34.92	-44.91	-37.51	-49.79	-54.10	-55.62	-42.67	-51.73
Net foreign financing c/	27.87	28.67	31.51	40.36	41.43	48.71	48.60	51.90	58.94	53.85
Project aid	13.31	14.40	20.17	29.63	25.01	27.20	35.50	35.20	36.37	40.57
Commodity aid	9.63	9.62	11.64	11.13	14.07	15.50	13.50	16.30	6.35	17.20
Food aid	6.97	4.92	4.99	6.94	7.64	9.33	6.20	9.70	8.81	4.65
Commercial food borrowing	-0.41	2.56	-2.27	-2.94	0.10	1.28	-0.80	-0.50	0.75	-0.73
Debt amortization	-1.63	-2.83	-3.02	-4.40	-5.39	-4.60	-5.80	-8.80	6.66	-7.84
Net domestic financing	4.36	1.30	5.58	4.68	1.19	-0.67	8.40	5.20	0.80	-2.10
Banking system	4.27	-1.90	0.95	3.37	-0.68	-4.47	6.50	1.70	-2.90	-12.0 e/
Other domestic	0.09	3.20	4.63	1.31	1.87	3.80	1.90	3.50	3.70	9.9
(Annual percentage change)										
Total Revenue	12.6	25.6	17.7	13.5	11.0	17.6	10.0	16.1	23.6	13.6
Total expenditure	4.9	8.6	17.6	20.1	3.1	14.8	14.3	8.8	5.0	1.6
Current expenditure a/	19.9	15.5	31.4	18.9	15.9	16.4	15.4	11.7	4.6	10.4
ADP	1.0	1.0	20.1	26.8	-18.0	16.3	6.9	10.2	9.6	17.3
(As percent of GDP)										
Total revenue	8.1	8.8	9.1	8.9	8.9	9.5	9.3	9.6	10.9	11.6
Tax revenue	6.7	7.1	7.1	7.2	7.1	7.5	7.8	7.8	8.8	9.3
Non-tax revenue	1.4	1.7	2.0	1.7	1.8	2.0	1.6	1.8	2.1	2.2
Total expenditure	17.2	16.2	16.6	17.3	16.1	16.7	17.1	16.4	15.9	15.1
Current expenditure a/	6.5	6.5	7.5	7.7	8.1	8.5	8.8	8.7	8.3	8.6
ADP	8.5	7.5	7.8	8.6	6.4	6.7	6.4	6.2	6.3	6.9
Overall budget deficit	9.1	7.4	7.5	8.4	7.1	7.2	7.7	6.8	5.0	3.5
Excluding food stocking	9.0	6.9	7.5	8.3	6.3	7.5	7.3	6.7	4.7	5.3
GDP Mkt. Prices	352.52	406.93	466.23	539.20	597.14	659.60	737.57	834.39	906.502	968.804

a/ Excludes food subsidies, which are included under the food account deficit.
b/ Comprises non-ADP project expenditure, the Food for Work program, miscellaneous investment (non-development) and net loan and advances.
   A major part of gross lending by Government is included within the ADP.
c/ Including foreign grants.
d/ Tk 3.1 billion of ADP expenditure has been reallocated from FY93 to FY92 per Gov't. estimates.
e/ Includes Tk9.2 billion of financing through National Saving schemes, prize and wage bonds and the surplus of the government
   employee pension fund. The remaining -3 billion taka may reflect errors in recording revenue and expenditure.

Source: Ministry of Finance and IMF and Bank Staff Estimates.

Table 5.4
ANNUAL DEVELOPMENT PROGRAMME
(Taka crore)

	1986/87 Revised Budget	1986/87 IMED Estimate	1987/88 Revised Budget	1987/88 IMED Estimate	1988/89 Revised Budget	1988/89 IMED Estimate	1989/90 Revised Budget	1989/90 IMED Estimate	1990/91 Revised Budget	1990/91 IMED Estimate	1991/92 Revised Budget	1991/92 IMED Estimate	1992/93 Revised Budget	1992/93 IMED Estimate
Agriculture, Rural Development and Water Resources	838.0	759.8	1030.5	798.4	1156.0	1016.0	1316.7	1325.4	1414.4	1208.9	1600.7	1278.0	1944.8	1354.14
(Agriculture)	252.0	190.9	333.2	258.7	363.4	280.0	384.4	262.7	424.92	307.2	468.53	423.45	534.29	370.89
(Rural Development)	143.9	108.3	137.6	91.0	130.8	99.9	256.7	177.8	286.1	222.3	392.13	318.77	529.53	365.67
(Water and Flood Control)	442.1	460.6	559.7	448.7	661.8	636.1	675.6	884.9	703.4	679.3	740.0	535.8	880.93	617.58
Industry	667.1	696.9	419.9	430.7	286.1	479.4	263.3	440.9	102.9	96.4	119.4	119.2	145.1	73.0
Power, Scientific Research and Natural Resources	1048.3	1153.0	1023.7	977.1	815.9	985.0	829.4	985.2	1146.4	747.72	1274.6	1069.4	2018.7	1490.4
Transport	435.1	441.1	468.6	466.3	604.5	684.2	539.7	750.2	622.6	630.1	856.6	837.1	1263.8	962.5
Communications	43.6	37.0	95.8	96.7	127.7	164.8	171.8	170.6	110.6	113.6	183.3	164.2	172.0	185.6
Physical Planning and Housing	158.5	139.0	198.0	167.5	179.4	161.5	190.5	286.4	251.04	231.1	360.7	314.6	380.0	235.5
Education and Training	214.6	197.6	251.5	213.3	257.6	209.5	303.9	224.9	335.29	173.4	492.2	298.9	603.4	528.4
Health	80.4	73.3	87.0	83.3	183	85.1	127.8	97.5	164.95	141.1	178.2	137.3	278.8	205.8
Family Planning	142.4	104.8	170.4	140.9	214.1	168.6	296.2	125.9	295.4	310.4	338.7	271.0	351.1	282.9
Social Welfare	21.9	20.1	19.9	15.9	41.5	36.6	27.6	25.8	38.4	30.6	36.4	28.5	92.1	30.6
Manpower and Employment	9.0	7.4	5.5	2.6	4.0	2.9	4.8	2.9	7.3	4.7	7.2	2.5	10.4	1.9
Upazilas	335	322.1	370	379.6	200.0	204.4	200.6	286.7	120	118.8	232.2	235.7	0.0	0.0
Other	519.5	487.0	509.8	374.1	525.5	417.0	830.0	816.3	1511.7	1463.2	1469.8	1267.5	860.6	1203.9
Total ADP	4513.4	4439.1	4650.6	4146.4	4595.3	4615.0	5102.3	5538.7	6121.0	5269.9	7150.0	6024.0	8120.7	6554.43

Note: Data used in the text differ from those shown above. The text data used IMED estimates on taka expenditures and ERD estimates on project aid disbursements.

Source: Ministry of Finance and Planning Commission.

Table 5.5:
Financial Performance of State-Owned Enterprises
Taka million

Corporation	1982-83	1983-84	1984-85	1985-86	1986-87	1987-88	1988-89	1989-90	1990-91	1991-92	1992-93
Manufacturing											
BSEC	-273	-202	-135	-85	-49	-62	-78	-365	-861	-1069	-1000
BSFIC	218	189	-234	-336	-315	-95	-255	164	-129	-692	-924
BCIC	158	121	131	105	-86	198	374	455	343	-548	-66
BTMC	23	112	42	-566	-245	-354	-22	-175	-574	-434	-959
BJMC	134	-310	-1462	-1583	-420	-1431	-1882	-3709	-2473	-3122	-3679
Subtotal	260	-90	-1657	-2466	-1115	-1743	-1864	-3629	-3695	-5865	-6628
Utilities											
BPC	597	1600	1817	1051	1473	938	1273	369	2492	3512	3134
BOGMC	72	136	101	-29	-71	95	-191	-272	302	633	648
BSC	24	4	6	-117	-101	37	-245	-244	-527	-383	38
BJMAN	123	163	-23	-57	-352	-266	33	117	-400	263	194
PDB	417	453	199	-285	172	-89	652	-3375	-2802	-7749	-7848
Subtotal	1233	2356	2099	563	1122	715	1522	-3405	-935	-3724	-3834
Other:											
BRTC	-120	-113	-137	-80	-182	-226	-237	-258	-246	-238	-298
DWASA	-11	-20	0	-10	20	14	19	16	4	5	7
CWASA	-3	6	5	-2	6	-2	-31	-63	-64	-57	-46
MPA	-18	-36	67	74	118	216	199	197	193	197	167
CPA	239	132	242	207	366	431	392	468	508	486	100
BJC	-271	-148	-444	-1623	-118	-1821	-1477	-1324	-1442	-1675	-2178
BFDC	2	-2	-25	-17	3	-18	-28	12	-15	0	-6
TCB	18	28	11	24	47	41	45	34	16	22	5
BFFWT	2	5	6	-5	-11	-26	27	33	32	5	-18
DESA	0	0	0	0	0	0	0	0	0	-18	-842
BADC	-34	-130	-176	56	46	78	152	109	78	-853	-221
BFIDC	-6	30	15	12	4	-16	7	-40	63	-105	21
BFDC (FILM)	2	2	1	2	2	2	2	1	-20	-142	-9
BIWTC	-20	-7	-11	-45	-55	-53	-78	-37	-37	-59	-47
EPZA	0	0	-9	-10	-8	1	3	-12	0	15	17
BSCIC	4	-3	-5	0	0	0	0	0	1	-6	-7
CDA	1	2	4	-4	28	42	89	71	49	20	7
RAJUK	48	78	78	92	133	0	0	79	75	130	57
KDA	8	7	20	2	4	-1	15	11	14	8	6
BIWTA	-11	-13	19	-52	-48	-5	-1	-21	-31	-9	-24
REB	0	0	0	0	0	0	0	31	79	109	187
BPRC	1	3	20	16	4	30	13	13	10	9	13
BSB	0	0	-1	-2	-2	0	-1	1	-2	-2	-7
BHB	0	0	0	0	2	0	0	-2	-5	-4	0
Subtotal	-176	-178	-320	-1366	356	-1312	-891	-681	-741	-2161	-3117
Total	1316	2087	122	-3267	364	-2339	-1232	-7716	-5371	-11851	-13578
Total excluding Petroleum (BPC)	719	487	-1695	-4319	-1110	-3277	-2505	-8085	-7863	-15363	-16713

Source: Monitoring Cell, Autonomous Bodies Wing, Ministry of Finance.

Table 6.1
MONEY SUPPLY AND DOMESTIC LIQUIDITY
(Tk billion)

	June 30, 1983	June 30, 1984	June 30, 1985	June 30, 1986	June 30, 1987	June 30, 1988	Dec 31, 1988	June 30, 1989	Dec 31, 1989	June 30, 1990	Dec 31, 1990	June 30, 1991	June 30, 1992 b/	June 30, 1992	June 30, 1992 c/	June 30, 1993 b/
1. Credit (net) to Government	16.1	20.7	19.9	18.5	18.9	18.2	14.5	17.3	21.4	20.2	19.9	21.9	19.0	36.3	36.3	24.2
2. Credit to Other Public Sector	24.6	25.5	32.2	39.7	41.6	43.6	45.2	46.3	50.6	50.1	52.1	53.6	56.9	56.4	56.4	60.3
3. Credit to Private Sector	31.0	49.1	68.9	83.6	89.6	109.0	119.6	133.6	148.6	160.0	168.1	178.2	191.2	179.4	179.4	199.6
4. Total Domestic Credit (1+2+3)	71.7	95.3	121.0	141.8	150.1	170.8	179.3	197.2	220.6	230.3	240.1	253.7	267.1	272.1	272.1	284.1
5. Net Foreign Assets	-4.6	-0.8	-2.4	-1.4	1.8	6.0	10.1	7.8	0.2	4.3	10.2	17.5	40.2	40.2	40.2	59.6
6. Other Liabilities (net)	-8.1	-10.6	-13.3	-17.0	-13.3	-12.7		-14.2		-11.6		-21.2	-22.0	-27.1	-27.1	-26.0
7. Total Liquidity (M2)	75.2	105.1	131.9	157.4	165.2	189.5	189.4	219.2	220.8	246.2	250.3	292.4	329.3	285.3	285.3	369.7
8. Currency Outside Banks	11.4	15.6	17.2	19.5	20.7	24.2	25.3	26.2	27.3	31.9	30.0	36.1	40.7	40.7	40.7	44.8
9. Demand Deposits	14.9	19.9	25.1	29.8	22.8	26.3	27.9	28.5	32.7	31.8	35.8	35.9	41.8	41.8	41.8	45.8
10. Currency and Demand Deposits (M1)	26.3	35.5	42.3	49.3	43.5	50.5	53.2	54.7	60.0	63.7	65.8	72.0	82.5	82.5	82.5	90.6
11. Time Deposits	32.7	48.4	63.0	74.1	95.1	113.6	125.9	136.1	150.5	159.3	168.5	178.0	202.7	202.7	202.7	224.7
Changes for Major Components (%) a/																
1. Credit (net) to Government and Public Sector																
Government	-0.7	13.5	12.8	11.7	4.0	2.1	-3.4	2.9	13.2	10.5	2.4	7.4	0.7	22.8		-8.8
Other Public Sector	-3.0	28.6	-3.9	-7.0	2.2	-3.7	-20.3	-4.9	23.7	16.8	-1.5	8.4	-13.2	65.8		27.4
2. Credit to Private Sector	0.8	3.7	26.3	23.3	4.8	4.8	3.7	6.2	9.3	8.2	4.0	7.0	6.2	5.2		6.0
3. Total Domestic Credit (1+2)	31.4	58.4	40.3	21.3	7.2	21.7	9.7	22.6	11.2	19.8	5.1	11.4	7.3	0.7		11.3
4. Total Liquidity (M2)	11.0	32.9	27.0	17.2	5.9	13.8	5.0	15.5	11.9	16.8	4.3	10.2	5.3	5.3		5.4
	29.7	39.8	25.5	19.3	5.0	14.7	-0.1	15.7	0.7	12.3	1.7	18.8	12.6	14.1		12.3

a/ Percent changes over preceding period.
b/ Data are adjusted (a) to exclude write-down of industrial loans and recapitalization of state banks which involved issuance of Tk 17.3 billion in long-term Treasury bonds (1991/92) and (b) to exclude the impact of mis-reporting of Bangladesh Krishi Bank and BCCI as well as Tk 15 billion of bonds issued by the government to NCBs for loan write-off and recapitalization and provisioning requirements, (1992/93).
c/ Actual.

Data prepared on the basis of revised reporting system.
Source: Bangladesh Bank, Statistics Department.

Table 6.2
AGRICULTURAL CREDIT ISSUED BY MAJOR CREDIT INSTITUTIONS
(Tk crore)

	1983/84	1984/85	1985/86	1986/87	1987/88	1988/89	1989/9	1990/91	1991/92	1992/93
Commercial Banks a/										
Short-term agricultural loans h/	288.1	349.0	164.2	156.3	227.20	199.85	204.8	167	224.5	206.9
Other agricultural financing b/	77.1	103.6	50.8	20.0	13.34	10.13	28.04	47.08	34.87	24.14
Fisheries financing	3.4	4.4	18.2	5.2	3.78	6.39	4.82	2.37	7.41	7.16
Tea production and development financing	2.7	6.7	6.3	6.0	5.23	5.48	6.35	4.96	5.7	5.82
Cold storage facilities for agricultural products	10.3	25.0	13.2	20.8	13.57	17.88	17.88	10.68	15.6	21.56
Total	381.54	488.67	252.7	208.3	263.12	239.73 d/	261.9	232.1	288	265.6
Bangladesh Krishi Bank & RAKUB										
Short-term agricultural loans h/	329.8	192.8	101.8	143.3	144.43	126.59	153.4	134	121.9	181.5
Other agricultural financing b/	198.3	312.2	137.6	105.6	114.46	172.47	128.6	91.87	222.5	219.7
Fisheries financing	24.2	15.3	10.4	5.2	6.23	4.79	3.2	2.45	2.6	4.58
Tea production and development financing	33.3	81.4	100.8	92.7	99.38	110.61	117.2	123.9 f/	145.9	145.2
Cold storage facilities for agricultural products	6.9	13.0	14.5	18.1	14.72	25.89	20.65	9.07	10.55	12.92
Total	592.4	614.7	365.1	364.9 c/	379.2	440.35	423	361.2 g/	503.5	563.9
Bangladesh Samabaya Bank										
Short-term agricultural loans h/	18.0	23.0	9.6	12.9	11.46	13.52	1.68	1.51	-	-
Other agricultural financing b/	3.3	5.3	4.4	4.2	2.51	4.13	0.22	0.76	3.06	3.43
Total	21.3	28.3	14.0	17.1	14.0	17.7	1.9	2.27	3.06	3.43
Totals by loan type										
Short-term agricultural loans h/	635.9	564.8	275.6	312.5	383.1	340.0	359.8	302.5	346.4	388.5
Other agricultural financing b/	278.7	421.1	192.8	129.8	130.31	186.73	156.9	139.7	260.4	247.2
Fisheries financing	27.6	19.8	28.6	10.4	10.01	11.18	8.02	4.82	10.01	11.74
Tea production and development financing	36.0	88.1	107.1	98.7	104.61	116.09	123.6	128.8	151.6	151
Cold storage facilities for agricultural products	17.2	38.0	27.7	38.9	28.29	43.77	38.53	19.75	26.15	34.48
Total	995.3	1131.7	631.8	590.3 c/	656.31	697.73 e/	686.8	595.6	794.6	832.9
Of which: Channelled through Cooperatives Under										
Bangladesh Rural Development Board										
Paddy	289.5	120.2	57.1	46.6	64.71	41.19	25.12	17.81	3.87	6.92
T. Aman	96.5	120.2	18.5	10.0	20.60	5.53	4.59	4.23	-	-
Boro	96.5	0.0	33.1	31.2	38.31	32.28	17.99	13.94	-	-
Aus/B. Aman	96.5	0.0	5.5	5.4	5.80	3.38	2.54	0.64	-	-
Wheat	33.2	0.0	0.7	0.4	0.27	0.20	-	-	-	-
Potato	0.0	0.0	1.8	1.1	0.63	1.20	1.1	1.53	-	-
Total	322.8	120.2	59.6	48.1	65.61	42.59	26.22	19.34	17.35	10.55

a/ Includes refinancing provided by Sonali Bank to TCCAs/KSSs through the IRCP/RDB.
b/ Includes agricultural term credit as well as financing for marketing, transport and agro-industries.
c/ Includes Tk 54.28 crore under BKB and Tk 22.67 crore under Rajshahi Krishi Unnayan Bank for which breakdown by type of loan is not available.
d/ Including Tk 62.26 crore disbursed by BRDB, for which breakdown is not available.
e/ Including Tk. 46.50 crore disbursed by RAKUB for which breakdown is not available.
f/ Including loans of Pubali Bank Ltd.
g/ Includes Tk. 324.17 crore under BKB Tk. 37.06 under RAKUB.
h/ Includes only crop loans.
Sources: Bangladesh Bank, Agricultural Credit Department; Bangladesh Krishi Bank; Bangladesh Samabaya Bank, Ltd.; and commercial banks.

Table 6.3
LOANS SANCTIONED BY DEVELOPMENT FINANCE INSTITUTIONS
(Tk crore)

	1985/86	1986/87	1987/88	1988/89	1989/90	1990/91	1991/92	1992/93
A. BANGLADESH SHILPA BANK (BSB)								
Loans sanctioned								
Food and allied products	0.9	0.1	0.2	1.4	17.7	0.8	3.6	0.9
Specialized textiles and handloom sector /a	69.9	56.9	35.6	85.3	190.4	72.6	2.7	31.4
Paper, board, printing and publishing b/	0.4	0.5	2.8	1.6	68.3	0.3	0.0	0.0
Tannery, leather and rubber industries	15.2	1.4	2.1	1.6	41.4	2.9	1.3	0.2
Chemicals, pharm, and allied industries	6.5	9.9	0.8	7.9	18.2	7.2	3.8	0.5
Engineering industries	2.4	3.3	3.3	3.1	8.7	6.8	0.2	1.7
Non-Metallic minerals c/	1.1	0.2	3.7	0.1	44.3	3.5	0.0	1.5
Miscellaneous industries	0.6	0.2	0.4	16.6	3.5	13.1	0.0	0.0
Sub-total	97.0	72.5	48.9	117.6	392.5	107.2	11.6	36.2
Service industries d/	2.1	2.8	3.1	2.6	10.9	6.1	0.8	1.8
Total Sanctions	99.1	75.3	52.0	120.2	403.4	113.3	12.4	41.0
Private sector	99.1	75.3	52.0	120.2	403.4	113.3	12.4	41.0
Public sector	0.0	0.0	0.0	0.0	0.0	0.0	0.0	0.0
Total Disbursements	12.2	27.9	30.9	46.8	63.1	81.5	35.4	66.2
End-fiscal year Resource Position								
Foreign Currency Resources (US$ million)								
Resources available from aid agreements	73.6	65.3	66.7	59.3	55.1 f/	46.3 f/	32.9	30.7
(-) Disbursements	2.3	7.0	7.0	9.4	8.1	3.8	1.4	5.7
Resurces available for disbursement	71.3	58.3	59.7	49.9	47.0	42.5	31.5	25.0
(-) Funds committed but not yet disbursed	32.7	18.3	27.3	12.0	4.9	5.4	3.8	9.8
Resources available for commitment	38.6	40.0	32.4	37.9	42.1 f/	37.1 f/	27.7	15.2
(+) Cancellations & withdrawals	5.5	0.0	0.0	0.0	0.0	0.0	0.0	0.0
(-) Approvals not yet committed	32.5	20.1	9.8	25.5	19.5	18.4	8.7	0.9
Foreign currency resources avail. for approval	11.6	19.9	22.6	12.4	-19.5	18.7	19.0	0.1 f/
Local Currency Resources (Tk crore)								
Cash on hand/in banks	90.9	104.3	130.6	191.5	115.4	50.0	57.4	120.6
(+) Money at call e/	6.8 e/	4.5 e/	6.0	0.0	-4.7	-19.0	-22.0	-7.0
(-) Reserves on deposit	6.7	5.3	5.5	9.5	8.8	8.5	7.9	12.1
(-) Commitments & approvals not yet disb.	27.1	33.8	27.0	18.3	39.7	62.5	23.3	49.1
Local currency resources avail. for disb.	63.9	69.7	104.1	163.7	62.2 g/	-40 /g	4.2	52.4

Continued....

Table 6.3 (Continued)
LOANS SANCTIONED BY DEVELOPMENT FINANCE INSTITUTIONS
(Tk crore)

	1985/86	1986/87	1987/88	1988/89	1989/90	1990/91	1991/92	1992/93
A. BANGLADESH SHILPA RIN SANGSTHA (BSRS) h/								
Loans sanctioned								
Food and allied products	1.0	0.2	-	1.2	21.3	0.6	0.3	1.4
Specialized textiles and handloom sector a/	10.3	0.0	-	8.3	58.6	1.6	0.8	2.9
Paper, board, printing and publishing b/	0.0	0.0	-	1.7	-	-	-	-
Tannery, leather and rubber industries	0.0	0.0	-	-	1.5	-	-	-
Chemicals, pharm, and allied industries	0.2	0.0	-	7.9	13.9	-	-	-
Engineering industries	0.0	0.3	-	0.5	0.2	-	-	-
Non-Metallic minerals c/	0.8	0.0	-	3.7	16.0	0.6	1.7	-
Miscellaneous industries	0.0	0.2	-	0.4	0.3	-	-	-
Sub-total	12.3	0.7	-	23.7	110.5	-	2.8	4.3
Service industries d/	0.4	0.0	-	-	0.8	0.8	0.3	0.8
Total Sanctions	12.7	0.7	-	23.7	111.3	3.6	3.1	5.1
Private sector	12.7	0.7	-	23.7	111.3	3.6	3.1	5.1
Public sector	0.0	0.0	-	-	-	-	-	-
Total Disbursements	8.9	5.2	3.0	3.7	20.0	42.9	27.4	24.0

a/   Includes jute and allied fibres.
b/   Includes forestry and wood products.
c/   Includes glass and ceramics.
d/   Includes inland water and road transport, cinemas, hotels, and clinics.
e/   Includes amount invested in the Government securities.
f/   Includes Tied Loans
      -Romanian Credit
      -Exim-Bank of India
      -CMC Chinese Suppliers Credit
g/   Includes customers' deposits of short term maturities.
h/   Net of subsequent cancellations and adjustments.
i/   As the validity of the Romanian credit expired on 30/6/93, unutilized balance amount of US$14.82 million has not
      been shown in the resources available for approval.

Source: Shilpa Bank & Shilpa Rin Shangstha.

Table 6.4
NOMINAL INTEREST RATES ON SELECTED SAVINGS
ACCOUNTS AND CERTIFICATES
(percent per annum)

	Jan 1985	Sept 1985	July 1986	Sept 1987	Aug 1988	Dec 1989	Jan 1990	July 1990	Jan 1991	July 1991	Dec 1991	June 1992	Jan 1993	April 1993	June 1993
Scheduled Banks' Deposit Rates:															h/
Special Notice Accounts	4.50	4.50	4.50	4.50	4.50	4.50	4.50	4.50	4.50	4.50	4.50	4.50	4.5	4.5	5.(min)g/
Savings Accounts with Checking	8.50	8.50	8.50	9.00 a/	9.00	9.00	8.5-12	8.5-11.75	8-11.50	8.5-12	8-11.5	6(min.)g/	5.5(min)g/	5.(min)g/	5.(min)g/
Fixed Deposits:															
Three months to under six months	12.00	12.00	12.00	12.00	12.00	12.00	10-14	10-13.75	10-13.75	10-13.75	9-13	7.5(min)g/	7(min)g/	6(min)g/	6(min)g/
Six months to under one year	13.00	13.00	13.00	12.50 b/	12.50	12.50	10-14	10-13.75	10-13.75	10-13.75	10-13.75	g/	7(min)g/	6(min)g/	6(min)g/
One year to under two years	14.00	14.00	14.00	13.25 b/	13.25	13.25	10-14	10-13.75	10-13.75	10-13.75	10-13.75	g/	7(min)g/	6(min)g/	6(min)g/
Two years to under three years	14.50	14.50	14.50	13.75 b/	13.75	13.25	10-14	10-13.75	10-13.75	10-13.75	10-13.75	g/	7(min)g/	6(min)g/	6(min)g/
Three years and over	15.00	15.00	15.00	14.25 b/	14.25	14.25	10-14	10-13.75	10-13.75	10-13.75	10-13.75	g/	7(min)g/	6(min)g/	6(min)g/
Post Office Savings Bank Deposit Rate:															
Ordinary Deposits	11.50	11.50	11.50	11.50	11.50	11.50	11.50	11.50	11.50	11.50	11.50	8.00	8.00	8.00	8.00
Fixed Deposits:															
One year to under two years	15.00	15.00	15.00	15.00	15.00	15.00	15.00	15.00	15.00	15.00	15.00	15.00	12.36	12.36	12.36
Two years to under three years	15.50	15.50	15.50	15.50	15.50	15.50	15.50	15.50	15.50	15.50	15.50	15.50	13.55	13.55	13.55
Three years and over	16.00	16.00	16.00	16.00	16.00	16.00	16.00	16.00	16.00	16.00	16.00	16.00	15.00	15.00	15.00
Government Borrowing:															
Treasury Bills	8.50	9.00	9.00	8.00	8.00	8.00	8.00	7.50	7.50	7.50	7.00	7.00	6.25	4.75	4.75
Tap Treasury Bills c/	9.50	8.00	8.00	8.00	8.00	8.00	8.00	8.00	11.50	11.50	11.50	11.50	10.50	9.00	9.00
Ways and Means Advances	10.50	10.75	10.75	10.25	10.25	10.25	10.25	9.25	9.25	9.25	8.75	8.75	8.00	6.50	6.00
Two-year Special Treasury Bonds: d/															
Issued at discount	15.70	15.70	15.70	15.70	15.70	15.70	15.70	15.70	15.70	15.70	15.70	15.70			
Issued at par	14.20	14.20	14.20	14.20	15.70	14.20	14.20	14.20	14.20	14.20	14.20	14.20			
Savings Certificates:															
Eight-year Defense Savings Certificates	21.00	21.00	21.00	21.00	21.00	21.00	21.00	21.00	21.00	21.00	21.00	18.00	18.00	18.00	18.00
Six-year Bonus Savings Certificates	22.00	22.00	22.00	22.00	22.00	22.00	22.00	22.00	22.00	22.00	22.00	/i			
Five-year Wage Earners Development Bo	23.00	23.00	23.00	23.00	23.00	23.00	23.00	23.00	23.00	23.00	23.00	23.00	23.00	23.00	23.00
Five-year Savings Deposits	12.20	18.00	18.00	18.00	18.00	18.00	18.00	18.00	18.00	18.00	18.00	16.00	16.00	16.00	16.00
Three Year Savings Certificate f/	-	19.55	-	-	19.55	19.55	19.55	19.55	19.55	19.55	19.55	15.00	15.00	15.00	15.00

a/ 10.0% for rural areas.
b/ Effective from January 17, 1987.
c/ Since repaid by August 1985.
d/ With effect from February 5, 1984 and repaid by June 1988.
e/ With effect from February 24, 1981.
f/ With effect from November 1, 1988.
g/ With effect from June 3, 1992 minimum rates were established as shown above: the maximum interest rate to be decided by the banks themselves.
h/ Banks are free to determine their rates.
i/ No money would be invested/deposited in the Bonus Savings Certificate (Bonus Sanchaya Patra) from June 3, 1992. The Government has decided to discontinue the scheme.

Source: Bangladesh Bank, Research Department.

Table 6.5
NOMINAL INTEREST RATES ON ADVANCES
(percent per annum)

	Aug. 1977	Oct. 1980	Jan. 1985	Sept. 1985	Jul. 1985	Sept. 1987	Aug. 1988	Dec. 1989	Jan. 1990	Jul. 1990	Jan. 1991	Jul. 1991	Dec. 1991	Jun. 1992	Apr. 1993
Bank Rate (Bangladesh Bank's lending and discount rate)	8.00	10.50	11.00	11.26	10.75	10.75	10.75	10.75	9.75	9.75	9.75	9.75	9.25	8.5 f/	6.50
Schedule Banks Interest Rates on Loans and Advances:															
- Export credit for traditional items a/	10.50	12.00	12.00	12.00	9.00	9.00	9.00	9.00	8.0-11	8.0-11	8.5-11.5	8.0-12	7.5-11	7.5-10.5	7.5-10.5
- Export credit for non-traditional items a/	10.50	9.00	9.00	9.00	9.00	9.00	9.00	9.00	8.0-11	8.0-11	8.5-11.5	8.0-12	7.5-11	7.5-10.5	7.5-10.5
- Export credit other a/	10.50	9.00	7.00	7.00	7.00	7.00	7.00	7.00	8.0-11	8.0-11	8.5-11.5	8.0-12	7.5-11	7.5-10.5	7.5-10.5
- Agriculture (production) including forestry and fishery b/	-	16.00	16.00	16.00	16.00	16.00	16.00	16.00	16.00	16.00	16.00	12-16	11-15	11-15	11-15
- Industry	11.00-12.00	14.00	14.50	12.00-14.50	9.00-14.00	9.00-14.00	9.00-14.00	9.00-14.00	13.0-17.00	12.5-16.5	12.5-16	12-17	11-15	d/	d/
- Industry in less developed areas	11.50	13.00	13.00	13.00	10.00-13.50	10.00-13.50	10.00-13.50	10.00-13.00	10.00	10.00	10.00	9-12	8-13	8-13	8-13
- Loans for construction of houses:															
- in rural areas	5.00	5.00	5.00	5.00	5.00	5.00	5.00	5.00	..	..	..	..	..	..	..
- in urban areas	16.00	16.00	16.00	16.00	16.00	16.00	16.00	16.00	12-15	12-15	12-15	12-15	11-14	..	d/
- Special credits:															
- loans given in the Special Economic Zone of Chittagong Hill Tracts region	11.00	5.00	5.00	5.00	5.00	5.00	5.00	5.00	5.00	5.00	5.00	5.00	5.00	5.00	d/
- small loan schemes, special credit for salt growers, self-employment, etc. c/	-	13.00	13.00	13.00	13.00	13.00	13.00	13.00	13.00	13.00	13.00	13.00	13.00	d/	d/
- Advances for internal trading purposes	-	15.50	16.00	16.00	16.00	16.00	16.00	16.00	16.00	16.00	16.00	12-17	12-17	d/	d/

a/ Traditional = jute, jute goods and loose tea, non-traditional = packet tea & jute carpets; other = newly emerging industries. From July 7, 1986 to Dec. 1989, a rate of 7 percent was applied to a small number of newly emerging non-traditional export items (engineering & electrical goods, handicrafts and handlooms). This special rate was abolished effective Jan. 1990.

b/ Includes service charge of 4%.

c/ Does not include services charges of 2% over the rate of 13% applied with effect from April 1, 1984.

d/ Effective April 1, 1992, BB removed all ceiling on deposit rates and all floors and ceiling on all lending rates with the exception of export, agriculture and small and cottage industries sectors.

.. = not available;   - = not applicable.

Source: Bangladesh Bank.

Table 7.1
LAND UTILIZATION STATISTICS
000 Hectares

	1988/89	1989/90	1990/91
Total area	14839	14839	14839
Not available			
for cultivation	3094	3150	3221
Forest	1903	1903	1899
Cultivatable waste	359	349	584
Current fallow	1329	1087	963
Net cropped area	8154	8350	8174
of which:			
Single cropped area	3571	3634	3294
Double cropped area	3605	3719	3899
Triple cropped area	977	997	981
Memo Item:			
Total cropped area	13714	14063	14034

Source: Agricultural Statistics Wing, BBS.

Table 7.2
AREA UNDER MAIN CROP
('000 hectares)

	1983/84	1984/85	1985/86	1986/87	1987/88	1988/89	1989/90	1990/91	1991/92	1992/93
Foodgrains	11506	11307	11094	11325	11035	10897	11122	11145	10927	
- Rice	10784	10452	10399	10609	10323	10224	10486	10435	10244	
(Aus)	3209	3004	2845	2904	2789	2684	2265	2111	1916	1735
(Aman)	6142	5839	6020	6053	5591	5101	5708	5776	5693	5844
(Boro)	1433	1610	1534	1652	1943	2439	2513	2548	2635	-
- Wheat	538	691	540	585	597	560	592	599	575	637
- Other Cereals	185	163	155	131	115	113	44	111	108	102
Pulses	763	744	708	683	699	564	704	696	689	659
- Gram	113	109	104	104	103	99	103	97	92	68
- Khesari	242	244	232	222	231	159	243	244	246	245
- Mashkalai	84	75	69	66	70	67	70	69	68	68
- Masur	240	233	223	213	217	163	209	210	209	207
- Matar	24	23	21	21	20	19	19	18	18	18
- Mung	60	60	59	57	58	57	60	58	56	53
Oilseeds	606	598	591	564	546	544	573	568	565	544
- Rape and mustard	364	385	370	343	318	334	339	339	340	338
- Til	102	86	92	85	82	76	86	83	81	64
- Groundnut	32	28	30	30	39	36	39	38	39	36
- Linseed	77	68	68	74	75	66	77	77	75	75
- Coconut	31	31	31	32	32	32	32	31	31	31
Fibres	612	705	1075	785	524	560	563	603	607	520
- Jute	594	691	1058	772	512	543	542	583	588	500
- Cotton	18	13	17	13	12	17	21	20	19	20
Drugs & Narcotics	148	147	145	139	142	141	140	135	134	
- Tea	46	46	45	46	47	47	47	48	48	
- Tobacco	53	53	54	46	47	46	45	38	37	36
- Betelnuts	36	36	34	34	35	35	35	36	36	75
- Betel leaves	13	13	12	13	13	13	13	13	14	31
Spices	132	131	125	122	124	125	127	127	124	124
- Rabi chillies	71	68	63	60	61	62	63	63	61	61
- Onion	34	35	34	33	34	34	35	35	34	34
- Garlic	13	13	13	13	13	13	13	13	13	13
- Turmeric	14	15	15	16	16	16	16	16	16	16
Tubers	179	177	165	157	174	163	169	174	177	175
- Potato	113	114	109	106	123	111	117	124	128	130
- Sweet potato	67	63	56	51	51	52	52	50	49	45
Sugar Plants	182	178	170	175	182	181	196	201	197	197
- Sugarcane	170	167	160	165	173	172	187	191	187	187
- Date palm	11	11	10	10	9	9	9	10	10	10
Fruits	125	124	122	124	129	125	127	127	127	
- Banana	43	41	40	41	41	38	39	39	39	39
- Mango	46	46	46	47	49	49	49	49	49	
- Pineapple	14	14	13	13	14	13	14	14	14	14
- Jackfruit	22	23	23	23	25	25	25	25	25	25
Vegetables										
- Brinjal	29	27	26	26	27	18	29	29	29	29

Note: Crops with less than 10,000 ha average not shown separately.
Source: Bangladesh Bureau of Statistics.

Table 7.3
PRODUCTION OF MAIN CROPS
(thousand metric tons (unless noted otherwise)

	1982/83	1983/84	1984/85	1985/86	1986/87	1987/88	1988/89	1989/90	1990/91	1991/92	1992/93
Foodgrains	15311	15865	16210	16189	16590	16547	16650	18827	18936	19395	13071
- Rice	14216	14508	14623	15039	15406	15413	15544	17857	17852	18251	11821
(Aus)	3066	3222	2783	2828	3130	2993	2856	2488	2328	2178	2075
(Aman)	7603	7936	7931	8542	8267	7690	6857	9202	9167	9269	9680
(Boro)	3546	3350	3909	3671	4010	4731	5831	6167	6357	6804	66
- Wheat	1095	1211	1463	1043	1091	1048	1022	890	1004	1065	1176
- Other cereals	..	146	124	107	93	86	84	80	80	79	74
Pulses	..	527	534	496	487	515	395	490	503	499	484
- Gram	..	86	81	77	82	75	64	70	71	65	53
- Khesari	..	170	183	167	164	182	118	170	177	185	172
- Mashkalai	..	60	55	45	43	52	47	52	52	50	51
- Masur	..	162	165	160	149	159	125	155	157	153	163
- Matar	..	14	15	14	14	14	13	12	14	14	14
- Mung	9	35	35	33	35	33	28	31	32	32	31
Oil seeds	..	468	484	469	438	448	420	437	449	461	474
- Rape and mustar	..	254	286	261	229	222	207	217	228	243	244
- Til	..	57	47	54	49	49	43	49	49	45	49
- Groundnut	..	33	31	34	34	48	45	41	41	42	39
- Linseed	..	41	37	37	43	43	41	48	55	49	49
- Coconut	..	83	83	83	83	86	84	82	76	82	93
Fibres											
- Jute ('000 bales)	4881	5216	5111	8660	6753	4701	4436	4639	5302	5273	4919
- Cotton ('000 bale	58	46	29	28	22	39	39	85	146	77	87
Drugs & narcotics											
- Tea	41	43	38	44	38	41	44	39	46	45	
- Tobacco	51	48	50	47	40	42	39	38	34	34	36
- Betelnuts	24	24	22	23	22	22	22	23	24	24	24
- Betel leaves	72	61	62	61	62	65	63	65	67	69	70
Spices	251	246	251	246	240	256	256	272	267	272	269
- Rabi chillies	43	42	42	41	39	41	43	47	47	46	49
- Onion	140	136	140	136	130	141	139	148	143	144	140
- Garlic	43	43	40	38	36	39	38	39	38	40	39
- Turmeric	25	25	29	31	35	35	36	38	39	41	41
Tubers	1893	1879	1842	1715	1617	1834	1633	1578	1720	1849	1818
- Potato	1167	1166	1159	1103	1069	1276	1089	1066	1237	1379	1384
- Sweet Potato	725	713	683	612	548	558	544	512	483	470	434
Sugar plants											
- Sugarcane a/	7477	7169	6878	6640	6896	7207	6707	7423	7682	7446	7506
- Date palm (juice)	343	343	312	279	268	221	201	206	206	206	214
Fruits	1280	1181	1207	1207	1226	1243	1156	1223	1218	1213	
- Banana	710	675	690	691	703	684	609	637	624	626	636
- Mango	199	159	163	159	155	160	159	175	179	183	
- Pineapple	159	136	132	128	133	145	137	157	162	148	148
- Jackfruit	212	211	222	229	235	254	251	254	253	255	257
Vegetables											
- Brinjal	187	182	171	167	162	164	116	182	186	185	189

a/ Based on total area and mill farm yield estimates; probably substantially overestimated.

Source: Bangladesh Bureau of Statistics.

Table 7.4
AUS AND AMAN PRODUCTION BY DISTRICT
('000 metric tons rice equivalent)

	1983/84	1984/85	1985/86	1986/87	1987/88	1988/89	1989/90	1990/91	1991/92	1992/93
AUS										
Rajshahi	895.9	827.9	803.2	748.1	611.6	605.0	471.1	446.5	430.8	352.7
Dinajpur	196.0	196.5	169.9	145.7	145.9	133.0	82.1	88.5	77.7	49.2
Rangpur	279.5	261.1	290.3	245.3	247.7	217.0	156.7	155.0	152.7	120.3
Bogra	112.7	85.7	84.3	90.9	39.4	31.0	21.0	24.2	10.0	5.2
Rajshahi	200.0	178.9	154.8	168.8	103.4	162.0	156.0	137.1	155.5	150.7
Pabna	107.7	105.8	103.9	97.4	75.2	62.0	55.3	41.7	34.9	27.3
Khulna	636.8	516.5	601.8	759.4	869.6	787.0	639.2	628.0	624.4	580.7
Kushtia	136.5	159.3	170.3	197.8	209.6	194.0	150.0	166.4	140.6	130.3
Jessore	168.0	141.7	156.7	240.4	227.0	230.0	172.1	150.7	189.0	130.5
Khulna	58.0	30.2	32.2	37.4	50.3	59.0	46.0	48.3	57.1	86.7
Barisal	192.1	139.3	172.0	195.6	263.9	213.0	202.8	181.5	169.8	154.2
Patuakhali	82.2	46.0	70.6	88.2	118.8	91.0	68.3	81.1	67.9	79.0
Dhaka	958.0	800.0	812.9	873.9	852.4	728.0	680.7	564.3	538.7	537.9
Jamalpur	130.0	114.5	119.8	107.5	87.0	70.0	60.6	58.8	55.1	52.7
Mymensingh a/	378.0	352.1	343.5	331.7	366.6	253.0	254.2	229.1	241.9	213.4
Tangail	93.8	71.8	76.0	79.1	64.9	64.0	49.6	47.3	37.6	40.1
Dhaka	195.8	154.6	123.7	143.9	109.0	108.0	109.5	90.1	73.1	65.8
Faridpur	160.3	107.0	149.8	211.7	224.9	233.0	206.8	139.0	131.0	165.9
Chittagong	730.9	638.1	609.2	748.0	659.5	736.0	696.7	689.4	584.6	603.6
Sylhet	178.4	147.5	163.1	230.2	177.4	227.0	263.2	269.0	182.7	238.0
Comilla	239.8	197.4	160.5	202.3	208.8	209.0	162.0	177.2	173.4	151.9
Noakhali	164.2	146.5	149.8	204.5	157.9	225.0	172.7	128.0	107.0	98.3
Chittagong	118.1	116.3	103.6	80.5	87.9	54.0	73.2	87.8	92.9	89.2
Chittagong H.Tracts b/	30.4	18.9	21.6	17.2	14.2	11.0	10.9	12.0	12.3	11.5
Bandarban	::	11.5	10.5	13.3	13.3	10.0	14.7	15.4	16.3	14.7
Total	3221.5	2782.5	2827.1	3129.4	2993.1	2856.0	2487.7	2328.2	2178.5	2074.9
AMAN										
Rajshahi	2594.9	2566.1	2692.2	2536.7	2245.2	2353.0	3141.9	3326.6	3254.7	3405.5
Dinajpur	506.2	529.1	546.8	525.1	504.8	624.0	763.1	793.4	713.6	735.4
Rangpur	885.9	928.1	930.0	887.8	868.4	844.0	1070.7	1112.2	1129.2	1132.0
Bogra	395.6	425.7	445.6	410.1	351.5	326.0	458.7	486.2	506.8	537.3
Rajshahi	560.5	525.4	557.3	510.1	420.2	450.0	675.6	731.0	710.8	766.8
Pabna	246.7	157.7	212.5	203.6	100.3	109.0	173.8	203.8	194.3	234.0
Khulna	1778.0	1897.1	2067.3	1917.5	1942.6	1711.0	2338.1	2207.2	2351.6	2349.7
Kushtia	81.6	107.1	119.0	114.1	128.1	141.0	176.7	185.4	190.2	199.0
Jessore	333.0	322.4	412.6	380.7	361.3	344.0	538.6	529.2	630.8	591.3
Khulna	528.8	622.7	607.9	497.0	524.0	461.0	654.6	627.9	655.3	643.2
Barisal	463.2	481.0	531.5	546.5	518.6	453.0	573.2	531.9	484.3	509.5
Patuakhali	371.3	363.9	396.3	379.2	410.6	312.0	395.0	332.8	391.0	406.7
Dhaka	1639.0	1587.0	1763.5	1760.4	1551.3	1062.0	1523.9	1496.3	1550.4	1666.8
Jamalpur	240.5	242.5	263.5	263.1	228.1	175.0	218.2	218.8	246.0	244.1
Mymensingh a/	634.8	698.5	756.7	709.5	693.9	524.0	698.5	656.7	651.7	721.8
Tangail	205.1	158.9	177.9	193.5	160.5	40.0	170.4	176.9	145.2	168.0
Dhaka	317.1	301.3	309.7	335.5	257.1	148.0	241.6	249.0	261.3	266.4
Faridpur	241.5	185.9	255.7	258.8	211.7	175.0	195.2	194.9	246.2	266.5
Chittagong	1925.0	1880.6	2019.2	2052.2	1951.2	1730.0	2198.2	2136.9	2112.2	2257.9
Sylhet	573.5	505.6	583.7	552.6	578.8	375.0	576.0	627.1	580.1	650.5
Comilla	501.7	482.5	533.4	524.3	496.5	424.0	667.9	611.9	528.3	586.3
Noakhali	385.1	423.1	418.6	418.9	316.7	372.0	379.3	303.8	368.8	381.8
Chittagong	415.1	422.8	430.3	509.5	514.4	514.0	526.5	537.7	580.4	581.5
Chittagong H.Tracts b/	49.6	46.6	53.2	46.9	44.8	45.0	48.5	56.4	54.6	57.8
Total	7936.9	7930.8	8542.2	8266.8	7690.3	6856.0	9202.1	9167.0	9268.9	9679.9

a/ Kishoreganj included in Mymensingh.
b/ Khaghrachari and Rangamati included in Chittagong Hill Tracts.
:: = Not Available

Source: Bangladesh Bureau of Statistics.

Table 7.5

PRODUCTION OF BORO AND WHEAT BY DISTRICT

('000 metric tons, rice equivalent)

	1983/84	1984/85	1985/86	1986/87	1987/88	1988/89	1989/90	1990/91	1991/92	1992/93
BORO										
Rajshahi	666.4	738.4	1022.4	1113.9	1394.0	1602.7	1757.9	1885.9	1975.1	1983.7
Dinajpur	35.2	38.4	52.6	71.3	87.2	142.9	166.1	169.9	204.7	172.4
Rangpur	128.2	154.5	280.7	340.9	391.8	439.3	461.8	452.7	471.9	515.0
Bogra	193.0	225.1	270.5	249.7	376.0	428.8	438.9	473.9	489.9	503.9
Rajshahi	169.8	159.1	237.9	289.2	319.8	346.1	418.8	512.7	522.7	537.2
Pabna	140.3	161.3	180.7	162.8	219.2	245.6	272.3	276.7	285.9	255.1
Khulna	215.9	355.4	234.1	246.6	365.0	609.2	615.0	667.3	709.2	728.3
Kushtia	6.9	10.2	19.4	21.1	26.9	45.6	53.1	61.0	67.5	66.1
Jessore	78.1	151.2	81.0	115.3	210.3	401.3	316.7	356.1	367.4	365.9
Khulna	42.4	80.0	74.9	59.6	78.4	90.5	90.9	100.3	117.2	159.9
Barisal	75.1	94.5	50.0	45.3	45.1	67.7	151.3	146.1	146.4	124.1
Patuakhali	13.4	19.5	8.8	5.3	4.3	4.1	3.0	3.8	10.7	12.3
Dhaka	1262.6	1525.3	1278.9	1472.2	1717.3	2081.4	2180.1	2244.1	2287.7	2256.0
Jamalpur	117.9	172.4	140.6	169.5	222.4	236.2	246.2	262.0	276.9	281.2
Mymensingh a/	528.7	647.4	503.0	603.0	731.1	816.1	815.3	814.5	898.3	909.1
Tangail	223.9	235.1	229.5	229.8	217.3	237.4	255.0	237.9	245.1	249.6
Dhaka	301.2	298.5	263.0	309.9	330.8	430.9	512.2	580.8	567.0	552.6
Faridpur	90.8	171.8	142.8	160.0	215.7	360.8	351.4	348.9	300.5	263.5
Chittagong	1204.6	1290.0	1135.6	1177.5	1254.5	1538.0	1613.8	1559.4	1832.2	1617.8
Sylhet	430.0	464.0	379.2	386.9	351.0	430.1	394.7	467.2	535.3	456.8
Comilla	287.5	317.7	303.1	304.0	436.7	577.1	592.7	555.4	616.0	610.4
Noakhali	151.4	186.5	135.1	170.8	179.7	245.2	314.9	321.6	364.7	246.0
Chittagong	308.4	292.2	293.1	284.4	264.8	267.0	290.3	196.6	293.8	282.5
Chittagong H. Tracts b/	27.2	29.5	25.1	31.4	22.3	18.6	21.2	18.6	22.4	22.2
Total:	3349.5	3909.1	3671.0	4010.2	4730.8	5831.3	6166.8	6356.7	6804.2	6585.7
WHEAT										
Rajshahi	598.1	684.3	454.0	535.2	435.3	443.0	437.2	530.7	557.3	583.3
Dinajpur	143.1	119.2	88.6	114.8	95.5	110.0	134.4	156.6	146.4	171.5
Rangpur	173.6	196.2	109.4	165.3	131.1	133.3	116.9	122.5	134.7	112.9
Bpgra	61.7	79.8	61.1	49.3	44.4	39.2	38.6	40.7	33.7	35.4
Rajshahi	112.3	154.4	108.4	109.8	93.2	87.2	78.5	92.3	104.7	124.4
Pabna	107.4	134.7	86.5	96.0	71.1	73.3	68.8	118.6	137.8	139.1
Khulna	197.8	246.7	170.2	157.8	222.8	203.9	149.0	156.7	166.5	228.0
Kushtia	131.9	136.1	94.3	73.2	97.4	96.2	67.5	72.4	80.5	117.6
Jessore	59.3	100.5	58.6	70.8	104.5	91.2	66.2	74.2	75.5	98.2
Khulna	4.7	5.6	10.4	9.7	6.8	7.3	6.5	5.1	5.7	3.6
Barisal	1.8	4.4	6.7	4.0	13.9	9.0	8.7	4.8	4.7	8.4
Patuakhali	0.0	0.1	0.2	0.1	0.2	0.2	0.1	0.2	0.1	0.2
Dhaka	261.6	359.1	265.8	242.5	255.0	250.0	206.5	223.5	253.3	263.5
Jamalpur	30.6	46.5	31.9	39.7	37.4	36.8	33.6	39.3	42.0	51.2
Mymensingh a/	40.2	47.8	43.2	41.2	39.3	42.2	35.8	37.8	43.3	48.6
Tangail	39.8	46.6	49.5	47.1	39.7	37.0	31.7	28.6	33.7	41.9
Dhaka	50.5	78.0	75.5	51.6	64.1	51.6	48.4	50.2	61.3	57.4
Faridpur	100.5	140.3	65.7	62.9	74.5	82.4	57.0	67.6	73.0	64.4
Chittagong	154.0	173.8	152.9	155.6	134.9	125.1	97.3	93.4	87.9	100.8
Sylhet	8.8	15.8	9.3	11.5	10.5	11.2	8.5	12.1	10.8	14.5
Comilla	143.7	154.7	140.9	141.7	122.3	112.6	86.9	81.1	76.7	85.2
Noakhali	1.3	3.0	2.4	2.1	2.0	1.3	1.9	0.2	0.4	1.1
Chittagong	0.2	0.2	0.2	0.3	0.1	-	-	-	-	-
Chittagong H. Tracts b/	0.0	0.0	0.1	0.0	0.0	-	-	-	-	-
Bandarban	0.0	0.0	0.0	0.0	0.0	-	-	-	-	-
Total:	1211.4	1463.9	1042.9	1091.1	1048.0	1022.0	890.0	1004.3	1065.0	1175.6

a/ Kishoreganj included in Mymensingh

b/ Khagrachari and Rangamati included in Chittagong Hill Tracts.

- = Not available

Source: Bangladesh Bureau of Statistics.

Table 7.6
JUTE PRODUCTION BY DISTRICT

	1983/84	1984/85	1985/86	1986/87	1987/88	1988/89	1989/90	1990/91	1991/92	1992/93
					('000 bales of 400 lb.)					
Rajshahi	1625.8	1773.4	3067.2	2384.8	1616.7	1687.0	1578.7	1874.4	1839.9	1623.8
Dinajpur	142.2	177.0	215.6	242.9	250.5	179.0	126.6	189.7	169.5	115.4
Rangpur	1014.7	1097.7	1634.3	1447.5	917.6	897.0	877.9	1166.3	1126.4	1062.0
Bogra	121.1	119.6	356.3	176.8	96.3	165.0	171.9	142.4	131.2	117.1
Rajshahi	161.4	188.7	481.4	343.2	182.6	190.0	166.7	180.3	166.7	137.9
Pabna	186.4	190.5	379.6	174.4	169.7	256.0	235.6	195.7	246.1	196.5
Khulna	992.5	1061.7	1571.0	1052.5	933.4	895.0	957.3	1101.1	1186.3	926.9
Kushtia	289.4	378.6	474.9	299.9	237.9	299.0	347.5	394.6	428.7	377.1
Jessore	567.0	501.4	888.1	584.3	605.4	459.0	487.4	570.7	623.3	451.2
Khulna	121.8	169.8	198.1	150.0	74.6	111.0	107.5	120.5	120.0	86.2
Barisal	12.5	10.4	8.2	16.3	13.4	25.0	13.5	13.6	12.1	9.9
Patuakhali	1.8	1.5	1.7	2.0	2.1	1.0	1.4	1.7	2.2	2.5
Dhaka	2281.5	1968.7	3427.4	2674.0	1911.2	1668.0	1850.3	2064.0	2017.2	2121.9
Jamalpur	263.7	211.5	292.6	222.4	209.7	258.0	294.9	322.6	264.1	257.4
Mymensingh	738.1	614.9	1207.0	893.1	535.3	377.0	377.3	446.7	388.4	323.1
Tangail	277.7	194.7	340.5	289.7	259.6	237.0	313.2	334.6	359.3	379.8
Dhaka	419.7	431.3	811.2	583.5	379.6	346.0	323.2	385.0	338.9	387.9
Faridpur	582.4	516.3	776.1	685.3	527.0	450.0	541.7	575.1	666.5	773.7
Chittagong	315.8	307.1	594.4	642.2	239.7	186.0	252.9	262.3	229.8	246.7
Sylhet	11.5	10.1	46.7	23.8	8.7	3.0	8.1	7.7	3.6	5.3
Comilla	292.7	286.3	530.5	610.7	223.9	175.0	227.1	244.6	220.7	237.8
Noakhali	10.7	10.0	16.1	7.4	6.8	8.0	11.1	3.4	5.3	3.2
Chittagong	0.3	0.2	0.0	0.0	-	-	-	-	-	-
Chittagong H. Tracts	0.5	0.5	1.1	0.3	0.3	-	6.6	6.6	0.2	0.4
Total:	5215.7	5110.9	8660.0	6753.5	4701.0	4436.0	4639.2	5301.8	5273.2	4919.3
					('000 metric tons)					
Rajshahi	295.0	321.8	556.5	432.7	293.3	306.1	286.4	340.0	333.7	288.6
Dinajpur	25.8	32.1	39.1	44.1	45.4	32.5	23.0	34.4	30.7	20.5
Rangpur	184.1	199.2	296.5	262.6	166.5	162.7	159.3	211.6	204.4	188.8
Bogra	22.0	21.7	64.6	32.1	17.5	29.9	31.2	25.8	23.8	20.8
Rajshahi	29.3	34.2	87.3	62.3	33.1	34.5	30.2	32.7	30.2	23.6
Pabna	33.8	34.6	68.9	31.6	30.8	46.4	42.7	35.5	44.6	34.9
Khulna	180.1	192.6	285.0	191.0	169.4	162.4	173.7	199.8	215.3	164.8
Kushtia	52.5	68.7	86.2	54.4	43.2	54.2	63.0	71.6	77.8	67.1
Jessore	102.9	91.0	161.1	106.0	109.8	83.3	88.4	103.5	113.1	80.2
Khulna	22.1	30.8	35.9	27.2	13.5	20.1	19.5	21.9	21.8	15.3
Barisal	2.3	1.9	1.5	3.0	2.4	4.5	2.4	2.5	2.2	1.8
Patuakhali	0.3	0.3	0.3	0.4	0.4	0.2	0.3	0.3	0.4	0.4
Dhaka	414.0	357.2	621.9	485.2	346.8	302.6	335.7	374.5	366.0	377.4
Jamalpur	47.8	38.4	53.1	40.4	38.0	46.8	53.5	58.5	47.9	45.8
Mymensingh	133.9	111.6	219.0	162.0	97.1	68.4	68.5	81.1	70.5	57.5
Tangail	50.4	35.3	61.8	52.6	47.1	43.0	56.8	60.7	65.2	67.5
Dhaka	76.1	78.3	147.2	105.9	68.9	62.8	58.6	69.9	61.5	69.0
Faridpur	105.7	93.7	140.8	124.3	95.6	81.6	98.3	104.3	120.9	137.6
Chittagong	57.3	55.7	107.8	116.5	43.5	33.7	45.9	47.6	41.6	43.8
Sylhet	2.1	1.8	8.5	4.3	1.6	0.5	1.5	1.4	0.6	0.9
Comilla	53.1	51.9	96.3	110.8	40.6	31.8	41.2	44.4	40.0	42.3
Noakhali	1.9	1.8	2.9	1.3	1.2	1.5	2.0	0.6	1.0	0.6
Chittagong	0.1	0.0	0.0	0.0	0.0	0.0	0.0	0.0	0.0	0.0
Chittagong H. Tracts	0.1	0.1	0.2	0.1	0.1	0.0	1.2	1.2	0.0	0.0
Total:	946.3	927.3	1571.2	1225.3	852.9	804.9	841.7	961.9	956.6	874.6

Note: i) Kishoreganj included in Mymensingh.
   ii) Bandarban, Khagrachari and Rangamati included in Chittagong Hill Tracts.
Source: Bangladesh Bureau of Statistics.

Table 7.7
IRRIGATION SUMMARY
('000 hectares)

	1982/83	1983/84	1984/85	1985/86	1986/87	1987/88	1988/89
BY METHOD							
Modern methods	1340	1506	1705	1721	1841	2390	2577
Tubewells	421	667	879	963	982	1467	1512
Low-lift pumps	763	667	681	609	660	527	658
BWDB gravity schemes	156	172	145	149	199	396	407
Traditional methods	549	586	513	526	557	353	569
Swing-baskets	87	84	79	84	94	238	a/
Doons	300	238	184	170	179	n.a.	a/
Canals	8	134	147	163	155	115	170
Other	154	130	103	109	129	n.a.	399
Total, net	1889	2092	2218	2247	2398	2743	3146
of which:							
modern (%)	71.0	72.0	76.9	76.6	76.8	87.1	81.9
traditional (%)	29.0	28.0	23.1	23.4	23.2	12.9	18.1
BY CROP							
Aus	128	145	141	165	164	119	145
Aman	199	159	156	190	190	160	211
Boro	1165	1198	1285	1259	1363	1678	1867
Wheat	198	214	283	267	264	196	261
Other cereals	4	6	3	3	3	a/	a/
Pulses	2	2	3	4	3	a/	a/
Oilseeds	5	7	11	12	11	18	12
Potato	75	74	70	68	68	57	77
Vegetables	51	44	49	53	57	34	63
Sugarcane	7	8	8	11	11	7	12
Cotton	3	7	4	3	4	-	4
Others	53	56	60	63	61	79	88
Total, gross	1889	1920	2073	2098	2199	2348	2740
Errors and omissions	0	-39	1	0	0	-	-
IRRIGATED AREA AS PERCENT OF TOTAL AREA UNDER PARTICULAR CROP							
Aus	4.0	4.6	4.5	5.8	5.6	4.3	3.4
Aman	3.2	2.6	2.7	3.2	3.1	2.9	4.1
Boro	79.5	85.5	81.6	82.1	82.5	86.4	76.5
Wheat	37.3	40.7	41.9	49.4	45.1	32.8	46.6
Other cereals	27.3	3.9	1.8	1.9	2.3	n.a.	n.a.
Pulses	0.6	0.2	0.4	0.5	0.4	n.a.	0.8
Oilseeds	1.6	1.1	1.8	2.0	1.9	3.3	2.2
Potato	66.4	67.3	63.1	62.4	64.2	46.3	69.4
Vegetables	52.0	32.4	35.5	37.6	39.3	n.a.	n.a.
Sugarcane	3.9	4.8	4.9	6.9	6.7	4.0	7.0
Cotton	16.8	41.2	36.4	17.6	30.8	-	23.5

a/ Included under "others"

Note: Irrigated area and percentage of total area under a particular crop
has been changed due to the Agriculture c

Source: Bangladesh Bureau of Statistics.

Table 7.8

COMMERCIAL FERTILIZER DISTRIBUTION BY TYPE AND REGION
('000 metric tons)

	1984/85	1985/86	1986/87	1987/88	1988/89	1989/90	1990/91	1991/92	1992/93
BY TYPE									
Urea	831.8	794.9	915.1	1028.5	1135.1	1367.7	1323.3	1529.5	1547.0
Triple super-phosphate [TSP]	345.7	297.4	335.7	389.8	416.0	480.7	514.7	458.7 d/	407.0
Di-ammmonium phosphate [DAP]	0.4	0.10	65.9	0.0	0.0	0.0	0.0	4.0	2.9
Muriate of potash [MP]	60.3	59.90	0.0	86.0	94.2 a/	119.0	149.7	138.9 e/	126.1
Hyper-phosphate [HP]	0.3	0.20	0.0	0.0	0.0	0.0	0.0	0.0	0.0
Super phosphate [SP]	0.0	0.0	0.0	0.0	0.0	0.0	11.4	34.2	119.8
Ammonium sulfate [AS]	0.0	0.0	0.0	6.4	b/	b/	0.8	4.5	5.5
Potassium sulfate [PS]	0.0	0.0	0.0	0.0	61.6	70.4	0.0	0.0	0.0
NitroPhosKa [NPK]	10.2	0.0	0.0	0.0	0.0	0.0	0.0	0.0	0.0
Triple phosphate [TP]	0.0	0.0	0.0	0.0	b/	b/	0.0	0.0	0.0
Zinc sulfate and oxy-sulfate	1.2	0.7	1.4	1.8	2.8	5.2	2.7	3.8	0.7
Gypsum	1.4	3.3	2.8	1.4	b/	b/	101.7	115.4	112.5
Others							3.1	2.3	-
Total	1251.2	1156.5	1320.9	1513.9	1709.7	2043.0	2107.4	2291.3	2321.6
BY REGION d/									
Rajshahi	404.1	390.0	454.4	510.6	544.5	422.0	157.1	844.8 f/	389.2
Dinajpur	79.2	57.40	65.30	89.3	102.1	89.5	34.6	n.a.	n.a.
Rangpur	84.1	83.30	98.80	92.6	97.1	93.1	30.2	n.a.	n.a.
Bogra	84.3	93.10	113.30	100.3	118.4	94.5	24.4	n.a.	n.a.
Rajshahi	94.9	80.40	96.20	93.6	106.9	71.7	38.9	n.a.	n.a.
Pabna	61.6	75.80	80.80	134.8	120.0	73.2	29.0	n.a.	n.a.
Khulna	188.9	166.6	200.3	258.7	314.3	212.3	307.4	625.2	414.4
Kushtia	60.5	55.4	60.3	78.6	88.8	34.6	14.7	n.a.	n.a.
Jessore	66.6	52.9	68.8	79.8	64.0	21.1	4.8	n.a.	n.a.
Khulna	27.8	28.1	29.4	51.0	109.1	126.2	272.5	n.a.	n.a.
Barisal	27.7	25.3	33.5	38.9	43.1	19.5	10.5	n.a.	n.a.
Patuakhali	6.2	4.9	8.3	10.4	9.3	10.9	4.9	n.a.	n.a.
Dhaka	355.3	352.8	360.6	407.1	418.5	165.2	434.6	516.4	714.3
Jamalpur	42.1	43.0	47.5	53.2	56.6	29.8	6.5	n.a.	n.a.
Mymensingh	118.3	100.4	122.2	131.4	111.4	39.6	16.6	n.a.	n.a.
Tangail	50.5	41.2	51.9	44.2	55.8	19.1	3.9	n.a.	n.a.
Dhaka	113.9	139.0	107.9	141.6	155.1	59.4	400.2	n.a.	n.a.
Faridpur	30.5	29.2	31.1	36.7	39.6	17.3	7.4	n.a.	n.a.
Chittagong	311.9	247.0	305.6	337.4	270.1	970.2	1208.0	296.8	803.3
Sylhet	46.6	35.3	43.3	54.5	45.8	84.2	99.8	n.a.	n.a.
Comilla	127.7	105.4	134.6	147.4	110.6	338.7	476.9	n.a.	n.a.
Noakhali	39.4	34.7	44.9	57.1	48.0	11.8	14.2	n.a.	n.a.
Chittagong	85.2	58.0	71.8	65.4	50.6	529.8	611.9	n.a.	n.a.
Chittagong HT	13.1	13.6	11.0	13.0	15.1	5.7	5.2	n.a.	n.a.
Total	1260.2	1156.4	1320.9	1513.8	1547.4 c/	2836.7	2107.1	2283.3	2321.2

a/ Including PS, TP and other types of fertilizer.

b/ Included under PS

c/ Does not include 162.13 thousand MT sold directly by BCIC for which districtwise breakdown is not available.

d/ Detailed district wise offtake from 1991/92 cannot be shown accurately in an open market situation where distributors are free to buy and sell wherever there is demand.

Source: Bangladesh Agricultural Development Corporation,IFDC/ Bangladesh Bureau of Statistics.

Table 7.9
PUBLIC FOODGRAIN DISTRIBUTION SYSTEM OPERATIONS
('000 metric tons)

	1982/83	1983/84	1984/85	1985/86	1986/87	1987/88	1988/89	1989/90	1990/91	1991/92	1992/93
Opening Stocks	616	611	800	1017	976	751	1498	909	1148	1040	1162
Domestic Procurement	192	268	349	349	188	375	416	959	783	1015	229
Imports	1843	2028	2590	1202	1767	2922	2137	1534	1577	1563	828
Total Availability	2651	2907	3739	2568	2931	4048	4051	3402	3508	3618	2219
Statutory rationing	308	293	282	160	210	189	203	156	235	169	56
Priority categories a/	648	641	712	467	668	585	724	623	673	976	329
Modified rationing	368	399	465	103	257	307	334	0	0	0	0
Relief	156	120	452	205	248	603	815	881	918	427	249
Food-for-Work & Canal Digging	338	441	458	468	480	468	611	457	458	498	369
Marketing Operations b/	0	51	8	8	40	0	0	0	0	0	0
Open Market Sales c/	118	107	201	129	217	344	255	47	87	275	72
Total Distribution	1936	2052	2578	1540	2120	2496	2942	2164	2371	2345	1075
Losses	104	57	139	52	62	55	148	90	97	66	79
Exports & repayments in kind	0	0	0	0	0	0	0	0	0	0	
Closing Stocks	611	800	1017	976	751	1498	962	1148	1040	1229	1067

a/ Includes: essential priorities; other priorities; large employers; & direct sales to flour mills.
b/ Marketing operations involve direct sale of grains to dealers at subsidized prices.
c/ OMS in paddy and rice were initiated during 1981/82; wheat OMS began in 1978/79.

Source: Food Planning and Monitoring Unit, Ministry of Food.

Table 7.10
SEASONALITY OF PUBLIC FOODGRAIN DISTRIBUTION SYSTEM OFFTAKE
('000 metric tons)

Month	1982/83	1983/84	1984/85	1985/86	1986/87	1987/88	1988/89	1989/90	1990/91	1991/92	1992/93
July	116	87	223	84	92	166	112	145	140	170	82
August	131	99	258	93	109	219	148	162	145	184	82
September	196	171	292	125	151	295	248	159	155	228	81
October	281	214	286	164	240	292	278	187	236	295	75
November	171	175	262	132	196	233	255	172	216	216	59
December	123	129	236	115	121	217	235	148	182	162	58
January	178	162	251	148	197	204	316	242	262	223	108
February	191	218	222	155	220	234	343	225	241	234	134
March	187	232	196	159	246	249	329	258	240	181	129
April	140	227	152	161	243	187	300	191	178	173	106
May	128	202	122	139	171	121	238	152	212	164	106
June	93	135	77	65	135	78	140	123	163	115	51
Total	1935	2051	2577	1540	2121	2495	2942	2164	2370	2345	1071
(Monthly Average)	161	171	215	128	177	208	245	180	198	195	89

Source: Ministry of Food and World Food Programme, Dhaka.
         Food Planning and Monitoring Unit.

Table 7.11

SUPPLY AND DISPOSITION OF RAW JUTE

('000 bales)

	1982/83	1983/84	1984/85	1985/86	1986/87	1987/88	1988/89	1989/90	1990/91	1991/92	1992/93
Opening stocks	1850	1339	730	1000	4265	3899	3207	2343	1095	1244	1352
Production, total	4920	5256	5150	8660	5461	4338	4439	4639	5302	5273	4919
- Jute	4881	5216	5111	8610	5422	4310	4403	4604	5262	5223	4849
- Mesta	39	40	39	50	39	28	36	35	40	50	70
Adjustment a/	594	0	612	-	14	-	-	-	-	330	-
Market arrivals	5514	5256	4538	8458	5261	3968	4039	4216	4682	4543	4619
Total supply	7364	6595	5268	9458	9526	7867	7246	6559	5777	5787	5971
Mill consumption	3329	3369	3050	2850	3356	3224	3168	3327	2888	2870	2993
- BJMC mills	3150	1880	-	-	1866	1857	1798	1827	1490	1393	1571
- Private mills	179	1489	-	-	1490	1367	1370	1500	1398	1477	1422
Other consumption	400	350	400	250	200	400	400	400	400	400	300
Losses	50	30	20	30	30	61	118	96	44	32	43
Total domestic uses	3779	3749	3470	3130	3586	3685	3686	3823	3332	3302	3336
Registered exports	2246	1902	1410	2301	2241	1345	1617	2064	1600	1533	1569
Total disposition	6025	5651	4880	5431	5827	5030	5303	5887	4932	4835	4905
Closing stocks	1339	944	1000	4279	3899	3207	2343	1095	1244	1352	1366

Total supply = market arrivals + opening stocks.

Total domestic uses = mill consumption + other consumption + losses.

Total disposition = total domestic uses + registered exports.

a/ Difference between estimated crop size and estimated market arrivals.

Source: Ministry of Jute, BJMC.

Table 7.12
PUBLIC FOODGRAIN PROCUREMENT BY DISTRICT
('000 metric tons, rice equivalent)

Division/District	1982/83	1983/84	1984/85	1985/86	1986/87	1987/88	1988/89	1989/90	1990/91	1991/92
Rajshahi	121.3	227.3	260.7	281.3	159.9	303.1	326.2	854.4	721.9	910.2
Dinajpur	54.8	99.5	81.8	96.7	42.2	85.9	90.4	280.1	260.4	373.4
Rangpur	26.3	67.0	65.3	62.0	34.0	62.6	52.0	118.7	116.4	141.1
Bogra	20.5	35.8	51.8	57.3	51.9	83.9	131.7	277.6	215.4	213.8
Rajshahi	14.4	14.2	36.8	44.9	22.7	53.2	41.3	138.9	89.3	103.6
Pabna	5.4	10.8	25.0	20.4	9.1	17.5	10.8	39.1	40.4	78.2
Khulna	12.0	13.9	32.9	31.9	4.3	27.5	56.5	38.1	28.9	49.1
Kushtia	0.3	1.4	8.0	6.4	1.2	4.2	10.0	1.8	1.2	7.0
Jessore	2.7	5.1	21.5	13.4	2.5	20.8	41.1	22.9	15.1	26.7
Khulna	1.0	1.0	2.6	1.7	0.1	2.1	5.2	9.6	12.6	14.8
Barisal	2.0	2.4	0.8	4.1	0.5	0.4	0.2	1.9	0.1	0.0
Patuakhali	6.0	3.9	0.1	6.4	0.0	0.0	0.0	1.9	0.0	0.7
Dhaka	31.4	16.3	29.6	20.6	8.9	20.1	18.2	55.4	25.1	42.0
Jamalpur a/	5.5	5.1	4.3	0.8	0.1	1.8	1.0	6.9	2.1	6.2
Mymensingh	17.9	8.4	9.7	3.7	7.8	15.3	15.3	44.4	21.4	33.6
Tangail	2.2	1.4	9.4	8.0	0.1	1.8	0.6	2.3	1.0	1.2
Dhaka	5.3	1.2	1.8	2.2	0.4	0.6	0.1	1.5	0.5	1.0
Faridpur	0.5	0.2	4.4	6.0	0.5	0.6	1.2	0.3	0.1	0.1
Chittagong	27.3	9.2	25.8	15.3	15.4	23.8	15.3	11.8	9.8	13.6
Sylhet	12.2	3.1	6.5	2.2	9.3	17.0	9.3	6.3	7.9	8.8
Comilla	8.2	3.0	15.9	9.0	4.5	2.9	2.4	3.3	0.4	0.2
Noakhali	3.4	1.6	0.9	1.1	0.1	0.1	0.0	0.4	0.2	0.0
Chittagong	1.6	0.3	0.1	1.4	0.7	0.9	0.4	0	0.0	2.7
Chittagong Hill Tracts	1.9	1.2	2.4	1.6	0.8	2.9	3.1	1.8	1.3	1.8
Total	192.1	266.7	349.0	349.1	188.5	374.5	416.2	959.7	785.6	1014.9

a/ Jamalpur was a subdivision of Mymensingh until December 26, 1978.

Note: 1.0 ton rice equivalent = 1.0 ton wheat = 1.5 ton paddy.

Source: Ministry of Food.

Table 7.13
PUBLIC PROCUREMENT OF AMAN RICE AND PADDY BY DISTRICT
(metric tons, rice equivalent)

	1982/83	1983/84	1984/85	1985/86	1986/87	1987/88	1988/89	1989/90	1990/91	1991/92
Rajshahi	60308	71393	71651	122341	21179	45562	49382	384244	160075	327936
Dinajpur	36537	43668	44602	62419	12614	23455	26659	163072	86088	161210
Rangpur	15847	11275	9436	27105	7777	8611	9486	65869	36553	59757
Bogra	4422	8219	5424	17105	374	7137	11125	90797	25445	56648
Rajshahi	3398	7512	12170	14277	357	6333	2102	51578	8666	27627
Pabna	104	719	19	1435	57	26	10	12928	3323	22694
Khulna	8361	7374	397	10896	55	472	319	17511	1344	27294
Kushtia	53	58	25	111	1	37	17	672	51	3195
Jessore	65	40	46	532	0	288	229	7372	283	14715
Khulna	258	950	35	91	1	34	6	5755	944	8730
Barisal	1966	2414	240	3811	34	107	63	1827	66	1
Patuakhali	6019	3912	51	6351	19	6	4	1885	-	653
Dhaka	11162	1646	1385	1822	23	462	16	13819	139	5732
Jamalpur a/	1502	522	44	556	0	10	0	3798	103	1696
Mymensingh	9022	773	1057	616	6	365	16	8816	36	3829
Tangail	61	27	63	21	1	15	0	1071	-	64
Dhaka	249	170	124	0	4	60	0	103	-	143
Faridpur	328	154	97	629	12	12	0	31	-	
Chittagong	13549	3367	2440	3496	1262	2148	2987	3180	1116	2041
Sylhet	5365	246	33	284	2	22	2	1157	-	4
Comilla	2092	359	200	42	19	74	0	594	-	
Noakhali	3405	1562	601	1074	11	13	25	422	-	25
Chittagong	1222	130	57	656	720	2	376	-	-	287
Chittagong Hill Tracts	1465	1070	1549	1440	510	2037	2584	1007	1116	1725
Total	93380	83780	75873	138555	22519	48644	52704	418754	162674	363003

a/ Jamalpur was a subdivision of Mymensingh until December 26, 1978.

Note: 1.0 ton rice equivalent = 1.0 ton wheat = 1.5 ton paddy.
Source: Ministry of Food.

Table 7.14
PUBLIC PROCUREMENT OF BORO AND IRRI RICE AND PADDY AND WHEAT
(metric tons, rice equivalent)

	1982/83	1983/84	1984/85	1985/86	1986/87	1987/88	1988/89	1989/90	1990/91	1991/92
BORO AND IRRI										
Rajshahi	44695	37185	41249	70850	94584	198243	225801	435410	511543	511530
Dinajpur	11070	13998	11800	19813	17089	47572	56650	103186	159253	182534
Rangpur	5185	10084	4235	11372	11828	29119	39926	41607	57163	58556
Bogra	13664	7603	18755	22785	44178	71093	119291	182573	182940	151987
Rajshahi	10729	2203	4110	13446	17828	39778	36849	82149	77106	67682
Pabna	4047	3297	2349	3434	3661	10681	9934	25895	35081	50771
Khulna	636	7	921	26	929	3275	7970	13581	21573	16819
Kushtia	55	0	85	0	247	147	40	534	647	2096
Jessore	0	0	26	6	311	2130	7765	9879	10934	9563
Khulna	575	7	705	0	110	627	58	3116	9992	5160
Barisal	6	0	105	20	248	331	107	52	0	0
Patuakhali	0	0	..	0	13	40	0	0	0	0
Dhaka	17950	9744	9144	4850	8407	16848	17875	41618	24754	35447
Jamalpur a/	5228	1831	82	45	69	527	952	3084	1892	3750
Mymensingh	7832	6170	6233	2755	7810	14787	16251	35552	21328	29690
Tangail	1110	725	2020	1426	84	879	559	1272	1006	1158
Dhaka	3779	1018	672	449	287	412	83	1415	521	820
Faridpur	1	0	137	175	157	243	30	295	7	29
Chittagong	9829	3740	5069	3691	10588	20690	11962	8630	8615	11535
Sylhet	6486	2434	3848	1886	8035	16972	9330	5132	7878	8832
Comilla	2499	1066	440	930	2180	2854	1994	2668	357	190
Noakhali	18	3	302	0	113	104	7	19	162	0
Chittagong	418	125	25	711	0	88	69	0	0	2455
Chittagong Hill Tracts	408	112	454	164	260	672	562	811	218	58
Total	73110	50676	56383	79417	114508	239056	263608	499239	566485	575331
WHEAT										
Rajshahi	13254	109756	147642	87182	44135	59296	12138	34980	50242	70746
Dinajpur	6269	35468	25287	14464	12506	14847	5117	13828	15080	29700
Rangpur	5252	44547	51668	22629	14369	24883	2627	11220	22676	22821
Bogra	240	19440	27579	17363	7331	5644	1272	4464	7036	5217
Rajshahi	272	4387	20427	17176	4565	7118	2302	5164	3480	8311
Pabna	1221	5914	22681	15550	5364	6804	820	304	1970	4697
Khulna	3015	6270	31582	14463	3339	23885	38162	6953	6006	5022
Kushtia	232	1370	7928	6313	968	4033	9978	589	498	1694
Jessore	2598	4848	21427	6313	2169	18415	23050	5608	3845	2443
Khulna	181	52	1811	1578	0	1436	5134	756	1663	885
Barisal	4	0	416	257	202	0	0	0	0	0
Patuakhali	0	0	..	2	0	1	0	0	0	0
Dhaka	1203	3323	19105	13597	427	2579	1245	62	168	863
Jamalpur a/	730	2582	4193	160	55	1242	62	15	84	769
Mymensingh	14	15	2374	299	1	70	0	21	0	61
Tangail	29	567	7357	6263	50	805	3	1	0	0
Dhaka	248	18	1040	1708	45	79	3	14	0	0
Faridpur	182	141	4141	5167	276	383	1177	11	84	33
Chittagong	3956	1931	16858	8017	3537	1003	436	16	27	0
Sylhet	313	324	1595	71	1198	0	0	0	0	0
Comilla	3643	1603	15263	7937	2339	0	436	16	27	0
Noakhali	0	0	0	9	0	0	0	0	0	0
Chittagong	0	4	0	0	0	847	0	0	0	0
Chittagong Hill Tracts	0	0	0	0	0	156	0	0	0	0
Total	23592	121280	215187	123259	51438	86763	51981	42011	56443	76631

a/ Jamalpur was a subdivision of Mymensingh until December 26, 1978.
Note: 1.0 ton rice equivalent = 1.0 ton wheat = 1.5 ton paddy.
Source: Ministry of Food.

Table 8.1
QUANTUM INDEX OF MEDIUM AND LARGE SCALE MANUFACTURING INDUSTRIES
(1981/82 = 100)

	Weight	1982/83	1983/84	1984/85	1985/86	1986/87	1987/88	1988/89	1989/90	1990/91	1991/92	1992/93
Food Beverages and Tobacco	14.9	91.9	83.3	81.1	86.1	106.0	112.6	110.2	145.2	146.6	140.1	134.4
Fish & Seafood (Shrimps and Froglegs)	1.1	85.3	38.1	158.5	250.6	227.5	270.8	366.0	594.4	480.4	512.9	460.8
Vegetable Oil	1.1	118.0	94.5	58.7	55.5	77.8	116.8	97.0	117.8	113.5	115.0	32.4
Tea	3.6	98.5	99.0	109.2	101.5	101.0	103.2	107.1	106.2	113.9	116.9	126.2
Flour Milling	0.6	83.6	94.2	111.6	126.0	140.2	163.4	169.3	161.1	145.1	154.2	173.7
Sugar	5.7	87.9	74.8	43.8	40.8	90.0	88.2	59.1	90.9	121.7	96.7	92.4
Beverage Industries	0.7	74.4	84.8	97.6	118.0	125.5	136.7	135.6	333.3	239.7	281.8	275.0
Tobacco Manufacturing	2.1	88.9	93.2	91.2	91.0	93.6	88.9	87.2	77.9	86.2	80.1	71.5
Textile Wearing Apparel and Leather	41.4	100.4	104.7	133.0	133.2	184.5	168.6	167.2	192.9	206.4	236.2	273.8
Cotton textile	8.3	101.7	104.6	109.5	97.6	101.9	105.6	119.0	113.3	120.1	128.1	120.5
Jute textile	30.2	97.2	92.8	88.6	77.1	92.0	89.9	87.2	90.1	74.0	71.0	77.9
Garments	0.7	182.0	526.2	2274.8	2796.1	4962.2	4077.7	4046.3	5464.7	6894.1	8645.6	10579.4
Leather & leather products	1.0	88.1	133.7	117.4	101.3	207.1	222.3	198.2	243.9	166.9	184.0	215.2
Mfg. of footwear	0.6	138.5	150.1	181.4	210.9	210.9	223.3	80.2	79.9	104.9	79.8	80.0
Jute bailing	0.6	131.8	110.2	103.4	231.4	195.1	176.6	202.1	172.2	199.9	203.5	158.0
Manufacture of Wood and Wood Products Including Furniture	0.7	132.7	152.0	189.3	187.5	186.3	199.1	187.1	180.4	176.9	175.6	171.3
Wood product except furniture	0.5	130.3	146.8	172.7	179.7	171.8	183.6	160.3	137.7	130.2	128.1	125.1
Wooden furniture	0.2	137.8	163.5	180.0	204.4	217.9	232.9	252.2	273.8	278.9	279.0	276.7
Manufacture of Paper Products: Printing & Publishing	3.0	93.9	104.7	133.4	146.4	153.0	163.0	161.3	185.6	199.5	249.6	260.1
Mfg. of paper & paper products	1.7	76.3	81.2	119.2	127.9	128.5	129.9	68.3	130.4	126.1	123.7	125.7
Printing, publishing & allied product	1.4	115.3	133.1	150.6	168.8	182.6	203.1	323.5	252.4	288.4	402.2	423.2
Manufacture of Chemicals and Chemical Petroleum & Rubber	23.2	101.1	140.8	137.7	149.2	124.6	155.5	161.5	175.4	173.6	200.3	230.4
Drugs and pharmaceuticals	10.2	84.1	92.0	98.2	103.1	53.1	53.8	128.3	83.1	97.5	127.9	150.2
Mfg. of industrial chemicals	7.4	103.0	191.0	192.2	213.6	201.2	310.1	204.2	345.0	328.8	307.6	433.5
Fertilizer	6.5	109.2	197.2	194.5	227.4	211.2	338.7	389.2	389.9	368.7	417.3	493.3
Mfg. of other chemical products	4.5	279.9	168.4	136.8	147.9	153.2	131.6	141.1	117.0	105.9	113.7	110.1
Petroleum refining	0.2	81.0	89.9	83.1	83.7	85.8	83.7	92.4	86.7	95.7	89.6	109.2
Mfg. of rubber products	0.8	138.4	153.7	154.7	163.7	173.5	168.6	127.2	130.3	103.8	77.0	77.7
Manufacture of Non-Metalic Mineral Products	1.7	111.8	83.8	100.1	186.5	213.4	216.9	239.2	239.7	217.5	189.5	213.6
Pottery china and earthen ware	0.3	190.2	122.2	139.5	537.7	537.7	318.6	837.2	823.1	787.2	527.8	673.1
Glass and glass products	0.4	96.9	109.1	112.0	97.2	145.6	192.6	200.6	132.4	101.2	190.2	204.1
Other non-metalic mineral products	1.0	93.8	61.2	83.9	115.7	141.8	195.8	106.8	104.6	90.4	85.4	75.5
Bricks	0.3	93.5	81.2	109.5	180.1	256.9	444.1	108.1	107.4	105.9	89.7	104.7
Cement	0.7	94.0	53.0	73.6	89.5	95.0	95.0	105.1	103.4	84.2	83.5	63.6
Basic Metal Industries	9.6	60.4	61.6	82.1	64.4	58.4	52.8	60.2	63.5	57.5	39.4	41.3
Iron and steel basic industries	9.6	60.4	61.6	82.1	64.4	58.4	52.8	60.2	63.5	57.5	39.4	41.3
Manufacture of Fabricated Metal Products Machinery & Equipments	5.6	119.9	126.2	159.3	161.5	153.2	148.2	144.3	149.1	134.2	144.2	137.5
Fabricated metal	0.5	91.3	106.9	135.9	204.2	204.1	132.3	121.3	121.0	121.5	123.7	137.6
Fabricate metal & equipment	0.6	92.0	149.6	226.8	221.6	225.1	248.4	225.6	183.5	181.0	186.9	168.9
Machinery (non-electric)	1.6	198.1	144.0	166.7	141.9	135.8	140.1	135.2	103.2	118.0	132.3	114.1
Electric machinery	2.2	102.7	129.4	153.5	161.3	162.8	155.7	150.4	195.1	149.2	149.3	161.1
Transport equipments	0.8	48.8	75.9	124.8	129.2	74.7	78.0	88.1	106.6	98.1	100.6	94.6
TOTAL	100.0	97.0	108.0	123.0	126.0	145.0	147.0	151.0	170.0	174.0	189.0	210.0

1992/93 figures are preliminary.

Source: C.M.I. (Current Production), B.B.S.

Table 8.2
PRODUCTION OF SELECTED INDUSTRIAL GOODS

Goods	Units	1988/89	1989/90	1990/91	1991/92	1992/93
Shrimps & froglegs	000 MT	5	5	5	6	6
Sugar	000 MT	110	184	246	195	188
Veg.oils	000 MT	25	30	29	30	9
Tea	000 MT	42	41	44	46	49
Beverage	M doz.bt	7	11	8	10	10
Cotton yarn	M KG	49	51	56	61	58
Cotton cloth	M meters	65	69	60	59	46
Jute goods	000 MT	509	528	434	416	457
Garments	M doz	8	11	14	18	22
Leather	M sq meter	12	15	10	11	13
Paper	000 MT	86	93	90	88	90
Fertilizer	000 MT	1598	1621	1533	1736	2051
Soap & detergent	000 MT	37	36	30	30	29
Petro products	000 MT	1048	984	1086	1017	1321
Footwear	M doz pr	386	397	316	235	237
Cement	000 MT	344	337	275	272	207
Steel ingots	000 MT	86	75	58	37	7
Textile machinery	000 NO.	1965	1314	3580	4484	3319
Radio	000 NO.	102	68	21	16	7
TV	000 NO.	79	83	57	44	61
Telephone	000 NO.	26	38	33	26	31
Dry cell Battery	M NO.	66	74	62	58	58
Bicycles	000 NO.	30	34	34	17	14

Note on units used: M = million, MT = metric ton, NO. = number
bt = bottles, pr = pair
Source: Bangladesh Bureau of Statistics.

Table 8.3
CHITTAGON EXPORT PROCESSING ZONE STATISTICS

Year	No. of Enterprise		Actual Investment Million US$		Actual Local Employment		Export (Million US$)	
	Current	Cumulative	Current	Cumulative	Current	Cumulative	Current	Cumulative
1983-83	2	2	0.874	0.874	624	624	0.164	0.164
1984-85	4	6	1.598	2.472	1156	1780	4.450	4.614
1985-86	8	14	3.602	6.074	732	2512	7.593	12.207
1986-87	2	16	6.631	12.705	728	3240	15.272	27.479
1987-88	2	18	1.791	14.496	198	3438	13.927	41.406
1988-89	4	22	2.722	17.218	769	4207	16.081	57.487
1989-90	6	28	8.580	25.798	2794	7001	34.213	91.700
1990-91	13	41	22.054	47.852	2363	9364	48.024	139.724
1991-92	7	48	34.659	82.511	5250	14614	76.661	216.385
1992-93	6	54	21.048	103.559	3114	17728	127.608	343.993

Source: Bangladesh Export Processing Zone Authority.

Table 8.4
NATURAL GAS STATISTICS
(million MMCF)

	1983/84	1984/85	1985/86	1986/87	1987/88	1988/89	1989/90	1990/91	1991/92	1992/93
PRODUCTION										
Sylhet	3829	3080	3795	3744	4384	3513	2389	2016	1896	1844
Chhatak	1778	1187	0	31	0	0	0	0	0	0
Rashidpur	0	0	0	0	0	0	0	0	0	0
Titas	57825	57367	45030	53099	60126	70248	78235	82158	91967	101226
Kailastila	2901	5007	4265	5911	6089	7037	7785	8261	7335	7941
Habiganj	16762	18124	32736	33741	34111	32380	29763	27660	28195	45771
Bakhrabad	355	6693	15290	24190	38799	41127	48423	51540	52961	48688
Semutang	0	0	0	0	0	0	0	0	0	0
Kutubdia a/	0	0	0	0	0	0	0	0	0	0
Begumganj	0	0	0	0	0	0	0	0	0	0
Feni	0	0	0	0	0	0	0	0	5940	5408
Beanibazar	0	0	0	0	0	0	0	0	0	0
Kamta	0	3134	5141	4657	3934	1619	1236	1200	180	0
Jalalabad	0	0	0	0	0	0	0	0	0	0
Belabo	0	0	0	0	0	0	0	0	0	0
Fenchuganj	0	0	0	0	0	0	0	0	0	0
Meghna	0	0	0	0	0	0	0	0	0	0
	0	0	0	0	0	0	0	0	0	0
	0	0	0	0	0	0	0	0	0	0
Total	83450	94592	106257	125373	147443	155924	167831	172835	188474	210878
CONSUMPTION BY SECTOR										
Power	30164	38293	39778	51821	62071	65138	74499	81559	91940	93308
Fertilizers	31834	30896	35401	37987	50978	53406	55905	54185	57903	68912
Industrial	10447	13362	16618	19392	17351	15358	15335	14917	14568	15129
Commercial	2058	2232	2456	2730	2930	3126	3102	2937	2908	2982
Households	5785	6320	6797	6841	7590	9262	10175	10525	11469	13165
Total	80288	91103	101050	118771	140920	146290	159016	164123	178788	193496

MEMORANDUM ITEMS:

Field	Year of Discovery	Estimated Recoverable Gas Reserves	Condensate Recovery BBL/MMCF)	Methane Content (vol %)	Calorific Value Gross (BTU/CFT)
Sylhet	1955		3.4	96.63	1050.68
Chhatak	1959		0.1	97.90	1005.71
Rashidpur	1960		3.6	98.00	1012
Titas	1962		1.4	97.33	1031.55
Kailastila	1962		10.9	95.57	1056
Habiganj	1963		0.1	97.60	1023.91
Bakhrabad	1969		1.6	94.20	1057.73
Semutang	1969		0.4	96.94	-
Kutubdia a/	1977		N/A	95.72	1041.66
Begumganj	1977		0.4	95.46	1045.61
Feni	1981		3.0	95.71	1049.13
Kamta	1982		0.2	95.36	1061.95
Beanibazar	1981		16.0	93.68	1043.33
Fenchuganj	1988		2.5	95.66	-
Jalalabad	1989		17.5	93.5	-
Belabo	1990		2.5	-	-
Meghna	1990		2.06	-	-
Total					

BBL = barrel.
BTU = British Thermal Unit is = 0.25 kilocalories
CFT = cubic feet.
MMCF = million standard cubic feet.
Note: (i) The estimated recoverable gas reservesis on the basis of abandonment ofpressure at 110 PSI.
    (ii) Net gas reserve position after adjustment of cumulative production till January 1992
a/ Offshore field.
Source: Petrobangla.

Table 8.5
ELECTRICITY PRODUCTION AND CONSUMPTION
[GWH EXCEPT AS NOTED]

	1985/86	1986/87	1987/88	1988/89	1989/90	1990/91	1991/92	1992/93
Installed capacity [MW]	1171.2	1607.2	2146.2	2365.3	2352.2	2349.9	2397.7	2607.7
Gross Generation	4800.3	5586.9	6541.4	7114.8	7731.9	8270.2	8890.0	9206.4
Net Generation	4572.3	5301.9	6140.6	6717.1	7301.6	7823.4	8378.5	8699.6
Final consumption	3306.8	3485.3	3772.7	4695.0	4704.7	4870.6	6021.4	6906.3
Billed consumption [million Taka]	5771.6	6278.4	7661.8	9674.0	10291.0	11498.4	12220.1	13295.9
CONSUMPTION BY SECTOR								
Domestic	715.8	825.6	885.4	1044	1164.7	1383.5	1070.2	1089.4
Commercial	278.1	308.7	391.1	531.4	380.1	425.0	421.2	362.3
Industrial	1562.5	1728.1	1843.2	2330.5	2504.4	2256.3	1471.1	1255.8
Agriculture	51.1	56.2	62.9	95.3	73.7	91.4	85.3	101.1
Others a/	699.3	565.8	590.2	693.8	581.9	714.4	2973.5	4097.8
Total	3306.8	3484.4	3772.8	4695.0	4704.8	4870.6	6021.3	6906.4
Losses (Utility only) b/	1493.5	2101.6	2768.6	2419.7	3027.2	3399.6	2868.6	2300.1
as % of gross generation	31.1	37.6	42.3	34.0	39.1	41.1	32.3	25

a/ Includes bulk sale to DESA (Dhaka Electric Supply Authority seperated from the Bangladesh Power Development
   Board and functioning since October 1 1991); and REB (Rural Electrification Board).
b/ Includes station auxiliary use.

Source: Bangladesh Power Development Board.

Table 8.6
RAILWAY STATISTICS

	1984/85	1985/86	1986/87	1987/88	1988/89	1989/90	1990/91	1991/92	1992/93
Route length [km] a/	2892	2918	2792	2746	2746	2746	2746	2746	2746
Broad gauge	978	980	970	924	924	924	924	924	924
Meter gauge	1914	1938	1822	1822	1822	1822	1822	1822	1822
Narrow gauge	0	0	0	0	0	0	0	0	0
Locomotives, total	306	290	291	307	307	307	307	308	287
Diesel, total	288	290	291	307	307	307	307	308	287
Broad gauge	75	75	75	75	75	75	75	75	73
Meter gauge	213	215	216	232	232	232	232	233	214
Steam, total b/	18	0	0	0	0	0	0	0	0
Broad gauge	18	0	0	0	0	0	0	0	0
Meter gauge	0	0	0	0	0	0	0	0	0
Broad gauge	4080	4073	4073	4073	4073	3798	3788	3711	3289
Meter gauge	12434	12357	12283	11884	11884	11738	11760	11451	11143
Total units	16514	16430	16356	15957	15957	15536	15548	15162	14432
Total 4-wheeler units	19720	19629	19545	19095	19077	18673	18634	18292	17739
Freight Carried ['000 metric tons]	2995	2341	1984	2518	2495	2410	2517	2506	2350
Rice	262	203	132	185	192	186	345	422	279
Paddy	75	51	47	47	34	20	15	14	11
Wheat	674	427	373	643	621	471	571	593	301
Raw jute	226	171	166	143	133	113	79	80	110
Jute goods	30	12	14	21	15	9	6	12	12
Sugarcane	215	218	254	307	143	285	299	74	44
Sugar	56	37	26	51	32	13	17	19	15
Salt	113	82	62	61	65	65	58	57	47
Fertilizer	419	404	317	362	457	408	248	403	400
Cement	130	116	77	83	91	132	114	108	390
Coal	29	59	34	72	69	99	74	63	151
Petroleum products c/	84	100	75	117	88	120	119	103	141
Total ton-km	822917	612225	502594	678267	665939	643478	650933	718388	673745
Fuel Consumption [metric tons]									
Coal	16886	14763	1767	1180	1422	1766	1399	1883	1578
Diesel oil	44998	44696	50417	50344	50238	49902	45957	44374	39289
Furnace oil	2191	1122	839	927	854	808	808	559	433

a/ Total track mileage in 1978/79 was 4503 km.
b/ Including 6 narrow gauge steam locomotives.
c/ Excluding fuel for the railways and for the military.

Source: Ministry of Communications.

Table 8.7
TRANSPORT STATISTICS

	1980/81	1981/82	1982/83	1983/84	1984/85	1985/86	1986/87	1987/88	1988/89	1989/90	1990/91
INLAND WATER TRANSPORT											
BIWTC Fleet											
Total	591	586	555	544	533	524	484	430	419	378	343
Self-propelled barges	6	6	6	3	8	8	8	8	8	8	7
Inland & river barges b/	287	255	229	232	246	239	246	198	194	166	147
Inland tugs	29	29	29	27	25	24	24	22	34	33	30
Mainland tugs	23	23	23	21	19	19	19	19	16	19	18
Coasters c/	23	23	25	21	20	20	20	20	20	20	20
Country Boats											
Cargo	94	96	98	202	209	217	226	236	246	256	261
Passenger	177	180	183	374	389	404	421	437	456	475	484
ROAD TRANSPORT STATISTICS											
Road Mileage, total a/	3536	4095	4618	4969	6446	6950	7341	7655	8053	8463	::
high	2662	2686	2968	3188	3862	4041	4213	4484	4697	4915	::
low	874	1409	1650	1781	2584	2909	3128	3171	3356	3548	::
Buses operating, private	6362	6383	7330	15164	15971	16860	17644	18472	20948	23886	23693
Trucks operating, private	11413	13263	14236	23430	24053	24719	25449	26154	29424	30329	31538
Bullock carts (est.)	138	139	141	609	621	632	643	653	665	677	689

a/ Data cover only roads constructed and maintained by the Roads and Highways Department. "High" roads are
roads with cement, concrete, bituminous concrete or bituminous surface; "low" roads are roads with
stone, gravel, brick, or earth surface, but which are properly aligned and have drainage structures.

b/ Including jute boats and flats.

c/ Can travel up the main river routes.

:: = Not available.

Source: Bangladesh Bureau of Statistics.

Table 9.1
CONSUMER PRICE INDICES

	1983/84	1984/85	1985/86	1986/87	1987/88	1988/89	1989/90	1990/91	1991/92	1992/93
DHAKA MIDDLE INCOME [1973/74 = 100]										
Food	350.47	387.89	429.46	483.42	535.4	565.88	606.2	647.9	683.8	676.5
Fuel & Lighting	466.39	502.64	539.30	542.20	562.1	621.16	674.3	945.1	1008.4	1054.6
Housing	416.81	453.74	506.62	550.78	647.7	723.31	808.1	867.2	892.9	946.1
Clothing	224.98	255.15	274.23	292.59	319.1	347.98	374.5	399.4	410.3	421.6
Miscellaneous	335.36	392.25	419.38	459.52	524.4	597.62	707.5	720.6	755.9	787.9
Overall	357.47	396.58	436.03	481.18	536.0	578.89	632.7	689.3	724.4	734.0
Percent increase	9.7	10.9	9.9	10.4	11.4	8.0	9.3	8.9	5.1	1.3
DHAKA GOVERNMENT EMPLOYEES [1969/70 = 100]										
Food	824.25	933.53	1024.32	1169.7	1255.5	1362.97	1461.3	1557.9	1641.6	1622.4
Fuel & Lighting	894.14	1057.34	1210.31	1263.7	1329.7	1508.50	1806.2	1908.6	1955.4	2000.7
Housing	1057.00	1113.86	1268.60	1415.9	1690.0	1882.78	2055.2	2212.9	2275.5	2433.6
Clothing	837.05	925.93	967.90	1034.3	1132.9	1269.03	1337.0	1394.2	1467.9	1537.1
Miscellaneous	712.58	795.78	817.96	877.2	977.3	1109.58	1263.4	1329.8	1416.5	1515.1
Overall	832.94	931.47	1014.33	1129.7	1241.2	1370.48	1497.8	1592.1	1671.1	1746.4
Percent increase	9.9	11.8	8.9	11.4	9.9	10.4	9.3	6.3	5.0	4.5
CHITTAGONG INDUSTRIAL WORKERS [1969/70 = 100]										
Food	801.25	907.99	980.11	1116.6	1187.9	1242.69	1325.1	1417.3	1477.3	1422.0
Housing	947.63	1066.91	1264.60	1409.4	1487.6	1542.33	1701.3	1893.8	1974.9	1423.1
Clothing	929.86	1037.50	1082.19	1123.0	1139.9	1189.20	1268.5	1364.5	1383.0	1997.9
Miscellaneous	606.47	695.44	718.19	741.5	759.3	811.26	951.2	1001.4	1080.7	1135.6
Overall	807.03	913.98	989.60	1105.20	1166.0	1219.85	1315.2	1412.7	1472.4	1445.9
Percent increase	14.1	13.3	8.3	11.7	5.5	4.6	7.8	7.4	4.2	-1.8
KHULNA INDUSTRIAL WORKERS [1969/70 = 100]										
Food	712.87	789.09	878.96	1029.00	1081.3	1183.39	1266.2	1290.2	1358.0	1359.3
Housing	781.90	862.94	1057.42	1269.65	1397.0	1550.49	1619.3	1847.7	1947.4	1246.6
Clothing	736.45	867.51	942.56	998.42	1012.6	1081.80	1126.5	1236.4	1249.9	1978.6
Miscellaneous	562.34	600.82	689.23	737.89	736.3	820.24	952.2	1038.8	1096.3	1162.3
Overall	706.01	784.37	882.33	1017.75	1067.4	1169.04	1251.8	1310.4	1374.4	1384.8
Percent increase	11.0	11.1	12.5	15.3	4.9	9.5	7.1	4.7	4.9	0.8
NARAYANGANJ INDUSTRIAL WORKERS [1969/70 = 100]										
Food	774.72	862.97	930.58	1052.18	1159.1	1229.25	1318.1	1399.1	1456.3	1451.5
Housing	891.11	1078.96	1257.59	1371.20	1536.0	1681.96	1832.6	2058.3	2115.5	1564.3
Clothing	809.38	913.53	1035.11	1131.55	1179.8	1259.72	1332.0	1483.8	1547.3	2220.2
Miscellaneous	604.44	674.08	725.19	757.69	789.8	866.74	1013.7	1062.6	1160.0	1259.9
Overall	770.96	868.73	950.45	1059.36	1157.8	1236.66	1335.7	1434.1	1496.3	1515.0
Percent increase	9.0	12.7	9.4	11.5	9.3	6.8	8.0	7.4	4.3	1.3
RURAL CONSUMER PRICE INDICES FOR										
SELECTED DISTRICTS [1973/74 = 100]										
Dhaka	315.0	356.0	369.0	420.0	454.0	479.60	510.3	556.0	591.5	592.8
Chittagong	344.0	380.0	391.0	456.0	489.0	507.80	539.9	581.7	616.9	622.6
Rajshahi	295.0	340.0	364.0	408.0	439.0	467.40	495.9	543.0	576.6	585.7
Khulna	284.0	320.0	333.0	391.0	415.0	445.40	470.0	524.5	559.6	565.9
Sylhet	329.0	354.0	375.0	437.0	477.0	::	::	::	::	::
Rangpur	305.0	368.0	381.0	430.0	465.0	::	::	::	::	::
Bangladesh [rural]	312.0	353.0	369.0	424.0	456.0	475.1	504.0	551.3	586.2	591.6

Notes: Dhaka middle income index refers to families with 1973/74 incomes of Tk 300 to Tk 999.

Dhaka government employees index refers to non-gazetted employees with monthly salaries of
Tk 100 to Tk 400 in 1969/70.

:: = Not available

Source: Bangladesh Bureau of Statistics.

Table 9.2
NATURAL GAS AND PETROLEUM PRODUCT PRICES

NATURAL GAS - TITAS SYSTEM	Effective Dates							
	June 30, 1985	June 27, 1986	June 18, 1987	July 1, 1988	July 1, 1989	July 1, 1990	July 1, 1991	May 1, 1992
BULK USERS								
Cost of Gas/MCF (ex-field),	13.80	16.85	21.72	24.97	28.18	29.66	30.86	31.99
including excise duty	12.80	15.72	20.30	23.28	25.96	25.96	27.25	27.25
INDUSTRIAL								
Cost of Gas/MCF (ex-field),	29.13	37.06	37.06	43.79	51.02	54.17	58.89	61.44
including excise duty	28.13	35.73	35.73	41.99	48.01	48.01	52.81	52.81
OTHER USERS								
Cost of Gas/MCF (ex-field),	49.25	61.06	61.06	71.17	-	-	58.89	61.44
including excise duty	46.45	57.76	57.76	67.16	-	-	52.81	52.81
END USERS PRICES/MCF INCLUDING EXCISE DUTIE								
Bulk Cunsumers								
Power Generation	15.66	19.09	24.82	28.54	33.00	37.95	39.07	43.04
Fertilizer Production	15.66	19.09	24.82	28.54	28.54	32.82	33.98	37.37
Industrial Consumers	43.20	52.14	52.14	59.96	70.00	80.50	85.23	93.72
Commercial Consumers	54.24	65.39	85.00	97.75	110.00	126.50	134.22	134.22
Household Consumers								
Metered	40.80	44.88	56.10	56.10	65.00	74.75	74.75	82.11
Unmetered/month								
- Stove (one burner)	60.00	66.00	80.00	92.00	100.00	115.00	115.00	126.00
- Stove (two burners)	100.00	110.00	130.00	150.00	170.00	195.00	195.00	215.00
- Additional burner (each)	41.00	45.00	56.00	64.00	74.00	85.00	85.00	93.00
- Oven (each)	89.00	97.00	121.00	139.00	161.00	185.00	185.00	203.00
- Additional oven (each)	45.00	49.00	61.00	70.00	81.00	93.00	93.00	102.00
- Grill (each)	89.00	97.00	121.00	139.00	161.00	185.00	185.00	203.00
- Additional grill (each)	45.00	49.00	61.00	70.00	81.00	93.00	93.00	102.00
- Water heater up to 20 gallons	177.00	194.00	242.00	278.00	322.00	370.00	370.00	407.00
- Water heater above 20 gallons	221.00	242.00	303.00	348.00	403.00	463.00	463.00	509.00
- Dryer (each)	265.00	291.00	364.00	419.00	485.00	558.00	558.00	614.00
- Refrigerator (each)	177.00	194.00	242.00	278.00	322.00	370.00	370.00	407.00
- Gas light, garden/external use	41.00	45.00	56.00	64.00	74.00	85.00	85.00	93.00
- Gas light, internal use	21.00	23.00	28.00	32.00	37.00	43.00	43.00	47.00
Minimum Charges/Month								
Domestic (unmetered)	41.00	63.00	84.00	97.00	112.00	129.00	85.00	93.00
Commercial	272.00	327.00						

Source: Titas Gas Company.

Table 9.3
RETAIL PRICES OF PETROLEUM PRODUCTS a/

	1986/87	1987/88	1988/89	1989/90	1990/91	1991/92	1992/93 Estimate
				(Taka per liter)			
Premium gasoline	13.86	13.86	13.86	8.58	14.95	14.95	14.65
Regular gasoline	13.20	13.20	13.20	8.20	14.00	14.00	13.70
Kerosene	7.40	7.40	7.40	7.30	14.00	14.00	13.70
Diesel oil	6.90	6.90	6.90	7.30	14.00	14.00	13.70
Fuel oil	4.70	4.70	4.70	5.10	7.41	7.41	7.11
Jet oil	8.67	8.67	8.67	9.07	16.92	16.92	16.62
				(U.S. dollars per gallon)			
Premium gasoline	1.71	1.68	1.63	0.99	1.59	1.59	1.64
Regular gasoline	1.63	1.60	1.55	0.94	1.49	1.49	1.54
Kerosene	0.92	0.89	0.87	0.84	1.49	1.49	1.54
Diesel oil	0.85	0.83	0.81	0.84	1.49	1.49	1.54
Fuel oil	0.58	0.57	0.55	0.59	0.79	0.79	0.80
Jet oil	1.07	1.05	1.02	1.04	1.80	1.80	1.87

a/ End year data.

Source: Bangladesh Petroleum Corporation.

Table 9.4
WHOLESALE PRICES OF CONSUMER GOODS IN URBAN AREAS
(Taka per unit shown)

Items	Traditonal Units	1983/84	1984/85	1985/86	1986/87	1987/88	1988/89	1989/90	1990/91	1991/92
Masur	maund	419.42	396.42	585.03	700.33	749.78	754.98	822.16	899.51	911.45
Khesari	maund	301.09	239.45	245.81	412.07	354.48	409.77	561.67	529.63	427.73
Potatoes, local (best quality)	maund	122.99	124.36	142.23	192.97	156.66	226.91	245.57	168.33	164.97
Rohu fish (large cut pieces)	maund	1272.78	1460.00	1905.13	2371.17	2284.87	2208.60	2542.61	2457.06	2506.31
Chicken eggs, fresh	100	121.69	144.46	177.93	182.33	183.36	215.00	225.00	230.45	242.13
Chillies, dry (superior quality)	maund	1152.06	1441.36	619.69	964.00	1592.01	1297.99	1288.29	1887.48	2483.17
Turmeric (Haldi, best quality)	maund	1325.84	1574.16	1441.00	958.33	936.35	1252.83	1279.70	1267.53	1606.43
Mustard oil, local (best quality)	maund	1394.27	1463.53	1320.57	1487.33	1473.45	1570.05	1745.83	1734.08	1959.52
Ghee (cow)	maund	3326.90	4218.38	5107.47	5390.80	5741.00	6314.54	6872.10	6940.00	6925.49
Coconut oil, imported (sup. quality)	maund	1485.57	1884.91	1480.11	1297.17	1662.11	1941.01	2065.66	2039.77	2415.62
Vegetable oil (Pakvan)	35 lbs.	569.02	754.08	697.26	694.38	734.58	724.26	708.00	699.17	1873.67
Tobacco leaf (Motihari, sup. quality)	maund	994.86	1111.54	1079.12	1038.60	1095.81	1341.28	1543.56	1371.29	1464.60
Betelnut (Tanti, whole, dry, sup. quality)	maund	1230.83	1801.39	2038.51	1691.17	1575.38	1457.72	1889.51	2776.92	2566.41
Betel leaf (medium size)	6400	461.55	544.76	529.69	538.33	817.80	1184.00	1442.00	757.18	1107.20
Firewood, Gazari	100 maunds	2908.09	3698.21	5341.73	5715.98	5748.77	6102.50	4079.53	5153.54	5264.48
Kerosene, white	4 gallons	135.72	136.65	136.13	130.16	131.92	132.00	132.00	213.84	243.12
Cigarettes (Capstan)	250	123.30	128.86	159.99	150.56	164.63	175.50	216.00	213.01	235.98
Matches (box of 40)	gross	38.75	40.80	64.52	68.17	59.35	70.17	87.00	78.22	78.89
Paper, 10 lbs. foolscap	ream	115.40	120.82	117.39	119.83	120.74	142.25	173.00	173.13	173.39
Cycle tyre, imported (Master Service)	dozen	1473.69	1722.05	2027.50	1968.79	2294.51	2594.00	2529.00	2516.04	2609.52
Cycle tubes (Deshi)	dozen	257.03	345.91	413.78	443.23	358.39	836.00	880.00	1442.40	821.28
Longcloth (medium quality)	40 yards	645.00	727.00	712.07	748.94	737.45	810.53	819.31	763.72	838.74
	Metric Units									
Masur	kg	15.66	14.80	15.67	18.76	20.09	20.23	22.03	24.10	24.42
Khesari	kg	11.24	8.94	6.59	11.04	9.50	10.98	15.05	14.19	11.46
Potatoes, local (best quality)	kg	4.59	4.64	3.81	5.17	4.20	6.08	6.58	4.43	4.42
Rohu fish (large cut pieces)	kg	34.15	39.17	51.11	63.53	61.22	59.18	68.13	65.83	67.15
Chicken eggs, fresh	hundred	121.69	144.46	177.93	182.33	183.36	215.00	225.00	230.45	242.13
Chillies, dry (superior quality)	kg	43.00	53.80	16.60	25.83	42.65	34.78	34.52	50.57	66.53
Turmeric (Haldi, best quality)	kg	49.49	58.76	38.61	25.67	25.09	33.57	34.29	33.80	43.04
Mustard oil, local (best quality)	kg	52.04	54.63	35.38	39.85	39.48	42.07	46.78	46.46	52.50
Ghee (cow)	kg	89.27	113.19	136.84	144.43	153.83	169.20	184.14	185.96	185.55
Coconut oil, imported (sup. quality)	kg	55.45	70.36	39.66	34.75	44.53	52.01	55.35	54.65	64.72
Vegetable oil (Pakvan)	kg	35.84	47.50	43.92	43.73	46.27	45.62	44.60	44.04	50.20
Tobacco leaf (Motihari, sup. quality)	kg	37.13	41.49	28.91	27.82	29.36	35.94	41.36	36.74	39.24
Betelnut (Tanti, whole, dry, sup. quality)	kg	45.94	67.24	54.62	45.31	42.21	39.06	50.63	74.40	68.76
Betel leaf (medium size)	thousand	72.12	85.12	82.76	84.11	127.78	185.00	225.31	118.31	173.00
Firewood, Gazari	metric ton	779.12	1060.24	1431.24	1531.45	1540.29	1635.00	1093.00	1380.75	1411.39
Kerosene, white	liter	7.46	7.51	7.48	7.16	7.26	7.26	7.26	11.76	13.37
Cigarettes (Capstan)	thousand	493.20	515.44	639.96	602.24	658.52	702.00	864.00	852.02	943.92
Matches (box of 40)	thousand	269.10	283.33	443.10	473.40	412.15	486.11	604.00	543.19	525.90
Paper, 10 lbs. foolscap	thousand	230.80	241.64	244.56	249.65	251.54	295.83	380.42	360.48	403.23
Cycle tyre, imported (Master Service)	each	122.81	143.50	168.96	164.07	191.21	216.17	210.75	209.67	217.46
Cycle tubes (Deshi)	each	21.42	28.83	34.48	36.94	29.87	69.67	73.33	120.20	68.44
Longcloth (medium quality)	meter	17.57	19.81	19.40	20.48	20.16	22.16	22.40	20.86	22.91

Note: All prices shown represent simple averages of weekly average prices during the fiscal year for the urban centers covered.

Source: Bangladesh Bureau of Statistics.

Table 9.5
WHOLESALE PRICE INDICES OF AGRICULTURAL AND INDUSTRIAL PRODUCTS
(1969/70 = 100)

	Weights, in % of total	1979/80	1980/81	1981/82	1982/83	1983/84	1984/85	1985/86	1986/87	1987/88	1988/89	1989/90	1990/91	1991/92	1992/93
DHAKA															
AGRICULTURAL PRODUCTS	67.87	499.12	535.83	605.80	616.30	751.76	929.00	933.00	1050.43	1148.25	1221.95	1329.41	1374.48	1429.17	1453.35
Food	41.08	548.14	561.27	635.22	631.79	742.62	839.00	912.00	1072.20	1118.05	1196.22	1271.57	1307.59	1388.38	1400.36
Raw materials	25.94	422.23	494.72	557.13	594.47	763.97	1069.00	952.00	1005.92	1184.38	1253.98	1410.60	1471.59	1484.32	1526.25
Fuel	0.85	476.76	561.18	669.41	534.12	797.74	1092.00	1298.00	1358.63	1417.35	1488.24	1647.06	1647.16	1717.65	1789.41
INDUSTRIAL PRODUCTS	32.13	565.91	594.09	652.60	728.01	780.95	857.00	911.00	930.50	969.56	1057.80	1134.92	1241.91	1348.66	1366.95
Food	7.96	517.63	567.08	590.45	611.15	780.28	957.00	1038.00	1025.44	1111.60	1269.43	1378.77	1426.00	1500.00	1517.71
Raw materials	6.38	581.24	503.29	517.24	587.54	683.87	726.00	769.00	801.80	809.95	901.88	954.23	975.24	986.23	1033.70
Fuel and lighting	6.16	543.67	621.92	769.80	960.47	956.42	977.00	1020.00	1021.92	1043.74	1054.52	1068.51	1490.91	1660.59	1681.66
Manufactures	11.63	602.32	647.64	707.31	762.02	733.85	798.00	843.00	888.08	920.59	999.51	1102.32	1130.35	1277.82	1279.88
ALL PRODUCTS	100.00	520.58	554.55	620.84	652.20	760.96	906.00	926.00	1011.93	1090.84	1169.21	1266.92	1331.91	1403.24	1425.59
CHITTAGONG															
AGRICULTURAL PRODUCTS	67.87	512.28	541.20	622.47	644.23	760.26	895.00	1004.00	1136.53	1146.81	1232.31	1340.22	1364.82	1390.81	1420.32
Food	41.08	558.34	576.63	682.59	674.76	776.09	844.00	1023.00	1167.69	1156.47	1219.01	1314.51	1335.52	1372.31	1347.08
Raw materials	25.94	433.17	485.43	528.10	593.68	738.97	977.00	967.00	1080.62	1126.91	1247.40	1374.71	1404.63	1412.61	1525.56
Fuel	0.85	518.92	531.76	596.47	711.76	642.35	877.00	1210.00	1265.69	1287.45	1414.90	1530.59	1565.88	1619.42	1748.24
INDUSTRIAL PRODUCTS	32.13	537.96	603.67	667.01	760.91	806.56	864.00	915.00	932.12	990.44	1057.58	1148.33	1315.90	1349.99	1351.17
Food	7.96	595.87	596.10	633.54	676.00	841.83	954.00	1058.00	1112.24	1202.14	1286.06	1422.24	1564.95	1490.17	1438.82
Raw materials	6.38	475.55	526.80	523.35	599.37	704.70	760.00	784.00	785.25	805.97	900.18	1045.92	1114.26	1161.63	1182.13
Fuel and lighting	6.16	577.27	642.86	809.09	1017.05	1067.33	1083.00	1112.00	1085.04	1154.87	1155.51	1096.75	1554.15	1727.95	1711.53
Manufactures	11.63	542.51	630.18	693.46	771.97	709.37	744.00	783.00	808.43	859.67	935.68	1044.37	1129.84	1157.20	1192.61
ALL PRODUCTS	100.00	519.00	561.27	636.78	681.73	774.87	885.00	975.00	1070.25	1096.57	1176.17	1278.57	1349.10	1377.70	1398.10
BANGLADESH															
AGRICULTURAL PRODUCTS	67.87	481.41	508.93	580.79	596.20	726.93	883.00	919.00	1023.29	1087.18	1174.59	1276.10	1297.24	1332.56	1352.78
Food	41.08	527.78	545.40	623.95	633.35	725.02	817.00	911.00	1029.86	1073.04	1152.50	1231.28	1236.27	1285.04	1288.88
Raw materials	25.94	406.67	449.42	508.48	533.96	729.51	989.00	919.00	1002.69	1096.93	1200.82	1338.55	1385.47	1399.67	1443.41
Fuel	0.85	520.00	531.76	701.18	689.41	770.79	1013.00	1291.00	1327.65	1399.04	1442.38	1536.47	1549.41	1580.34	1675.29
INDUSTRIAL PRODUCTS	32.13	543.95	603.02	667.44	740.83	788.23	854.00	904.00	915.10	964.32	1033.84	1118.43	1232.52	1302.61	1331.12
Food	7.96	516.59	562.94	594.72	627.76	779.10	937.00	1014.90	1019.90	1103.27	1212.31	1326.88	1375.88	1411.63	1415.45
Raw materials	6.38	515.67	529.78	513.79	582.44	697.18	722.00	736.00	753.15	774.72	881.03	978.88	1011.91	1028.69	1079.62
Fuel and lighting	6.16	548.86	661.04	834.90	993.02	978.30	999.00	1039.00	1004.65	1054.95	1071.75	1063.31	1470.74	1620.63	1620.29
Manufactures	11.63	575.75	644.63	712.21	771.37	747.00	794.00	848.00	892.02	924.78	974.70	1081.51	1129.23	1209.81	1258.30
ALL PRODUCTS	100.00	501.51	540.99	608.63	642.67	746.86	875.00	914.00	988.54	1047.75	1129.37	1225.44	1276.45	1322.94	1345.82
Annual Increase (%)		12.40	7.90	12.50	5.60	16.20	17.20	4.50	8.16	5.99	7.79	8.51	4.16	3.64	1.73

Note: The wholesale price indices (base 1969/70 = 100) are prepared for six urban centers in Bangladesh (Dhaka, Chittagong, Khulna, Rajshahi, Sylhet and Rangpur) and cover 44 individual items. Weights are assigned in proportion to the gross value of production for each item in the base year 1969/70. The national index represents the unweighted average of the indices for the six urban centers.

Source: Bangladesh Bureau of Statistics.

Table 9.6
DAILY WAGES FOR UNSKILLED LABOR a/
(Tk/day)

		1983/84	1984/85	1985/86	1986/87	1987/88	1988/89	1989/90	1990/91	1991/92
AGRICULTURE [WITHOUT FOOD]										
	current	19.58	24.29	29.53	32.92	32.30	31.39	::	::	::
	1973/74 prices b/	6.28	6.88	8.00	7.76	7.08	6.51	::	::	::
	Index, 1973/74 = 100	94	103	120	116	106	98	::	::	::
FISHERY										
	current	19.80	22.51	25.42	31.27	::	::	::	::	::
	1973/74 prices b/	6.35	6.38	6.89	7.38	::	::	::	::	::
	Index, 1973/74 = 100	93	94	101	109	::	::	::	::	::
SMALL SCALE RURAL INDUSTRY d/										
	current	24.25	28.86	31.45	39.50	40.16	43.69	50.17	52.59	57.68
	1973/74 prices b/	7.77	8.18	8.52	9.32	9.53	9.70	10.35	10.18	10.67
	Index, 1973/74 = 100	154	162	169	185	189	192	205	202	212
COTTON TEXTILE WORKERS										
	current	21.63	24.04	28.68	32.17	35.67	38.95	43.71	46.64	48.40
	1973/74 prices c/	7.62	7.54	8.17	8.12	8.51	8.64	9.01	9.03	8.97
	Index, 1973/74 = 100	138	136	148	147	154	156	163	163	162
JUTE TEXTILE WORKERS										
	current	20.22	20.81	28.29	32.71	33.10	39.12	43.9	45.78	47.96
	1973/74 prices c/	7.12	6.52	8.06	8.26	7.86	8.68	9.05	8.86	8.89
	Index, 1973/74 = 100	94	86	107	109	104	115	119	117	117
MATCH INDUSTRY WORKERS										
	current	20.12	20.57	22.01	24.36	30.53	35.59	40.75	44.88	48.64
	1973/74 prices c/	7.08	6.45	6.27	6.15	7.25	7.90	8.4	8.69	8.97
	Index, 1973/74 = 100	111	101	99	97	114	125	132	137	141
ENGINEERING INDUSTRY WORKERS										
	current	22.78	26.00	36.43	34.40	30.64	38.69	48.12	53.54	58.17
	1973/74 prices c/	8.02	8.15	10.38	8.69	7.27	8.59	9.92	10.36	10.78
	Index, 1973/74 = 100	128	130	166	139	116	137	159	166	172
VEGETABLE OIL INDUSTRY WORKERS										
	current	16.47	18.14	20.93	23.43	26.30	30.69	36.13	39.33	43.52
	1973/74 prices c/	5.80	5.69	5.96	5.92	6.24	6.81	7.45	7.61	8.06
	Index, 1973/74 = 100	105	103	108	107	113	123	135	138	146
CONSTRUCTION WORKERS										
	current	24.56	26.36	33.32	38.98	45.24	50.84	52.35	52.53	56.62
	1973/74 prices c/	8.65	8.26	9.49	9.84	10.74	11.28	10.79	10.17	10.49
	Index, 1973/74 = 100	122	117	134	139	152	159	152	144	148

a/ Based on average wage rates for Dhaka, Chittagong, Rajshahi and Khulna Divisions.
b/ Deflated by rural consumer price index.
c/ Deflated by the average of the consumer price indices for industrial workers in Chittagong, Khulna and Narayanganj.
d/ Refers to skilled workers.
:: = Not available
Note: BBS has discontinued wage series for agriculture and fishery sector.

Source: Bangladesh Bureau of Statistics.

Table 9.7
WAGE DIFFERENTIALS

	1978/79	1979/80	1980/81	1981/82	1982/83	1983/84	1984/85	1985/86	1986/87	1987/88	1988/89	1989/90	1990/91	1991/92	1992/93
UNSKILLED INDUSTRIAL WORKERS : UNSKILLED AGRICULTURAL WORKERS															
Agriculture	1.00	1.00	1.00	1.00	1.00	1.00	1.00	1.00	1.00	1.00	1.00	n.a	n.a	n.a	n.a
Fishing	0.91	1.23	1.31	1.39	1.26	1.01	0.93	0.86	0.95	n.a.	n.a.	n.a	n.a	n.a	n.a
S.S. Industry	0.88	0.96	0.99	1.01	0.96	1.24	1.19	1.07	1.20	1.24	1.39	n.a	n.a	n.a	n.a
Cotton Textile	1.09	1.19	1.21	1.16	1.17	1.10	0.99	0.97	0.98	1.10	1.24	n.a	n.a	n.a	n.a
Jute Textile	0.99	1.07	1.18	1.14	1.13	1.03	0.86	0.96	0.99	1.02	1.25	n.a	n.a	n.a	n.a
Matches	0.93	1.01	0.99	1.06	1.10	1.03	0.85	0.75	0.74	0.95	1.13	n.a	n.a	n.a	n.a
Engineering	0.99	1.07	1.10	1.18	1.19	1.16	1.07	1.23	1.04	0.95	1.23	n.a	n.a	n.a	n.a
Vegetable Oil	0.91	0.99	0.98	0.99	0.94	0.84	0.75	0.71	0.71	0.81	0.98	n.a	n.a	n.a	n.a
Construction	1.26	1.38	1.38	1.40	1.37	1.25	1.09	1.13	1.18	1.40	1.62	n.a	n.a	n.a	n.a
SKILLED WORKER : UNSKILLED WORKER															
INDUSTRY															
Cotton textiles	1.28	1.27	1.31	1.35	1.33	1.37	1.31	1.40	1.55	1.42	1.36	1.31	1.27	1.27	1.28
Jute textile	1.35	1.27	1.20	1.24	1.29	1.37	1.31	1.36	1.47	1.52	1.33	1.28	1.27	1.27	1.28
Matches	1.26	1.22	1.23	1.34	1.44	1.36	1.35	1.39	1.43	1.39	1.32	1.33	1.29	1.31	1.34
Engineering	1.81	1.87	1.80	1.83	1.80	1.66	1.56	1.37	1.68	1.79	1.97	1.36	1.40	1.38	1.27
Vegetable oils	1.24	1.26	1.26	1.20	1.26	1.44	1.45	1.45	1.52	1.58	1.44	1.38	1.32	1.27	n.a
CONSTRUCTION	1.98	1.94	1.98	1.98	2.04	2.04	1.98	1.90	1.97	2.05	1.95	1.90	1.92	1.85	1.84
AGRICULTURE	1.18	1.17	1.17	1.23	1.30	1.44	1.40	1.51	1.50	n.a.	n.a.	n.a.	n.a.	n.a.	n.a.
FISHERY	1.34	1.30	1.26	1.28	1.31	1.62	1.64	1.69	1.98	n.a.	n.a.	n.a.	n.a.	n.a.	n.a.

Note: BBS has discontinued wage series for agricultural workers.

Source: Bangladesh Bureau of Statistics.

Table 9.8
AGRICULTURAL WAGE RATES
(Tk/day, without food)

Division/District	1980/81	1981/82	1982/83	1983/84	1984/85	1985/86	1986/87	1987/88	1988/89
Rajshahi	12.23	13.88	14.82	15.70	21.97	26.22	27.00	25.87	24.03
Dinajpur	10.50	11.83	14.00	14.33	22.50	25.00	27.91	27.15	23.86
Rangpur	14.80	15.17	14.33	16.83	24.00	26.25	24.33	22.49	20.65
Bogra	10.00	12.08	15.00	15.00	19.33	25.00	25.83	25.35	24.64
Rajshahi	14.00	15.67	14.92	14.42	19.00	24.83	27.75	26.47	25.48
Pabna	11.83	14.67	15.83	17.92	25.00	30.00	29.16	27.90	25.54
Khulna	13.57	13.93	14.73	18.37	22.47	28.04	28.67	28.86	28.67
Kushtia	11.17	10.92	11.58	18.67	19.17	28.33	21.25	23.84	25.15
Jessore	12.50	12.92	13.58	16.58	19.50	24.16	32.50	28.74	25.92
Khulna	15.00	15.17	15.58	15.58	22.00	30.00	29.58	28.48	29.39
Barisal	15.42	15.83	16.00	19.00	23.75	27.72	32.50	32.51	33.72
Patuakhali	13.75	14.83	16.92	22.00	27.92	30.00	27.50	30.71	29.17
Dhaka	13.80	15.11	16.58	19.27	21.68	27.45	30.67	30.60	30.52
Mymensingh a/	11.87	14.17	14.71	17.38	20.96	28.96	30.96	30.91	29.31
(Mymensingh)	12.50	13.50	15.00	18.75	20.67	33.33	30.25	30.52	29.31
(Kishoreganj)	11.33	14.83	14.42	16.00	21.25	24.58	31.66	31.29	-
Tangail	14.50	15.00	15.00	21.33	25.00	27.33	29.00	29.81	29.34
Dhaka	16.25	21.25	23.50	25.75	25.00	29.09	32.42	32.63	35.41
Faridpur	12.58	14.08	15.00	14.50	16.50	22.91	30.00	29.03	28.01
Chittagong	16.43	18.60	22.08	24.98	31.68	36.43	41.79	40.51	42.35
Sylhet	15.00	15.42	20.00	23.92	29.50	30.16	34.58	34.79	35.98
Comilla	15.00	17.08	18.75	25.42	30.08	32.27	35.42	30.70	30.70
Noakhali	16.42	19.42	22.75	24.75	33.33	37.50	40.42	37.24	45.72
Chittagong	18.50	20.25	24.25	21.25	33.83	42.08	48.75	52.17	55.43
Chittagong Hill Tracts	17.25	20.83	24.75	29.58	31.67	40.16	44.44	47.64	43.9
Country Average	14.01	15.38	17.05	19.58	24.45	29.53	32.92	32.30	31.39

REAL WAGE RATES
(Tk/day, without food, 1973/74 prices)

Division/District	1980/81	1981/82	1982/83	1983/84	1984/85	1985/86	1986/87	1987/88	1988/89
Rajshahi	5.83	5.34	5.39	5.25	6.25	7.11	6.37	5.67	4.99
Dinajpur	5.17	4.73	5.07	4.70	6.11	6.78	6.58	5.95	4.95
Rangpur	6.93	6.07	5.19	5.52	6.52	7.11	5.74	4.93	4.28
Bogra	4.57	4.52	5.47	5.08	5.69	6.78	6.09	5.56	5.11
Rajshahi	7.08	5.87	5.44	4.89	5.59	6.73	6.54	5.80	5.29
Pabna	5.40	5.49	5.77	6.07	7.35	8.13	6.88	6.12	5.30
Khulna	6.65	5.62	5.66	6.47	7.02	7.60	6.76	6.33	5.95
Kushtia	5.47	4.81	4.45	6.57	5.99	7.68	5.01	5.23	5.22
Jessore	6.13	5.13	5.22	5.84	6.09	6.55	7.67	6.30	5.38
Khulna	7.35	6.02	5.99	5.49	6.88	8.13	6.98	6.25	6.10
Barisal	7.56	6.28	6.15	6.69	7.42	7.51	7.67	7.13	7.00
Patuakhali	6.74	5.88	6.51	7.75	8.73	8.13	6.49	6.73	6.05
Dhaka	6.46	6.12	6.07	6.37	6.12	7.44	7.23	6.71	6.38
Mymensingh a/	5.73	5.17	5.32	5.95	5.81	7.85	7.30	6.78	6.08
Tangail	6.65	5.75	5.32	6.77	7.02	7.41	6.84	6.54	6.09
Dhaka	7.45	8.14	8.33	8.17	7.02	7.88	7.65	7.16	7.35
Faridpur	6.00	5.40	5.32	4.60	4.63	6.21	7.08	6.37	5.81
Chittagong	7.44	6.81	7.67	7.46	8.70	9.87	9.86	8.88	8.79
Sylhet	6.69	5.61	6.90	7.27	8.33	8.17	8.16	7.63	7.46
Comilla	6.69	6.36	6.46	7.73	8.50	8.75	8.35	6.73	6.37
Noakhali	7.33	6.60	7.84	7.52	9.42	10.16	9.53	8.17	9.49
Chittagong	8.52	7.64	8.48	6.18	8.90	11.40	11.50	11.44	11.50
Chittagong Hill Tracts	7.95	7.85	8.65	8.60	8.33	10.88	10.48	10.45	9.11
Country Average	6.53	5.90	6.13	6.34	6.93	8.00	7.76	7.08	6.51

a/ Including Jamalpur.

Note: National, division, and district figures shown are unweighted averages of wage
rates in constituent administrative units. The series has been discontinued by BBS.
Source: Bangladesh Bureau of Statistics.

Distributors of World Bank Publications

ARGENTINA
Carlos Hirsch, SRL
Galeria Guemes
Florida 165, 4th Floor-Ofc. 453/465
1333 Buenos Aires

Oficina del Libro Internacional
Alberti 40
1082 Buenos Aires

**AUSTRALIA, PAPUA NEW GUINEA,
FIJI, SOLOMON ISLANDS,
VANUATU, AND WESTERN SAMOA**
D.A. Information Services
648 Whitehorse Road
Mitcham 3132
Victoria

AUSTRIA
Gerold and Co.
Graben 31
A-1011 Wien

BANGLADESH
Micro Industries Development
　Assistance Society (MIDAS)
House 5, Road 16
Dhanmondi R/Area
Dhaka 1209

BELGIUM
Jean De Lannoy
Av. du Roi 202
1060 Brussels

BRAZIL
Publicacoes Tecnicas Internacionais Ltda.
Rua Peixoto Gomide, 209
01409 Sao Paulo, SP

CANADA
Le Diffuseur
151A Boul. de Mortagne
Boucherville, Québec
J4B 5E6

Renouf Publishing Co.
1294 Algoma Road
Ottawa, Ontario
K1B 3W8

CHINA
China Financial & Economic
　Publishing House
8, Da Fo Si Dong Jie
Beijing

COLOMBIA
Infoenlace Ltda.
Apartado Aereo 34270
Bogota D.E.

COTE D'IVOIRE
Centre d'Edition et de Diffusion
　Africaines (CEDA)
04 B.P. 541
Abidjan 04 Plateau

CYPRUS
Center of Applied Research
Cyprus College
6, Diogenes Street, Engomi
P.O. Box 2006
Nicosia

CZECH REPUBLIC
National Information Center
P.O. Box 668
CS-11357 Prague 1

DENMARK
SamfundsLitteratur
Rosenoerns Allé 11
DK-1970 Frederiksberg C

DOMINICAN REPUBLIC
Editora Taller, C. por A.
Restauración e Isabel la Católica 309
Apartado de Correos 2190 Z-1
Santo Domingo

EGYPT, ARAB REPUBLIC OF
Al Ahram
Al Galaa Street
Cairo

The Middle East Observer
41, Sherif Street
Cairo

FINLAND
Akateeminen Kirjakauppa
P.O. Box 128
SF-00101 Helsinki 10

FRANCE
World Bank Publications
66, avenue d'Iéna
75116 Paris

GERMANY
UNO-Verlag
Poppelsdorfer Allee 55
53115 Bonn

GHANA
Greenwich Mag. and Books
Rivera Beach Hotle
PO Box 01198
Osu-Accra

GREECE
Papasotiriou S.A.
35, Stournara Str.
106 82 Athens

HONG KONG, MACAO
Asia 2000 Ltd.
46-48 Wyndham Street
Winning Centre
7th Floor
Central Hong Kong

HUNGARY
Foundation for Market Economy
Dombovari Ut 17-19
H-1117 Budapest

INDIA
Allied Publishers Ltd.
751 Mount Road
Madras - 600 002

INDONESIA
Pt. Indira Limited
Jalan Borobudur 20
P.O. Box 1181
Jakarta 10320

IRAN
Kowkab Publishers
P.O. Box 19575-511
Tehran

IRELAND
Government Supplies Agency
4-5 Harcourt Road
Dublin 2

ISRAEL
Yozmot Literature Ltd.
P.O. Box 56055
Tel Aviv 61560

R.O.Y. International
P.O.B. 13056
Tel Aviv 61130

Palestinian Authority/Middle East
P.O. Box 19502, Jerusalem

ITALY
Licosa Commissionaria Sansoni SPA
Via Duca Di Calabria, 1/1
Casella Postale 552
50125 Firenze

JAMAICA
Ian Randle Publishers Ltd.
206 Old Hope Road
Kingston 6

JAPAN
Eastern Book Service
Hongo 3-Chome, Bunkyo-ku 113
Tokyo

KENYA
Africa Book Service (E.A.) Ltd.
Quaran House, Mfangano Street
P.O. Box 45245
Nairobi

KOREA, REPUBLIC OF
Pan Korea Book Corporation
P.O. Box 101, Kwangwhamun
Seoul

Daejon Trading Co, Ltd.
P.O. Box 34, Youido
Seoul

MALAYSIA
University of Malaya Cooperative
　Bookshop, Limited
P.O. Box 1127, Jalan Pantai Baru
59700 Kuala Lumpur

MEXICO
INFOTEC
Apartado Postal 22-860
14060 Tlalpan, Mexico D.F.

NETHERLANDS
De Lindeboom/InOr-Publikaties
P.O. Box 202
7480 AE Haaksbergen

NEW ZEALAND
EBSCO NZ Ltd.
Private Mail Bag 99914
New Market
Auckland

NIGERIA
University Press Limited
Three Crowns Building Jericho
Private Mail Bag 5095
Ibadan

NORWAY
Narvesen Information Center
Book Department
P.O. Box 6125 Etterstad
N-0602 Oslo 6

PAKISTAN
Mirza Book Agency
65, Shahrah-e-Quaid-e-Azam
P.O. Box No. 729
Lahore 54000

Oxford University Press
P.O. Box 13033
Karachi - 75350

PERU
Editorial Desarrollo SA
Apartado 3824
Lima 1

PHILIPPINES
International Book Center
Suite 1703, Cityland 10
Condominium Tower 1
Ayala Avenue, H.V. dela
　Costa Extension
Makati, Metro Manila

POLAND
International Publishing Service
Ul. Piekna 31/37
00-677 Warszawa

PORTUGAL
Livraria Portugal
Rua Do Carmo 70-74
1200 Lisbon

SAUDI ARABIA, QATAR
Jarir Book Store
P.O. Box 3196
Riyadh 11471

SLOVAK REPUBLIC
Slovart G.T.G Ltd.
Krupinska 4
P.O. Box 152
852 99 Bratislava 5

**SINGAPORE, TAIWAN,
MYANMAR,BRUNEI**
Gower Asia Pacific Pte Ltd.
Golden Wheel Building
41, Kallang Pudding, #04-03
Singapore 1334

SOUTH AFRICA, BOTSWANA
For single titles:
Oxford University Press
　Southern Africa
P.O. Box 1141
Cape Town 8000

For subscription orders:
International Subscription Service
P.O. Box 41095
Craighall
Johannesburg 2024

SPAIN
Mundi-Prensa Libros, S.A.
Castello 37
28001 Madrid

Librería Internacional AEDOS
Consell de Cent, 391
08009 Barcelona

SRI LANKA AND THE MALDIVES
Lake House Bookshop
P.O. Box 244
100, Sir Chittampalam A.
　Gardiner Mawatha
Colombo 2

SWEDEN
Fritzes Customer Service
S-106 47 Stockholm

Wennergren-Williams AB
P. O. Box 1305
S-171 25 Solna

SWITZERLAND
Librairie Payot
Case postale 3212
CH 1002 Lausanne

Van Diermen Editions Techniques - ADECO
P.O. Box 465
CH 1211 Geneva 16

TANZANIA
Oxford University Press
Maktaba Street
P.O. Box 5299
Dar es Salaam

THAILAND
Central Department Store
306 Silom Road
Bangkok

TRINIDAD & TOBAGO
Systematics Studies Unit
#9 Watts Street
Curepe
Trinidad, West Indies

UGANDA
Gustro Ltd.
1st Floor, Room 4, Geogiadis Chambers
P.O. Box 9997
Plot (69) Kampala

UNITED KINGDOM
Microinfo Ltd.
P.O. Box 3
Alton, Hampshire GU34 2PG
England

ZAMBIA
University of Zambia Bookshop
Great East Road Campus
P.O. Box 32379
Lusaka

ZIMBABWE
Longman Zimbabwe (Pvt.) Ltd.
Tourle Road, Ardbennie
P.O. Box ST 125
Southerton
Harare